101 Endgame Masterclasses
Rooks and Material Imbalances

Alexander Galkin

101 Endgame Masterclasses: Rooks and Material Imbalances

Author: Alexander Galkin

Translated from the Russian by Grigory Baranov

Typesetting by Andrei Elkov

Cover page drawing by Julia Ryzhova

Follow us on Twitter: @ilan_ruby

www.elkandruby.com

ISBN 978-5-604784877

Contents

Introduction

This book aims to give you a wealth of self-study knowledge about handling different types of endings that occur frequently but on which there is not much literature analyzing recent games. Imbalanced material endgames involving rooks are a key focus of the book, covering three-fifths of the material, and all endings in the book feature at least one rook. The vast majority of games are taken from the last few years, including many from 2021-2022. Like my previous endgame book published with Elk and Ruby, *101 Endgame Crimes and Punishments*, this one is aimed at strong tournament players (1900-2300 Elo) and fast improving juniors.

Specifically, this book covers the following endings: rook vs. minor piece (chapter 1), rook vs. a pair of minor pieces (chapter 2), rook and minor piece vs. rook and minor piece, rook and minor piece vs. rook, rook and minor piece vs. two minor pieces, rook and minor piece vs. a pair of rooks, and rook and minor piece vs. queen (all in chapter 3).

The material arrangement principles applied for this book are largely consistent with those adopted for my books published earlier. I select examples only from games played over the board and in which at least one of the players is a grandmaster. I see this as their quality stamp. Eight of the 101 examples in this book come from my own games.

Nearly all of these examples are from games played in the last three years. Being a fan of cutting edge methods of learning chess, it makes sense to me to familiarize the reader with the creative achievements of modern grandmasters. New times give rise to new names. Technological innovations bring new resources to the training process. It's true that the games of earlier periods offer much interesting and instructive material as well. However, who wants to see the same old, famous games and positions migrating from one book to the next? Even if not with "borrowed" commentary, but readily recognizable by many readers nonetheless. In writing this book, I believe I filled it entirely with proprietary and unique material.

I have used all the examples from this book in my coaching work, both with groups of young chess players and in one-to-one lessons. In other words, I am offering you the reader proven materials with hands-on experience of using them. This is of no small importance for coaches. When using the book in the coaching process you already know that the material has passed the required practical testing.

Endgame positions have been selected so that a person studying the book can see the critical moments of play, such as a single or a series of errors that led to a loss or when one of the sides missed a winning move, with the reader challenged to find the correct continuation. At the same time, I have set a goal of not drowning the reader in an endless sea of lines. Therefore, you might have ideas of your own to add to the content of some examples.

I wish you pleasant and fruitful study of my latest book!

Grandmaster Alexander Galkin
October 2022

About the Author

Alexander Galkin was born in 1979 in Rostov-on-Don, Russia. Grandmaster (1997). Russian junior champion in his age-groups (1989 and 1993). Russian under-20 champion (1999). Second in the Soviet junior championship in his age-group (1991). Second in the European junior championship in his age-group (1991). Member of the winning Russian team in the world junior Olympiad (1994). World under 20 champion (1999). Member of the winning Khimik team in the Russian team championship (1999). Prize-winner in other Russian team championships for various teams (1996, 1998, 2003, and 2008). Participant in two FIDE world championships (2000 and 2004) and the FIDE world cup (2007). Member of the Russian team in the European team championship (1999). Outright winner or prize winner in a number of international tournaments.

His pupils include outright winners or prize winners in Russian, European and world championships among juniors and junior girls across the age-groups. He was named Children's Trainer of the Year in 2016 by the Russian Chess Federation. Possesses three university degrees. This is his third book for Elk and Ruby.

Chapter 1

ROOK VS. MINOR PIECE

The first rule to keep in mind for this type of endgame is that if there are no pawns left on the board then a king and rook defeat a king and minor piece in only a handful of cases. It happens either when the minor piece falls to a pin or a fork, or when the weaker side's king is cut off on the last rank or on the rook file while the king of the stronger side helps create mating threats. Moreover, we specifically highlight king and rook vs. king and knight endgames in which the weaker side's king has been pushed to the last rank and his knight is located by it, as defying such "rule of thumb" evaluation over the board.

The advent of strong computer programs and special endgame tablebases has opened up new horizons for the stronger side in terms of playing for a win in such endings. In the past, almost all such positions were considered to be a draw. At present, however, an engine can produce an exact chain of moves which in some positions sets a combination of mating threats to the king and threats to win the knight that force the weaker side's knight to move away from its king, resulting in the stronger side's successful hunt for the knight using the combined forces of his rook and king. However, to determine the point of no return between a drawn and a lost endgame of this type is a challenge even for a top chess player.

In this book we analyze endings in which the strongest grandmasters of our time prove in practice every conclusion stated above by the author. It is also important to note that, in the overwhelming majority of cases, the minor piece stops the stronger side's king and rook from edging the weaker side's king away from the center and to the edge of the board, unless the defending side commits grave errors. Therefore, when defending such endgames, it is of high importance to avoid making careless moves from the very beginning, so as not to find yourself in a position that can be saved with nothing but "only" moves. You may find this a tall order given the situation of an over-the-board game and the likelihood of finding yourself pressed for time by the time you reach the endgame. On the other hand, all the above points in reverse can apply in equal measure to the stronger side, especially if they lack belief in their ability to execute such endings. You absolutely need to test your opponents for mastery of such endings and exploit any errors they might commit.

It is only natural that the addition of pawns dramatically increases the winning chances of the stronger side, if, of course, we mean positions with an equal number of pawns and the weaker side doesn't have any dangerous passers. In this case, we can add at least two winning methods to those stated above: (i) transition to a winning pawn endgame, and (ii) grabbing a pawn (pawns) from the weaker side with the subsequent queening of the stronger side's pawn. Accordingly, the total number and location of pawns become important factors when it comes to evaluating such endgames. All other things being equal, more often than not the presence of pawns on one flank only increases the defending side's chances. This has to do, among other things, with the rook being a more mobile piece and requiring less effort to swing between flanks to attack different enemy pawns. The chances are that, in positions with pawns on both flanks, a minor piece will simply not make it to help its pawns, which is especially true for a knight.

You clearly need to evaluate each specific position, taking into account not only the location of the pawns, rook and minor piece, but of both kings as well. We should never forget that the king becomes a key and independent piece in an endgame and that its active role has a huge influence on the evaluation of any ending, the only exceptions being some major- and many-piece endings in which the offensive potential of the remaining pieces is still capable of creating mating threats to the king. The side looking for ways to make its king active in an endgame cannot ignore this circumstance.

If the king and rook vs. king and minor piece endgame has pawns as well, you need to know at least the basic positions classified as theoretical draws.

 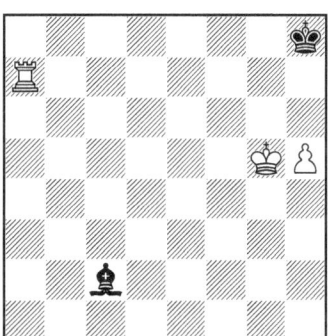

Known theoretical draws

This knowledge will facilitate correct evaluation and decision-making in particular endgame positions. Moreover, this book will help you to see how strong grandmasters take advantage of their knowledge of drawn setups in this type of endgame. This knowledge is of vital importance and in no way inferior to that of opening lines.

Also important to note is that besides general knowledge of endgame handling, a strong chess player cannot do without the knowledge of techniques inherent to solving study positions. The vast majority of studies feature imbalanced-material endgames. Indeed, this book contains examples that show how knowledge of studies solving techniques allows grandmasters to create a work of art during actual play.

It goes without saying that being an exchange up in the type of endgames in question is not an automatic guarantee that the side having the rook can play for a win. The side lacking the exchange may have one, two or even three pawns by way of compensation. In this case, the tables may turn in favor of the side possessing a minor piece. This book provides lots of examples to help you understand the inner workings of the struggle between the sides. Similarly to the cases described above, the ability to save a half-point in this type of endgame (where the side with the initiative is an exchange down but with extra pawns) largely depends on the activity of the defending side's rook and king, as well as on the number of squares between the opponent's extra passed pawns and the promotion square. Is there enough time to eliminate or stop them before they reach a critical square for getting promoted, after which saving the game is possible no longer?

Yet another key factor in saving such endgames for the defending side with a rook is the ability to get rid of all the opponent's pawns even at the cost of the rook. This is because we know that a single minor piece cannot normally deliver checkmate, i.e. unless there is a blunder or in rare cases of a study-like win in a position with a rook's pawn on the board. Another way to reach a draw in such a situation would be to transpose into a position with a bishop and a rook's pawn for the stronger side, in which the lone king of the weaker side controls the promotion square of the opponent's pawn and the bishop is of the color opposite to this promotion square. To promote a pawn in this situation becomes impossible, and the extra bishop is useless.

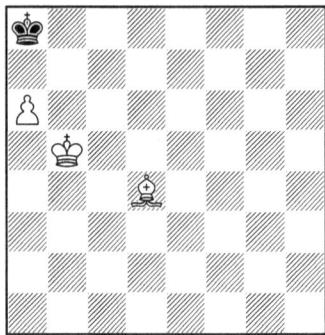 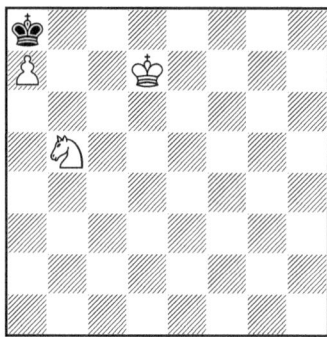

Typical drawn positions

Positions with a knight and rook's pawn vs. a lone king when the pawn stands on the penultimate rank with the knight defending it also belong to this case, even if on a much less frequent basis. The weaker side's king controls the promotion square and any attempts to reassign pawn protection duties to the king result in stalemate.

Finally, this type of position also includes the stronger side having a knight and any pawn other than a rook's pawn, but its king being far away and unable to help his pieces while the weaker side's king is well-placed to attack simultaneously both the only remaining pawn and the knight protecting it. This enables it to drive the knight away and capture the pawn, or, alternatively, to start by capturing the knight and then switch to dealing with the pawn.

Draw   **Win**

To meet this condition, it is crucial for the defending side that the opponent's knight be posted above the pawn in its custody. Otherwise, capturing the knight results in the weaker side's king stepping out of the square of the pawn and allowing it to queen.

We may continue adding to the list of potential positions with different material imbalances and some theoretically drawn positions that might happen along the way. However, that would exceed the scope of this book and they are better served as input material for other types of endgame.

We wrap up the introduction to this chapter by demonstrating yet another important theoretical endgame position that any chess player should know.

White wins easily with Black to move because the black king cannot avoid letting his white counterpart out of the corner with the subsequent queening of the pawn. However, it is a draw with White to move. The black king keeps his white counterpart boxed in by shuffling between the f7 and f8-squares. The white knight is unable to pass the turn to move on to his opponent to take over control of the above squares in the starting position no matter the route chosen. This distinctive feature of a knight – an inability to pass the turn to move – is a crucial piece of knowledge for any chess player.

Rook vs. Minor Piece

We begin by reviewing example positions from grandmaster games in which the side having a minor piece against the rook attempts to make a draw by resorting to such factors as reaching a drawn position (a "positional draw") or reaching a small number of pawns (allowing the game to reach a drawn rook vs. minor piece endgame without any pawns on the board), among others.

Example No. 1
Jung Min Seo – A. Rasmussen
Catez 2021

White to move

Which approach is better suited to saving the game – active counterplay or passive resistance? This dilemma is relevant to nearly every type of endgame, and the answer to this question is not always straightforward.

101.♞xf5?

White errs in believing that his pawn, supported by the king, will make it to the queening square to secure him a draw.

101.♔d4? ♔f2−+ is bad, of course.

There is no allowing the black king a free run across the home rank: 101.♞h5? ♔f1 102.♞g3+ (102.♔f3 ♖a3#) 102...♔g2 103.♞h5 ♖a3+ 104.♔e2 (104.♔d4 ♔f3 105.♔e5 ♖a5+ 106.♔e6 ♔g4−+) 104...♔h3 105.♞f6 (105.♞g7 ♔g4 106.♞e6 ♖a6 107.♞c5 ♖a2+ 108. ♔e3 ♖a3+ 109.♞d3 ♖xd3+ 110.♔xd3

♔xf4−+ with a winning pawn ending) 105...♔g3 106.♞d5 ♖a5−+ and Black wins a pawn.

White should have maintained the drawn position by preventing the black king from encroaching on the f4-pawn: 101.♔f3!

a) 101...♔d2 *(here and further in this book, "a)" is the main line if there is a main line, unless otherwise stated)*

102.♞h5. It is also fine for White to mark time with his king – 102.♔f2 ♔d3 103.♔f3=.

102...♔d3 103.♞g3 ♔d4

104.♘e2+. 104.♘h5? ♖a3+ 105. ♔f2 ♔e4 106.♔g2 ♖b3 107.♔h2 ♔f3 108.♔h3 ♖b6 109.♔h4 ♖h6 110.♔g5 ♖xh5+ 111.♔xh5 ♔xf4−+ would be a mistake landing White in a lost pawn ending.

104...♔d5 105.♘g3 ♔e6 106. ♘h5=, holding the position.

b) 101...♖a3+ 102.♔g2 ♖a5 103. ♔f3 yields nothing;

c) Accordingly, the attempt to test the drawn position for viability by passing the turn to move 101...♖b5 fails to 102.♘h5!

c1) 102...♖b3+ 103.♔g2 ♔d2 (103... ♔e2? 104.♘g3+) 104.♘g7 ♖b5 (104... ♔e3 105.♘xf5+ ♔xf4 106.♘d4!= ♖d3 107.♘e2+!) 105.♔f3 ♔d3 106.♘h5 ♔d4

107.♘g3! ♖a5 108.♘e2+ ♔d5 109.♘g3 ♔e6 110.♘h5=. Black has

completed the king march to relieve the rook of its pawn defending duties. However, it has not become any clearer as to how to turn this into an asset in the struggle for victory;

c2) 102...♔d2 103.♘g7 ♖a5 104. ♘h5= is harmless;

c3) In case of 102...♔f1 103.♔g3! ♔g1 (103...♔e2 104.♔h4 ♔f3 105. ♔g5 ♖a5 106.♘f6 ♔e3 107.♘h5 ♔e4 108.♘g3+=) 104.♔h4! ♔f2 105.♔g5 ♔f3 106.♘f6 ♖a5 107.♘h5 ♔e3 108. ♘f6= the active white king guarantees an easy draw.

101...♖xf5 102.♔e4

102...♖f8!

This is the only correct move; it places the rook on an ideal square from which to combat the opponent's passed pawn.

103.f5

In case of 103.♔e5 ♔f2 104.f5 ♔g3 105.f6 ♔g4 106.♔e6 ♔g5 107.f7 ♔g6−+ Black is just in time to eliminate the passed pawn.

103...♔e2!

White definitely overlooked this rejoinder. Now Black forces White to commit to a route for his king, choosing the opposite direction and bringing about the passed pawn's liquidation at the doorstep of the queening square.

103...♚f2? 104.♚f4! is bad.

and there is no winning this position with Black to move:

a) 104...♚g2 105.♚g4!=;

b) 104...♖a8 105.f6=;

c) 104...♖f7 105.♚e5 ♚g3 106.♚e6 ♖f8 107.f6=;

d) 104...♚e2 105.♚e4! ♚d2 106. ♚e5 ♚e3 107.f6! ♚f3 108.♚e6 ♚g4 109.f7 ♚g5 110.♚e7=.

104.♚f4

104.♚e5 ♚f3 105.f6 ♚g4 106. ♚e6 ♚g5 107.f7 ♚g6−+ loses immediately.

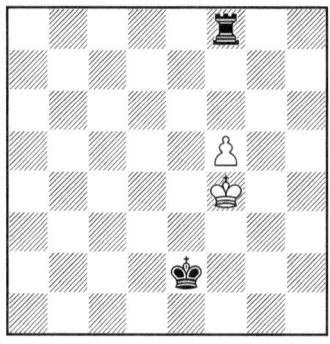

104...♚f2!−+

And White is in zugzwang. 104... ♚d3? fails to 105.♚e5!=.

105.♚e5

Or the other way around: 105.♚g5 ♚e3 106.f6 ♚e4 107.♚g6 ♚e5 108.f7 ♚e6−+.

105...♚g3 106.f6 ♚g4 107.♚e6 ♚g5 and White resigned.

Example No. 2
P. Eljanov − J. Arizmendi Martinez
Skopje, 2019

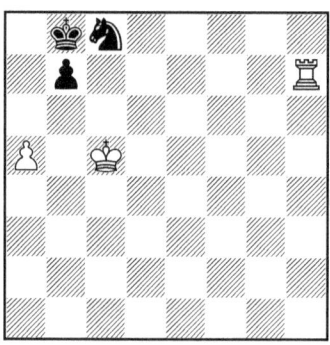

Black to move

Despite White's exchange superiority the position is a draw because there are too few pawns left. The white king cannot cross the road to the b7-pawn, while the only remaining white pawn is subject to attack from the black pieces at any moment. However, Black needs to demonstrate proper defensive accuracy.

81...♚a7?

And Black failed to demonstrate it.

81...♞a7! 82.♖h8+ (82.♚b6 ♞c8+!; 82.♚d6 ♞b5+ 83.♚d7 ♞d4=; 82.♖g7 ♞c8!) 82...♚c7! 83.♖g8 ♞c8! was the only way to hold the game, since White cannot improve his position here.

82.♖h8! ♚b8?

Black drops a piece and collapses quickly following 82...b6+? 83.axb6+ ♞xb6 84.♖h7+ ♚a6 85.♖h6+−.

82...♞e7 83.a6! is correct.

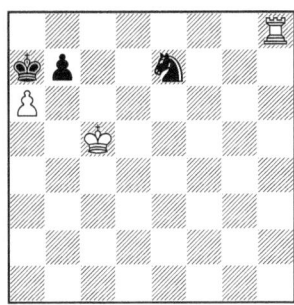

a) 83...♘g6 84.♖e8! ♘f4 (84...b6+ 85.♔b5+−; 84...bxa6 85.♖e6 ♘f4 86.♖e7+ ♔b8 87.♖e4 ♘h5 88.♔c6+− ♘f6 89.♖f4 ♘h5 90.♖f7 a5 91.♖b7+ ♔a8 92.♖b5 ♘g7 93.♖g5 ♘e6 94.♖e5 ♘d8+ 95.♔c7 ♘b7 96.♖b5) 85.axb7 ♔xb7 86.♖e7+ ♔c8 (86...♔a6 87.♔c6 ♔a5 88.♖e5+ ♔a6 89.♖e4+−)

87.♔d6!+− and White succeeds thanks to a combination of two threats: checkmating the cutoff black king and trapping the knight. For example, 87... ♘d3 88.♖f7! ♘b4 89.♖c7+! ♔b8 (89... ♔d8 90.♖b7 ♘a6 91.♖b6+−) 90.♖c4 ♘a6 91.♔c6! ♘c7 (91...♔a7 92.♖a4+−) 92.♖e4 ♘a6 (92...♘a8 93.♖e7+−; 92... ♔c8 93.♖e7+−) 93.♖h4 ♔a7 94.♖a4, and the game is over.

b) 83...♔xa6 84.♖a8#;

c) 83...bxa6 84.♖h7+−;

d) 83...♘c6 84.axb7 ♔xb7 85.♖h7++−;

e) 83...b6+ 84.♔b5+−;

f) 83...♘f5 84.♖h5 ♘g3 85.♖e5 bxa6 86.♔c6+−

83.a6! and Black resigned: 83...bxa6 (83...♔c7 84.♖xc8+! ♔xc8 85.a7+−) 84.♔c6 a5 85.♔d7.

Example No. 3
I. Rogers − D. Antic
Adelaide 2007

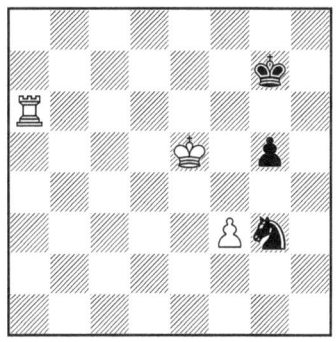

White to move

As in the previous positions, there is every reason to believe that Black's defense should be impregnable. His king, knight and pawn guard the f-file squares against infiltration by his opponent's king. Is there any way for White to prevail?

61.♖b6!

The Australian grandmaster is spot-on in skipping a move, giving Black an opportunity to find any move that keeps his fortress from falling apart. Yet there is no such move. The position is a zugzwang!

Hence, one important rule: *the proof of any drawn position is in the "passing the move" test.* This is when you should never forget to ask yourself the question as to whether skipping a move has any bearing on the position's evaluation.

61...♔h7

A king move in the opposite direction

loses as well: 61...♔f7 62.♖h6! ♔g7 63.♖h3 ♘e2 64.♔f5+−.

In case of 61...♘e2 62.♔f5 ♘d4+ 63.♔g4! ♔f7 64.♖d6 ♘b5 65.♖d5+− White wins the pawn anyway.

62.♔f6 ♔h6 63.♖b2

63.♖b8   ♘h5+   64.♔f7   ♔h7 65.♖b2+− was also winning.

63...♘h5+

White checkmates after 63...♔h5 64.♖h2#.

64.♔f7 g4

64...♘f4 65.♖h2+ ♘h5 66.♖h1+− lands Black in yet another deadly zugzwang.

65.fxg4 ♘g3 66.♖b5 and Black resigned.

The above examples serve to highlight the significance of studying pure rook versus knight endings without any pawns. This ending is a rare guest in grandmaster tournaments. The stronger side takes its winning chances from one of the two following circumstances or their combination: a checkmate threat to the weaker side's cutoff king or the knight's misplaced position.

Example No. 4
V. Topalov — Ding Liren
Baku 2019

White to move

The white king is cut off on the last rank, so Black should try to weave a mating net. However, as long as the knight is near the king, Black's plan is extremely hard to execute. In fact, such endings are nearly impossible for a human player to evaluate. The thin line between a routine draw and a winning position with this material balance does not lend itself to easy detection.

96.♘g7?

This natural move is an error.

96.♘d6?   ♔f6   97.♘e8+   ♔e7 98.♘g7 ♖h3 99.♘f5+ ♔f6 100.♘d6 ♖d3! 101.♘e8+ ♔e7 102.♘g7 ♖d5! 103.♔h7 ♔f8! was losing as well.

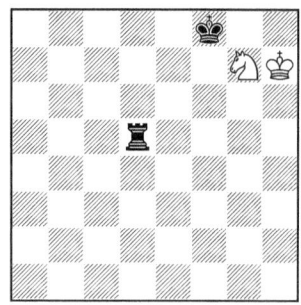

104.♘e6+. The line 104.♔g6 ♖d6+ 105.♔h7 ♖d7 106.♔h8 ♔f7! 107.♔h7 ♔f6 108.♔h8 ♖d1 109.♔h7 ♖h1+! 110.♔g8 ♖g1 111.♔h8 ♔f7−+ produces the same result.

104...♔f7 105.♘g7 ♖g5 106.♔h8 ♖g1−+, checkmating the white king along the h-file.

The correct move is 96.♘c7! ♖c3 (96... ♖f2 97.♘e8!; 96...♖d3 97.♔f8!) 97.♘e8 maintaining the drawn position for White.

96...♔f6!

The underwhelming 96...♖d3? keeps White in the game after 97.♘e8!.

97.♘h5+ ♔e6?

Engine precision is also not something that Black is capable of maintaining.

The correct 97...♔f5! 98.♘g7+ ♔e5! (98...♔g6 99.♘e8!) 99.♘e8 ♔e6! 100.♘g7+ ♔e7 101.♔h7 ♔f6−+ wins the game.

98.♔h7?

Returning the compliment. Staying in the game required 98.♔g7! ♔f5 99.♘f6!=.

98...♔f5 99.♘g7+

Both 99.♔g7? ♔g5−+ and 99.♔h6? ♖h3−+ are bad.

99...♔f6 100.♘h5+

100.♔g8? ♖g3 101.♔h8 ♔f7! 102. ♘h5 ♖h3 −+ is an immediate failure.

100.♘e8+ ♔f7 101.♘d6+ ♔e7 102. ♘e4 ♖f4 103.♘g5? (103.♘c3 ♖c4 104. ♘d5+ ♔f7! 105.♔h6 ♖c6+! 106.♔h7 ♖c5 107.♘f4 ♖f5−+) 103...♔f6! 104. ♘h3 ♖h4+−+ does not save the game either.

100...♔g5 101.♘g7

101...♖h3+!

There is no doing without this precision!

102.♔g8 ♔f6! 103.♘e8+

The king cannot escape: 103.♔f8? ♖h8#

103...♔e6

104.♘g7+

In the same manner, White fails to sort out his problems with 104.♘c7+ ♔d6 105.♘b5+ ♔e7 106.♘d4 ♖g3+ 107.♔h7 ♖g4! 108.♘f5+ ♔f6 109.♘d6 (109.♘h6 ♖h4−+) 109...♖d4 110.♘b5 ♖d7+

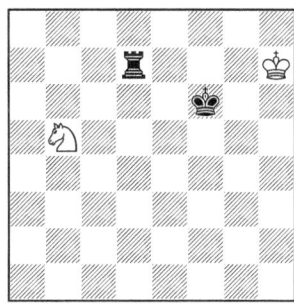

111.♔g8 (111.♔h6 ♖d3 112.♔h7 ♔e5 113.♔g6 ♖b3 114.♘c7 ♖b8 115. ♔g5 ♔d6 116.♘a6 ♖b6−+) 111... ♖g7+! 112.♔f8 (112.♔h8 ♔g6−+) 112...♖b7 113.♘d6 ♖b8+ 114.♘e8+ ♔e6−+.

104...♔e7 105.♘f5+ ♔f6 106.♘d6

106.♘g7 ♖g3 107.♔h8 ♔f7−+ loses the game immediately.

The game is over following 106. ♘d4 ♖g3+! 107.♔h7 (107.♔h8 ♔f7−+; 107.♔f8 ♖d3 108.♘c6 ♖d6−+) 107...♖g7+ 108.♔h6 ♖g4! 109.♘f3 ♖f4!−+.

106...♖h5

Among other continuations, 106...♖h4 107.♘e8+ ♔e7 108.♘g7 (108. ♘c7 ♖g4+ 109.♔h7 ♖g5−+) 108...♖e4 109.♘f5+ ♔f6 110.♘d6 ♖e6 111. ♘c4 ♖e8+ 112.♔h7 ♖e7+ 113.♔g8 ♖d7−+ was also winning.

107.♘f7?!

107.♘e8+ ♔e7 108.♘g7 ♖g5 109. ♔h7 (109.♔h8 ♔f7−+) 109...♔f7 110. ♔h8 ♖g1−+ is no better than the text.

107.♘e4+! ♔e6 108.♔g7 puts up tougher resistance even if White is still lost after 108...♖e5!−+.

107...♖d5! 108.♘h6

108.♘h8 ♖d7−+ and 108.♔f8 ♖d7−+ are just as bad.

108...♖d8+! 109.♔h7 ♖d7+! 110. ♔g8

110.♔h8 ♔g6 111.♘g8 ♖h7# results in a cute-looking checkmate.

110...♔g6 and White resigned. Not only is this endgame attractive, but it

comes from world class chess players at that.

It is also worth noting that computer chess programs and special endgame databases have given us much insight into the "king and rook vs. king and knight" ending. If earlier they believed this ending to be nearly impossible to win, each piece's location and the side having the right to move are now clearly seen as extremely important in terms of final evaluation of the particular endgame in question.

Example No. 5
Z. Tsydypov − G. Prithu
Moscow, 2019

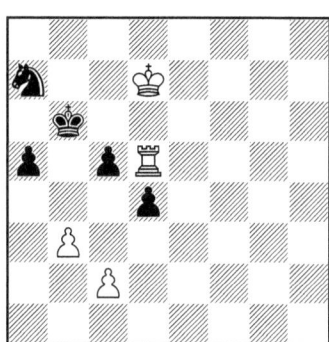

White to move

The white king is very active, while the black knight is misplaced. Is White in time to win before all the queenside pawns are exchanged off?

70.♖d6+?

This is an ill-advised decision. White trains his guns on the black knight and overlooks his opponent's counterplay.

70.♖h5! is correct:

a) 70...♘b5

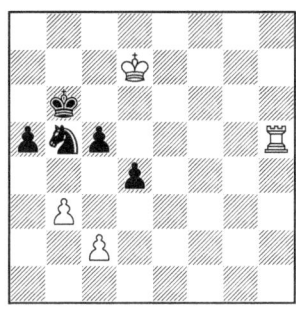

71.♖h6+! ♔b7 72.♖c6! d3 (72...♘a3 73.♖xc5 ♔b6 74.♔d6 ♘b5+ 75.♔d5+−) 73.cxd3 ♘d4 74.♖xc5

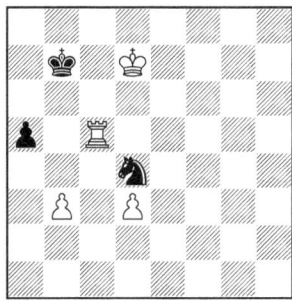

74...♔b6 (74...♘xb3 75.♖b5++− is bad, 74...♔a6 also fails to 75.♖c4 ♘xb3 76.♔c6 ♘d2 77.♖f4 ♘b3 78.d4 a4 79.d5+−) 75.♖c8 ♔b7 (75...♘xb3 76.♖b8++−; 75...♔b5 76.♖b8+ ♔c5 77.♔c7+−) 76.♖c4!? ♘xb3

77.d4! The white pawn advances, whereas Black cannot establish coordination among his pieces.

77...♔b6 78.d5 ♔b5. After 78...a4 79.d6 a3 (79...♔b5 80.♖c3 ♘c5+ 81.♔e7+−) 80.♖b4++− Black is also in bad shape.

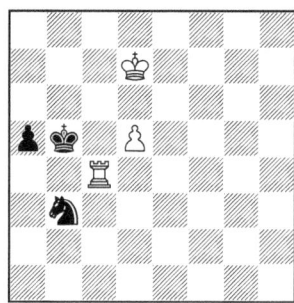

79.♖c8! ♘c5+ (79...♘d4 80.d6 ♘f5 81.♔e6+−) 80.♔d6 ♘e4+. After 80...♘b7+ 81.♔e7 a4 82.♖b8 ♔b6 83.d6 a3 84.d7+− White queens his pawn with check.

81.♔e5 ♘c5 82.♖xc5+ ♔xc5 83.d6 ♔c6 84.♔e6+− and the white pawn is the first to queen.

b) 70...♘c6? fails to 71.♖h6+−;

c) 70...♔b5 71.♔d6 ♘c8+ 72.♔c7! ♘b6 (72...♘e7 73.♖e5 ♘g6 74.♖e6 ♘f4 75.♖b6#) 73.♖h8! ♘d5+ 74.♔d6 ♘b6 75.♖b8+− is of no help either;

d) There is no exchanging off all pawns via 70...a4 71.bxa4 c4 72.♖d5 d3 73.cxd3 cxd3 (73...c3 74.d4 c2 75.♖c5+−) 74.♖xd3 ♔a5 75.♖d6+−, and the knight is bound for captivity.

70...♔b5!

70...♔b7? fails to 71.♖e6 ♘b5 72.♖c6+−.

71.♔c7 ♔b4! 72.♔b7 ♘b5

72...♔c3? was ill-timed due to 73.♔xa7 ♔xc2 74.♔b6 ♔xb3 (74...d3 75.♔xc5 d2 76.♔b5 ♔xb3 77.♖xd2 a4 78.♖d3++−) 75.♔xc5 a4 76.♖xd4 a3 77.♖d3+! ♔b2 78.♔b4 a2 79.♖d2+ ♔b1 80.♔b3 a1=♘+ (80...a1=♕ 81.♖d1#) 81.♔c3+−, and White wins.

73.♖b6

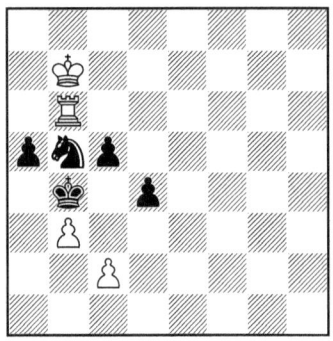

73...♔c3!

The black king completes his mission no matter the cost. 73...c4? is bad because of 74.♔a6+−.

74.♖xb5 ♔xc2 75.♖xc5+, and the opponents agreed a draw without producing the following sequence: 75... ♔xb3 76.♖xa5 d3 77.♖d5 ♔c2.

Example No. 6
H. Nakamura – S. Karjakin
Stavanger, 2018

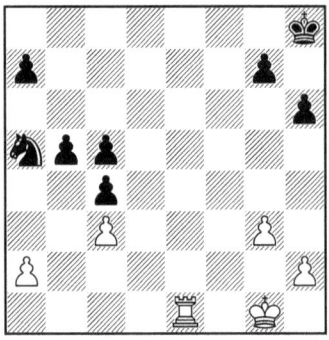

White to move

Black has two pawns for the exchange and potentially dangerous passed pawns

on the queenside. However, it is the white king's active play that proves a decisive factor in this position.

27.♔f2!

The white king is on his way to combat the black passed pawns. In case of 27.♖e5 ♘b3 28.axb3? cxb3 29.♖xc5 b4! 30.♖b5 a5 31.cxb4 a4−+ the white rook cannot handle the black passed pawns.

27...b4

Both 27...♘c6 28.♖e6 ♘a5 29.♖a6+− and 27...♘b7 28.♖e7 ♘d6 29.♖e6+− lose the game.

28.♔e3! bxc3

Black is helpless after 28...b3 29.♔e4! bxa2 30.♖a1+−.

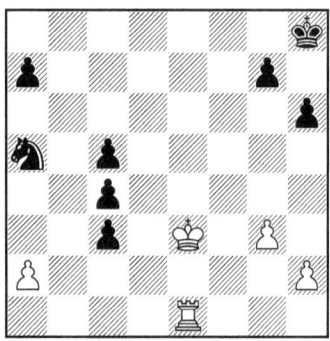

29.♖c1!?

It is also fine to play 29.♔e4 c2 (29... ♘b3? 30.axb3 cxb3 31.♔d3 c2 32.♔c3 c4 33.♔b2 a5 34.♖a1 ♔h7 35.♖xa5 c3+ 36.♔c1+−) 30.♖c1 (30.♔d5? ♘b3−+) 30...♘c6 31.♖xc2 ♘b4 32.♖xc4 ♘xa2 33.♖xc5+−, developing similarly to the game.

29...♘c6 30.♖xc3 ♘b4 31.♖xc4 ♘xa2 32.♖xc5+−

The a-pawn is doomed, and the knight has yet to make it in time to escape from encirclement.

32...♘b4

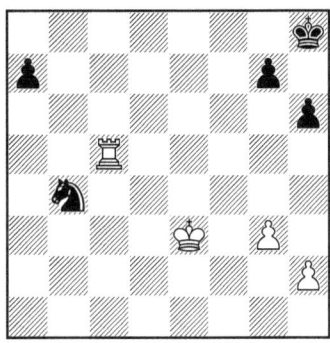

33.♔e4! ♔h7

33...a6 34.♖c4 a5 35.♖c5 a4 36.♖a5+− makes no difference.

34.♖c4 a5

The knight is trapped in the line 34...♘a6 35.♔d5 ♘b8 36.♖c7 ♘a6 37.♖b7 ♔g6 38.♔c4+−.

White also wins after 34...♘a2 35.♔f5!? a5 36.♖a4 ♘c3 37.♖xa5+−.

35.♖c5 a4 36.♖a5

The knight cannot be trapped after 36.♖c4 ♘a6! 37.♔d5 a3 38.♖a4 ♘c7+.

36...♘c6

It does not help to set the forking mechanism in action: 36...♘a2 37.♔d4 ♘c1 38.♖xa4 ♘e2+ 39.♔e5+−.

37.♖xa4 ♘d8

Black also loses the endgame after 37...♘e7 38.♖a6 ♘g8 (38...♘g6 39.♔f5 ♘e7+ 40.♔e6+−) 39.♔e5 ♘e7 (39...♘f6 40.♖xf6! gxf6+ 41.♔xf6+−) 40.♔e6 ♘g8 41.♔f7+−.

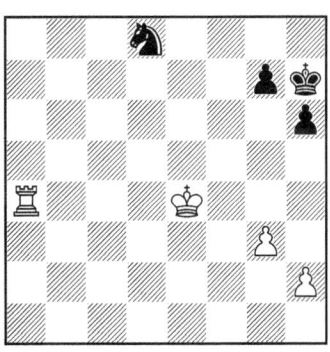

38.♖a6! ♘f7 39.♔f5! ♘h8

In case of 39...♘d8 40.h4+− the pawns onslaught is decisive.

40.h4 ♘f7

Black's pieces are stuck on the bottom ranks. Black is in bad shape in all lines: 40...g6+ 41.♔f6+−; 40...h5 41.♔g5+−; 40...♔g8 41.g4+−

41.g4! , and Black resigned in the face of 41...♘h8 42.g5 hxg5 43.hxg5 ♘f7 44.g6+

Example No. 7
S. Vidit − V. Artemiev
Poikovsky, 2018

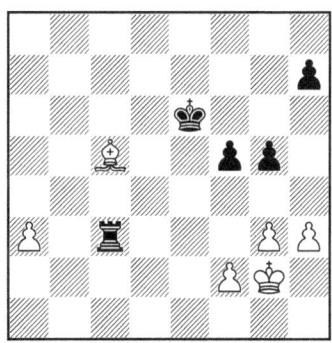

White to move

At first glance, White has no choice but remove the bishop from en prise while keeping an eye on the a3-pawn, which spells White's long suffering in this ending. This is likely the path the majority of titled chess players would have taken.

46.♗e3!

However, the Indian GM takes a different decision. He cracks down on his opponent's pawn, initiating further inevitable pawn exchanges on the kingside.

46...h6

46...♔f6? would be a blunder due to 47.♗d4++−.

In case of 46...g4 47.hxg4 fxg4 48.♗d4 ♖xa3 49.♗b6= Black cannot convert his exchange advantage due to a lack of reasonable winning ideas.

At the same time, keeping his position together would be simple for White after 46...f4 47.gxf4 gxf4 48.♗xf4 ♖xa3 49.♗g3=.

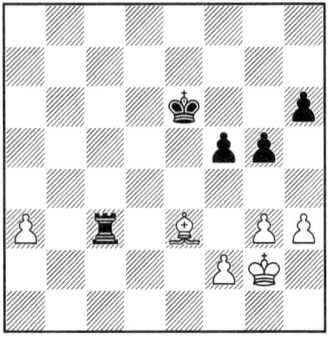

47.h4!

Attacking the g5-pawn yet again.

47...gxh4

47...g4? 48.♗xh6= is bad.

Likewise, no real winning chances result from 47...f4 48.gxf4 gxh4 (48...g4 49.f5+ ♚xf5 50.♗xh6=) 49.f5+!? ♚xf5 50.♗xh6 ♖xa3 (50...h3+ 51.♚h2=) 51.♗e3= since this endgame is a theoretical draw.

48.♗xh6! hxg3

There are no winning prospects after 48...♖xa3 49.gxh4=.

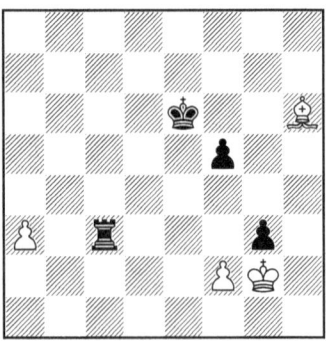

49.f3!

A splendid move! Black gets a winning endgame after 49.fxg3? ♖xa3−+.

49...♖xa3 50.♚xg3=

This position turns out to be a draw. Black cannot gang up on the white pawn and keep his last pawn alive at the same time. It's amazing how the Indian GM saw it all when deciding to part with his a-pawn!

50...♖a4 51.♗g5 ♚e5 52.♗h6 ♖c4

Black drops the pawn after 52...♚d4 53.♚f4 ♖a5 54.♗g7+ ♚d3 55.♗e5=.

After 52...f4+ 53.♚g4 ♖c4 54.♗g5= all of Black's resources are tied down to the defense of his weak pawn.

An attempt to redirect the rook via 52...♖a7 53.♗f4+! ♚d5 54.♗d2 does not promise any benefits for Black.

53.♗g7+ ♚d5

53...♚e6 54.♗h6 ♚f7 55.♗g5 ♚g6 56.♗d2 ♚f6 57.♗h6 ♖a4 58.♗f4 ♖a1 59.♗d2 ♖g1+ 60.♚f4= makes no difference for the positional evaluation.

54.♗h6 ♚c6 55.♗g5

White is marking time to see which winning plan Black is going to come up with.

55...♚b5 56.♗h6 ♚b4 57.♗g5 ♚c3 58.♗h6 ♚d3 59.♗g5 ♚e2 60.♗h6

The black king has travelled far to approach the f3-pawn, but his efforts fall short of bringing success nonetheless.

60...♖c3

61.♔f4! ♖xf3+ 62.♔e5!

In addition to being up the exchange Black has also pocketed a pawn, but this success proves temporary. Now the black pieces cannot stop the encirclement and annihilation of their last pawn.

63...♖h3

63...♔d3 64.♗f4= changes nothing.

64.♗g5!

The careless 64.♗f4? fails to 64...♖h5!−+.

64...♖h5 65.♔xf5 and the opponents agreed a draw.

Example No. 8
I. Miladinovic − A. Beliavsky
Ohrid 2001

Black to move

Black seems winning no matter which way he captures the white pawn. Moreover, capturing with his pawn seems more advantageous as the pawn advances towards the center and gets closer to the queening square at that. However, it turns out to be not as simple as that...

99...gxf3?

Surprisingly, this error costs Black victory.

He needed to capture with the rook: 99...♖xf3+! 100.♔g2 (100. ♔h4 ♖h3#) 100...♖d3! 101.♗c7 ♔g5! 102.♗e5 (102.♗g3? ♖d2+ 103. ♔f1 ♔f5−+; 102.♗b8? ♔h4−+) 102...♖d5!, restricting the bishop's defensive potential (102...♔h4 103. ♗f6+!) 103.♗c7 (103.♗c3 ♔f4−+; 103.♗g7 ♖d2+ 104.♔g3 ♖d3+ 105. ♔g2 g3 106.♔h3 ♔f4−+) 103... ♖d2+! (103...♔h4 104.♗g3+!) 104. ♔g3 ♖d3+!, and preparing his king's decisive inroad: 105.♔g2 ♔h4! 106. ♗f4 ♖c3 107.♗d6 ♖c2+ 108.♔g1 ♔h3−+.

100.♗c5 ♔e4

101.♔f2!

This position turns out to be a draw. Black cannot coordinate his pieces so as to advance and not drop the pawn.

101...♖c3

Likewise, there is no headway after 101...♖b2+ 102.♔f1! ♔f4 (102...f2 103.♔g2!) 103.♗d6+ ♔e3 104.♗c5+ ♔e4 105.♗a7 ♔f4 106.♗c5= ♔g3 107. ♗d6+.

102.♗a7 ♖c7 103.♗b6 ♖c2+ 104. ♔f1 ♖c6 105.♗a7 ♖a6 106.♗c5 ♔f4 107.♗d4

107...♖a4

The bishop drives the king away after 107...♔g3 108.♗e5+!

108.♗c5 ♖c4

or after 108...♔g3 109.♗d6+!

109.♗a7 ♖b4

or after 109...♔g3 110.♗b8+!

110.♗c5 ♖b5 111.♗d4 ♔g4

or after 111...♔g3 112.♗f2+!

112.♔f2 ♖b4 113.♗c5 ♖b2+ 114. ♔f1 ♖c2 115.♗a7 ♖b2 116.♗c5 ♖b5 117.♗d4 ♔f4 118.♗f2 ♖d5 119.♗b6 ♖d7 120.♗e3+ ♔g4 121.♗b6 ♖b7 122. ♗c5 ♖b5 123.♗d4 ♖h5 124.♗b6 ♖h2+ 125.♔f1 f2

With no profits from long maneuvering, Black finally makes up his mind to advance the pawn.

126.♔e2!

Yet another precise move! 126.♗xf2?

loses to 126...♔f3 127.♗b6 ♖h1+ 128. ♗g1 ♔g3−+.

126...♔g3 127.♗c5

Since there is no headway for the black pieces without dropping the f-pawn, the position is a draw.

Example No. 9
R. Rapport − Wei Yi
Tbilisi 2017

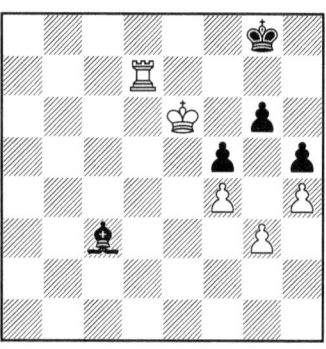

White to move

The pawn structure is completely symmetrical. The g6-pawn is the only link in the black pawn chain that could come under attack. However, the black bishop and king exercise control over all access squares. Meanwhile, there is no way to drive the black king away, and the bishop has no shortage of squares along the key diagonal. Therefore, there is no destroying this drawn position via zugzwang.

58.♖d3!

This is an important preliminary move to take control of the third rank.

58...♗b2

Both 58...♗g7? 59.♖d8+ ♔h7 60.♔f7+−,

and 58...♖h8? 59.♖d8+ ♔g7 (59...♔h7 60.♔f7+−) 60.♖c8 ♔h7

61.♔f7+− fail immediately because the king and rook eliminate the black pawns.

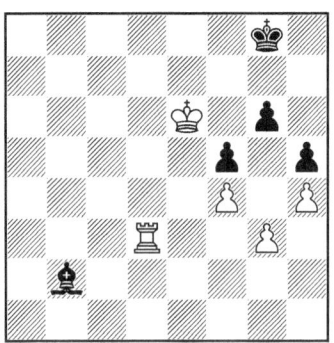

59.g4!

A brilliant break! By sacrificing the pawn on what is seemingly the best defended square, White destroys the protective shield of black pawns and clears the path for his king to attack the resulting weaknesses.

59...hxg4

59...fxg4 60.f5! gxf5 61.♔xf5 ♔f7 62.♔g5 ♗e5 63.♔xh5 g3 64.♖d2! (64. ♔g4? g2 65.♖d1 ♗h2=) 64...♔g7 65.♔g4 ♔f6 also fails.

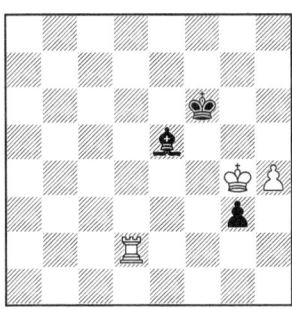

66.♖e2! ♗b8 (66...♗d6 67.h5+−) 67.♖b2 ♗c7 (67...♗d6 68.♖b6 ♔e7 69.♔f3 ♗e5 70.h5 ♔f7 71.♖g6 ♗b8 72.♔e4 ♗c7 73.♔f5 ♗b8 74.h6+−)

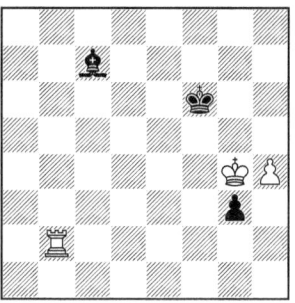

68.h5 ♗e5 69.♖b6+ ♔g7 (69...♔f7 70.♖g6+−) 70.♔f5+−.

60.h5! ♔g7

In case of 60...gxh5 61.♔xf5 ♔g7 (61...♔f7 62.♖d7+ ♔e8 63.♔h7 g3 64.♖xh5 ♗d4 65.♖g5 ♗f2 66.♔e6 ♔f8 67.f5+−) 62.♔g5 ♗c1 White comes up with an excellent rejoinder

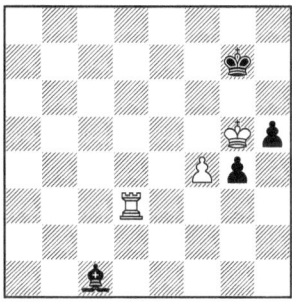

63.♖g3! ♔f7 (63...♔h7 64.♖c3! ♗d2 65.♖c7+ ♔g8 66.♔g6 ♔f8 67.f5 g3 68.f6+− is no better; 63...♗d2 loses to 64.♔xh5 ♗xf4 65.♖xg4+) 64.♖g1! ♗e3 (64...♗d2 65.♔xh5! ♗xf4 66.♖f1+−) 65.♖g2! ♗c1 (65...♔g7 66.♔xh5 ♗xf4 67.♖xg4+; 65...♔e6 66.♖e2+−) 66.♔xh5 ♗xf4 67.♖f2+−, winning the bishop.

61.♖d7+ ♔h6 62.hxg6 ♔xg6

Black is checkmated after 62...g3 63.♔xf5 ♔g7 (63...g2 64.♖h7#) 64.♖d3 g2 65.♖h3#

63.♖f7 ♗c1

White eliminates all of his opponent's pawn after 63...g3 64.♖xf5 g2 65.♖g5++−.

64.♖xf5 ♔h6 65.♔e5

Reintroducing the threat of ♖g5.

65...♗b2+

65...g3 66.♖g5+− drops the pawn.

66.♔e4 and Black resigned.

Example No. 10
M. Bagi − V. Zvjaginsev
Budva 2019

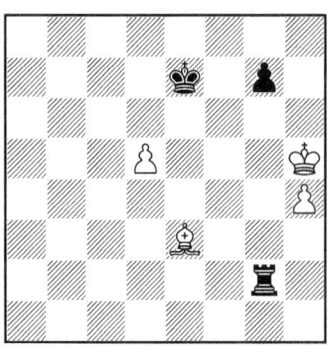

Black to move

In this position, the Moscow grandmaster managed to put into practice a well-known, beautiful, study-like checkmating idea.

60...♔f6!

The straightforward 60...♔d6? leads to a draw after 61.♗g5 ♔xd5 62.♔g6=.

60...♔f7? results in a draw after 61.♗g5! (61.d6? ♔g8 62.d7 ♔h7 63.d8=♕ g6#) 61...♔g8 (61...g6+ 62.♔h6 ♖g3 63.d6 ♖d3 64.♗e7 ♖d5 65.♗g5 ♖xd6 66.h5=) 62.♔g6! ♖e2 63.♗f4!=.

61.d6

The same checkmating idea is implemented after 61.♗g5+ ♔f5 62.d6 ♖e2! 63.d7 ♖e6! 64.d8=♕ (64.♗f6

♖xf6! 65.d8=♕ ♖h6#) 64...♖h6+! 65.♗xh6 g6#.

61...♖g6!

and White disappointingly resigned instead of allowing the beautiful checkmate 62.d7 ♔f5 63.d8=♕ ♖h6+ 64.♗xh6 g6#.

Example No. 11
Z. Medvegy − P. Prohaszka
Hungary 2021

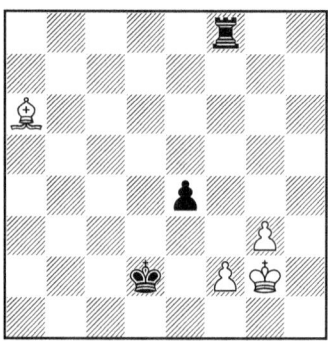

White to move

If White had a dark-squared bishop instead of a light-squared one, then making a draw would have been simple as the bishop would have moved to the a7-g1 diagonal to reliably secure the f2-pawn. The black king's attack on the f-pawn looks critical for White in this situation. Therefore, care must be taken against its showing up on e1.

95.♗b7?

White attempts to counter this threat by challenging the only remaining black pawn, only to miss a deadly blow.

95.♔f1? e3 96.f4 ♖a8−+ is also bad and gives Black an easy win.

The following lines show what comes of White's hopes for the passed pawn in an attempt to save the rook vs. pawn ending − 95.g4? ♔e1 96.g5 ♖xf2+

97.♔g3 ♖f3+ (97...e3? 98.g6 ♖f6 99.♗d3!) 98.♔g4 ♖a3

99.♗c4

(99.♗b5 e3 100.g6 ♖a7 101.♗d3 [101.♗c4 ♖a4−+; 101.♔g5 ♖a5−+] 101...♔d2−+)

99...e3 100.♔h5 (100.g6 ♖a4−+; 100.♔f5 ♖c3! 101.♗a6 ♖c5+ 102.♔f4 ♔f2 103.g6 ♖c6 104.g7 ♖g6−+) 100...♖a4 101.♗d3. 101.♗b5 also loses to 101...♖a5 102.♗c4 ♔f2 103.♔h6 ♖a4 104.♗b5 ♖b4 105.♗d3 ♖h4+ 106.♔g6 ♖d4 107.♗b5 ♖d6+ 108.♔h5 ♔f3 109. ♗c4 ♖d4 110.♗f1 ♔f4 111.g6 ♖d1−+.

101...♔d2 102.♗f1

(102.♗b5 ♔c3! 103.♔h6 [103.g6 ♖a5−+; 103.♗f1 ♖a1 104.♗b5 ♖b1 105.♗e2 ♖b2 106.♗f1 ♖f2 107.♗b5 ♖g2 108.g6 ♔d4 109.♔h6 ♔e5 110. g7 ♔f6−+; 103.♗xa4 e2−+] 103... ♖h4+! 104.♔g7 ♖c4!−+ and there

is no stopping the black pawn from promoting)

102...♖a1   103.♗b5   (103.♗c4 ♔c3−+)

103...♔c3! The black king joins the battle against the white passed pawn.

104.♔h6 ♖b1 105.♗e2 (105.♗a6 ♖b6+−+) 105...♖h1+ 106.♔g7 ♖h2 107.♗a6 ♔d4! 108.g6 ♔e5! 109.♔f7 ♖f2+ 110.♔e7 ♖f6! 111.g7 (111.♗d3 ♖xg6 112.♗xg6 e2−+) 111...♖xa6! 112.g8=♕ ♖a7+ 113.♔f8 ♖a8+−+ − Black eliminates the newly promoted white queen and promotes his pawn afterwards.

Furthermore, the pawn provocation is not going to help: 95.f4? ♖a8! (both 95...exf3+? 96.♔f2= and 95...e3? 96.♔f3= are bad) 96.♗b5 ♖a5 97.♗f1 (97.♗c4 ♖a3!? 98.f5 ♖c3! 99.♗a6 e3 100.g4 e2 101.♗xe2 ♔xe2 102.f6 ♖f3 103.g5 ♔e3−+) 97...♖a3

98.g4. 98.f5 ♖f3 99.g4 ♖xf1! 100. ♔xf1 e3−+ makes no difference.

98...♖f3 99.f5 ♖xf1! 100.♔xf1 e3−+ and White is a tempo behind with his pawn promotion because of the black pawn's check on the king.

The way to go is to retreat the king from the potential check via 95.♔g1! ♖b8. Black tries to prevent the white bishop from attacking its pawn.

(Following 95...♔e1 96.♗b7! ♖e8 97.g4!? [97.♔g2=] 97...♔d2 98.♔g2 ♔d3 99.♔g3 ♔d4 [99...♖f8 100.g5 ♖f3+ 101.♔g4 ♖xf2 102.g6=] 100. g5 ♔e5 101.♗a6! ♖f8 [101...♔f5 102. f3 e3 103.f4 ♔e4 104.♗e2=] 102.♗e2 ♖f5 [102...♔f5 103.f4=] 103.♗g4! ♖xg5 104.f4+! exf3 105.♔xf3= White succeeds in exchanging off the only remaining black pawn)

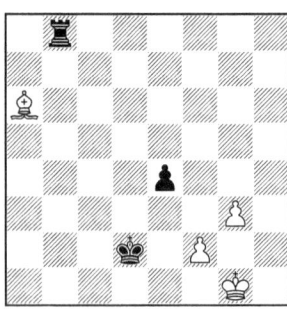

96.♗c4! Nevertheless, White finds another square for his bishop's potential offensive against the e4-pawn (96.g4? ♖g8−+; 96.♔f1? ♖b1+ 97.♔g2 ♔e1 98.g4 ♖b6 99.♗c4 ♖f6−+).

96...♖b1+ (96...♔e1 97.♗d5=) 97.♔g2 ♖b2 (97...♔e1 98.♗d5 ♖b4 99.g4=) 98.♗d5 (98.g4 e3 99.fxe3? ♔c3+!−+) 98...♔d3 99.♔g1=.

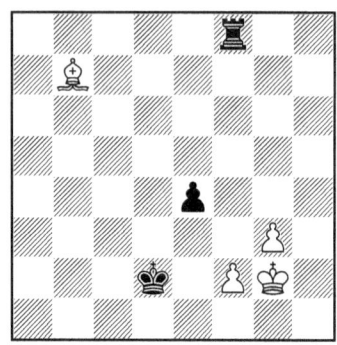

95...♖xf2+!, and White resigned in the face of the black pawn's promotion following 96.♔xf2 e3+ 97.♔g2 e2.

Example No. 12
K. Alekseenko − A. Sarana
Khanty-Mansiysk 2018

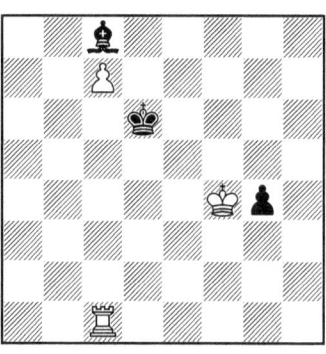

White to move

Black tries to hold together a drawing formation, in which his bishop doubles as his only pawn's defender and the dangerous opponent's pawn's blockader, whereas the black king never abandons the white pawn to prevent his opponent's rook from activating. Black intends to meet the white king's long-distance transfer to the queenside by deflecting the rook with the g-pawn's advance. Can Black really hold this position an exchange down?

58.♔e4

The main winning idea has so far escaped White. The way to victory is 58.♔g3! ♔d5 (both 58...♔e5? 59.♖d1+− and 58...♔d7? 59.♔xg4+− lose on the spot) 59.♖c2 ♔d6

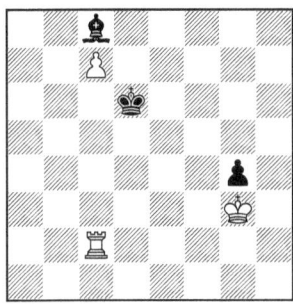

60.♖c4!, and Black is in zugzwang.

60...♔d5 (60...♔d7 61.♔xg4+−; 60...♔e7 61.♖d4!+−; 60...♔e5 61.♖xg4!+−) 61.♖xg4!+− ♔d6 (61... ♗xg4 62.♔xg4+− and the pawn is going to promote) 62.♖c4! (62.♖g7? ♗d7= is ill-advised) 62...♔d5 63.♖c1, and the white king's march to his pawn seals the game's outcome.

58...♗b7+ 59.♔e3 ♗c8

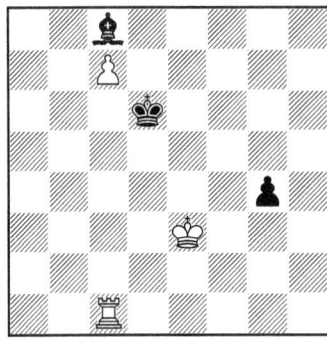

60.♔d4?

Yet another deviation from the correct plan. White needed to return his king to attacking the black pawn via

60.♔f4! ♔d5 61.♔g3 ♔d6 62.♖c4!+−, forcing Black into the zugzwang position that we now know

60...♔d7

60...g3? goes down to 61.♔e3 g2 62.♔f2+− as the white king is in the square of the passed pawn.

61.♖c3

61.♔e5? would have given the win away to 61...g3! 62.♔f4 g2 63.♔g3 g1=♕+ 64.♖xg1 ♔xc7=.

61...♔d6 62.♖c2 ♔d7 63.♔e3 ♔d6 64.♔e4 ♗b7+

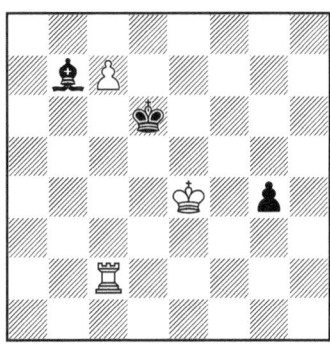

65.♔d4

White again needed to go for 65.♔f4!

65...♗c8 66.♖c3 ♔d7 67.♖c5 ♔d6 68.♔c4?

Long maneuvering has panned out with no gains for White. On failing to find the correct plan, White lets the victory escape.

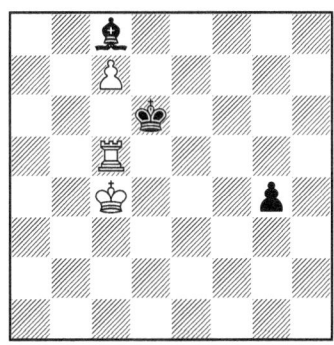

68...g3!

A saving exchange of pawns is about to take place.

69.♔b5 g2 70.♖c1 g1=♕! 71.♖xg1 ♔xc7, and the game ended in a draw.

Example No. 13
G. Garcia – V. Mikhalevski
Montreal 2004

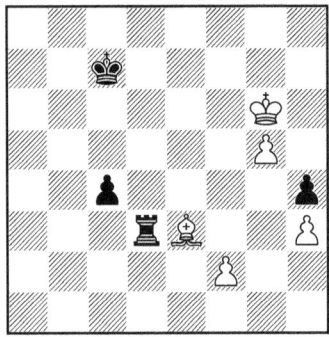

Black to move

This position demonstrates an instance of advantage conversion by means of transposing from a more complex endgame into a less complex one. The skill of precise calculation of long lines and, indeed, to the required depth, is of great help in anybody's endgame victories to come!

60...♖xe3!

Black exploits the opportunity to transpose into a less complex winning pawn ending that lends itself to precise calculation.

61.fxe3 c3 62.♔h7!

The most resilient. Black wins easily after the underwhelming 62.♔f7? c2 63.g6 c1=♕ 64.g7 ♕f1+ 65.♔e7 ♕g2 66.♔f8 ♕f3+.

62...c2 63.g6 c1=♕ 64.g7 ♕c2+!

If we begin delivering checks from the bottom rung of the ladder with 64...

♕b1+ 65.♔h8 ♕b2 66.♔h7 ♕c2+ we land in the same position via a transposition of moves.

65.♔h8

Black delivers checkmate after 65.♔h6? ♕b3 66.♔h7 ♕f7! 67.♔h8 ♕h5+ 68.♔g8 ♔d7 69.♔f8 ♕e8#.

65...♕c3! 66.♔h7 ♕d3+! 67.♔h8 ♕xe3! 68.g8=♕

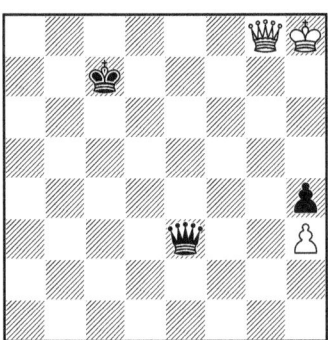

68...♕e5+!

It is this strong move that Black had in mind when going for the exchange sacrifice.

Both 68...♕h6+? 69.♕h7+ ♕xh7+ 70.♔xh7= and 68...♕d4+? 69.♕g7+= yield no more than a draw. 68...♕xh3? is also bad, as it leads to a well-known drawn queen ending after 69.♕g7+=.

69.♔h7

Similarly, another way of defending from the checks 69.♕g7+ ♔d6! 70.♔h7 (70.♕xe5+ ♔xe5 71.♔g7 ♔f4 72.♔f6 ♔g3–+) 70...♕xg7+! 71.♔xg7 ♔e5 72.♔g6 ♔f4–+ is of no help as the resulting pawn ending is lost.

69...♕h5+

And White resigned in the face of the black pawn's unstoppable promotion after 70.♔g7 ♕g5+ 71.♔h7 ♕xg8+ 72.♔xg8 ♔d6 73.♔f7 ♔e5 74.♔g6 ♔f4 75.♔h5 ♔g3 76.♔g5 ♔xh3 77.♔f4 ♔g2.

Example No. 14
M. Carlsen – V. Anand
Morelia/Linares.2008

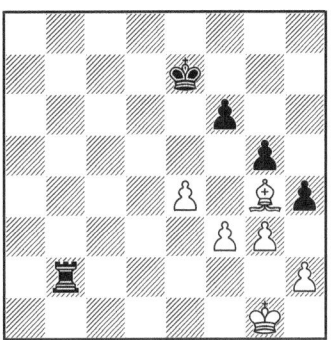

Black to move

The white king is cut off. The decisive inroad of the black king into White's home turf is about to take place with the idea of attacking the white pawns and creating checkmate threats to his white counterpart.

White's chance to save the game lies in reducing the number of remaining pawns to as few as possible.

34...♖e2!

An excellent decision! Black aims to throw a wrench into the gears of the f-pawn's advance.

If the black king heads to the white pawns immediately, then after 34...♔d6?! 35.gxh4 gxh4 36.f4 ♖d2 37.♗h3 ♔c5?! 38.e5 ♖d4 39.exf6 ♖xf4 40.♔g2! ♖xf6

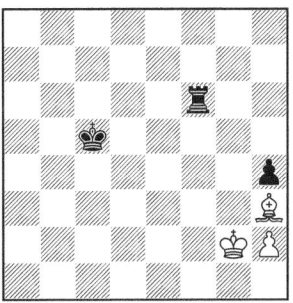

41.♗c8!= we arrive at a theoretical position that is a draw, the key aspect being the white pawn not having moved to h3, which gives the white king access to this square not only to hide from rook checks, but also to disturb the h4-pawn.

35.gxh4

It does not help to avoid the immediate exchange of pawns: 35.♗f5 ♔d6 (35...hxg3 36.hxg3=) 36.f4 gxf4 37.gxf4 ♔c5 38.e5 fxe5 39.fxe5 ♖xe5

40.♗c8. Black forces White to commit his pawn to h3 anyway after 40.♗g4 ♖g5! 41.h3 ♔d4–+; 40.♗h3 ♖e2!–+ is not a game-changer either.

It is now instrumental to stop the white king from showing up on g2: 40...♖e2! (40...♔d4? 41.♔g2!=) 41.♗d7 ♔d4 42.♗c8 ♔e3 43.♗d7 (43.♗g4 ♖b2–+) 43...♔f3! 44.♗c6+ ♔f4 45.♗d7

45...♖d2! The black rook marks the white bishop as much as possible.

46.♗c8   ♖d8!   47.♗e6.   Neither 47.♗b7 h3! 48.♔f2 ♖d2+ 49.♔g1 ♔e3!−+, nor 47.♗h3 ♖d1+! 48.♔g2 ♖d2+ 49.♔g1 ♔f3!−+ are of any help.

47...♔f3!, and if White persists in not advancing his pawn to h3 with 48.♗b3, then Black completes the mating net for the white king via 48...h3! 49.♗a4 ♔e3 50.♔f1 ♖a8−+.

35...gxh4 36.h3

After 36.♗f5 ♔d6 37.f4 ♔c5 the position transposes to the 35.♗f5 continuation.

36...♔d6 37.♔f1 ♖b2 38.f4 ♔c5 39.e5 ♖b4 40.exf6 ♖xf4+ 41.♔e2 ♔d4 42.♗f3 ♖xf6

Black's preceding play has forced White to part with the pawn. However, there is still much work to do to win the game. Anand handles this ending superbly and demonstrates the correct winning plan.

43.♗b7 ♖b6 44.♗c8

44.♗g2 ♖b3−+ is no better than the text.

44...♔e4   45.♗g4   ♖b2+   46.♔e1 ♔e3 47.♔f1 ♔f4 48.♔e1 ♔g3 49.♔f1

49...♖f2+!

After getting his own king active, Black switches to the plan of driving his

opponent's king as far away from the h3-pawn as possible.

50.♔e1

50.♔g1   ♖f7   51.♗c8   (51.♗e6 ♖e7−+; 51.♗h5 ♖c7−+) 51...♖c7−+ is an immediate failure.

50...♖f4 51.♗c8

Not walking into a prearranged trap 51.♔e2? ♖xg4! 52.hxg4 h3−+.

51...♖f8 52.♗g4 ♔g2 53.♔e2 ♖e8+ 54.♔d3 ♔f2!

It is yet premature to execute the exchange   sacrifice   idea: 54...♖e1 55.♔d2 ♖h1? 56.♔e2 ♖xh3 57.♗xh3+ ♔xh3 58.♔f2=.

55.♗f5 ♖e3+ 56.♔d4

The white king is also pushed away after 56.♔d2 ♖e5 57.♗g4 ♖d5+−+.

56...♔f3!

Black is consistent in implementing his winning plan.

57.♗g4+ ♔f4 58.♔d5

The   white   king   is   once   again thrown back after 58.♗c8 ♖e8 59.♗g4 ♖d8+−+.

58...♖e5+! 59.♔d4

Black   captures   the   white   pawn to decisive effect with the rook after 59.♔d6 ♖g5 60.♗c8 ♔g3 61.♔e7 ♔h2 62.♔f6 ♖g3−+.

59...♖g5 60.♗e6

Neither 60.♗d7 ♖g8! nor 60.♗c8 ♖g8 61.♗e6 ♖d8+−+ make any difference.

60...♖g6

and the future world champion resigned in the face of the pawn queening after 61.♗c8 ♖d6+ 62.♔c5 ♖d2 63.♗e6 ♔g3 64.♔c4 ♖h2 65.♔d3 ♖xh3 66.♗xh3 ♔xh3 67.♔e2 ♔g2.

Example No. 15
G. Jones − K. Mekhitarian
Batumi 2018

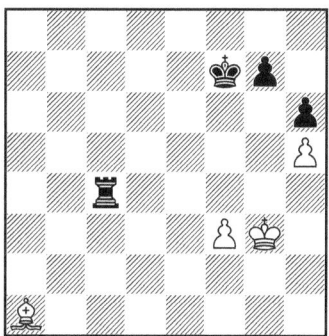

Black to move

Despite both sides having pawns on one flank only, Black should seemingly experience no problems prosecuting his material advantage. The white pawns are disconnected, which makes them easier targets to attack for Black and bigger liabilities to defend for White.

61...♖c7?!

Black attempts to reassign the defense of his g7-pawn to enable his king's advance.

However, as long as the white f-pawn remains where it is, Black can get to the h5-pawn without dropping his own one: 61...♖c5! 62.♔h4. Likewise, White faces the same problems after 62.♔g4 ♖c1 63.♗b2 ♖b1 64.♗c3 ♖g1+

65.♔h4 ♔e6 66.♗d4 ♖d1 67.♗c3 (67.♗xg7? ♖h1+ 68.♔g4 ♖g1+−+) 67...♖h1+ 68.♔g4 ♖g1+ 69.♔h4 ♔f5 70.♗d4 ♖h1+ 71.♔g3 ♖xh5 72.♗xg7 ♖g5+−+.

62...♖c1! 63.♗e5. Both 63.♗b2 ♖b1! 64.♗c3? ♖b3−+ and 63.♗d4? ♖c4−+ do White a disservice.

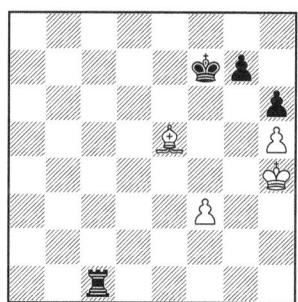

63...♔e6! 64.♗b2. There is no taking the pawn: 64.♗xg7? ♖h1+ 65.♔g4 ♖g1+−+. White is also defenseless after 64.f4 ♔f5 65.♔h3 ♖g1 66.♔h2 ♖g4 67.♔h3 ♖xf4! 68.♗xg7 ♔g5−+.

64...♖h1+ 65.♔g4 ♖g1+ 66.♔h4 (66.♔f4 ♖g5 67.♔e4 ♔f7−+; 66.♔h3 ♔f5 67.♔h2 ♖g5−+) 66...♔f5! 67.♗d4 ♖h1+ 68.♔g3 ♖xh5 69.♗xg7 ♖g5+−+.

62.♗b2 ♔e6?! 63.♔f4 ♖c4+ 64.♔g3 ♖c5

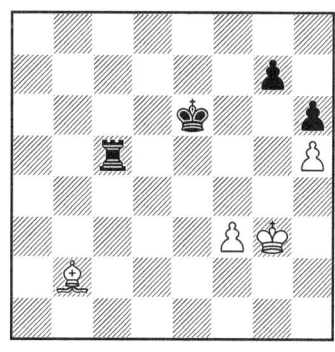

65.f4!

White goes down quickly both with 65.♗xg7? ♖g5+−+ and 65.♔h4 ♖g5−+.

65...♖c7 66.♗e5 ♖b7 67.♔g4 ♖b1

The correct way to go is 67...♖d7! 68.♗b2 ♖d1 69.♔f3 (69.♗xg7? ♖g1+−+) 69...♖f1+! 70.♔e4 (70.♔g4 ♖g1+ 71.♔f3 ♔f5−+; 70.♔g3 ♔f5 71.♗e5 ♔e4! 72.♔h2 ♖xf4! 73.♗xg7 ♖h4+ 74.♔g3 ♖xh5−+) 70...♖g1 71.♗c3 (71.♔f3 ♔f5 72.♗e5 g5 73.hxg6 ♖xg6 74.♗c7 h5−+; 71.f5+ ♔f7−+)

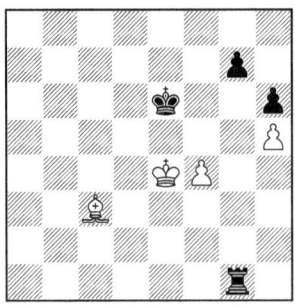

71...♖g4! It is equally important not only to attack the h5-pawn, but to prevent the white king from defending it as well. 72.♗e5 (72.♔f3 ♔f5 73.♗e5 g6−+; 72.♗d4 ♔f7 73.♗f2 ♖g2! 74.♔f3 ♖h2−+) 72...♔f7! 73.♔f5 (73.♔f3 ♖h4−+) 73...♖h4−+ and Black gets the upper hand.

68.♔f3 ♖g1 69.♗d4 ♖f1+

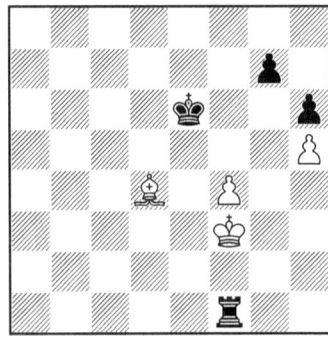

70.♔e4! ♔f7

70...♖h1 71.♗xg7 ♖xh5 72.f5+ ♔f7 73.f6 ♔g6 74.♔f4! leads to a positional draw after 74...♖a5. There is no cutting off the white king: 74...♔g5 75.♗xh6! ♔xh6 76.f7=.

75.♔g4 h5+ 76.♔h4 ♖a3 77.♗h8! ♖a4+ 78.♔g3 ♖g4+ 79.♔h3 (79.♔f3? ♖g5−+) 79...♖f4 80.♗g7 ♔g5 81.♔g3 h4+ 82.♔h3 ♖f3+ 83.♔g2 ♔g4 84.f7! ♖xf7 (84...h3+ 85.♔g1 ♖xf7 86.♗e5=) 85.♗e5=.

71.♔f5!

71.♗e5? ♖h1−+ is an error.

71...♖h1 72.♔g4 ♔e6 73.♔f3

There is no touching the pawn this time either: 73.♗xg7? ♖g1+−+.

73...♖xh5?! Black has abandoned all hopes of avoiding the exchange of pawns.

73...♔f5 74.♗xg7 ♖h3+ 75.♔g2 ♖xh5 76.♔g3= would have transposed to the text. Meanwhile, White is in time to keep his pawn alive after 73...♔f7 74.♔g4!.

74.♗xg7 ♔f5

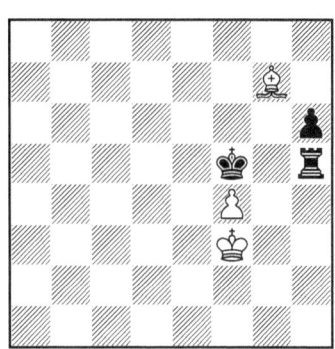

75.♔g3!

There is no doing without this precision. 75.♗e5? loses to 75...♖h3+ 76.♔g2 ♔g4−+.

75...♖h1 76.♗e5=

This is a drawn ending. However, this game has many adventures in store for us yet.

76...♖b1 77.♔h4 ♖g1

77...♖h1+ 78.♔g3 h5 79.♗c7 h4+ 80.♔g2 ♖c1 81.♗e5 ♔g4 82.f5 ♖c2+ 83.♔h1 (83.♔g1=) 83...♔xf5 (83...♔h3 84.♔g1 ♖c1+ 85.♔f2 ♖c5 86.♗d6 ♖xf5+ 87.♔g1=) 84.♗d6= does not make any difference because the resulting position is a drawn one, as we already know.

78.♔h3 ♔e4 79.♔h4

79...♔f5

79...♔f3 does not promise much in the way of success – 80.♔h5! ♖h1+ 81.♔g6 h5 82.f5 ♔e4 (82...h4 83.f6=) 83.♗c7 ♔d5 84.f6 ♔e6 85.♗f4 h4 (85...♖f1 86.♗g5=) 86.f7 ♖g1+ 87.♗g5 ♖f1 (87...♖xg5+ 88.♔xg5 ♔xf7 89.♔xh4=) 88.♗xh4 ♖xf7=.

80.♔h3 ♖g4 81.♗c7 h5 82.♗e5 ♔g6 83.♗d6 ♔f6 84.♗c7 ♔e6 85.♗b8 ♖g1 86.♗e5 ♔f5 87.♔h2 ♖d1 88.♔g3 ♔e4 89.♗c7 ♖g1+

90.♔h4!

Black wins after the underwhelming 90.♔h2? ♖c1 91.♗e5 ♔f3! 92.♗d6 (92.f5 ♖c5–+) 92...♔g4–+.

90...♔f5 91.♗e5

The pawn is poisonous: 91.♔xh5? ♖h1#.

91...♖h1+ 92.♔g3 ♖c1 93.♔h4 ♔g6 94.♔h3 ♖b1 95.♔g3 ♔f5 96.♔h4 ♖f1 97.♔g3 ♖h1 98.♔g2 ♖h4 99.♔g3 ♖g4+ 100.♔h3 ♔e4 101.♗c7

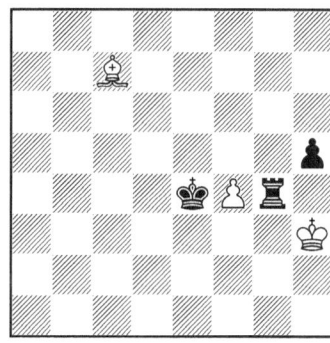

101...♖g1

101...♔f3 leads nowhere again because White is in time to deal with the black pawn after 102.♗e5 ♖g1 103.♔h4! (103.♔h2? ♖b1 104.♗d6 ♔g4–+) 103...♖h1+ 104.♔g5 h4 105.f5 ♔e4 (105...h3 106.f6 h2 107.♗xh2 ♖xh2 108.f7=) 106.♗f6! (106.♗c7? ♖c1–+; 106.♗d6 ♖d1–+; 106.♗b8 ♖b1–+) 106...h3 107.♔g4! h2 108.♔g3! ♔xf5 109.♗h8 ♔e4 110.♔g2=.

102.♔h4 ♖c1 103.♗d6 ♖h1+ 104.♔g5

White would have had an easier time with 104.♔g3! h4+ 105.♔g4 h3 106.♗e5 h2 107.♔g3=.

104...h4

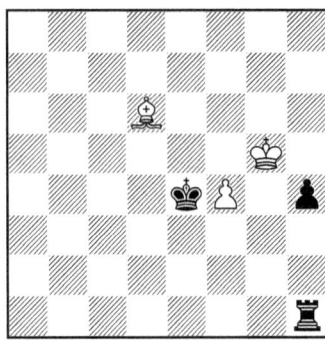

105.f5? White has been patiently fighting back for a very long time – for nearly 50 moves – only to blunder a step away from a draw.

White needed to play 105.♔g4! h3 (105...♔e3 106.f5=) 106.f5 (106.♗e5 h2 107.♔g3=) 106...h2 (106...♖d1 107.♗g3=) 107.♔h3!=.

105...h3?

Black returns the favor. Surgical precision was required of the rook to bring the game home by driving the white bishop to a square that allowed Black to gain a decisive tempo: 105...♖d1!

a) 106.♗h2 ♖d2! 107.♗b8 h3 108. f6 ♖g2+! 109.♔h6 ♖f2! 110.♔g6 (110. ♔g7 ♖b2 111.♗d6 ♔d5! 112.♗f4 ♔e6 113.f7 ♖b7–+ and Black catches up with the white passed pawn)

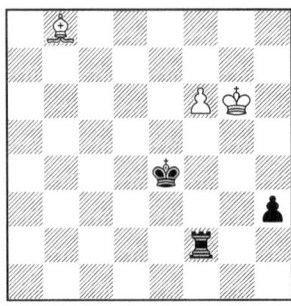

110...♖b2! Getting at the white bishop once again.

111.♗c7 (111.♗g3 ♖g2–+; 111. ♗d6 ♖g2+ 112.♔h5 ♖f2! 113.♔g6 ♔d5! 114.♗c7 ♔e6–+) 111...♖g2+! 112.♔h7 ♖f2! 113.♔g7 (113.♔g6 ♔d5 114.f7 ♔e6–+) 113...♖c2! 114. ♗b8 ♖b2! 115.♗d6 (115.♗c7 ♖b7–+) 115...♔d5! 116.f7 ♖g2+ 117.♔h6 (117. ♔f6 ♖f2+ 118.♔e7 ♖xf7+ 119.♔xf7 ♔xd6–+) 117...♖f2–+, winning. This is nearly a study-like sequence!

b) 106.♗b8 ♖b1 107.♗c7 ♖b7 108. ♗d6 ♔d5 109.♗h2 ♖b2 110.♗c7 h3–+ loses the game;

c) 106.♗c7 ♖d7! 107.♗b8 ♖b7! 108. ♗h2 ♖b2! 109.♗c7 h3 110.f6 ♖g2+!

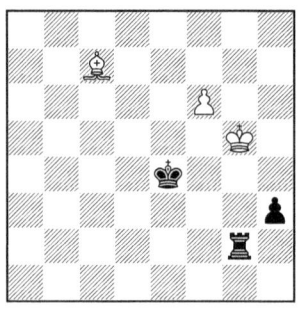

111.♔h6 (111.♔h4 h2 112.♗xh2 ♖xh2+ 113.♔g5 ♔e5 114.f7 ♖f2 115. ♔g6 ♔e6–+) 111...♖f2! 112.♔g7 (112. ♔g6 ♔d5–+) 112...♖c2! 113.♗b8 (113.♗g3 ♖g2–+; 113.♗d6 ♖g2+ 114. ♔h7 ♖f2 115.♔g7 ♔d5–+) 113...♖b2! 114.♗d6 (114.♗c7 ♖b7–+; 114.♗g3 ♖g2–+) 114...♖g2+ 115.♔f8 (115. ♔h7 ♔d5 116.f7 ♖f2–+) 115...♔d5–+ is no better than the previous line.

106.f6! ♖f1

The game also ends in a draw after 106...h2 107.♗xh2 ♖xh2 108.f7 ♖f2 109.♔g6 ♔e5 110.♔g7=.

107.♗c7

107.♔g4? ♖xf6–+ is an error that leaves the bishop hanging.

107...♖f2

107...♔d5 108.♔g4= leads to the exchange of pawns.

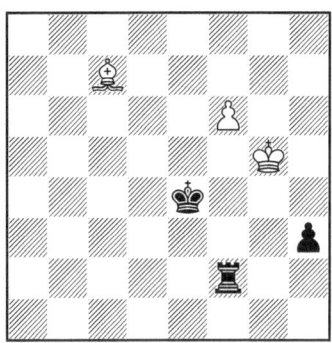

108.♗b8?

This is yet another instance of White blundering on the verge of a draw.

The correct 108.♗g3! ♖g2 109.♔g4 h2 110.f7 h1=♕ 111.f8=♕ ♕d1+ 112.♔h3= leaves Black with no opportunity to exploit his right to move to create real threats against the white king.

108...♖g2+?!

A speedier way to deliver victory was 108...♔d5! 109.f7 (109.♔g6 ♔e6-+; 109.♔g4 h2 110.♗xh2 ♖xh2-+) 109...♖xf7 110.♔g4 ♖h7 111.♗h2 ♔e4 112.♔g3 ♖g7+ 113.♔xh3 ♔f3-+, and White is doomed.

109.♔h6

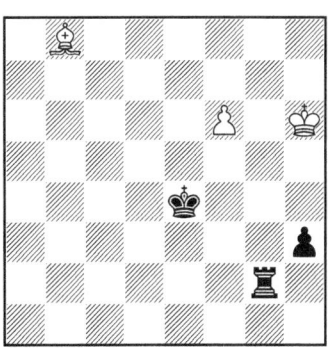

109...h2?

This move is a final farewell to victory. 109...♖b2? 110.♗g3! ♖f2 111.♔g5! was also a draw.

(111.♗xf2 leads to interesting lines: 111...h2 112.f7 h1=♕+ 113.♔g7 ♕a1+ [113...♕g2+ 114.♗g3! ♕xg3+ 115. ♔h7=]

114.♗d4! Getting rid of the useless bishop without further ado. 114... ♕xd4+ 115.♔g8 ♕d5 116.♔g7 ♕d7 117.♔h8! [117.♔g8? ♔f5 118.f8=♕+ ♔g6-+] 117...♔f5 [117...♕e7 118. ♔g8=] 118.f8=♕+ ♔g6 119.♕g8+=, with a draw)

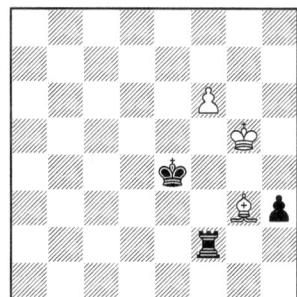

111...♖f5+ 112.♔g4! ♖xf6 113. ♔xh3 ♔f3 114.♔h4!=, and the white king manages to break free from the mating net.

Black catches up with the passed pawn and wins the game after 109...♖f2!

110.♔g5 (110.♔g6 ♖b2!–+; 110.♔g7 ♖b2–+) 110...♔d5! 111.♗g3 (111.f7 ♖xf7 112.♔g4 ♖h7 113.♗h2 ♔e4–+) 111...h2 112.♗xh2 ♖xh2 113.f7 ♖f2 114.♔g6 ♔e6–+.

110.♗xh2 ♖xh2+ 111.♔g7 ♖g2+ 112.♔h7

King retreats to the f-file are fatal: 112.♔f7? ♔f5–+; 112.♔f8? ♔f5 113. f7 ♔f6 114.♔e8 ♖e2+ 115.♔f8 ♖e7.

112...♖f2 113.♔g7!

The careless 113.♔g6? ♔e5 114. f7 ♔e6–+ would have cost White the game yet again.

113...♖g2+ 114.♔h7 ♔e5 115.f7 ♖f2 116.♔g7 ♖xf7+ 117.♔xf7 and, having exhausted the game's fighting potential, the opponents agreed a draw.

Example No. 16
D. Navara – H. Stefansson
Catez 2022

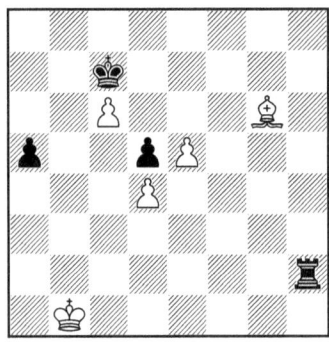

Black to move

The previous move saw the exchange of a pair of rooks, and now Black faces the dilemma of which pawn to take first to convert his material advantage.

48...♔xc6?

Black rushes with the move that begs to be played. However, it gives the win away.

It was correct to eliminate the more important pawn first with 48...♖d2! 49.e6 (White loses after both 49.♔c1 ♖xd4 50.e6 ♔d6! 51.♗f5 ♖c4+–+ and 49.♗f7 ♔xc6–+) 49...♖e2!–+ (49... ♖xd4? is a mistake that passes the victory to White after 50.e7 ♖b4+ 51.♔c2 ♖b8 52.e8=♕ ♖xe8 53.♗xe8+–), and the white pawns start dropping one after another.

49.♗e8+!

This is a strong rejoinder. It turns out that now White manages to do away with the d5-pawn.

49...♔c7

49...♔b6 50.♗f7! is no better than the text.

50.♗f7 ♖d2 51.♗xd5 ♖xd4

Black might have seen this position in his calculations and thought it to be a winning one since his pawn was still on a5. However, the remaining white pawn has a decisive say in this ending, which is a drawn position. Firstly, eliminating the white pawn is far from easy now. Secondly, as we are going to see in a while, White takes skillful advantage of his passed pawn to tether the black rook.

52.♗f7 ♖e4 53.e6 ♖e2 54.♗g8 ♔d6 55.♔c1 ♖f2 56.♗f7 ♖g2

57.♔b1!

There is no zugzwang in this position because White has a spare move. Both 57.♔d1?♖b2!–+ and 57.♗h5?♔xe6–+ lead to a theoretically won ending.

57...♖e2 58.♗c1 ♔c5 59.♔d1! ♖e4 60.♔c2 ♔b4 61.♗g8 ♖e2+ 62.♔d3 ♖e1

After 62...♖g2 63.♗f7= the black rook no longer prevents the white pawn's promotion.

63.♔d2 ♖e5 64.♔c2 ♖c5+

Neither 64...a4 65.♔b1= nor 64...♔a3 65.♔c3= make any difference to the evaluation of this position.

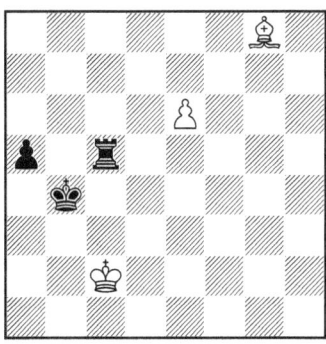

65.♔b2!

A great move. 65.♔d2? ♖c7–+ loses the game as the white king is cut off from the black passed pawn.

It would be a mistake to go for 65.♔b1? ♔a3! 66.♗f7 (66.♗h7 ♔b3 67.♗g8 ♖g5–+; 66.e7 ♖e5–+) 66...♖c7!, and Black scores with a surgically precise continuation: 67.♗g8 (67.♔a1 ♖c1#)

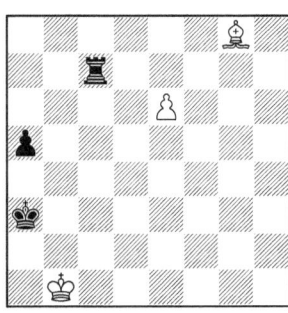

67...♖e7! The rook does a double job of blockading the pawn and keeping the opponent's bishop restrained, while being always available to join a mating net construction to finish off the white king.

68.♗f7 (68.♔c2 ♔a2–+; 68.♔a1 ♖g7–+) 68...♔b3! 69.♔a1 (69.♗g8 ♖g7!–+) 69...♖c7! 70.♔b1 (70.e7+ ♔a3! 71.e8=♕ ♖c1#) 70...♖b7! The rook lies in ambush for potential delivery of a discovered check.

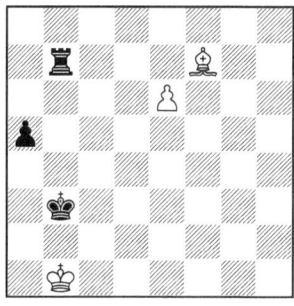

71.♔a1 (71.e7+ ♔a3+ 72.♔c2 ♖xe7–+) 71...♔a3 72.♗e8 ♖g7 73.♔b1 ♔b3 74.♔c1 ♖e7! 75.♗g6 (75. ♗f7 a4 76.♔b1 a3 77.♔a1 a2–+) 75...♔c3! 76.♗f5 ♖b7! Denying the king the opportunity of fighting against the black passed pawn.

77.♗e4 ♖b2! 78.♔d1 (78.e7 ♖e2!–+) 78...♖b6. The black rook has literally terrorized the white pieces with its never-ending threats.

79.♗f5 a4! Time has come for the pawn's victorious march.

80.e7 ♖b8 81.♗g6 a3! 82.♗f7 (Black gets a new queen following 82.e8=♕ ♖xe8 83.♗xe8 a2–+) 82...♖e8!–+, and Black wins. What impressive lines!

65...♖e5

65...♖c7 66.♗f7= makes no difference either.

66.♔c2 ♖c5+ 67.♔b2 ♖g5 68.♗f7 ♖g2+ 69.♔c1 ♔c3

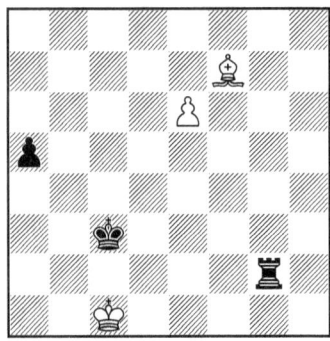

70.♔b1!

70.♔d1? fails to 70...♖g1+ 71.♔e2 ♖g5! 72.♔d1 ♖e5 73.♗g8 a4−+.

70...♖g1+ 71.♔a2 ♖e1 72.♗g8!

There is a move to spare yet again. White gets mated after 72.♔a3? ♖a1#.

72...♔b4 73.♔b2 ♖e2+ 74.♔c1 ♔c3 75.♔b1! ♔b3 76.♔c1! ♔a2 77.♗f7 ♔a1 78.♔d1 ♖e5 79.♔c2! a4

79...♖c5+ 80.♔b3= is also a draw.

80.♔c3 a3 81.♗g8 a2

82.♗h7!

This is another instance of a drawn position in which the black king cannot make it out of the corner.

82...♖xe6 83.♔b3 ♖e3+ 84.♔c2 ♖g3 85.♗e4 ♖g4 86.♗h7 ♖g2+ 87.♔c3!

It was not too late to lose the game after 87.♔c1? ♖g7 88.♗d3 ♖c7+ 89.♗c2 ♖c8 90.♔d2 ♔b2−+.

And here Black recognized the futility of further attempts to win and agreed to a draw.

We now move to reviewing a set of positions in which the side nominally the exchange down is nonetheless in the driver's seat.

Example No. 17
B. Notkevich − J. Tisdall
Norway 2021

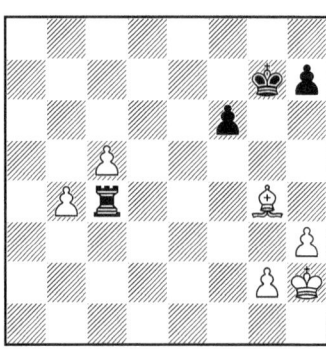

White to move

White has a pair of connected passed pawns as compensation for the exchange. That said, the black rook intends to capture the first pawn and stop the second pawn. White's job is to interfere with his opponent's plans.

49.♗e6!

And White is up to the task! Not only does the white bishop attack the crucial c4-square, but it continues to exercise control over the pawn promotion c8-square.

49...♖c3?

Black chooses the wrong square for his rook.

Naturally, it was a bad idea to take the pawn because it costs Black the rook after 49...♖xb4? 50.c6+−.

Black's attempt to dislodge the bishop from e6 does not work: 49...♖e4? 50.c6! (50.♗d5? ♖xb4 51.c6 ♖b5!; 50.♗d7? ♖xb4 51.c6 ♖c4!) 50...♖xe6 51.b5+− ♖e7 52.b6, and there is no stopping the white passed pawns.

To keep the position together Black needed to play either 49...♖c1! 50.♗d5 ♔f8 51.♗e4 (Black is in time to deal with the white passed pawns after 51.c6 ♔e7 52.b5 ♖b1!)

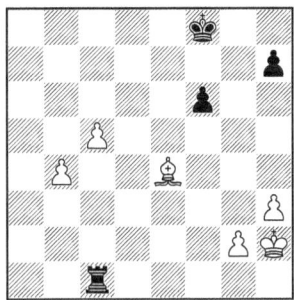

51...h6 (it was also fine to go for 51...♖c4 52.♗xh7 ♖xb4 53.♗d3 ♔e7 54.♗e2 ♖e4 55.♗f3 ♖c4 56.c6 f5=, with a likely draw) 52.c6 f5 53.♗d5 (53.♗xf5 ♖xc6=) 53...♔e7 54.♔g3 (54.b5 ♖b1!=) 54...♖b1 55.♔h4 ♖xb4+ 56.♔h5 ♖b5!? 57.♗f3 ♔f6 58.♔xh6 ♖b8! 59.♔h7 ♖c8 60.h4 ♖c7+ 61.♔g8 ♖c8+ 62.♔h7 ♖c7+ 63.♔h6 ♖c8 64.♔h7=, with a draw by repetition;

or 49...♖c2! 50.♗d5 ♔f8 51.c6 ♔e7 52.b5

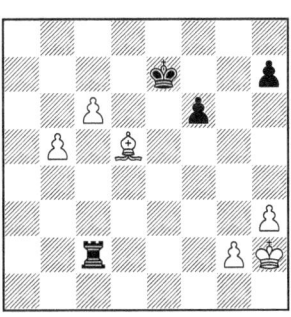

Contrary to the game, Black can now bail out with 52...♖b2! (52...♔d6? 53.b6!+−) 53.♗c4 ♔d6 54.♔g3 ♖b4 55.♗e2 ♔c7=, and the black king does a good job controlling the white passed pawns, while the rook, now relieved of its defensive duties, restricts the white king in its desire to assault the black kingside pawns.

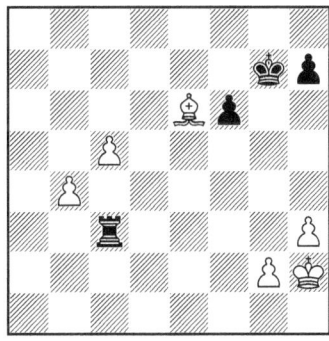

50.♗d5!+− ♔f8

The white pawns are equally unstoppable after 50...f5 51.c6 ♔f6 52.b5 ♔e5 53.b6 ♔d6 (53...♔xd5 54.b7 ♖b3 55.c7+−) 54.c7 ♔d7 55.♗e6+! ♔xe6 56.b7.

In a similar manner, 50...♖d3 51.c6 ♖xd5 52.c7+− is not going to be of any help.

51.c6! ♔e7 52.b5!

On realizing that the rook is denied access to the b-file, Black resigned in the face of 52...♔d6 53.b6! ♖xc6 (53...♔xd5 54.b7! ♖b3 55.c7+−) 54.♗xc6 ♔xc6 55.♔g3 ♔xb6 56.♔f4 ♔c6 57.♔f5, with a winning pawn ending.

Lessons from my Career

Example No. 18
O. Ivanov – A. Galkin
Rostov on Don 2010

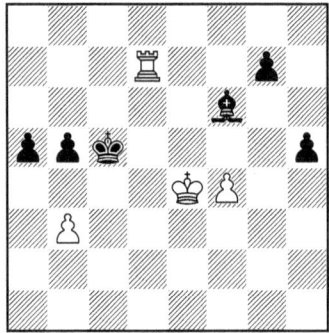

White to move

Let us look into this position from Black's point of view: in return for the exchange he has two pawns, each being a passed one or soon to be passed on opposite flanks. The black kingside passed pawn enjoys the bishop's support, while the potential queenside passed pawn has the king accompanying it. Further, the bishop is placed ideally. It is both protected by and protects the g7-pawn. Besides lending support to both his passed pawns, it stops the white f-pawn dead in its tracks. Further, the bishop will participate in shielding his king from the white rook's checks.

Now let us study this position through White's eyes. There is no doubt that he is fighting for a draw. Nevertheless, in addition to White having an active rook and a centralized king, Black's passed pawns have not advanced very far yet. All this contributes to White's optimism about his prospects of getting that draw.

41.♖b7?

White had to decide whether to deal with the future black queenside passer by placing his rook behind it or from the side. However, White's chosen plan for arranging his pieces is an error of judgement.

He needed to go for 41.♖d5+! ♔b4 42.♔d3! 42.♖xh5? is bad due to 42...a4 43.bxa4 bxa4 44.♔d3 a3 45.♖h2 ♔b3−+, and the pawn cannot be stopped.

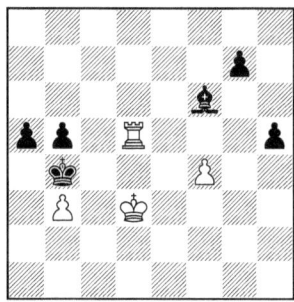

42...h4. Of course, nobody will let you create a pair of connected passed pawns just like that – 42...♔xb3? 43.♖xb5+ ♔a4 44.♖xh5, whereas 42...a4 43.bxa4 bxa4 44.♔c2! h4 (44...a3 45.♔b1=) 45.♖d3 leads to the same position.

43.♔c2 a4 44.bxa4 bxa4 45.♖d3 a3 (45...♔c4 46.♖a3=; 45...♗e7 46.♖d7 ♗f6 47.♖d3=) 46.♔b1 ♔c4 47.♖e3! ♔d4

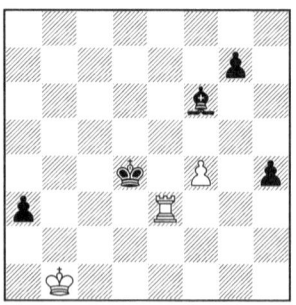

48.♖e8!=, and the white pieces have managed to keep the black passed pawns at bay, which can no longer count on their king's decisive transfer to the kingside because is it cut off by the rook.

41...h4!

To start pushing this particular pawn with the purpose of deflecting the white king from the queenside is the right decision.

In case of the incorrect 41...a4? 42.bxa4 bxa4 43.♖a7 ♔b4 (43...♔b5 44.♖b7+ ♔a6 45.♖b8=) 44.♖b7+ ♔c4 45.♖a7 ♔b3 46.♖b7+ ♔a2 (46...♔c2 47.♖a7!) 47.♔d3 h4 (47...a3 48.♔c2=; 47...♗b2 48.♔c2=) 48.♔c2= the white king is in time to stifle Black's play on the queenside, while the rook is capable of handling the kingside passed pawn on its own.

42.♖b8

42.♔f3 a4 43.bxa4 bxa4 comes to the rescue no longer.

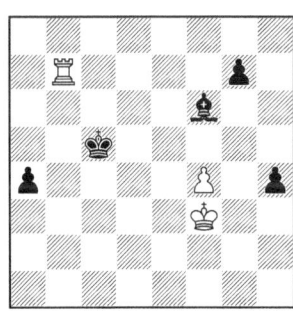

44.♖a7

(44.♔g4 a3 45.♖a7 ♔b4 46.♖b7+ ♔c3 47.♖a7 ♔b2 48.♖b7+ ♔a1 49.♔h3 a2 50.♔g4 ♗b2−+ and the king makes room for the pawn to queen)

44...♔b4 45.♖b7+ ♔c4 46.♖a7 ♔b3 47.♖b7+ ♔a2 48.♔e2 h3! The

premature 48...♗b2 49.♔d2 ♔b1 50.♖e7! ♗c1+ 51.♔e1! h3 52.♖xg7 h2 53.♖h7 ♗xf4 54.♔f2 a3 55.♔g2 a2 56.♖b7+= allows White to bail out.

49.♖b8 (49.♔f3 a3 50.♔g3 ♗b2 51.♔xh3 ♔b1−+) 49...a3−+ 50.♔d1 g5! 51.fxg5 h2 and the pawn is about to queen.

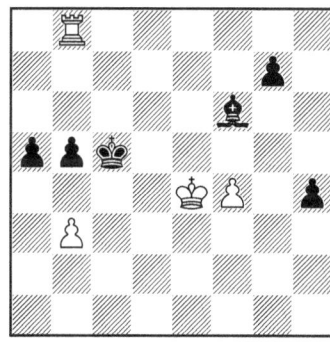

42...h3!

The suicide pawn presses on with its mission.

43.♔f3

In case of 43.♖h8 ♔b4 44.♖xh3 a4 45.bxa4 bxa4

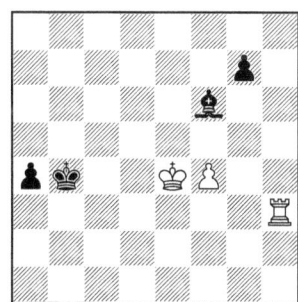

46.♔d3

(46.♖h8 a3 47.♖b8+ ♔c3 48.♖a8 ♔b2 49.♖b8+ ♔c2 50.♖a8 ♗b2 51.♔f5 ♔b1 52.♔g6 a2−+)

46...a3 47.♖h2 ♔b3 48.♖h8 a2 49.♖b8+ ♔a3 50.♖a8+ ♔b2 51.♖b8+

♔c1 52.♖c8+ ♚b1 53.♖b8+ ♗b2−+ the bishop, like an umbrella, shields the black king from bad weather, and there is no stopping the black passed pawn from taking its last step to becoming a queen.

43...h2 44.♔g2 a4 45.bxa4 bxa4 and White resigned in the face of 46.♖a8 ♚b4 47.♖b8+ ♚c3 48.♖a8 ♚b3 49.♖b8+ ♚a2 50.♔xh2 a3 51.♔g3 ♗b2, followed by the king stepping to b1 and the pawn queening.

Example No. 19
R. Haria − O. Kurmann
Catez 2021

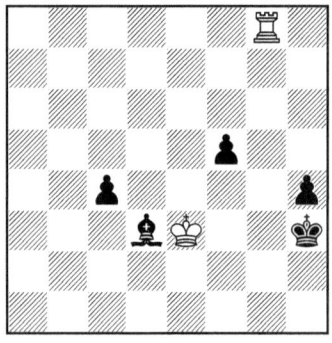

Black to move

In return for the exchange Black has as many as three pawns, each of which can become dangerous when supported by the bishop. White has nothing else but to pin his hopes on the black king's somewhat poor placement and his opponent's inaccurate play.

63...♚h2? This natural move is a blunder that puts White on the right tracks to engineer a drawn position.

The way to win was 63...♗e4!
a) 64.♖c8 c3!
Both 64...♚g2? 65.♖g8+! ♚f1 66.♖h8 c3 67.♖xh4 ♚e1 68.♖h8 c2

69.♖c8 ♚d1 70.♖d8+=, and 64...♚g3? 65.♖g8+ ♚h2 66.♖h8! h3 67.♔f2 c3 68.♖c8= would have missed the win.

65.♖xc3.

65...♚g3!−+. This square is ideal for the black king in terms of assisting his passed pawns and restricting the opponent's king. 65...♚g4? 66.♔f2 h3 67.♖g3+ ♚h4 68.♖g8= is bad, and 65...♚g2? 66.♔f4 h3 67.♖g3+= is an error as well.

66.♔e2+ (66.♖c1 h3 67.♖g1+ ♗g2−+; 66.♖c8 ♗f3! 67.♖g8+ ♗g4−+) 66...♚g2!

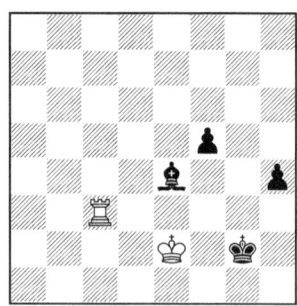

67.♖c8. White is in bad shape in the line 67.♔e3 h3 68.♔f4 h2 69.♖g3+ ♚f2 70.♖h3 ♚g1 71.♖g3+ ♗g2 72.♖a3 h1=♕ 73.♖a1+ ♗f1−+.

67...♗f3+! 67...h3? fails due to 68.♖g8+.

68.♔e3 ♔g3! Again, both 68...h3?
69.♔f4 h2 70.♖c2+=, and 68...♗g4?
69.♔f4 h3 70.♖c2+= blow the win.

69.♖g8+. 69.♖f8 ♗g4−+ is no
better than the text, and the frontal
rook offensive is also unproductive:
69.♖c1 h3 70.♖g1+ ♗g2−+, while
69.♔d4 h3 70.♔e5 h2 71.♖h8 (71.
♖c1 f4−+) 71...♗g4−+ is of no help
either.

69...♗g4−+, followed by the black
pawns' winning march to their queening
squares.

All below continuations are losing:

b) 64.♔f2 c3 65.♖c8 c2 66.♖c3+
♔g4 67.♖c8 h3 68.♔g1 f4, and
White cannot keep the black pawns
at bay,

c) 64.♔d4 c3!? 65.♔xc3 ♗f3!
66.♔d2 ♗g4 67.♔e3 (67.♔e1 ♔g2!−+)
67...♔g3!−+,

d) 64.♔f4 c3 65.♖c8 c2 66.♔g5 ♔g3
67.♖c3+ ♔f2 68.♔xh4 ♔e2 69.♖c8
♔d2 70.♖d8+ ♗d3−+ when White is
again understaffed to successfully fight
his opponent's passed pawns.

64.♖h8 h3

64...♔g3 no longer works because
of 65.♖g8+ ♔h3 66.♖c8! ♔g4
67.♖g8+ ♔h5 68.♔f4! c3 69.♖h8+
♔g6 70.♖xh4 c2 71.♖h1 ♗e2 72.♖c1
♗d1 73.♖a1= .

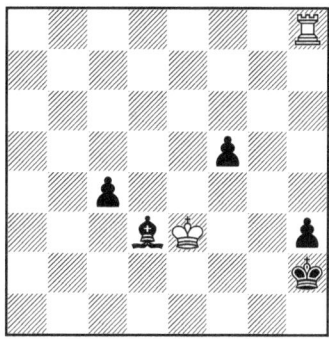

65.♔f2!

Not only paralyzing the black king,
but also both kingside passers.

**65...c3 66.♖c8 c2 67.♖c7 ♗e4
68.♖c5 ♗d3 69.♖c7 ♗e4**

The rook does a good job handling
the passed c-pawn, and, seeing no way
of improving his position further, Black
had to make do with a draw.

**Example No. 20
S. Sevian – A. Hakobyan
Saint Louis 2022**

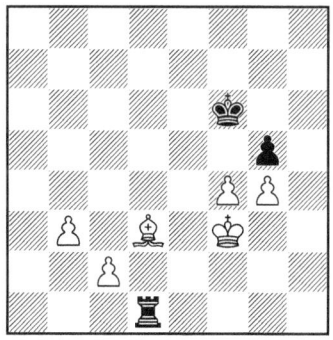

Black to move

White has three pawns for the
exchange. Not only that, but all three
extra white pawns are passers that are
ready to roll on different flanks to pull
Black's defensive resources apart. Black
seems to be doomed.

47...♖e1?

Black attempts to deny the white king access to the queenside to prevent it from assisting its passed pawns. In doing so, he misses a more important factor in this position.

47...gxf4? 48.♔xf4 ♖g1 49.b4+− is also bad.

Instead, it would have been correct to take the white queenside pawns under control to stop them from moving forward. Further, not only is the black king capable of challenging his opponent's kingside pawns, but he is also ready to go over to the opposite part of the board to assist his rook.

47...♖b1!

a) 48.fxg5+ ♔xg5 49.♗f5 (49.♔e4 ♔xg4 50.♔d5 ♔f4 51.♔c5 ♔e5 52.b4 ♔e6 53.b5 ♔d7 54.b6 ♔c8= is harmless as the black king's coming to the rescue is well-timed)

49...♖e1! It is time to restrict the white king.

50.c4. White drops a pawn after both 50.b4? ♖b1 51.c3 ♖b3= and 50.c3? ♖c1 51.c4 ♖c3+ 52.♔e4 ♖xb3 53.c5 ♔f6=. Likewise, 50.♔f2 ♖e7= 51.b4 ♖b7 52.c3 ♖c7 yields nothing.

50...♔f6! 51.♔f4 (51.c5 ♖c1! 52.b4 ♖c4=; 51.b4 ♖c1 52.♗d3 ♔e5! 53.g5 ♔d4 54.♗e2 ♖g1 55.♔f4 ♖e1=) 51...

♖f1+ 52.♔e3 (52.♔e4 ♖b1=) 52...♔e5! Restricting the white king yet again, this time with his own king.

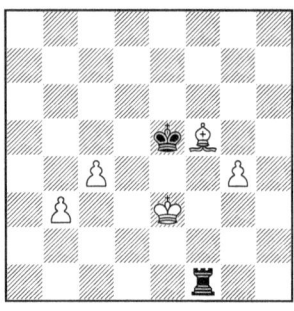

53.b4 (53.c5 ♖c1 54.b4 ♖c4=) 53...♖f4 54.♔d3 ♖f3+! 55.♔c2 (55.♔e2 ♖f4=) 55...♔d4 56.c5 (56.♗e6 ♖f6 57.♗d5 ♖g6=) 56...♖c3+ 57.♔b2 (57.♔d2 ♖c4 58.g5 ♔e5!=) 57...♔c4= and the position is a draw.

b) 48.♔e4 ♖e1+!;

c) 48.f5 ♔e5=;

d) 48.♔e3 ♖e1+! 49.♔d2 ♖g1 50.fxg5+ ♔xg5 51.♗f5

51...♖g3! 52.b4 ♔f4 53.b5 ♔e5! 54.b6 ♔d6 55.b7 ♔c7 56.♗c8 ♔b8 57.c3 ♔c7 58.♔c2 ♖e3 59.♔b3 ♖d3! 60.♔b4 ♖d1 61.c4 ♖c1 62.♔c5 ♖d1=.

48.b4!+−

Having withdrawn the rook from the b-file, Black allows the white pawns to start rolling.

48...♖b1

48...gxf4 49.♔xf4 ♔e6 50.g5+− is losing for Black as well.

49.b5 ♖e1 50.c4! ♖d1 51.fxg5+ ♔xg5

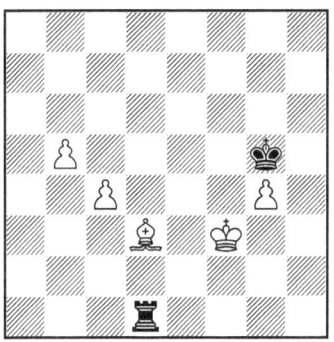

52.♔e4! ♖e1+. 52...♔xg4 53.♗e2++− is utterly bad.

53.♔d5 ♔xg4 − 53...♖d1 54.♔d4+− makes no difference.

54.b6 and Black resigned because ·there is no stopping the white pawns.

Example No. 21
A. Fier − Jimenez Garcia
Mexico 2022

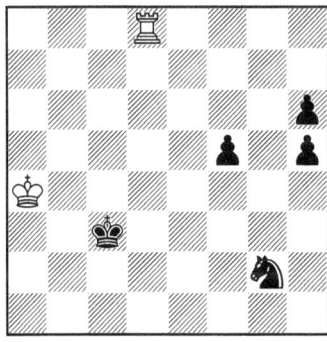

White to move

Black has three pawns for the exchange. However, his compromised pawn structure is one of the aspects that is likely to come to White's rescue. Also important is the remoteness of the black pawns from their king and from the queening squares. Nevertheless, White needs to demonstrate precise play.

47.♖f8?

Instead, this move is a big error.

The alternative way of assaulting the pawns from the bottom rank also fails: 47.♖h8? ♔d3 48.♖xh6 (48.♖g8 ♘e3 49.♖h8 ♘g4 50.♖f8 ♔e4−+) 48...h4 49.♖g6 (49.♔b4 f4−+) 49...♘f4 (49...h3? 50.♖g3+) 50.♖h6 (50.♖f6 h3 51.♖xf5 h2−+; 50.♖d6+ ♔e3−+) 50...h3

and the pawns gradually promote with support from the king and knight: 51.♔b4 ♔e3 52.♔c4 ♔f3 53.♔d4 ♔g4! 53...♔g3? would be an error because White eliminates the last pawn after 54.♖h8! h2 55.♖xh2 ♔xh2 56.♔e5=.

54.♔e3 (54.♔e5 ♔g5 55.♖h7 ♘h5−+; 54.♖h8 ♘g6 55.♖h7 ♘h4−+) 54...♔g3! 55.♔d4 (55.♖h8 ♘g2+ 56.♔e2 h2−+) 55...♘g2! 56.♖g6+ (56.♔e5 ♘h4 57.♖a6 h2 58.♖a1 f4−+) 56...♔f3 57.♖h6 (57.♔e5 ♘h4−+)

57...♔g4! A work of exquisite precision!

58.♖g6+ (58.♔e5 ♘h4−+) 58...♔h5! 59.♖g8 (59.♖g3 ♔h4 60.♖g8 h2 61.♔e5 ♔h3−+) 59...♘h4 60.♖h8+ (60.♖g1 ♘f3+−+) 60...♔g4 61.♖g8+ ♔f4 62.♖h8 ♘f3+ 63.♔d3 (63.♔d5 h2 64.♔e6 ♔g4−+) 63...h2 64.♔e2 ♔g4 65.♔f2 ♘h4−+.

White could have bailed out with 47.♖d5!?

a) 47...♘e3

48.♖d6! The white rook takes turns to get at the black pawns and the knight, thus keeping the black king from coming to their aid.

48...h4 (48...♘g4 49.♖d5 f4 50.♖f5= 50...♔d4 51.♖xf4+ ♔e5 52.♖f1) 49.♖xh6 ♘g2 50.♖g6! ♘f4 (50...h3 51.♖g3+=; 50...♘e1 51.♖f6=) 51.♖h6 (51.♖f6? h3 52.♖xf5? h2 53.♖c5+ ♔d2−+) 51...h3 52.♖h4=.

b) 47...f4? 48.♖xh5 f3 49.♖xh6 f2 50.♖f6=;

c) 47...♘h4? 48.♔b5 ♘f3 49.♔c5!=.

47.♖g8!? was also an option:

a) if Black gives up his knight in the hope of promoting his pawns with support from the king 47...f4 48.♖xg2 ♔d3 49.♖g6 f3 50.♖xh6 f2 51.♖f6 ♔e2 52.♖e6+ ♔f3 53.♖f6+ ♔g3

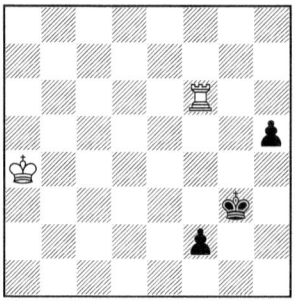

54.♖g6+, then the black pawns are disconnected, which means that there is no proper shield for the black king to hide behind from the white rook's checks: 54...♔h3 55.♖f6 ♔g2 56.♖g6+ ♔f1 57.♖h6=, and the white rook is capable of handling the passed pawns on its own;

b) 47...♘f4 48.♖f8=;

c) 47...♘e3 48.♖h8=;

d) 47...♘h4 48.♖f8 ♔d4 49.♖f6 ♔e4 50.♖xh6 f4 51.♖xh5 ♘g2 52.♖h1 ♘e3 53.♖h4=.

Lastly, 47.♖d6!? h4 (47...f4 48.♖xh6 h4 49.♖g6 f3 50.♖f6 ♘e1 51.♖f4 h3 52.♖h4 f2 53.♖xh3+ ♔d4 54.♖h1=) 48.♖g6! (48.♖xh6? ♔d3−+) 48...♔d3 (48...♘f4 49.♖xh6 h3 50.♖h4=; 48...h3 49.♖xh6=) 49.♖xg2 f4 could also draw the game.

50.♖b2!? Switching to checking the black king from the side. White fails after 50.♖h2? f3 51.♖xh4 f2 52.♖f4 ♔e2 because the rook is too close to the black king: 53.♖e4+ ♔f3−+.

50...♔e3

(50...h3 51.♖h2=; 50...f3 51.♔b4 ♔e3 52.♖b3+ ♔f2 [52...♔f4 53.♔c3 f2 54.♖b6=] 53.♔c3 ♔g2 54.♖b6 f2 55.♖g6+ ♔h2 56.♖f6=)

51.♖b3+ ♔e2 52.♖b2+. White strives to force the black king to the f-file to put it in the way of its own passed pawn.

52...♔f3 53.♖b6 h5 54.♔b3 h3 55.♔c3 h2 56.♖b1 ♔g2 57.♖b2+ ♔g3 58.♖b1 f3 59.♔d2 ♔g2 60.♔e3 f2 61.♔e2 h4 62.♖f1 h1=♕ 63.♖xh1 ♔xh1 64.♔xf2= with a drawn pawn ending.

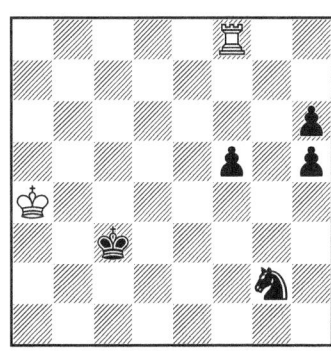

47...f4−+ 48.♖f6

48.♔b5 h4 49.♖f6 ♔d3−+ results in a transposition.

48...h4 49.♔b5

49.♖xh6 is of no help because after 49...♔d3 (49...f3? 50.♖f6 ♘e1 51.♖f4 h3 52.♖h4 f2 53.♖xh3+ ♔d4 54.♖h1=) 50.♖f6 (50.♔b4 f3 51.♖f6 ♔e2−+) 50...♔e2−+ the black king is there to assist his passed pawns.

49...♔d3

49...h3? 50.♖xh6 is an error that enables the white rook to deal with each pawn one by one.

50.♔c5

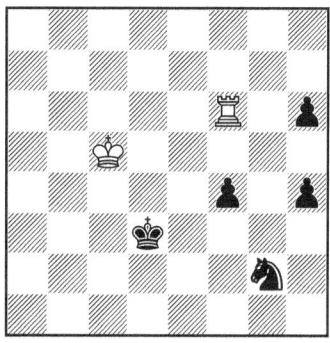

50...h5!

The black pawns are on their slow but unstoppable way to the promotion square.

51.♖a6

White falls to a fork after 51.♔d5 h3 52.♖h6 f3 53.♖xh5 ♘f4+−+.

51...f3 52.♖a3+ ♔e4 53.♖a4+ ♔e3 54.♖a3+ ♔f4 55.♖a4+ ♔g3

Now that the black king is safe from the rook checks, his pawns reaching the queening squares is only a matter of time.

56.♔d4 h3 57.♖a1 f2 58.♖f1

If the white king attempts to join the fray, then Black interposes and chases the rook out of play with 58.♔d3 ♘e1+

59.♔e2 ♔g2—+, after which the pawn will queen.

58...♔f3 and White threw in the towel.

Lessons from my Career

Example No. 22
A. Galkin – R. Kempinski
Saint Vincent 2000

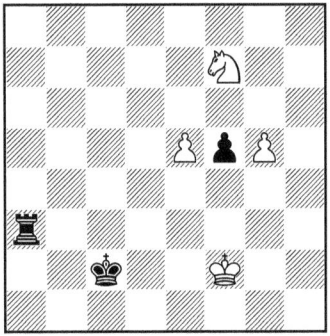

Black to move

Black executed a fierce middlegame attack against the enemy king, but White managed to fight it off at the cost of minor material losses. The Polish grandmaster tried for hours on end to destroy the drawn endgame position built by White, for which he launched a flanking maneuver to get around from the rear, advancing his king into the white camp but taking too much risk. There followed a pawn break, and it is now up to Black to demonstrate the precise move order to save this position, in which he is under pressure from the ever-melting clock time, from the drastic turnaround in the position's evaluation, and from fatigue from many hours spent at the board.

78...♔d3?

The king rushes to help his rook fight off the white passed pawns that are running in parallel to each other. However, this erroneous decision leads Black to disaster.

78...♔d2? 79.e6 ♖e3 80.♘d8 f4 81.g6 ♖g3 82.e7 ♖e3 83.g7+— was losing.

78...♖a6? could not save the game either because after 79.♔f3 ♔d3 (79...♖a1 80.e6 ♖e1 81.♘d8 ♔d3 82.g6+—) 80.♔f4 ♔d4 81.♔xf5 ♔d5 82.g6 ♖e6 83.g7 ♖e8 84.e6 ♖g8 85.e7+— the white pawns cannot be stopped.

It was correct to play either 78...♖a4!? 79.e6 (79.♔f3 ♖e4 80.g6 ♖g4 81.♘h8 ♖e4 82.g7 ♖g4=; 79.g6 ♖g4 80.♘h8 ♖e4=)

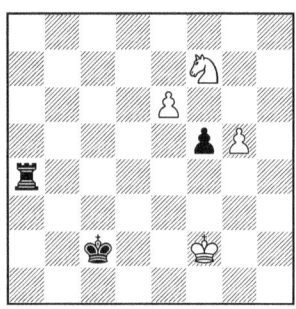

79...♖f4+ (alternatively, 79...♖e4 80.♘d8 ♔d3 81.g6 ♖f4+!=) 80.♔g3 (80.♔e3 ♖e4+=) 80...♖e4 81.♘d8 ♖g4+ 82.♔f3 ♖xg5 83.e7 ♖g8 84.♔f4 ♖e8 85.♘c6 ♖xe7=,

or 78...f4!?, preventing the white king from coming to his pawns' assistance in both cases and also using the f-pawn to help his rook combat the passed pawns: 79.e6 (79.g6 ♖g3 80.♘h8 ♖e3 81.g7 ♖g3=) 79...♖g3! (79...♖e3? 80.♘d8 ♖g3 81.e7 ♖e3 82.♘c6+—) 80.e7 ♖e3 81.g6 ♖xe7 82.g7 ♖e8 83.♘h6 ♔d3 84.♔f3 ♔d4 85.♔xf4

85...♔d5 (85...♖e1? 86.g8=♕ ♖f1+ 87.♔g5 ♖g1+ 88.♘g4) 86.♔f5 ♔d6 87.♔f6 (87.♔g6 ♔e6=) 87...♖e6+ 88.♔f7 (88.♔g5 ♖e8=) 88...♖e7+ 89.♔f8 ♖xg7=.

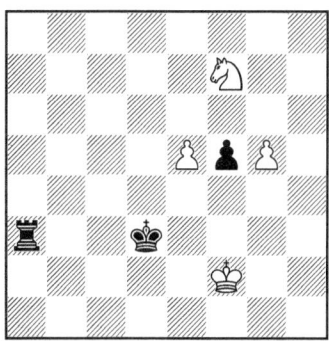

79.e6!

The passed pawns can be stopped no longer.

The wrong 79.g6? ♖a6 80.♘d6 ♖a7!= would have saved Black.

It would be equally bad to play 79.♔f3? ♔d4+ 80.♔f4 ♔d5 81.g6 (81. ♔xf5 ♖f3+ 82.♔g6 ♔e6=) 81...♖a1 82.g7 (82.♔xf5 ♖f1+ 83.♔g5 ♔e6 84.♘h6 ♖h1 85.♘g4 ♖g1=) 82...♖f1+ 83.♔g5 ♖g1+ 84.♔f6 ♖xg7! 85.♔xg7

♔e6 86.♔g6 f4=, and White cannot keep his last pawn alive.

79...♖a8 If one pawn is stopped, then the other pawn starts rolling after 79...♖a7 80.g6+−.

This sad evaluation for Black cannot be changed either by 79...♖a2+ 80.♔f3 ♖e2 81.♘d8 ♖e4 82.g6+−, or 79...♔d4 80.e7 ♖e3 81.♘d8! (81.♘d6? ♖xe7 82.♘xf5+ ♔e5 83.♘xe7 ♔e6=) 81...f4 (81...♖xe7 82.♘c6++−) 82.g6+−, and the pawns become queens again.

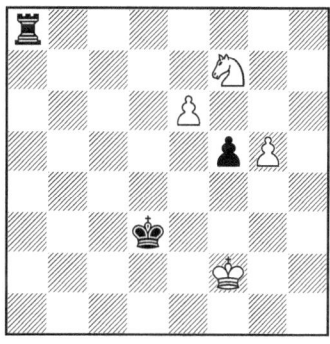

80.g6!

80.♘d6? ♖a7 81.♘xf5 (81.g6 ♖e7!=; 81.♔f3 ♖e7=) 81...♖a5= would have missed the win.

80...♔d4

If 80...♖e8, then 81.g7+−, and if 80...♖g8, then 81.e7+−.

81.e7 ♖e8

After 81...♔d5 82.♘d8+− the black rook would lose control over the white pawn's promotion square.

82.g7 and Black resigned: 82...♔d5 83.♘h6 ♔e6 84.g8=♕+ ♖xg8 85.♘xg8 ♔f7 86.♔f3.

Chapter 2

ROOK VS. A PAIR OF MINOR PIECES

Having studied endgame examples of a rook versus minor piece, it is logical to turn to examples from modern grandmaster games to study how to handle endings with a rook opposed by two minor pieces: two bishops, two knights, or a bishop and a knight.

First though, let's start from the very basics. Nominally, a pair of minor pieces outweighs a rook. However, a rook often comes with a makeweight of one or even two pawns. Everything is more or less clear about this imbalance in the middlegame because, due to the presence of queens and more rooks still on the board, a pair of minor pieces can help develop active play against the opponent's king or other weaknesses in his camp, which makes possessing a pair of minor pieces more promising than having a rook (but there may of course be specific exceptions). However, other factors come to the forefront in the endgame, including the presence of passed pawns for either or both sides and active kings.

If neither side has pawns in such endings, then a draw seems the most logical outcome. The weaker side will normally only need to trade his rook for either of his opponent's minor pieces. Of course, special features of the position may still change this outcome, such as if the rook is pinned by the bishop and there is no way to unpin it without dropping the whole rook. Then the resulting endgame passes to the technical stage, in which the stronger side needs to demonstrate its skills of checkmating a lone king with two bishops or a bishop and a knight (one more reason to revise or learn the mating techniques once and for all!). We transpose to the same ending if the rook drops to a knight fork, unless the stronger side has a pair of knights for the rook so that even elimination of the rook gives no win. As long as the defending side keeps exercising a basic amount of prudence, two knights cannot checkmate a lone king. This is an important point to remember.

That said, the majority of rook vs. pair of minor pieces endings initially begin with pawns on the board. As mentioned above, arrangement of both sides' pawns has a crucial influence on any positional evaluation. It depends, above all, on whether the side having a rook has a passed pawn or even connected passed pawns, and if such passed pawn is backed up by the rook or king, as well as on whether the enemy pawns are vulnerable to an actively posted rook, etc. Correct evaluation of the position is subject to many factors, and you need to take all of them into account. It is this approach that determines which side has the advantage in a rook vs. pair of minor pieces ending.

The bishop pair is more often than not a superior material ratio in an endgame like this. This is true, of course, about normally developed bishops in open positions and not blunted by your own or your opponent's pawn chains. A pair of bishops is a mobile and an easy-to-coordinate asset that is capable of raking the entire board, which makes for their successful use both in active operations and for defensive purposes. A pair of knights is less mobile in terms of quick relocation between opposite flanks. On the other hand, the knights can go a long way if proper outposts are available, especially in the center. Their forking capabilities are a powerful tool.

Everything is more or less clear in terms of conversion of a positional or even material advantage. The ultimate winning goal of the stronger side with two minor pieces is to win material (pawns or rook) or to queen a pawn and then deliver a checkmate. The same is true when specific features of a position give the rook holder superiority, such as winning material (a minor piece or a pawn) or promoting his own pawn to the queening square, followed by a routine checkmate procedure to crown the game.

We have already identified a number of drawn positions as part of the "rook vs. minor piece" section (which is of course far from exhaustive) that a competitive chess player needs to know to handle the endgame correctly. Obviously, some of those drawn positions can emerge from the "rook vs. a pair of minor pieces" ending as a result of exchanging the rook for one of the minor pieces. Meanwhile, the situation from the opposite side of the board holds true as well — one of the minor pieces can be sacrificed for the opponent's passed pawn in order to transpose into a theoretically drawn ending.

We also highlight that the presence of a small number of pawns and their location on one flank only, similarly to other types of endgame, significantly increases the weaker side's chances of saving the game. Again, these postulates are of a general nature and should only serve as helpful input for a chess player when evaluating a specific endgame on the board. I repeat, to hammer this point home, that correct evaluation depends entirely on concrete features of each particular position.

Rook vs. a Pair of Minor Pieces

Let us begin the topic by an example from a grandmaster game in which there is no debate as to who is better. The two pieces are superior to the rook and the only question is whether the stronger side is capable of increasing and converting the advantage.

Example No. 23
G. Meier – L. D. Nisipeanu
Dortmund 2018

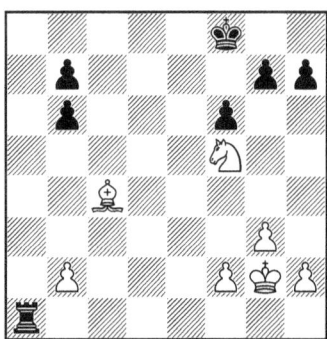

White to move

White has two minor pieces for a rook and pawn. Moreover, the black queenside pawns are doubled, which disables the potential to create a passed pawn on this part of the board. The bishop and knight are posted actively and are looking for an opportune moment to launch an offensive against the opponent's weak pawns. Objectively speaking, Black will find it hard to come up with anything against White's aggressive plans.

31.b3!

This is a sound prophylactic move. The bishop and pawn arrangement allows them to fend for each other.

The greedy 31.♘d6?!♖d1 32.♘xb7?! ♚e7 would have led to problems with the stray knight.

31...♖d1 32.♘e3 ♖d2 33.h4!

White shows the opponent his readiness to open a second front for active play on the kingside in order to create new weaknesses in the black camp.

33.♘d5? b5−+ would be yet another greedy attempt leading to disaster.

33...g6 34.g4! ♖b2

34...♚g7 35.♚g3!? would have made no significant difference

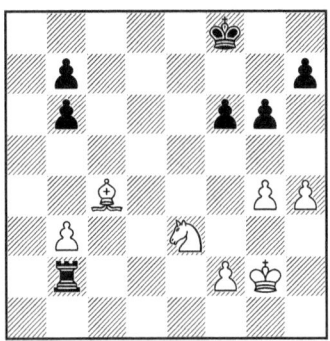

35.♘d1!

35.♘d5?! b5! 36.♗xb5 ♖xb3 37.♗c4 ♖b2!? 38.♘xf6 b5! would have given Black decent counterplay by setting his passed pawn in motion.

35...♖d2

In case of 35...♖c2 36.♚f3!? ♚g7 (36...♚e7? 37.♘e3) 37.♚e3 White dislodges his opponent's rook and starts attacking the exposed black pawns.

36.♘c3 ♖d4 37.♚g3 ♖d8

37...♚g7?! 38.♘d5! b5 39.♘c7! is a dubious continuation leading to Black's material losses due to the threatened fork

38.f3!

White is in no hurry. He improves his position gradually and prepares to activate his king.

38...♚g7 39.♚f4 ♖d2

The check 39...♖d4+ 40.♚e3 brings no dividends to Black.

40.♘e4 ♖d1 41.h5!? White is true to his plan and keeps increasing dynamic pressure all over the board.

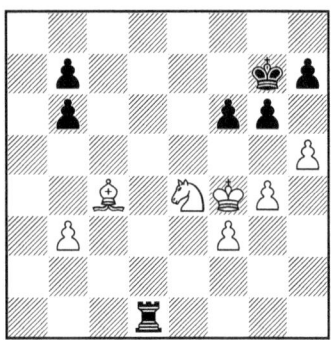

41...b5? Black caves in under heavy defensive duties and attempts to get at least some semblance of counterplay.

Of course, 41...g5+? is bad because the black king is in for checkmate after 42.♚f5 ♖d8 43.h6+! ♚xh6 44.♚xf6 ♖f8+ 45.♗f7+−.

Along the same lines, 41...♖d7?! 42.h6+ ♚xh6 43.♘xf6± is unsatisfactory for Black.

An uphill battle was in store for Black even after the relatively better 41...♖d4 42.♚e3 ♖d8 43.hxg6 hxg6 44.♘c3±.

42.♗e6

White is not lured by the pawn offering, quite reasonably believing that material gain is his for grabs whenever he feels like it.

42.♗xb5!? gxh5 43.gxh5 ♖d5 44.h6+! ♚xh6 (44...♚g6 45.♗e8+!? ♚xh6 46.♘xf6) 45.♗c4 ♖d4 46.♚f5 b5 47.♗e6+− was looking good for White, leaving Black in bad shape.

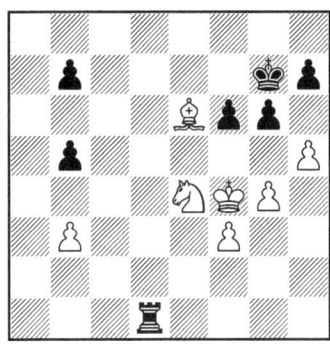

42...♖h1? Black is again in search for counterplay. He needed to fight back patiently with 42...♖d4! 43.♔e3 ♖d1.

43.♗d5!? Getting down to reaping the harvest of ripe pawns.

43...b6   43...gxh5? 44.♘g3 ♖d1 45.♘xh5+ ♔g6 46.♗e4++− is bad.

44.hxg6 hxg6 45.♘c3!? b4 After 45...g5+ 46.♔f5 ♖e1 47.♘e4+− White shifts the activity vector to grab another black pawn, this time on the kingside.

46.♘a2   g5+   47.♔e3   ♔f8 48.♘xb4+− ♔e7 **49.♗e4** and Black threw in the towel.

Example No. 24
N. Meskovs – D. Paravyan
Riga 2021

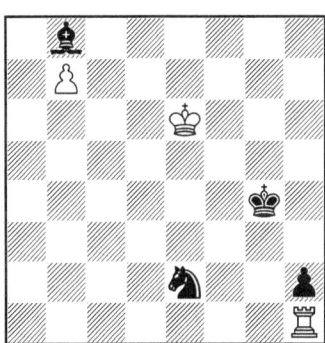

Black to move

White hopes to draw the game by giving up his rook for the black passed pawn, provided that his king is in time to help queen his only remaining pawn.

81...♔h3?

This blunder allows White to implement his plan.

The game could have been won by other king moves:

a) 81...♔g3! 82.♔d7 ♘d4! 83.♖d1. Black also gets the upper hand after 83.♔c8 ♘c6 84.♖c1 (84.♔d7 ♘b4 85.♔c8 ♘a6 86.♖a1 ♗e5!−+) 84... ♗f4!−+.

83...♔f3!? (83...♗f4 84.♖f1!, 83... ♗e5 84.♖e1! or 83...♔g2 84.♖d2+!) 84.♖b1. The premature 84.♔c8 ♘c6 85.♔d7 ♘b4 86.♔c8 ♘a6−+ gives Black time for a decisive regrouping of his pieces.

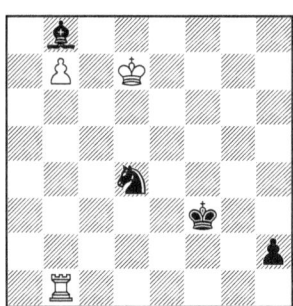

84...♗g3 85.♖c1 ♔e4. 85...♔g2? is ill-advised: 86.♔c8 ♘c6 87.♖c2+! ♔f3 88.♖xc6 h1=♕ 89.♖c3+!=

86.♖e1+ (86.♔c8 ♘c6! 87.♔d7 ♘b8+−+) 86...♔d3. 86...♗xe1? fails to 87.b8=♕ h1=♕? 88.♕a8+, while after 86...♔d5 87.♖c1! White cuts off the path of the black king's relocation.

87.♖d1+ (87.♖b1 ♔c4!; 87.♖c1 ♘b3 88.♖b1 ♘a5 89.♔c8 ♘c6−+)

87...♔c4 88.♖c1+ (88.♖b1 ♔c5!) 88...♔d5 89.♖b1

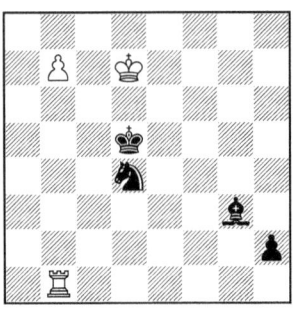

89...♔c5! 90.♖c1+ (90.♔c8 ♘c6−+) 90...♔b6! 91.♖b1+ (91.♔c8 ♘c6−+) 91...♔a7! The black king has travelled a long way to the queenside to assist in the regrouping of his minor pieces.

92.♔c8 ♘c6! 93.♖a1+. 93.♔d7 ♘b4! 94.♔c8 ♘a6 95.♖a1 ♔b6−+ makes no difference.

93...♔b6 94.♖b1+. White is in equally grim shape after 94.♔d7 ♘b4! 95.♖b1 ♔a7 96.♔c8 (96.♔e6 ♘d3 97.♔f5 ♘f2−+) 96...♘a6−+.

94...♔c5! – once the regrouping is successfully over, the king travels back to the kingside to help promote his passed pawn.

95.♔d7

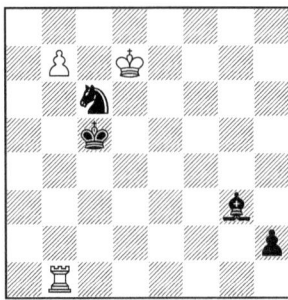

95...♘b4! One more precise move. 95...♘b8+? 96.♔e6 ♔d4 97.♔f5 ♔e3

98.♔g4 ♗c7 99.♔h3 ♔f2 100.♖h1= would be an error.

96.♖d1 White attempts to cut off the black king from the kingside. Likewise, there is no saving the game after 96.♔c8 ♘a6−+, while 96.♔e6 ♗b8 97.♔f5 ♘d3 98.♔g4 h1=♕ 99.♖xh1 ♘f2+ 100.♔f3 ♘xh1 101.♔g2 ♘g3−+ is of help no longer.

96...♔b6! A surgical precision job! (96...♘a6? 97.♔e6= is no good) 97.♖b1 (97.♔e6 ♘d3! 98.♖b1+ ♔c6!? 99.♔f5 ♘f2−+) 97...♔a7! 98.♔c8 ♘a6! 99.♖c1 loses again (similarly, there is no way to stay in the game after 99.♔d7 ♔b8! 100.♔e6 ♘c5+ 101.♔f5 ♘d3 102.♔g4 ♗e1!−+):

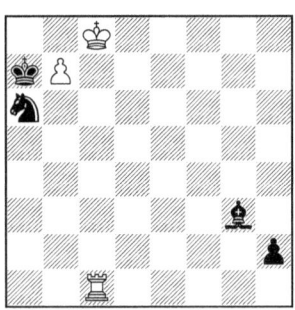

99...♔b6! Like an experienced animal tamer, the black king forces the opponent into submission via the same repetitive gestures.

100.♖a1 (100.♖b1+ ♔c6−+) 100...♘b8 101.♖c1 ♗f4! Forcing the rook to cede control over the c-file.

102.♖f1 ♗d6! The sloppy 102...♔c5? 103.♖xf4! h1=♕ 104.♔xb8= would have missed the win.

103.♖d1 ♔c6 104.♖e1 ♔d5 105.♖d1+ ♔e6 106.♖f1 ♗g3

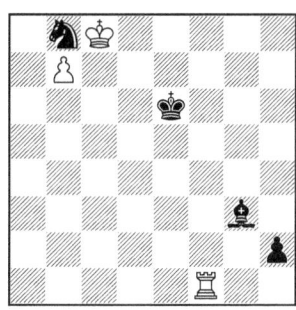

107.♖h1. 107.♔d8 ♘c6+ 108.♔c8 ♔e7!−+ would have unexpectedly woven a mating net.

107...♔f5 108.♖a1 ♔g4 109.♖c1 ♔h3 110.♖a1 ♔g2 111.♖a2+ ♔f1! 112.♖a1+ ♗e1 113.♔xb8 h1=♕ 114. ♔c7 (White is also lost after 114.♔a7 ♕h7−+) 114...♕h2+ 115.♔c8 ♕h8+ 116.♔d7 (116.♔c7 ♕xa1! 117.b8=♕ ♗g3+−+ is an immediate failure) 116... ♔e2−+, and the bishop joins the fray with decisive effect.

b) 81...♔f3! 82.♔d7 ♘d4 83.♖d1 was winning along the same lines

(83.♔c8 ♘c6 84.♔d7 ♘b4! 85.♔c8 ♘a6 86.♖a1 ♗e5 87.♖d1 ♗g3−+; 83.♖e1? ♔g2 84.♔c8 ♘c6 85.♖e2+ ♔f1 86.♖c2 h1=♕ 87.♖c1+ ♔g2 88.♖xh1 ♔xh1 89.♔d7 ♘a7−+)

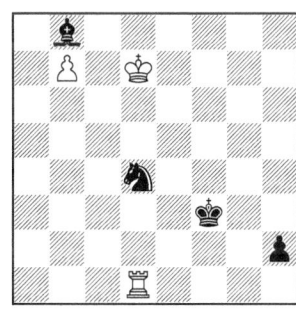

83...♔e3. (Not 83...♗g3? 84.♖d3+ ♔f2 85.♖xg3.)

b1) 84.♖b1 ♗g3

b1.1) 85.♖a1

85...♘b3! 86.♖b1 ♘a5 87.♔c8 ♘c6−+, followed by Black's taking the white rook for its passed pawn yet again.

b1.2) 85.♖c1 ♘b3 86.♖f1 ♘a5 87.♔c8 ♘c6! 88.♔d7 ♘b8+ 89.♔e6 ♗f2 90.♖h1 ♗g1 91.♔d6 ♘a6 92.♔c6 ♔f3−+;

b1.3) 85.♔c8 ♘c6−+;

b1.4) 85.♖h1 ♔d3 86.♖d1+ ♔c4−+

b2) 84.♔c8 ♘c6 85.♔d7 ♘b4−+;

b3) 84.♖c1 ♘b3 85.♖e1+ ♔d2 86.♖b1 ♘a5 87.♔c8 ♘c6 88.♔d7 ♘b4 89.♔e6 ♔e2 90.♔f5 ♘d3−+;

b4) 84.♖a1 ♘c2 85.♖b1 ♘b4−+

82.♔d7! ♘d4

A draw is inevitable after 82...♔g2 83.♖xh2+ ♗xh2 84.♔c8=.

83.♔c8 ♘c6

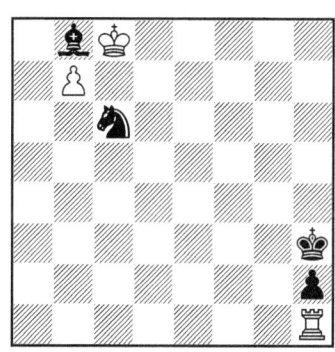

84.♖c1!?

An alternative way to make a draw was: 84.♔d7 ♘b4 85.♔c8 ♘a6 86.♖a1! ♔g4 (86...♗f4 87.♖xa6 h1=♕ 88.♖h6+! ♗xh6 89.b8=♕=) 87.♖xa6 h1=♕ 88.♔xb8=, and White is out of the woods with such an advanced passed pawn.

84...♔g4

After 84...♗f4 85.♖xc6 h1=♕ 86.♖h6+! ♗xh6 87.b8=♕= the endgame is drawn.

Black also achieves nothing after 84...♔g2 85.♖xc6 h1=♕ 86.♔xb8=.

85.♖xc6!

The careless check 85.♖c4+? ♗f4!−+ would have cost the game.

85...h1=♕

86.♖c4+!

This intermezzo is crucial. Both 86.♔xb8? ♕xc6 and 86.♖g6+? ♔f5 are bad.

86...♔f5 87.♔xb8=

and the position is drawn despite the presence of the black queen on the board.

87...♔e6 88.♔a7 ♕g1+ 89.♔a6 ♕a1+ 90.♔b6 ♕b2+ 91.♔c7 ♕e5+ 92.♔c8 ♕h8+ 93.♔c7 ♕g7+ 94.♔b6 ♕b2+ 95.♔c7 ♕e5+ 96.♔c8 ♕h8+ 97.♔c7 ♕g7+ 98.♔b6 ♕b2+

Or following 98...♕e5 99.♖e4!? ♕xe4 100.b8=♕ the position is an obvious draw.

99.♔c7 and the opponents agreed a draw after repeating the position several times.

Example No. 25
B. Firat − M. Zirkelbach
Catez 2022

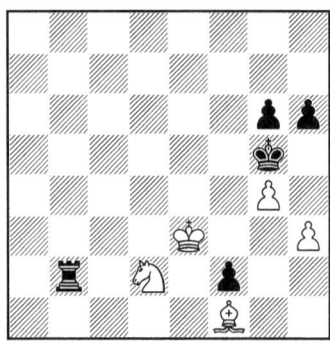

Black to move

Black has a rook and a pawn for a pair of minor pieces. At the same time, the f2-pawn is nearly encircled by the white pieces and is likely doomed. This means that Black should either exchange all the white pawns or else find other opportunities available in the position.

49...h5?!

This is not yet an error, but an inaccuracy.

A counter-intuitive exchange sacrifice would have secured a draw then and there: 49...♖xd2! 50.♔xd2 h5! 51.gxh5. White cannot hold on to the last pawn following 51.♗e2 hxg4 52.hxg4 f1=♕ 53.♗xf1 ♔xg4=.

51...gxh5= and given that White's pawn promotion square color is opposite to that of the bishop and that the black king faces no problems reaching the h8-square, the position is a draw.

Another good plan was to activate the king with 49...♔h4!? 50.♘e4 (White cannot improve his position via 50.♘f3+ ♚g3 51.♘d4 g5 52.♘e2+ ♚h2 53.♗xf2 ♖a2=) 50...h5 51.gxh5 (51.g5 ♖a2 52.♚f3 ♖b2 53.♗g2 ♖a2=; 51.♘xf2 ♖xf2 52.♚xf2 hxg4=) 51...gxh5 52.♘xf2 ♖xf2!? 53.♚xf2 ♚g5=, with a draw.

50.♘f3+

The alternative check is not as good as the text: 50.♘e4+?! ♚h4!=.

50...♚f6

The erroneous 50...♚h6? 51.g5+ ♚g7 52.♗e2 gives us a transposition to the actual game.

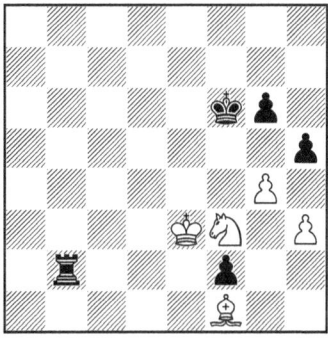

51.g5+!

51.gxh5 gxh5 52.♗e2 ♚f5 53.♚xf2 ♚f4= is harmless and poses Black no problems in maintaining the balance thanks to his active pieces

51...♚g7?

Black's play is overly passive, and his opponent punishes him for that.

The king was needed where the action was: 51...♚f5! 52.♗d3+. 52.h4? ♚g4! is bad, and after 52.♗e2 ♖b3+ 53.♚xf2 ♚f4 54.h4 ♖b2 55.♘e1 ♖a2 56.♘g2+ ♚e4 57.♚f1 ♖a1+ 58.♚f2 ♖a2= White cannot untangle his pieces in any satisfactory way.

52...♚e6 53.♘d2

(Black is in good shape after both 53.♗e2 ♚f5 54.♚xf2 ♚f4!= and 53.h4

♖a2 54.♘d2 ♖a3 55.♚e2 ♖a4 56.♘c4 ♖a2+ 57.♚f1 ♖a1+ 58.♚xf2 ♖h1 59.♚g3 ♚g1+ 60.♚h2 [60.♚h3 ♖h1+!] 60...♚g4 61.♚h3 ♖f4! 62.♘b2 ♖f2 63.♘a4 ♖f3+ 64.♚g2 ♖xd3! 65.♘c5+ ♚f5 66.♘xd3 ♚g4=.

Similarly, White gains nothing from 53.♘h2 ♖b3 54.h4 ♖a3 55.♚e2 ♚e5! 56.♗xg6 ♖h3 57.♘f1 [57.♘f3+? ♖xf3] 57...♖xh4 58.♗d3 [58.♘e3 ♚f4=] 58...♖g4 59.g6 ♚f6 60.♚xf2 ♖xg6=)

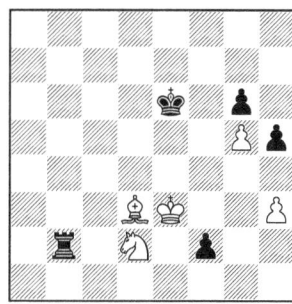

Now there follows the study-like 53...♖xd2! (53...♚e5? 54.♘c4+; 53...♖a2? 54.♗c4+) 54.♚xd2 f1=♕! 55.♗xf1 ♚f5 56.h4 (56.♚e3 ♚xg5=) 56...♚g4 57.♚e3 ♚xh4 58.♚f4= and stalemate.

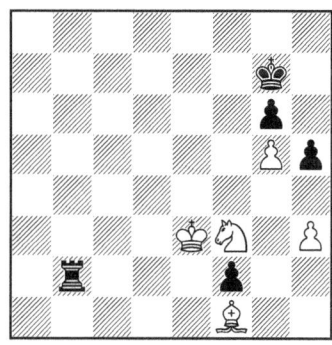

52.♗e2!

The first black pawn is encircled and eliminated.

52...♖a2

An attempt to stop White from forming a pawn chain only results in new weaknesses – 52...h4 53.♔xf2! (53. ♘xh4?! ♖b3+ 54.♔xf2 ♖xh3) 53...♖b4 54.♗d3 ♖a4 55.♔e3 ♖a8 56.♗e4 ♖h8

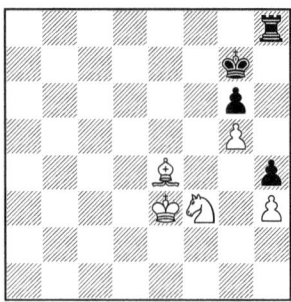

57.♔f4. A cute stalemate comes to Black's rescue in the line 57.♘e5 ♖e8 58.♘xg6 ? ♖xe4+ 59.♔xe4 ♔xg6 60.♔f4 ♔h5 61.♔f5.

57...♖f8+ 58.♔g4 ♖e8 59.♗d5 ♖d8 60.♗c6 ♖c8. An alternative way of attacking the bishop fails as well: 60... ♖d6 61.♗e4 ♖e6 62.♔f4+− and the black pawn drops.

61.♘e5 ♖h8 62.♘d3 ♖d8 (62... ♖c8 63.♗d5 ♖c3 64.♘f4+− is equally hopeless) 63.♘f4 ♖d4 64.♗e8+− and White has got at the black pawns.

53.♔xf2 ♖a3 54.♗c4 ♖c3 55.♗d5 ♖c2+ 56.♔g3 ♖c3 57.♔f4 ♖a3 58.♗e4 ♖b3 59.h4+−

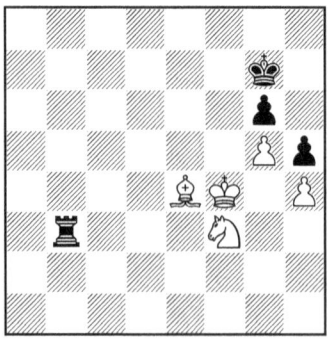

White has activated his pieces and is well placed for the upcoming decisive siege of the g6-pawn. Black has nothing to show for it.

59...♖a3 60.♘e5 ♖h3

The pawn ending arising after 60...♖a6 61.♗xg6 ♖xg6 (61...♖a4+ 62.♗e4+−) 62.♘xg6 ♔xg6 63.♔e5 ♔f7 (63...♔g7 64.♔f5 ♔f7 65.g6+ ♔g7 66.♔g5+−) 64.♔d6 is lost. 64.♔f5 ♔g7 65.g6? ♔h6 66.♔f6= is another instance of a cute stalemate.

64...♔g6 65.♔e6 ♔g7 66.♔f5 ♔h7 (66...♔f7 67.g6+ ♔g7 68.♔g5+−) 67.♔f6+−.

61.♘xg6 ♖h2

Black is also doomed after 61...♔f7 62.♘e5+ ♔g7 63.♘f3+−

62.♔g3 ♖a2

62...♖e2 63.♗f3+− is no better than the text.

63.♘f4 ♖a3+ 64.♗f3

Black resigned in the face of dropping his third pawn.

Example No. 26
D. Gordievsky – V. Fedoseev
Moscow 2019

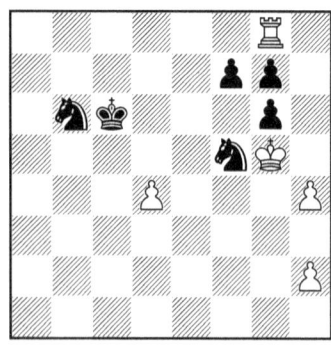

Black to move

Black is definitely the side playing for a win here. In return for a pair of knights, White has only a rook without any makeweight in the form of one let alone two pawns. Further, the d4-pawn looks doomed. On the other hand, with all pawns located on the same flank and White's king and rook being sufficiently active, White is not entirely devoid of chances of exchanging or eliminating those pawns. Besides, a potential transposition into a two knights vs. king ending is something to keep in mind.

44...♘xd4?!

Black is in a hurry to cash in, making conversion of his advantage a lot more difficult.

44...♘d7? was bad because of 45.h5! f6+ (White also holds a draw after 45...♘xd4 46.♖xg7! ♘e6+ 47.♔h6 ♘xg7 48.♔xg7 gxh5 49.♔xf7 ♘e5+ 50.♔f6 ♘f3 51.h4 ♘xh4 52.♔g5=)

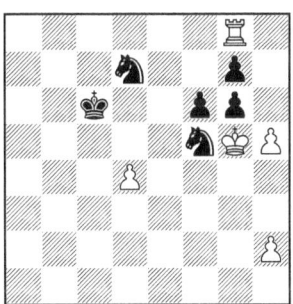

46.♔xg6! ♘e7+ 47.♔xg7 ♘xg8 48.♔xg8 f5 49.♔g7 f4 50.h6 f3 51.h7 f2 52.h8=♕ f1=♕ 53.♕a8+=.

Black should have gone for 44...♘d5! 45.♖f8 (45.h5 f6+ 46.♔xg6 ♘de7+ 47.♔h7 ♘xg8 48.♔xg8 ♔d5–+; 45.♖d8 ♘xd4–+) 45...♘d6 46.♖xf7. White drops the rook to 46.♖g8? ♘e4+ 47.♔g4 ♘ef6+–+. White's position is also hopeless after 46.♖a8 ♘c7 47.♖a4 ♘e6+ 48.♔g4 ♔d5–+ or 46.h5 gxh5

47.♔xh5 ♘f4+ 48.♔g4 ♘e6 49.♖g8 ♔d5–+.

46...♘xf7+ 47.♔xg6 ♘d6

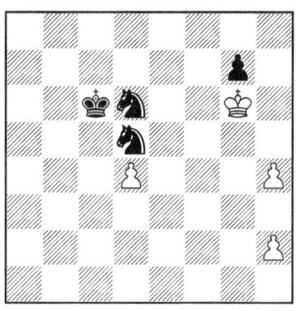

48.h5. Following 48.♔xg7 ♘f5+ 49.♔g6 ♘xh4+ 50.♔h5 ♘f3 51.h4 ♔d6 52.♔g4 ♘d2 53.♔f5 ♘f1 54.h5 ♔e7 55.♔e5 ♘fe3–+ Black eliminates the h-pawn and transposes into a theoretically won ending.

48...♘e8 49.h6 (there is no dislodging the knight from its defensive position with 49.♔f7 ♔d7–+) 49...gxh6 50.♔xh6 ♔d6–+, transiting into a known winning position.

45.♖xg7! ♘e6+ 46.♔f6! ♘xg7

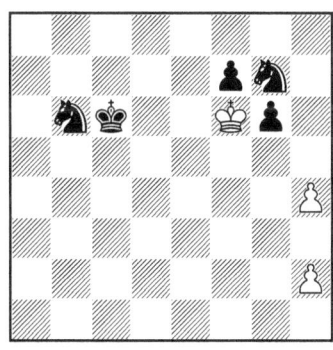

47.♔xf7!

47.♔xg7? f5! is losing (47...♘d5? misses the win to 48.♔xf7 ♘f4 49.♔f6 ♔d5 50.h5 gxh5 51.♔f5 ♘e6 52.♔g6 h4 53.♔f5=):

48.♔xg6 f4 49.h5 f3 50.h6 ♘d7! 51.♔g7. After 51.h7 ♘f8+−+ the white passed pawn is stopped, and its black counterpart is about to become a queen.

51...♘f8! Decoying the white king into a check from the future queen.

52.♔xf8 f2 53.h7 f1=♕+ 54.♔g7. But for the second h2-pawn the position would have been a draw. However, it is there, much to White's grief:

54...♕g2+ 55.♔f7 ♕h3 56.♔g8 ♕g4+ 57.♔f7 ♕h5+ 58.♔g7 ♕g5+ 59.♔f7 ♕h6 60.♔g8 ♕g6+ 61.♔h8 ♕f7 62.h4 ♕f8#.

47...♘e6?

This decision by a strong grandmaster is beyond understanding. It must be due to either a serious miscalculation or even disbelief in his own skill-set to win this endgame.

47...♘f5? 48.♔xg6 ♘xh4+ 49.♔g5 ♘f3+ (49...♘g2 50.h4=) 50.♔f4 ♘d4 51.h4= is also a draw.

It takes the following to succeed: 47...♘h5! 48.♔xg6 ♘f4+

49.♔g5. 49.♔h6 ♘bd5 50.h5 ♘f6−+ gives rise to another instance of a known winning ending. Yet another retreat of the king is also inferior to the text: 49.♔f5 ♘bd5 50.h5 ♘xh5 51.h4 ♔d6 52.♔g5 ♘df6!−+.

49...♘e6+! 50.♔f5 (50.♔f6 ♔d6

51.h5 ♘d5+ does not make any difference) 50...♔d6 51.h5 ♘f8! 52.h6 (Black also reaches a winning position after 52.♔f6 ♘bd7+ 53.♔f7 ♘h7 54.♔g7 ♘df6−+) 52...♘h7! 53.♔g6 (in case of 53.h4 ♘d5 54.♔e4 ♔e6 55.h5 ♘e7 56.♔d4 ♔d6 57.♔c4 ♘f5−+) 53...♔e7 and now White may continue 54.♔xh7

(Another doomed attempt would be 54.h4 ♘d7 55.♔f5

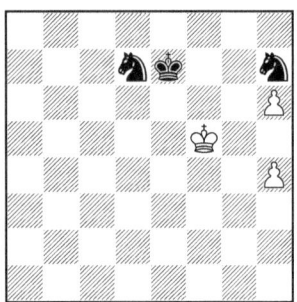

55...♔d6! A crucial moment. Black clearly intends to capture the h6-pawn with his knight. However, despite being mathematically winning, this position with a white rook's pawn on the fifth rank blocked by a knight is also known to defy the 50-move rule from time to time. This is the reason the stronger side should not be in a hurry to grab this pawn, instead centralizing his king as much as possible and edging the opponent's king out towards any of the corners prior to that. It is only at this moment that the winning mechanism should be set in motion.

56.♔e4 ♔e6! 57.h5 [57.♔d4 ♘df6 58.h5 ♔d6!−+] 57...♘e5 58.♔d4 ♔d6! 59.♔e4 ♘c6! 60.♔f5 ♔d5! 61.♔f4 [Black gets the upper hand along the same lines following 61.♔g6 ♔e6 62.♔xh7 ♔f7 63.♔h8 ♘e5

64.♔h7 ♘f3 65.♔h8 ♘g5 66.h7 ♔f8 67.h6 ♘f7#] 61...♘b4! 62.♔e3 ♔e5! 63.♔d2 ♔d4! 64.♔e2 ♘d3−+, and the endgame database shows that Black can deliver a checkmate without violating the 50-move rule.)

54...♔f7! 55.♔h8 ♘d7 56.♔h7 (White is immediately checkmated after 56.h7 ♘e5 57.h4 ♘g6#) 56...♘f6+ 57.♔h8 ♔f8! (here we have a known position with the knight superior to rook pawns because of the smothered mate of the misplaced king) 58.h3 (White is checkmated after 58.h4 ♔f7 59.h5 ♘d5 60.♔h7 ♘f4 61.♔h8 ♘e6 62.♔h7 ♘g5+ 63.♔h8 ♔f8! 64.h7 ♘f7#) 58... ♔f7 59.h4 ♔f8 60.h5

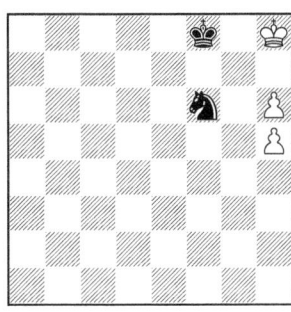

60...♘e4! 61.♔h7 (there is an alternative way to get checkmated: 61.h7 ♘d6 62.h6 ♘f7#) 61...♔f7! 62.♔h8 ♘g5! 63.h7 ♔f8 64.h6 ♘f7#.

48.♔xe6

and the opponents agreed to a draw without producing the sequence 48... ♘d5 49.h5 gxh5 (49...♘f4+ 50.♔f6 gxh5 51.♔g5=) 50.♔f5 ♔d6 51.♔g5, after which the last black pawn falls.

Lessons from my Career

Example No. 27
O. Karpeshov − A. Galkin
St. Petersburg 1997

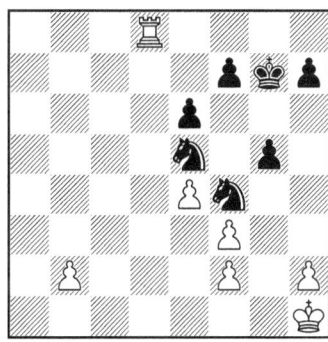

White to move

White has a rook and a pawn for two knights. Further, given that the pawn is a passed one and can move forward with the support of the rook, White played

27.♖b8

and offered a draw, believing the position to be approximately equal. Naturally, the hasty 27.b4? ♘c6−+ was bad.

27...♔f6!

However, Black turned the peace proposal down by reasonably evaluating his position as considerably superior due to his actively posted knights and White's compromised kingside pawn structure. His king is capable of handling the white passed pawn, and his knights will get down to reaping the harvest of his opponent's weak pawns.

28.b4?!

White persists in driving his passed pawn forward. 28.♖b7! was a stronger continuation.

28...♔e7! 29.b5?! ♔d7! 30.b6

There is no way to exploit the black king's relocation to the queenside and grab some pawns left unprotected as a result of his departure: 30.♖g8 h6 31.♖h8 h5 32.♖g8 ♘xf3 33.♖g7 ♔c7 34.h4 (34.♖xf7+ ♔b6−+) 34...♘xh4 35.♖xg5 ♘hg6−+.

30.♖h8 h5 was not a game-changer either.

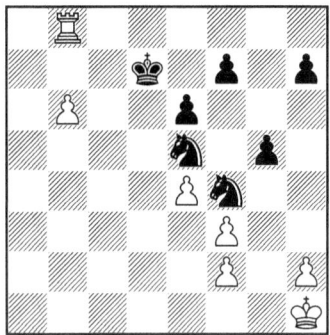

30...♘fg6!

An important prophylactic move. Restricting the opponent's rook, the black knight protects his kingside pawns.

31.♔g2

White cannot exchange his passed pawn, which seemed so formidable only a while ago: 31.b7 ♔c7 32.♖g8 ♔xb7 33.♖g7 h5−+.

31...h5!?

Now White is left with numerous weak pawns and no counterplay whatsoever.

32.♔f1 ♔c6! 33.♔e2 ♘d7 34.♖d8 ♘xb6−+

Encircled by the black pieces, the key pawn has fallen. The same fate is in store for its fellow pawns, too.

35.♖g8 ♘d7 36.♔e3 ♔d6 37.♖g7?!

White has entirely lost his sense of danger.

37...♔e7 38.♖h7 ♘f6 39.♖h6

The rook is immediately trapped after 39.♖g7 ♔f8−+.

39...h4!? 40.h3 e5

Black is in no hurry whatsoever. Having restricted his opponent's options to the maximum, he is now ready to let his king loose on its prey via f8-g7. Here, White resigned in the face of the imminent fall of his rook.

Let us now proceed to a rook vs. pair of bishops example. This ending is a good display of the two bishops' strong coordination and of the importance of opposing them with an active rook to enable saving counterplay.

Example No. 28
M. Schekhachikhin – I. Popov
Sochi 2022

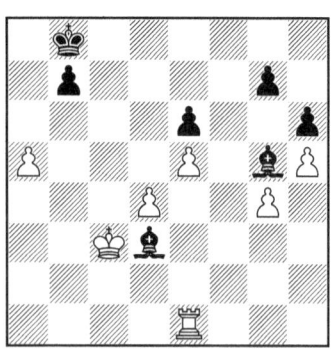

Black to move

White has a rook and a pawn for two bishops. Black's bishops are sufficiently active, and White's extra central pawn does not make itself felt yet. Further, White's kingside pawns will likely turn into easy targets for the light-squared bishop. Black will be obviously winning if he manages to adequately address the current threat to his queen's bishop while keeping the white rook out of his camp. Advantage conversion will only be a question of time.

47...♗b5?

Out of the three available bishop retreats Black chooses a bad one.

47...♗h4? 48.♖h1+− is a bad continuation that drops one of Black's bishops.

There is no ceding control over the f-file to the black rook: 47...♗h7? 48.♖f1! ♗e4. It is a draw by repetition after 48...♔c7 49.♖f7+ ♔c6 50.♖xg7 ♗e4 51.♖g6! ♔d5 52.♖g7 ♔c6 53.♖g6 ♗d5 54.♔d3 ♗c1 55.g5! ♗xg5 56.♖xg5 hxg5 57.h6 ♗a2 58.♔c2 ♗d5 59.♔d3=.

49.♖f7!? White can also transpose to the actual game via 49.♖f8+!?.

49...g6 50.♖f6! gxh5 51.gxh5 ♗d5 (51...♗f5 52.d5!=) 52.♖g6 ♔c7 53.♔d3! ♗f4 54.♖g4 ♗c1 55.♖g1 ♗a3. 55...♗g5 56.♖xg5 hxg5 57.h6 ♗a2 58.♔c2 ♗d5 59.♔d3= is a repetition of the drawing mechanism seen above.

56.♖g6 ♗c1 (56...♗f8? 57.♖f6) 57.♖g1= and White's counterplay is sufficient to make a draw.

The correct continuation is 47...♗a6! 48.♖b1. The pawn break 48.d5 does not work because after 48...exd5 49.♔d4 (49.e6 ♗f6+! 50.♔c2 ♗e7−+) 49...♗c4 50.♖b1 (White drowns in the bishops' nets following 50.e6 ♗f6+! 51.♔c5 ♗e7+ 52.♔b6 ♗h4! 53.♔c5 ♗f2+! 54.♔d6 ♗xe1 55.e7 ♗b4+−+) 50...♗h4! 51.♖b2 (51.♔e3 ♔c7−+; 51.e6 ♔c7−+) 51...♔c7−+ White gets

zero counterplay for the sacrificed pawn.

48...♗d8 49.♔b4. 49.d5 exd5 50.♔d4 ♗c4 51.a6 b5!? 52.♔c5 ♔c7 53.a7 ♗e7+ 54.♔d4 ♔b7 55.♖a1 ♔a8−+ is hopeless.

49...♔c7 50.♖b2 (50.♔c5? ♗e7#; 50.♖c1+ ♔d7!)

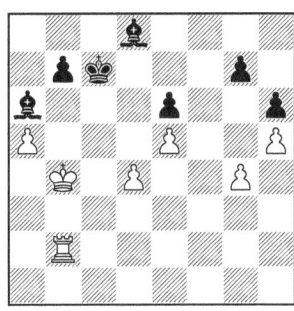

50...♗h4! Black again denies the white rook access to the f-file to create counterplay.

51.♔a4 (51.♔c5? ♗e7#; 51.d5 exd5 52.♔c5 ♗c4−+; 51.♖a2 ♔c6−+) 51...♔c6 52.♖b6+. White is doomed after 52.♖c2+ ♔d5 53.♖c7 ♔xd4 54.♖xg7 ♔xe5 55.♖g6 ♗g5−+.

52...♔d5! 53.♖d6+ ♔c4 54.♖xe6 (54.♔a3 ♗e7−+ is an immediate failure) 54...♗g5!?

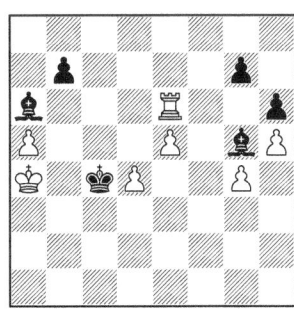

55.♖g6 (55.♔a3 ♔xd4−+; 55.♖d6 ♗b5+ 56.♔a3 ♗e7−+; 55.♖b6 ♔xd4 56.e6 ♔e5−+; 55.d5 ♔xd5 56.♖e8

♗f4!? 57.e6 ♗e5 58.e7 ♔e6–+) 55...♗e7! Setting up a decisive mating mechanism for the white king.

56.♖b6 (56.♖xg7? ♗b5#) 56...♔xd4 57.♖g6 ♗c4! 58.♖b6 ♔d5 59.♖g6 ♗f8 60.e6 ♔c4! 61.e7 ♗xe7 62.♖xg7 ♗b5#.

48.♖b1!

48.♔b4? ♗d2+–+ drops the rook.

48...♗c6

White gets unpleasant counterplay no matter the retreat of the black bishop's choosing.

The onus of solving problems in the endgame arising after the underwhelming 48...♗a6? 49.♖b6 ♗d8 (49...♗e2? 50.♖xe6 ♗xg4 51.♖g6 ♗xh5 52.♖xg7) 50.♖xe6 ♗xa5+ 51.♔c2 ♗e2 52.♖g6 is already with Black.

After 48...♗d7 49.♖f1 ♗c6 50. ♖f7= the rook's activity is sufficient to maintain equality.

Meanwhile, after 48...♗e2 49.♖b6 ♗xg4 50.a6! ♔a7 (Similarly, 50...♗f3 51.♖xe6 bxa6 52.♖xa6 ♗xh5 53.d5= is no better) 51.axb7 ♔b8 52.d5 exd5 53.♔d4 ♗f3 (53...♗xh5 54.♔xd5 ♗f3+ 55.♔d6 ♗xb7 56.e6 ♔a7 57.♖b4 ♗f3 58.e7 ♗h5 59.♔d7=) 54.♖b3 ♗e4 55.♔c5 ♗e7+ 56.♔d4 White's counterplay allows him to count on a draw.

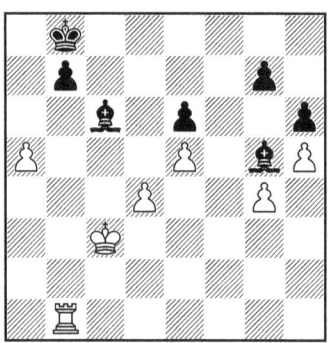

49.♖f1!

Gearing up for infiltration along the open file with the rook.

49...♗e4 50.♖f8+

The ramifications of 50.♖f7!? are analyzed above in the 47...♗h7 line.

50...♔c7

The alternative king retreat also has disadvantages: 50...♔a7 51.♖e8 ♗d5 52.♖g8 ♗f3 (52...♔a6 53.♖xg7 ♔xa5 54.♔d3 ♗f3 55.d5! ♗xd5 56.♖xg5 hxg5 57.h6 ♗a2 58.♔c2 ♗d5 59.♔d3=) 53.♖xg7 ♗xg4

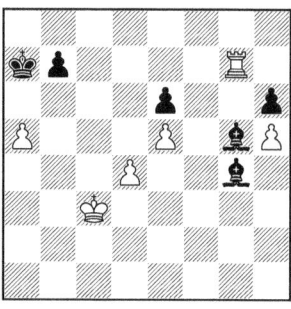

54.d5! Black can no longer play 54...exd5? 55.♖xg5 hxg5 56.h6 ♗f5 57.e6+– since one of White's passed pawns becomes a queen.

51.♖f7+ ♔c6 52.♖xg7 ♗f3=

52...♔b5 53.♖g6! ♗d5 54.♔d3 ♔xa5 55.♖xg5 hxg5 56.h6 ♗a2 57.♔c2 ♗d5 58.♔d3 ♗a2= leads to yet another draw by repetition.

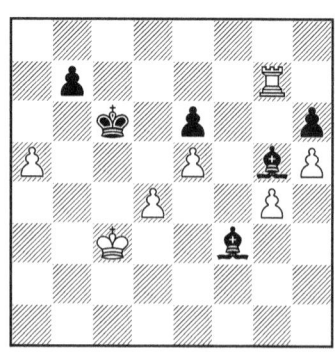

53.d5+!

This nice move places the pawn en prise to as many as three captures. It was also fine to play 53.♖g6!? ♗xg4 54.♔c4 ♗e2+ 55.♔c3 ♗g4 (55...♗d5? 56.♖xg5 hxg5 57.h6+−; 55...♗xh5 56.♖xe6+ ♔b5 57.♖b6+ ♔xa5 58.♖xb7=) 56.♔c4 ♔d7 57.♖g7+ ♔c6 (57...♔c8? 58.♔c5!) 58.♖g6 with an equal position.

53...exd5

White achieves a draw both after 53...♔xd5 54.♖xb7 ♗e2 55.♖b6 ♗e3 56.g5!=,

and after 53...♗xd5 54.♔d4 ♗b3 55.♖g6!? (55.♔c3 ♗a2!?) 55...♗b5 56.♔d3 ♗a2 (56...♗d1 57.♖xe6 ♔c5 58.a6 bxa6 59.♖xa6 ♗xg4 60.♔e4 ♗xh5 61.e6=; 56...♗c4+ 57.♔c3 ♗d5 58.♔d4=) 57.♔c2 (in this line each time reinstating the threat of sacrificing the rook on g5):

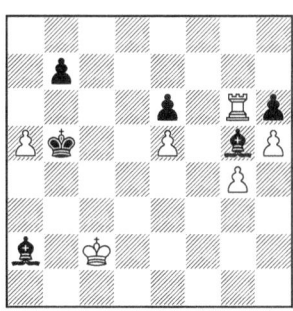

a) 57...♗f4 58.g5 ♗xg5 59.♖xg5 hxg5 60.h6 ♗d5 61.♔d3 ♗a2 62.♔c2=;

b) 57...♔xa5 58.♖xg5 hxg5 59.h6 ♗d5 60.♔d3 ♗a2 61.♔c2=;

c) 57...♗d5 58.♔d3 ♗f3 59.♖xe6 ♔c5 (59...♗xg4 60.♖b6+ ♔xa5 61.♖xb7 ♗xh5 62.e6=) 60.a6 bxa6 61.♖xa6 ♔d5 62.♖a5+ ♔e6 63.♖b5 ♗xg4 64.♔e4 ♗f5+ (or 64...♗xh5 65.♖b6+=) 65.♔d4=.

54.♔d4!

Activating his king.

54...♗xg4

Likewise, the position arising after 54...♗e4 55.♖f7 ♗h4 56.♔e3 ♗g5+ 57.♔d4 is equal.

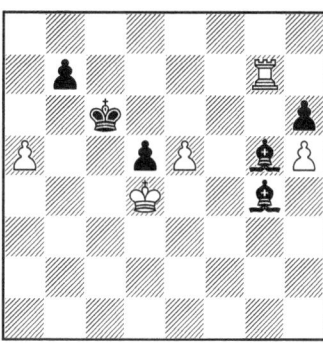

55.♖g6+!

Signaling to Black to give up any hope of winning the game.

55...♔d7 56.♖g7+ ♔c6

The pursuit of a non-existent victory could even cost the game: 56...♔e6? 57.♖xb7.

In the same fashion, Black has nothing to match the activity of White's pieces in the line 56...♔c8 57.♔xd5 ♗xh5 58.♔d6 ♗e8 59.♖g8 ♔d8 60.♖g7=.

57.♖g6+ ♔c7

A refusal to repeat moves could backfire for Black after 57...♔b5? 58.♖xg5! hxg5 59.h6 ♗f5 60.e6 ♔c6 61.♔e5! ♗e4 62.♔f6 d4 63.e7 ♔d7 64.♔f7+− and there is no stopping the white pawns.

58.♖g7+ ♔c8

58...♗d7? 59.e6+− is an error.

59.♖g8+ ♔d7 60.♖g7+ ♔c6 61.♖g6+ ♔d7 62.♖g7+ ♔c6 with a draw agreed.

Let us now review a case in which the stronger side in the rook vs. two minor pieces rivalry is the one with the rook.

Example No. 29
D. Berczes – E Li
USA 2022

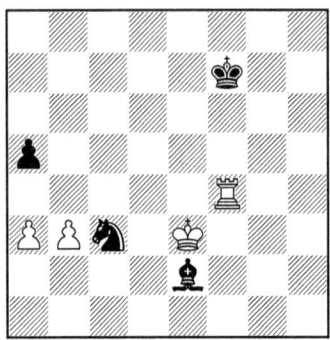

Black to move

White has delivered a check to the black king. After that, he plans to attack the opponent's minor pieces and the only remaining pawn in an attempt to win.

49...♔g6!

Both 49...♔e6? 50.♔d2 ♘d5 51.♖e4++− and 49...♔g7? 50.♔d2 ♘d5 51.♖f5 ♘e7 52.♖e5+− are bad.

50.♔d2 ♘d5 51.♖a4

In case of 51.♖f8 ♗g4 52.♖a8 ♔f6! 53.♖xa5 ♔e5 54.♔d3 (54.b4 ♔d4=; 54.a4 ♔d4=) 54...♔d6 55.♔d4 (55.♔c4 ♗e2+ 56.♔d4 ♘e7=) 55...♘e7= the black pieces can handle the pair of opposing passed pawns.

51...♗f3?!

A wrong decision. The correct continuation is 51...♗d1! 52.♖xa5. 52.♔xd1 ♘c3+ 53.♔d2 ♘xa4 54.bxa4 ♔f5 55.♔d3 ♔e6 56.♔c4 ♔d6 57.♔b5 ♔c7 58.♔xa5 ♔b7 is an elementary draw.

52...♗xb3 53.♖b5 ♗c4 54.♖c5 ♗b3= and elimination of the only remaining pawn will be easy for Black.

52.♔d3!

White improves his king first and intends to grab the pawn in more favourable conditions.

Perhaps Black counted on 52.♖xa5 ♗e4! 53.a4 (53.♖a4 ♔f5=; 53.b4 ♔f6 54.b5 ♔e7 55.b6 ♔d7=) 53...♔f6 54.♖b5 ♔e6 55.a5 ♔d6 56.a6 (56. b4 ♗g2 57.a6 ♔c6 58.a7 ♘b6 59.♖g5 ♗d5=) 56...♘c7= and his pieces are well-coordinated to save this ending.

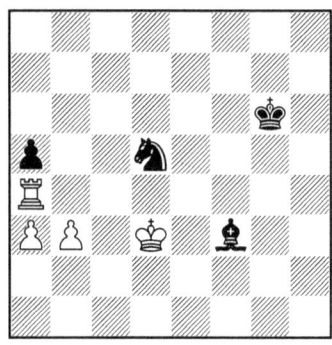

52...♗d1?

This is a losing error already.

52...♔f6? also loses because after 53.♖xa5 ♔e6 (53...♔e5 54.♔c4 ♔d6 55.♖a6+ ♔c7 56.♔c5+−) 54.♔d4! ♘c7 55.♔c5 ♔d7 56.♔b6+− the white king's activity helps disorganize his opponent's defensive formations.

It takes 52...♗e2+! to retain a draw. Now

a) 53.♔c2 ♔f6! 54.♖xa5 ♔e5! 55.b4 (55.a4 ♔d4=)

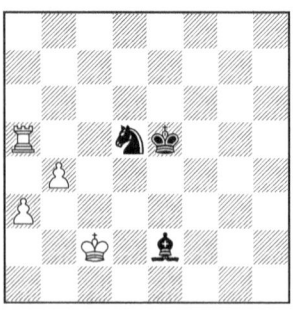

55...♔d4! 56.♖c5 ♗c4=, and the strong black king and two minor pieces again stop the white king and rook from promoting their pair of connected passed pawns.

b) The pawn ending after 53.♔xe2 ♘c3+ 54.♔d3 ♘xa4 55.bxa4 ♔f5 56.♔c4 ♔e5 57.♔b5 ♔d6 58.♔xa5 ♔c7= is again a draw,

c) 53.♔d4 ♘e7! 54.♔c5 (54.♔e3 ♗d1=) 54...♗d1 55.♖e4 (55.♔c4 ♘c6=) 55...♘f5 56.♖e6+ ♔f7 57.♖b6 ♔e7= does not hold much promise for White either.

53.♖xa5 ♗xb3?

Persisting with the wrong way chosen earlier. Having said that, the endgame after 53...♘e7 54.b4 is already lost for Black.

54.♖b5! ♘f4+

54...♗a2 55.♖b2 ♘f4+ 56.♔e4+− is equally bad.

55.♔e3! ♗a4

Both 55...♘d5+ 56.♔d4+− and 55...♘g2+ 56.♔f2+− lose the game.

56.♖a5! ♘g2+ 57.♔f2! ♗b3

In saving the knight with 57...♗c6 58.♖a6+− the bishop is lost.

58.♔xg2+− ♔f6 59.♖b5 ♗a4 60.♖b4 ♗c6+ 61.♔f2 ♔e5 62.a4 ♔d6 63. a5! ♔c5 64.♖b6 ♗b5 65.♔e3 ♗c6 65...♔b4 66.a6+−.

66.♔f4 ♗b5 67.♔e5 ♗c6 68.♔e6 ♗b5 69.♔e7 ♗c6 70.♔d8 ♗f3 71.♔c7

White has protected the rook and is ready to resume pushing his pawn towards the promotion square. Therefore, Black resigned.

Chapter 3

ROOK AND MINOR PIECE
AGAINST DIFFERENT FORCES

We now move on to the most in-depth subject matter of this book. This chapter includes examples from over-the-board games both with and without pawns for one or both sides.

The majority of examples in this chapter cover battle with a rook and minor piece vs. an opposing rook and minor piece. There are also several instructive examples with a rook and minor piece fighting against a rook. Further examples feature a rook and a minor piece vs. two minor pieces. The follow-up to that is battle between a rook and minor piece vs. two rooks, and we wrap-up with battle between the tandem in question and a queen.

In a nutshell, rook and a bishop teamplay in the endgame is more effective than that of a rook and a knight. This is similar to having a queen and knight versus a queen and bishop, in which the former combination of pieces is generally considered more advantageous than the latter. There is no doubt, however, that correct evaluation of a particular endgame primarily depends on specific features of the position, such as activity of the rook and minor piece, the location of pawns, activity of the king, presence of weaknesses in one side or the other, and so on. The numerous examples offered for consideration confirm this. That is why the author believes it incorrect to come up with simplistic rules of thumb about one of the above material balances being superior to the other.

At the same time, the presence of a minor piece alongside a rook renders the rook more productive both in terms of developing an initiative against the enemy king and the opponent's pawn weaknesses, and in terms of assisting their own passed pawns' promotion to the queening square. We will see, among other things, how the combination of these two factors helps experienced grandmasters attain the necessary result.

We also consider material ratios that feature opposite-colored bishops. On the one hand, this increases the potential for one of the sides (usually the stronger one) to seize the initiative, primarily attacking the opponent's king. However, it also increases drawish tendencies in the position should the rooks be exchanged off.

Further, we analyze in more detail exchanges or transpositions from one endgame to another. We have already touched upon these aspects earlier. However, in the topic under review we deal with more material on the board. Thus, a possible exchange of minor pieces in a rook and minor piece vs. rook and minor piece ending gives us a rook ending. The exchange of rooks leaves us in a minor-piece ending. And, finally, when reviewing endgames that begin with a more standard material balance, we cannot avoid mentioning the potential transition into a pawn ending in case of the exchange of both minor pieces and rooks of both opponents. In doing so, a player will naturally face having to evaluate the arising ending correctly. A player's insight into similar endings, experience and precise calculation of possible lines should be of help in this respect. In case of a rook sacrifice for a minor piece or when winning the exchange, a "rook versus minor piece" imbalance may arise that we covered in detail in chapter one.

A pawn promotion will naturally increase the number of pieces by one. It will obviously be a queen most of the time, unless, of course, such a promotion is impossible due to a stalemating idea set by the weaker side, or when the pawn is to be promoted with a check via underpromotion to a knight. In this case it will already be a multi-piece endgame, or even a middlegame, which is beyond our scope.

Besides possible transition into some type of standard endgame, the examples offered for studying may also lead to other endings with material imbalances. They include, for example, a minor piece vs. pawns or a queen vs. a rook and pawn. This once again highlights the multitude of situations that might arise on the chessboard.

The author has made what is intended to be a highly instructive selection of examples with rook and bishop vs. rook endings and rook and knight vs. rook endings. In his focus on such important aspects of handling this type of ending as location of the weaker side's king, activity of the defending side's rook, typical defensive drawn positions and, conversely, decisive rearrangement of pieces in already won positions, he also uses the selected examples to show that defending such types of endgame is a huge challenge in practice. We should also keep in mind that by the time this type of endgame appears on the board the defending side is likely to be experiencing a lack of thinking time as well as fatigue from the challenge of preceding defensive efforts. All these factors, coupled with tournament tension, largely interfere with successful defense of such endings.

When analyzing examples with the rook and minor piece vs. two pieces imbalance, we looked at the Vallejo Pons – Carlsen game played in Germany, in which the world champion confidently managed to win the endgame despite the absence of pawns. Despite the seemingly drawn material balance, these positions do not lend themselves to easy understanding. I would even go as far as to claim that they are mind-bending for the human, and that there is no other way but carrying out much work on databases to gain insight into many secret aspects of this type of ending. The engine demonstrates which positions are mathematically won, or how the defending side could avoid losing them.

The positions with a rook and minor piece opposing two rooks are important to study as well. A side enjoying an advantage and playing for a win in a position the exchange down largely relies on his pawns, activity of pieces and position of the kings. It is not always the side with the pair of rooks who should win, which the examples here of modern grandmasters serve to confirm.

Coordinating a rook and a minor piece

We start with examples which begin with an identical material balance of rook and bishop vs. rook and bishop. In these examples, the bishops are of the same color.

Example No. 30
E. Najer – I. Saric
Riga 2021

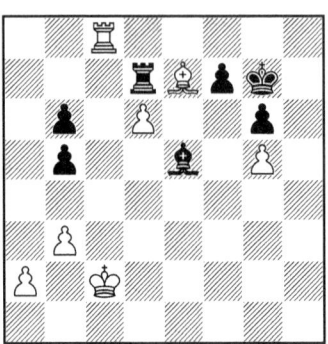

Black to move

Black's position produces a grim impression. His king is unsafe, he has weak doubled pawns on the queenside, and White has a far-advanced and dangerous passed pawn. The situation has become critical.

54...f5

Black undertakes a desperate attempt to free his king from the mating net.

54...♗xd6? 55.♗f6+ ♔h7 56.♖h8# is immediate failure.

Black is doomed after 54...b4 55.♖c6!? ♖b7 56.♔d3+−.

55.gxf6+?

An unfortunate slip. 55.♗f6+! was winning by force: 55...♗xf6 (55...♔f7 56.♗xe5+−) 56.♖c7!

a) 56...♖f7 57.gxf6+ ♔xf6 58.d7! ♖f8 (58...♔e7 59.d8=♕+ ♔xd8 60.♖xf7+−) 59.♖c8+−;

b) 56...♖xc7+ 57.dxc7+− and the pawn queens;

c) 56...♗xg5 57.♖xd7+ ♔f6 58.♖b7 ♗e3 59.♖b8+−.

55...♔f7

Black has improved significantly. The white pawns are under attack, and

a rook ending that he can save is already looming.

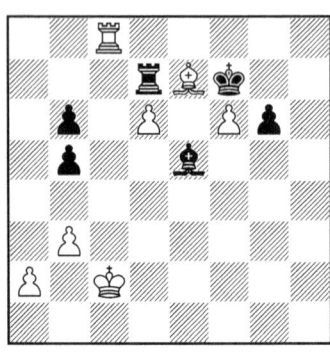

56.♖c6

After 56.♖b8 ♗xd6 57.♖xb6 ♗xe7 58.fxe7 ♖xe7 59.♖xb5 ♖e2+ (Black also holds the ending arising after 59...♔f6!? 60.a4 g5 61.a5 g4 62.a6 g3 63.♖a5 g2 64.♖a1 ♖g7 65.♖g1 [65.a7 ♖xa7!] 65...♔e5 66.♔c3 ♔d5=) 60.♔b1 ♔f6 61.a4 g5= a draw is obvious.

56.♖f8+! ♔e6 is stronger

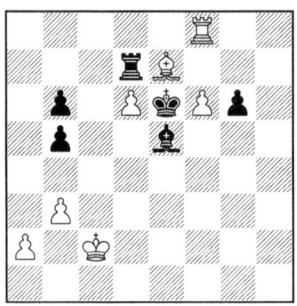

57.♖g8

(Black also saves the ending in case of 57.♖b8 ♖a7!? 58.♔b1 [58.♖xb6 ♖xa2+ 59.♔d3 ♗xf6 60.♗xf6 ♔xf6 61.♖xb5 ♔e6=] 58...♗xf6 59.♖xb6 ♗xe7 60.dxe7 ♔xe7 61.♖xg6 [61. ♖xb5 ♔f6 62.a4 g5=] 61...♖a5!

a) 62.♖g5 ♔d6 63.b4 [63.a4 ♔c6 64.♔b2 ♔b6=] 63...♖a4 64.♖xb5 ♔c6

65.♖c5+ [65.♖b8 ♔c7=] 65...♔b6 66.♖c4 ♔b5=;

b) 62.♔b2 ♔d7;

c) 62.♖b6 ♔d7 63.b4 ♖a4 64.♖xb5 ♔c6=).

57...♗xd6. Both 57...♗xf6? 58.♖xg6 and 57...♔f7? 58.♖g7+ ♔e6 59.♖xg6 are wrong.

58.♗xd6 (58.♖xg6 ♖c7+ 59.♔d3 ♗e5 and White has no way of making headway) 58...♖xd6 59.♖xg6 ♔f7 60.♖h6 (60.♖g5 ♔xf6 61.♖xb5 ♔e6=)

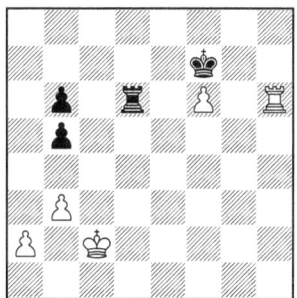

60...b4! Restricting the white king. 60...♖c6+? loses to 61.♔b2 b4 62.♖h4 ♔xf6 63.♖xb4 ♔e5 64.♔a3! ♔d6 65.♔a4 ♖c2 (65...♔c7 66.♖c4+−) 66.♔b5 ♖xa2 67.♖c4! (67.♔xb6? ♖a3! 68.♖e4 ♔d5 69.♖e3 ♖a8=) 67...♖a8 68.b4! ♖b8 69.♖c6+ ♔d7 70.♖xb6+−.

61.♖h4 ♖xf6 62.♖xb4 ♔e7! Not 62...♖f2+? 63.♔b1 ♖f1+ 64.♔b2 ♖f2+ 65.♔a3+−.

63.♖d4. White seems to have managed to cut the black king off and would have been winning if only his own king were more active. (63.a4 ♔d7=)

63...♖f2+! 64.♖d2 (64.♔c3? ♖xa2 65.♔b4 ♖a5!=) 64...♖f3! Black uses his rook to restrict white pieces' activity.

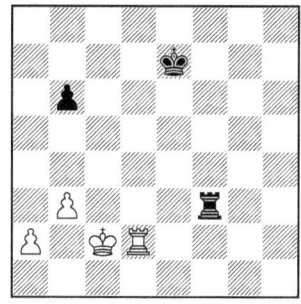

65.a4. There is also no winning after 65.♔b2 ♖h3 66.♔a3 ♖h4 67.♖d5 (67. b4 b5! 68.♖d5 ♖h3+ 69.♔b2 ♖h2+=) 67...♖h2 68.♖b5 ♖h6 69.♔a4 ♔d7=.

65...♖h3 (65...♔e6 66.♖d8 ♔e7 67.♖b8?! ♖f6 68.♔c3 ♔d7= is also fine) 66.♔b2. White's attempt to bring the king up to c4 and interpose along the fifth rank with the rook does not work: 66.♖d3 ♖h2+ 67.♔c3 ♖h5! 68.♔c4 (68.b4 ♖h4! 69.♖d4 ♖xd4 70.♔xd4 ♔d6=) 68...♖c5+! 69.♔b4 ♖h5=.

66...♖g3 67.♔a3 (67.♖d5 ♖h3 68.♖b5 ♖h6=) 67...♖g4 68.♖d5 ♖h4, and there is no visible headway for White in this position: 69.♖b5 ♖h6 70.♔b4 ♔d7= or 69.b4 ♖h3+ 70.♔b2 ♖g3 71.♖b5 ♖g6=.

56...♖a7! 57.♖c8

57.♖xb6 ♖xa2+ 58.♔d3 (58. ♔b1 ♖a1+) 58...♗xf6 59.♗xf6 ♔xf6 60.♖xb5 ♔e6= is also a draw.

In case of 57.♔b1 ♗xf6 58.♗xf6 ♔xf6 59.d7+ (59.♖xb6 ♖d7 60.♖xb5 ♖xd6 61.a4 g5=) 59...♔e7 60.♖xg6 ♖xd7 61.♖xb6 ♖d5 62.♔b2 ♔d7 63.♔c3 ♔c7 64.♖h6 ♔b7 65.♔b4 ♖d2 66.a3 (66.♔xb5 ♖xa2=) 66...♖d3 67.♖h5 ♔a6!= Black also holds the ending.

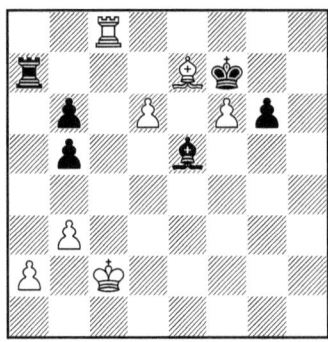

57...♔e6!

57...♖xa2+? 58.♔d3 ♔e6 (58...♖a7 59.♔e4+−) 59.f7 ♔xf7 60.d7+− is bad.

58.♖g8 ♖xa2+ 59.♔d3 ♖f2 60.♔e3 ♖f1 61.♖xg6

and the opponents agreed a draw without playing 61...♗xd6 62.♗xd6 ♔xd6 63.♔e4 b4 64.f7+ ♔c7 65.♖g7 ♔d6.

Example No. 31
G. Mitrabha – H. Gusain
Delhi 2022

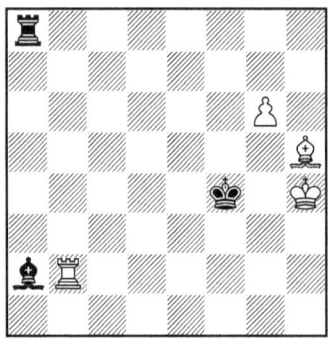

Black to move

In view of there being only one pawn and a potential rook and bishop vs. rook endgame that should end in a draw with the proper defense, it might seem that making a draw for Black is not such a big deal. However, a deeper look into the position points to White's intention

not to allow the black bishop to lurk in wait for the white pawn to show up on the promotion g8-square, instead planning full-scale support for his passer with all the remaining pieces so as to intervene in his opponent's control over the promotion square.

68...♖a4?

Black resorts to a discovered check to stop the white king's further progress up the board. However, this idea does not work.

Equally, White's plan cannot be stopped by 68...♖a7? 69.♖f2+! ♔e3 (69...♔e5 70.♔g5+−) 70.♖f3+ ♔e4 71.♖f8 ♔e7 72.♔g5+−,

by 68...♗g8? 69.♖f2+ ♔e5 70.♔g5+−,

or by 68...♔f5? 69.♖f2+ ♔e5 (69...♔e6 70.g7 ♔e7 71.♖xa2+−) 70.♔g5+−.

Rather, Black could stay in the game with 68...♗d5! 69.♖f2+ (69.g7? ♖g8=; 69.♖b5? ♖a1! 70.♖b4+ ♔f5=) 69...♔e3! (69...♔e5? 70.♔g5+−) 70.♖f6 (70.♖f5 ♗e4! 71.♖e5 ♔f4=; 70.♖e2+ ♔f4! 71.g7 ♖g8 72.♖e7 ♔f5=)

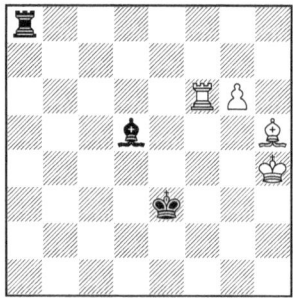

70...♖g8! 71.♔g5 ♗e4! 72.♖e6 ♔d4, and Black is in time to stop Black's passed pawn.

69.♗g4!

69.♖f2+? blunders the white pawn to 69...♔e3+ 70.♔g3 ♖a7! 71.♖b2 (71.♖xa2 ♖xa2 72.g7 ♖a8=) 71...♗d5.

69...♗d5

Black cannot avoid the decisive involvement of the white king with either 69...♖a6 70.♖b4+ ♔e5 71.♔g5+−, or 69...♗g8 70.♖f2+ ♔e5 71.♔g5+−.

70.♖f2+! ♔e5

Neither 70...♔e4 71.♔g5+−, nor 70...♔e3 71.♖f6+− are game-changers.

71.♔g5! ♖a7

Black is defenseless after 71...♖a8? 72.♖e2+! ♔d6 73.♖d2 ♖f8 (73...♔e5 74.♖xd5+ ♔xd5 75.♗f3++−) 74.g7 ♖g8 75.♔f6+−.

71...♖a1? also fails, to 72.♖e2+! ♔d6 73.♖d2 ♔e5 74.♖xd5+ ♔xd5 75.g7 ♖a8 76.♗f3+ ♔e6 77.♗xa8 ♔f7 78.♔h6+−.

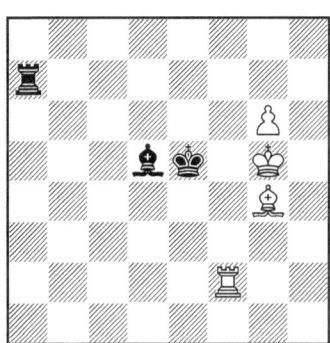

72.♖e2+!

White keeps widening the gap between the black king and the passed pawn.

72...♔d6

Black is also in bad shape after 72...♔d4 73.♔f6 ♖a6+ 74.♗e6 ♔d3 75.♖e5+−.

73.♔f6! ♖a8

In case of 73...♖a4 74.♗f5 ♖f4 75.g7!

a) 75...♗g8 76.♖e8 ♗a2 (76...♗h7 77.♔g5! ♖xf5+ 78.♔h6+−, White gives back the piece to promote his passed pawn) 77.♔g5 ♖f1 (77...♖a4 78.♗e6!+−) 78.♖e6+! ♗xe6 79.♗xe6 ♖g1+ (79...

♔xe6 80.g8=♕++−) 80.♗g4+− and there is no stopping the passed pawn,

b) Black goes down both after 75...♗c4 76.♖e4! ♖xe4 77.♗xe4 ♗b3 78.♗g6 ♗g8 79.♗f7 ♗h7 80.♗b3 ♔d7 81.♔g5 ♔e7 82.♔h6+−,

c) and after 75...♖f1 76.♖d2+−,

d) 75...♗b3 76.♔g5 ♖f1 77.♖e6+! ♗xe6 78.♗xe6 ♖g1+ 79.♗g4+− is no better.

74.g7 ♖a7

74...♗g8 75.♗e6 ♗h7 (75...♖e8 76.♖d2+ ♔c5 77.♗xg8 ♖xg8 78.♔f7+−) 76.♖h2+− will not save Black either.

75.♖d2! ♔c6

75...♖f7+? 76.♔g6+− is equally hopeless.

76.♗h5

The hasty 76.♖xd5? ♖xg7! 77.♗f3 ♖c7!? would have thrown the win away.

76...♖b7

76...♖a8 77.♖xd5! ♔xd5 78.♗f3++− was losing as well.

77.♗e8+ and Black resigned in the face of 77...♔c5 78.♖xd5+ ♔xd5 79.g8=♕+.

Example No. 32
A. Vaisser − R. Kasimdzhanov
Germany 2022

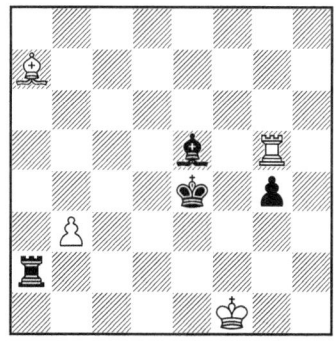

White to move

The white king is cut off and may fall into checkmating mechanisms in the future. Besides, the advance of Black's pawn which is so far still alive can create more problems. White needs to keep a cool head and demonstrate precision when defending this position.

101.♖xg4+?

White's immediate elimination of the last black pawn is an error stemming from misevaluation of the perils threatening his king's position.

It was worth considering 101.♗f2!? ♚f4 (there is no sense in 101...♚f3 102. ♖xe5 ♖xf2+ 103.♚g1=) 102.♖h5 (102. ♖g8? ♚f3) 102...♖b2 (102...♗b8 103. ♖h8=; 102...♗c7 103.♖h7=)

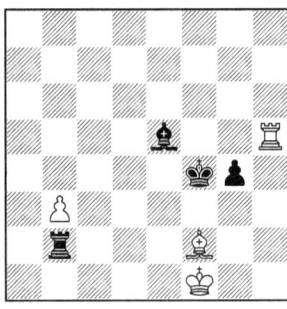

103.♗e1. Both 103.♗g3+? ♚xg3 104.♖xe5 ♖b1+ 105.♚e2 ♖xb3−+ and 103.♖h7? ♚f3 104.♖f7+ ♗f4−+ are bad.

103...♖xb3 104.♗d2+ ♚e4 105.♖g5 g3 (105...♖b1+ 106.♚f2 g3+ 107.♖xg3 ♗xg3+ 108.♚xg3=) 106.♚e2. White has dropped a pawn, but now his pieces are well-coordinated.

106...♖b2 107.♖g4+ ♚f5 108.♖g5+ ♚f6 109.♖g4 and Black has nothing better than 109...♗c3 110.♖xg3 ♖xd2+ 111.♚e3=, transposing into a drawn rook and bishop vs. rook ending.

It was also fine to go for 101.♗b6!?

a) 101...♚f4 102.♗e3+ (102.♖h5 ♖b2 103.♗a5!? is also fine) 102...♚f3.
(a drawn rook ending results from 102...♚xe3 103.♖xe5+ ♚f3

a1) 104.b4!
a1.1) 104...♖b2 105.b5 ♖b1+ 106. ♖e1 ♖xb5 107.♚g1=;
a1.2) 104...♖a1+ 105.♖e1 ♖xe1+ 106.♚xe1 g3 107.♚f1 ♚e4=;
a1.3) 104...♚g3 105.b5 ♖b2 106. ♖e3+ ♚h2 107.♖e2+ ♖xe2 108.♚xe2 g3 109.b6 g2 110.b7 g1=♕ 111.b8=♕+ ♕g3=;
a1.4) 104...g3 105.♖f5+ ♚g4 106. ♖f8=.
a2) 104.♚g1? ♖a1+ 105.♚h2 g3+ 106.♚h3 ♖h1#;
a3) 104.♖e8? ♖a1+ 105.♖e1 ♖xe1+ 106.♚xe1 ♚g2!−+;
a4) 104.♖f5+ ♚g3 105.♚g1? ♖a1+ 106.♖f1 ♖xf1+ 107.♚xf1 ♚h2−+.)
103.♖f5+! ♚e4

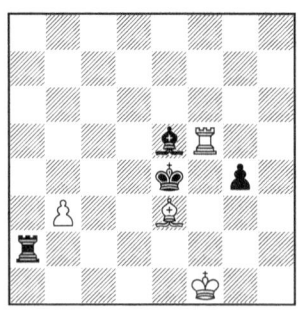

104.♖f2! An important defensive resource.

104...♖a1+ 105.♔e2 g3. White also keeps his position together after 105...♖b1 106.♖f8 ♖b2+ 107.♗d2 ♗c3 108.♖f4+!

106.♖f8 g2. 106...♖a2+ 107.♗d2 ♗c3 108.♖e8+ ♔f5 109.♖f8+ ♔e6 110.♔f3! is yet another transposition into a rook and bishop vs. rook ending.

107.♖g8 ♖a2+ 108.♗d2 ♗f4. 108...♗c3 109.♖g4+! ♔f5 110.♖g5+ ♔f6 111.♖xg2 ♖xd2+ 112.♔f3 make no difference either.

109.♖e8+ ♔f5. White acts similarly in the case of 109...♔d5 110.♖g8! ♖xd2+ 111.♔f3.

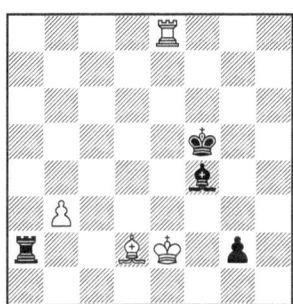

110.♖f8+ ♔e5 111.♖g8! ♖xd2+ 112.♔f3 ♖d3+ (112...♔f5 113.♖f8+! ♔e6 114.♖g8!) 113.♔xg2 ♔e4 114. ♖e8+ ♗e5 115.♔f2 ♖xb3 116.♔e2 ♖b2+ 117.♔e1!=, which gives us one of the typical key defensive positions to be analyzed in the following sections.

The alternatives for Black on move 101 also lead to a draw:

b) 101...g3 102.♖xe5+ ♔xe5 103. ♗c7+ ♔e4 104.♗xg3 ♔f3 105.♗e5! ♖c2 106.♔g1=;

c) 101...♗f4 102.♖xg4 ♔f3 103. ♖xf4+=;

d) 101...♗d6 102.♖xg4+ ♔f3 103. ♖a4! ♖b2 104.♖a1=.

101...♔f3 102.♖a4 ♖d2!

This rejoinder was obviously not on White's radar.

White holds the position easily after both 102...♖c2 103.♖c4= and 102...♖b2 103.♔e1=.

103.♔e1

103.♔g1 ♖d1# is a deadly alternative.

The mating net is complete after 103. ♗f2 ♖d1+ 104.♗e1 ♗g3−+.

103...♖d3!

The erroneous 103...♗c3? 104.♖c4 ♖d3+ 105.♖xc3= keeps White in the game.

104.♖a2

104.♖c4 ♗g3+ 105.♔f1 ♖d1# would be an alternative way to get checkmated.

104...♗c3+ and White resigned.

Example No. 33
A. Tabatabaei − K. Sasikiran
Moscow 2018

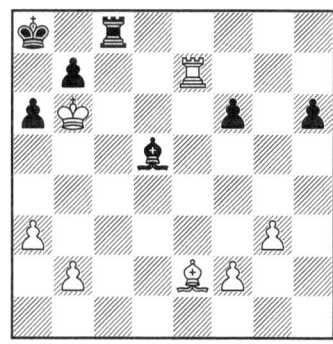

White to move

The white king enjoys clear superiority over his black counterpart in terms of activity. That said, Black intends to deliver a check from c6 with his rook.

42.♖c7!

In defending from the check, White gives Black the possibility of transposing into a less complex bishop ending that retains all the benefits of White's position.

42...♖d8

Black goes down after both 42...♖xc7 43.♔xc7+− and 42...♔b8 43.♖xc8+ ♔xc8 44.♔c5! ♗b3 45.♔d6 ♔d8 46.♗f3 b5 47.♗d5 ♗xd5 48.♔xd5 ♔d7 49.♔c5 ♔c7 50.b4 h5 51.f4 f5 52.♔d5+−.

Black is in equally bad shape following 42...♖h8 43.♖d7 ♗c6 44.♖f7+−.

43.♗g4!

Wanting to trade the rooks yet again.

43...♔b8

43...♖d6+ 44.♔c5 ♖c6+ 45.♖xc6 ♗xc6 46.♔d6+− loses as well.

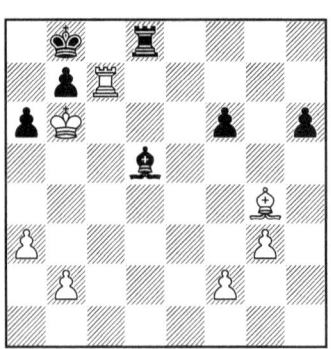

44.♖d7! ♖xd7 45.♗xd7 ♗f3 46.b4! ♗e4 47.a4! ♗f3

After 47...♗c2 48.♗e6 ♗xa4 49.♗d5+− White grabs both black pawns.

48.♗f5 ♗g2 49.f4!

White improves his position to the maximum prior to engineering a decisive break.

49...♗f3 50.b5! axb5

50...♗e2 51.♗e4+− makes no

difference. 50...♗d1 51.bxa6 bxa6 52.a5 ♗e2 53.♗e4 ♗b5 54.♗b7+− is also bad.

51.axb5 ♗e2

51...♗g2 52.♔c5 ♔c7 53.b6++− is no better than the text.

52.♗e4 ♗f1

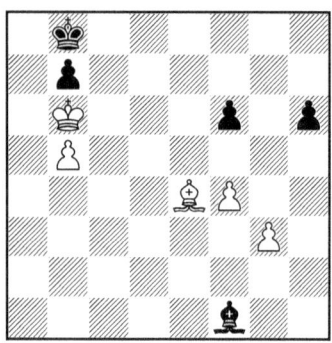

53.♔c5!

The hasty 53.♗xb7? ♗xb5 54.♔xb5 (54.♗c6 ♗e2 55.♗d5 ♔c8 56.♔c6 ♔d8 57.♔d6 ♗g4!) 54...♗xb7 55.♔c5 ♔c7 56.♔d5 ♔d7 57.g4 (57.f5 h5 58.♔c5 ♔c7=) 57...♔e7! 58.f5 ♔d7= would have missed the win.

53...♔a7

After 53...♔c7 54.b6+! ♔c8 55.♔d6+− the white king heads to the kingside to treat himself to the black pawns.

54.f5!

Bringing the potential passed pawn closer to the promotion square.

54...h5

54...b6+ 55.♔d6 ♗xb5 56.♔e7+− loses the game as well.

55.♔d6!

Perfect timing!

55...♗xb5 56.♔e7 ♗c4 57.♔xf6 b5 58.♔e7 ♔b6 59.f6 ♔c5 60.f7 ♗xf7 61.♔xf7 ♔d4 62.♗g6 b4 63.♔f6

White could win also via 63.♗xh5

♔e3 64.♔f6 b3 65.g4 b2 66.♗g6 ♔f4 67.g5+−.

63...♔e3 64.♔g5 ♔f2 65.♔f4 and Black resigned in the face of 65...b3 66.♗xh5 b2 67.♗g6.

Example No. 34
M. Carlsen – G. Ostmoe
Norway 2022

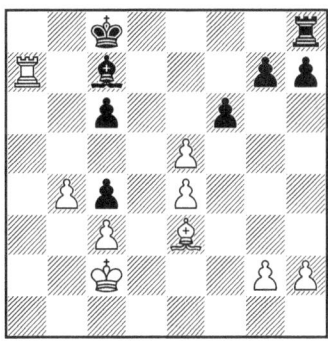

Black to move

White has just captured the black e5-pawn with his own pawn. How should Black react?

28...fxe5?

This error of judgement allows the world champion to achieve a decisive advantage.

a) 28...♗xe5?!

a1) 29.h4!

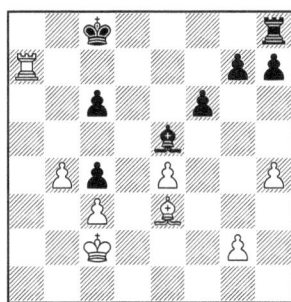

29...h5. White wins the pawn ending after both 29...♖g8? 30.♖a8+!

♗b8 31.♗a7 ♔b7 32.♖xb8+ ♖xb8 33.♗xb8 ♔xb8 34.♔d2 ♔c7 35.♔e3 ♔b6 36.♔d4 ♔b5 37.h5 g6 38.h6 g5 39.g4+− and 29...g6? 30.♖a8+ ♗b8 31.♗a7 ♔b7 32.♖xb8+ ♖xb8 33.♗xb8 ♔xb8 34.♔d2 ♔c7 35.♔e3 ♔b6 36.g4 h6 37.♔f4 ♔b5 38.g5 fxg5+ 39.hxg5 h5 40.e5 ♔b6 41.e6 ♔c7 42.♔e5 h4 43.♔f6 h3 44.e7 h2 45.e8=♕ h1=♕ 46.♔xg6+−.

30.♖xg7 ♖e8 31.g4± with an uphill battle for Black to make a draw with a pawn deficit.

a2) 29.♖xg7 ♗xh2 30.♗d4 (30.g3 h5!) 30...♗e5 is harmless.

a3) White gains nothing from transiting into the pawn ending after 29.♖a8+ ♗b8 30.♗a7 ♔b7 31.♖xb8+ ♖xb8 32.♗xb8 ♔xb8

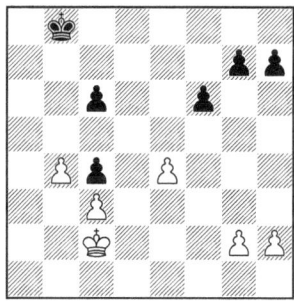

33.♔d2 ♔c7 34.♔e3 ♔b6 35.♔d4 ♔b5 36.g3 g6 37.h3 g5 38.g4 h6 39.e5 fxe5+ 40.♔xe5 ♔a4 41.♔d6 ♔b3 42.♔xc6 ♔xc3 43.b5 ♔d3 44.b6 c3 45.b7 c2 46.b8=♕ c1=♕+ 47.♔d7 ♕f4!?=.

b) White should convert his extra pawn after the underwhelming 28...♖e8?! 29.♖a8+ ♔d7 30.♖xe8 ♔xe8 31.exf6 gxf6 32.g3!?.

c) The correct approach is 28...♔b8! 29.exf6 (29.e6?! ♖e8!; 29.h4 ♖e8! 30.exf6 gxf6=) 29...gxf6 30.g3 (30.♗d4 ♖e8=) 30...♖e8 31.♖a1 ♖xe4 32.♔d2

♖e5, and White is only slightly better in the resulting endgame.

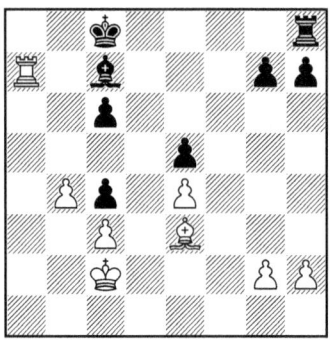

29.♖a8+?

This error is unusual for Carlsen. Most likely, Magnus could not bring a proper mindset to the game against a clearly inferior-rated opponent and planned to succeed without investing much effort along the way.

He can win with the simple 29.♗b6! ♗d8 (29...♗xb6? 30.♖a8++−; 29... ♗b8 30.♖xg7+−) 30.♗xd8 ♖xd8 (30... ♔xd8? 31.♖a8+) 31.♖xg7 ♖f8 (31...h5 32.h4 ♖f8 33.♖g5+−)

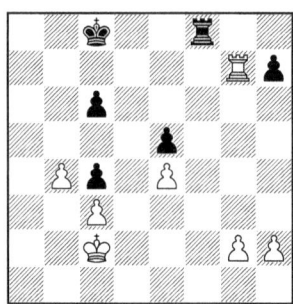

32.h4!? (32.♖xh7?! ♖f2+ 33.♔d1 ♖xg2 34.h4 ♖g1+ 35.♔c2 ♖g2+ 36.♔c1 ♖g1+ 37.♔d2 ♖g2+ 38.♔e1 ♖g1+ 39.♔f2 ♖c1 40.h5 ♖xc3 41.♖e7 ♖h3 42.♖xe5 ♔d7) 32...♖f2+ (32... ♖f4 33.h5 ♖xe4 34.h6+−; 32...h5 33.♖g5+−; 32...h6 33.h5+−) 33.♔d1

h5 (33...h6 34.h5+−) 34.♖g5+− and White is in for more material grabbing.

29...♗b8 30.♖a5

The world champion's earlier assumption of easy success in this position by transposing into the pawn ending was, perhaps, thoughtless.

Rather, after 30.♗a7 ♔b7 31.♖xb8+ ♖xb8 32.♗xb8 ♔xb8 the position is drawn.

Likewise, White has nothing to write home about following 30.♖a1 ♖f8=.

30...♔b7

30...♖f8!? 31.♖c5 ♗a7! 32.♖xc6+ (32.♖a5 ♗b8!) 32...♔b7 33.♗c5 ♖f4= was equally good.

31.b5

There is no attacking the black pawn with 31.♖c5? due to 31...♗a7.

31...♖c8 32.b6

32.bxc6+ ♔xc6!? 33.♖c5+ ♔d7= is no better than the text.

32...♖f8 33.♖a1 ♖f6 34.g3 h5

and Black went on to earn a deserved draw.

Lessons from my Career

Example No. 35
A. Galkin − A. Lastin
Krasnoyarsk 2007

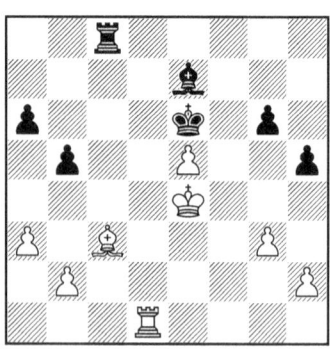

Black to move

White is up a pawn. However, it is blocked by the active black king, whereas the black bishop keeps an eye over the squares of potential rook infiltration. At the same time, the black rook is there to create counter-threats to the white king and pawns whenever possible.

36...♖c4+!

Black harasses the king in an attempt to disorganize the white pieces.

36...♗xa3? 37.bxa3 ♖xc3 38.♖d6+ is bad.

The pawn sacrifice 36...h4?! 37.gxh4 ♖h8 38.♗e1 ♖h5? 39.♗g3 is dubious and its purpose is not entirely clear.

37.♖d4

After 37.♔d3 ♖c8!? Black has managed to decentralize the white king.

37...♖c5 38.♖d3 ♖c4+ 39.♗d4

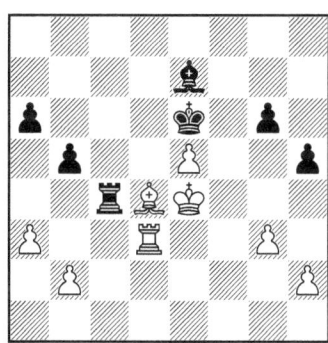

39...b4

39...♗c5? loses to 40.b3 ♖c2 41.♗xc5 ♖xc5 42.♖d6++−.

39...♖c2!? looks interesting, and after 40.♖c3 (40.h3 a5!? 41.♖c3 ♖e2+ 42.♔d3 ♖g2 43.♖c7 g5!?) 40...♖e2+! (40...♖xb2? 41.♖c6+ ♔d7 42.♖xg6 ♖xh2 43.♖xa6+−; 40...♖xh2? 41.♖c6+ ♔f7 42.e6+ ♔e8 43.♖c8+ ♗d8 44.♗f6+−)

41.♔d3 (41.♖e3 ♖xh2; 41.♗e3 ♗g5!?; 41.♔f3 ♖xb2!) 41...♖xh2. 41...♖xb2? fails to 42.♖c6+ ♔d5 43.♖d6+! ♗xd6 44.exd6 ♖b3+ 45.♔c2 ♖f3 46.d7 ♖f8 47.♗b6+−.

42.♖c6+ ♔f5 43.♖xa6? ♖g2 Black even starts playing for a win.

40.axb4 ♗xb4

40...♖xb4 41.♖c3! is inferior.

41.♖f3 ♗e7!

This is a prophylactic move. White is hard-pressed to find a winning plan. 41...♗c5?! 42.♖f6+ ♔e7 43.♔d5! is unsafe as White breaks into the black camp.

42.♖c3

White decides to transpose into a bishop ending. 42.♖b3? is bad: 42...♗c5 43.♖d3 a5= .

White gains nothing from attacking the rook with 42.♔d3 ♖c1!?.

It is also unclear how White is supposed to improve his position further after 42.♖f1!? a5!? (42...♗c5?! 43.♖f6+ ♔e7 44.♔d5; 42...♖c2?! 43.♖a1) 43.♔d3 ♖c8 44.♖a1 ♗b4.

42...♖xc3

Black cannot decline the swap: 42...♖a4? 43.b3 ♖b4 44.♖c6+ ♔d7 45.♖xa6 ♗c5 46.♖a4+−; 42...♖b4?! 43.♖c7!

43.♗xc3

43.bxc3 a5= is no better than the text.

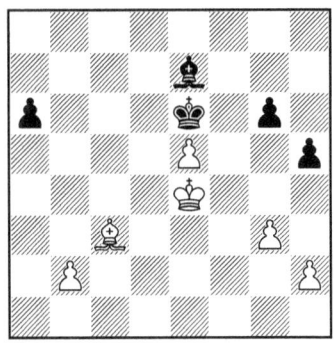

43...♗c5

Just as before, White is up a pawn but also facing the unsolvable problem of how to get to the black pawns.

44.♗d4

44.♔f4 ♗e7! gets the white king nowhere

44...♗b4 45.♗e3

Or the king will be harassed from below after 45.♔f4 ♗d2+!. 45.♔d3 ♔d5! is another instance of the black king restricting his white counterpart.

45...♗a5 46.♔f4 ♗d8 47.♗c5 ♔d5 48.♗a3

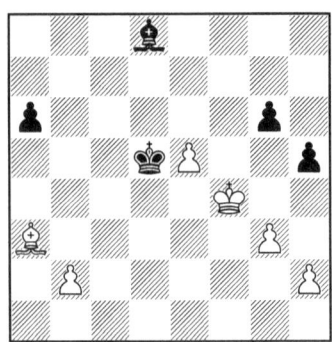

48...♔e6!

48...♗c7? would be a blunder after 49.♔g5 ♗xe5 50.♔xg6 h4 51.gxh4 ♗xh2 52.h5 ♗f4 53.♗e7+−.

49.♗f8 ♔f7 50.♗d6 ♔e6 51.♗c5 ♔d5 52.♗f8 ♔e6 53.♗h6 ♗e7 54.♗g5 ♗b4 55.♔e4

55.♗f6 ♗d2+! leads White nowhere yet again.

55...♗c5 56.♗f6 ♗g1 57.h3 ♗b6

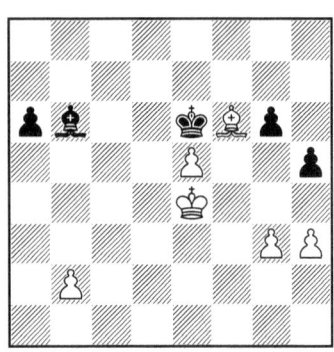

58.b3

White also achieves nothing with 58.♔f4 ♔f7! (58...♗d4?! 59.b3 ♗c3? 60.♔g5 ♔f7 61.e6+ ♔xe6 62.♗xc3+−) 59.b3 (59.♔g5 ♗e3+ 60.♔h4 ♗d4 61.b3 ♗c3 62.g4 ♗e1+ 63.♔g5 ♗d2+ 64.♔h4 ♗e1+=) 59...♗c5 60.♗d8 (60.♔g5 ♗e3+; 60.♔e4 ♔e6) 60...♗b4 61.♗b6 ♗c3 62.♗e3 ♗b2 63.♗d2 ♗a1!?.

58...♗c5 59.♗d8 ♗g1 60.♗c7

60.♔f4 ♔f7! 61.♗a5 (61.♔g5 ♗e3+!) 61...♗c5 62.♗d2 ♗e7! 63.♔e4 ♔e6 is running around in circles one more time.

60...♗c5 61.♗b8 ♗f2

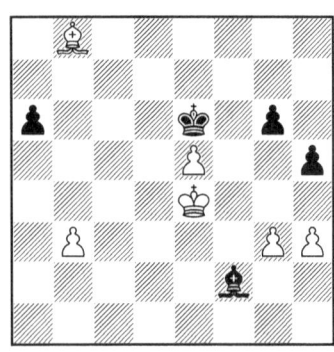

62.♔f4

62.g4 hxg4 63.hxg4 ♗c5!? makes no difference in this position.

62...♔f7! 63.♗d6 ♗e1 64.♗c5 ♗d2+ 65.♗e3

After 65.♔e4 ♔e6! the black king is again well-placed to guard his realm.

65...♗c3 66.♔e4

66.e6+ ♔xe6 67.♔g5 ♔f7= makes no sense.

66...♔e6 67.♗d4 ♗e1 68.g4

68.♔f4 ♗d2+! would be deja-vu.

68...hxg4 69.hxg4 ♗g3 70.♗b2 ♗h2

and White had to make do with the inevitable draw in this game.

Example No. 36
A. Sarana – D. Khismatullin
Satka 2018

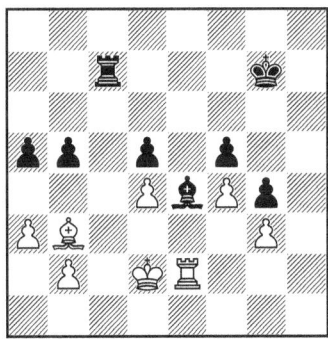

White to move

Black threatens to push his rook pawn and force the white bishop to surrender control of either the c2- or c4-squares. That will leave the square no longer defended by the bishop up for grabs by the black rook.

50.♖e1!

An excellent decision! White intends to exchange off the black rook to neutralize its activity.

50.a4? bxa4 51.♗xa4 ♖c4−+ is bad.

White is in for some hard work in the endgame arising after 50.♖e3 b4 (50...a4 51.♖c3! ♖xc3 52.♔xc3 axb3 53.♔xb3=) 51.axb4 (51.♖e1 bxa3 52.bxa3 a4 53.♗xa4 ♖c4 54.♗b5 ♖c2+ 55.♔d1 ♖c3∓) 51...axb4 52.♖e1 ♖c8 53.♔e3 ♖h8 54.♖e2 ♖h1 55.♔f2 ♔f6.

50...a4

50...♔f6 51.♖c1 ♖h7 52.♖c6+! ♔g7 53.♖c7+ yields nothing.

51.♖c1!

Ignoring the fact that his bishop is en prise.

Both 51.♗a2? ♖c2+−+ and 51.♗d1? ♖c4 52.♔e3 b4 53.♗e2 (53. axb4 ♖xb4 54.♖e2 ♗f3−+; 53.♗xa4 bxa3−+) 53...♖c2 54.axb4 ♖xb2 55.♖a1 ♖xb4 56.♗d1 ♖b2 57.♖xa4 ♔g2 lose.

51...♖xc1 52.♔xc1 axb3 53.♔d2

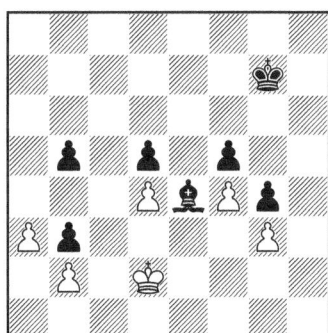

Black cannot win this endgame. The white pawns stand on dark squares and cannot be challenged by the bishop. Meanwhile, the pawn chains are formed in such a way that they preclude the black king's infiltration into the opponent's camp.

53...b4

There is no winning after 53...♔f6 54.♔c3 ♔e6.

(54...♗c2 also leads to a draw after 55.♔b4 ♔e6 56.♔xb5 ♔d7! 57.♔b6 ♗d3

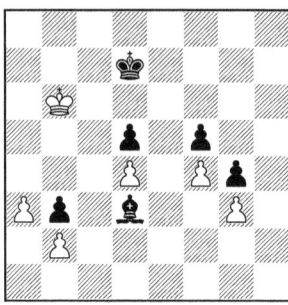

58.a4! 58.♔b7? is bad: 58...♗b5 59.♔b6 ♗c6 60.♔c5 ♔c7 61.♔b4 ♔b6 62.♔xb3 ♔b5 63.♔c3 ♔a4 64.♔c2 ♗b5 65.♔c3 ♗e2 66.♔c2 ♗f3 67.♔c3 ♗e4−+ 68.b4 ♗g2 69.♔b2 ♗f1 70.♔a2 ♗b5 71.♔b2 ♗c4.

58...♔c8 59.♔c5 ♗e4 [59...♗c4? 60.♔d6 ♔b7 61.♔e5] 60.♔b4 ♔b7 [60... ♗c2 61.♔c5=] 61.♔xb3 ♔b6 62.♔b4 ♗f3 [62...♗c2 63.a5+ ♔c6 64.♔c3 ♗d1 65.♔b4=] 63.a5+ ♔c6 [63...♔a6 64.♔c5 ♔xa5 65.b4+ ♔a6 66.♔c6! ♔a7 67.♔c7! ♗e2 68.♔d6 ♗f3 69.♔c7 ♔a6 70.♔c6=] 64.♔a4 ♗e2 65.♔b4 ♗d1 66.b3 ♗e2 67.♔a4 ♔b7 [67...♗f1 68.♔b4 ♗b5 69.♔c3=] 68.♔b4 ♔c6 [68...♔a6 69.♔c5] 69.♔a4=)

55.♔xb3 ♔d6 56.♔c3 ♔c6 (56... b4+ 57.♔xb4! ♔c6 58.♔a5 is only dangerous for Black) 57.b4!= sealing the last window of opportunity for the black king.

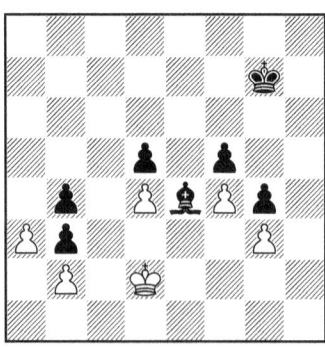

54.a4!

54.axb4? is a losing blunder after 54... ♔f6 55.♔c3 (55.b5 ♔e6 56.b6 ♔d6 57.b7 ♔c7−+) 55...♔e6! 56.♔xb3 ♔d6 57.♔a4 (57.b5 ♔c7 58.♔b4 ♔b6−+) 57...♔c6 58.♔a5 ♗d3−+.

54...♗g2

Lowering your guard is deadly: 54... ♔f6? 55.a5+−.

55.♔e2!

55.a5? ♗f1−+ is bad.

55...♗f3+! 56.♔e3

56.♔f2 ♗e4 57.♔e3 ♗g2= is also a draw via a different move order.

56...♗g2 57.♔f2 ♗e4 58.♔e3 and the opponents agreed to a draw.

Example No. 37
M. Krzyzanowski − B. Socko
Poland 2020

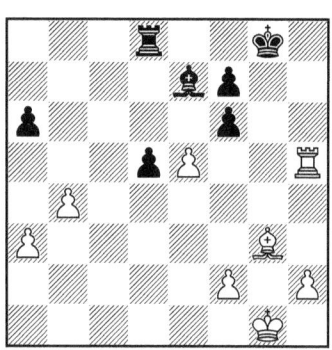

White to move

White is up a pawn in a technically winning position and only needs to keep the passed d-pawn supported by the rook from advancing too far, as that would allow Black saving counterplay.

34.♗h4?!

Unfortunately, White wants to take the opportunity to pin and grab yet another pawn. Not yet a decisive error, but a step in the wrong direction.

34.exf6 ♗xf6 35.♖h6! ♗c3 was stronger.

The game is lost after both 35...♔g7 36.♖xf6! ♔xf6 37.♗h4++−, and 35...d4 36.♖xf6 d3 37.♗f4+−

Further, after 35...♗b2 36.♖xa6 d4 37.♗f1 d3 38.♖d6 ♖xd6 39.♗xd6 ♗xa3 40.♔e1 ♗c1 41.b5+− the white pawn cannot be stopped.

36.♖xa6 d4 37.♗e5!? It is also fine to play 37.♔f1 ♖e8 (37...d3 38.♖d6+−) 38.♗f4 ♖e1+ 39.♔g2 d3 40.♖d6 ♖d1 41.b5, with a winning position.

37...♗b2 (37...♖e8 38.f4!? ♗b2 39.♔f2+− makes no difference) 38.♔f1 ♖e8 (38...d3 39.♖d6 ♖xd6 40.♗xd6 ♗xa3 41.♔e1 ♗c1 42.b5+−) 39.♗f4 d3 40.b5+−, and Black goes down.

34...d4!

Black plays his main trump card. An attempt to hold on to the pawn with 34...♔g7 loses to 35.♖f5 ♔g6 36.♖f3 d4 37.♔f1! d3 38.♔e1+−, and the white king neutralizes the threats coming from the black passed pawn.

35.exf6?

White is still unaware of the danger and goes on with his plan in the belief that he possesses sufficient time to deal with the black passed pawn.

35.♔f1! is stronger: 35...♖d5 (the pawn is blockaded following 35...d3 36.♔e1 d2+ 37.♔d1) 36.♔e2 d3+ 37.♔d1!? ♗d8 38.♖f5 fxe5. Black goes down to 38...a5 39.♗xf6 ♗xf6 40.♖xf6 axb4 41.axb4 ♖xe5 42.♔d2 ♖b5 43.♖f4 ♖d5 44.♖c4+−.

39.♗xd8 ♖xd8 40.♖xe5+− with a winning rook ending.

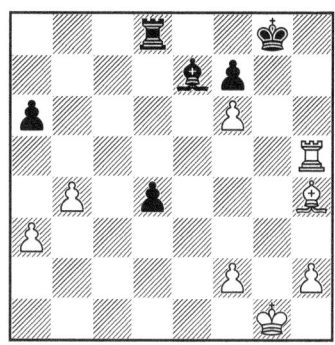

35...♗xb4!

White obviously missed this resource. The bishop sacrifices itself to step out of en prise, bereaving White of a tempo to fight the passed d-pawn.

Both 35...♗f8? 36.♔f1!? (36.♖e5? d3 37.♖e1 ♗h6; 36.♗g5? ♖d5) 36...d3 37.♔e1 d2+ 38.♔d1+− with an easy win, and 35...♗d6? 36.♗g5 d3 37.♗d2+− are bad.

36.axb4 d3 37.♗g5 ♖d5!

Not the premature 37...d2? 38.♗xd2 ♖xd2 39.♔g5+ ♔h8 (39...♔f8? fails to 40.♖a5 ♖d6 41.b5+−) 40.♖g7

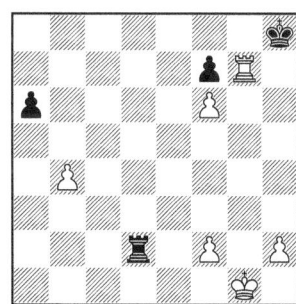

40...♖d6. Both 40...♖b2 41.♖xf7 ♖xb4 42.♖a7, when 42...♖b6? 43.♖a8+ ♔h7 44.f7 is of no help, and 40...♖d7 41.♔g2 ♖b7 42.♔g3 ♖xb4 43.♖xf7+− lose the game.

41.♖xf7 ♖b6 42.♔g2 ♖xb4 (a theoretically winning ending arises after 42...♔g8 43.♖g7+ ♔f8 44.♖a7 ♖xf6

45.h4 ♖b6 46.♔g3 ♖xb4 47.f4+−)
43.♖a7 ♔g8 (43...♖b6 44.♖a8+
♔h7 45.f7+−; 43...♖f4 44.♖xa6+−)
44.♖xa6+− and a rook ending in which
being up three pawns is sufficient for
White to win the game.

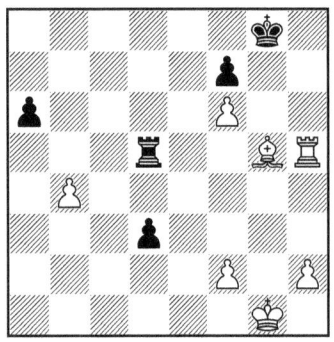

38.♖h3

38.♔f1? is wrong: 38...d2 39.♗xd2
♖xh5∓. Meanwhile, 38.♖h4 ♖xg5+
39.♔f1 ♖d5 40.♔e1 d2+ 41.♔d1
♖d6= leads to a draw.

**38...♖xg5+ 39.♔f1 ♖d5 40.♔e1
♖d4 41.♖g3+ ♔f8 42.♖f3 d2+ 43.♔d1
♖xb4 44.♖d3**

44.♔xd2 a5= is also a draw.

44...♔g8 45.♖g3+   and   the
opponents agreed to a draw.

Example No. 38
M. Sieciechowicz – R. Edouard
England 2020

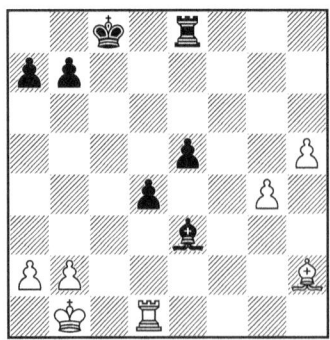

White to move

Each side has a pair of passed
pawns. However, Black's pieces are
better coordinated to assist their pawns.
Holding this ending takes precise play
by White.

36.♔c2?

This king's centralization in fact
exposes him to a tempo check.

36.♗g1?! is dubious in view of
36...♗f4 37.♔c2?! (37.♖f1 d3!?)
37...♖g8 38.♗f2 ♖xg4 39.♖g1 ♖xg1
40.♗xg1 ♔d7 41.♔d3 ♔e6 42.♔e4
♗g3! 43.♔f3 (43.h6 ♔f6−+) 43...d3
44.♗e3 (44.♗xa7 e4+ 45.♔e3 ♗f4+
46.♔f2 ♔f5 47.a4 ♔g4 48.a5 ♔xh5
49.b4 ♗d2 50.♗c5 ♔g4−+) 44...
♗f4!−+.

The correct move is 36.♖f1! e4 (36...
d3?! 37.♖f3 d2 38.♔c2 ♗h6 39.♖f6
♗e3 40.♔d1! ♔d7 41.♔e2) 37.♗g1!
(37.♖f7? d3 38.♖c7+ ♔d8 39.♖xb7
♖e6!−+)

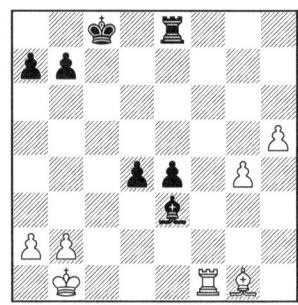

37...♗d2.

(The exchange of bishops also results
in a draw: 37...♗xg1 38.♖xg1 d3 [38...
e3? 39.♔c2] 39.♔c1 e3 40.g5 ♔d7
[40...♔b8? 41.♔d1 ♖c8 42.♖e1!]
41.♔d1 ♔e7 [41...♖c8 42.♖e1!] 42.g6
♔f8 43.h6 ♔g8 44.♖h1=.)

38.♔c2!?

(It is fine to play 38.♗xd4 e3 39.♖f5
♖e4 40.♗e5 e2 41.♗g3

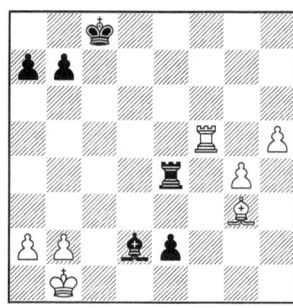

41...e1=♕+ [41...♖xg4? 42.♖c5+
♔d7 43.♖d5+ ♔c6 44.♖xd2 ♖xg3
45.♖xe2; 41...♖c4 42.a3] 42.♗xe1
♖xe1+ 43.♔c2 ♗e3 [43...♗h6?
44.g5] 44.♖e5 ♔d7 45.♔d3= [45.h6?
♖c1+] 45...♗f2 46.♖f5 ♗g3 [46...♗b6
47.g5=] 47.♖f3 and the pair of passed
pawns compensates for the bishop
deficit.)

38...e3 39.♖b1!? ♖g8 40.h6! ♖xg4

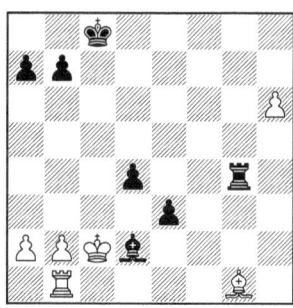

41.♗f2! An excellent rejoinder!
41...exf2. 41...♖g6 42.♖h1! ♖xh6
43.♖xh6 exf2 44.♖f6 ♗e3 45.♔d3=
does not influence the evaluation.
42.♔xd2 ♖h4 (42...♖g1? 43.h7+−
♖xb1 44.h8=♕+ ♔c7 45.♕h7+)
43.♖f1 ♖xh6 44.♖xf2 with a drawn rook
ending.

**36...e4! 37.♗g1 d3+! 38.♔c3 ♗g5
39.♗d4**

Following 39.♗xa7 ♔d7! 40.♗g1
(40.♗d4 ♖c8+ 41.♔b3 ♔e6 42.♗c3 e3

43.♖xd3 ♖xc3+! 44.♖xc3 e2−+) 40...
♔c6! 41.b4 (41.♔d4 d2 42.♗e3 ♖d8+
43.♔xe4 ♖e8+−+) 41...♔d5−+ White
has nothing to counter the onslaught of
the pair of black passed pawns: 42.a4
♖c8+ 43.♔b3 d2.

39...♖e7
39...♔d7!? is also fine
40.♖h1

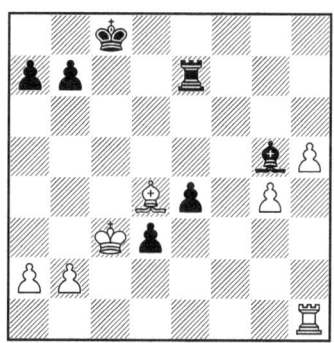

40...d2
40...♖c7+! 41.♔b3 d2 42.♗c3 e3−+
was an immediate winner.
41.♔c2
41.h6? ♖c7+ 42.♔b3 ♖c1−+ was
bad, too.
41...e3 42.♗c3 ♖e6
It was again more precise to play 42...
♖f7! 43.♔d3 (43.h6 e2 44.♗xd2 ♗xd2
45.♔xd2 ♖f1 46.♔xe2 ♖xh1 47.g5
♖h5−+) 43...♖f2 44.h6 ♖h2!−+.
43.♔d3 ♗e7
White stays in the game after 43...
e2? 44.♗xd2 ♖d6+ 45.♔xe2 ♖xd2+
46.♔f3.
44.a3
White loses after both 44.♔e2
♖f7−+ and 44.♔c2 ♖f7! 45.h6 (45.
♔d3 ♖f2−+) 45...e2 46.♗xd2 ♗xd2
47.♔xd2 ♖f1−+.
**44...♖d7+! 45.♔e2 ♖f7! 46.♔d3
♖f2 47.h6 ♗xh6 48.♔c2 e2 49.♗xd2**

e1=♕ 50.♖xe1 ♖xd2+ 51.♔b1 ♗g7
52.♖e8+ ♔d7 and White resigned.

Example No. 39
A. Mishra − R. Baskin
Reykjavik 2022

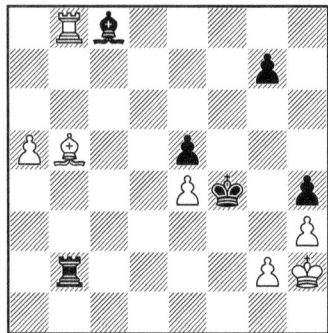

Black to move

This position is rich in dynamic factors, such as weak pawns, a dangerous passed pawn, various pins, intermediate checks, and misplaced kings. Black needs to find his way through this maze and come up with the right solution.

58...♔e3?

Black avoids a check along the f-file, but misses his opponent's strong rejoinder as a result.

The pawn is not to be touched: 58...♔xe4? 59.♗c6++−.

There is no exploiting the pin either with 58...♗d7? 59.♖f8+−+ or 58...♗a6? 59.♖f8+−+.

58...♗e6? 59.a6 ♖a2 60.♖b7+− is equally poor.

Holding the position can be achieved via 58...♔g5!? 59.♖b6 (59.a6? ♗xa6) 59...♔f4! 60.♗c6 (60.a6? ♗xa6; 60.♗d3 ♖xb6 61.axb6 ♔e3 62.♗c2 ♔d4 63.g3 g5=) 60...♖a2 61.♖b8 (61.♖b5 ♗a6 62.♖b3 ♗e2!=) 61...♗a6 62.♖h8 (62.♖f8+ ♔e3=)

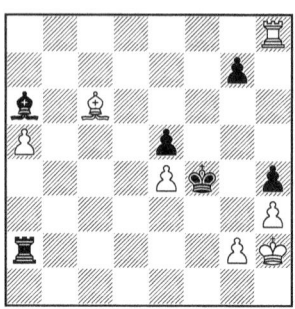

62...g5. 62...♗f1? blunders to 63.♖f8+, whereas after 62...♔g5 63.♖g8!? ♔h6 64.♗d5 ♖xa5? 65.♖a8!+− Black falls to a deadly pin.

63.♗d5 ♖xa5 64.♖a8. White cannot improve his position following 64.♖f8+ ♔e3 65.♖f5 ♗d3 66.♖xe5 ♖b5 67.♖f5 (67.♖xg5 ♗xe4 68.♖e5 ♖xd5 69.♖xd5 ♗xd5 70.g3=; 67.♖e8 ♔d4 68.♗a8 ♖e5=) 67...♔d4 68.♔g1 ♖b1+ 69.♔h2 (69.♔f2? ♖f1#) 69...♖b5=.

64...♖a4 65.♖f8+. The pin cannot be exploited after 65.♗b7 ♗b5=, 65.♗b3 ♖b4!, or 65.♗c6 ♖a2! 66.♗b5 ♖xg2+! 67.♔xg2 ♗xb5=.

65...♔e3 66.♖f5 (66.♖f3+ ♔d4 67.♖f5 ♗c4!?=) 66...♗c4 67.♖xe5. A drawn rook ending also comes about after 67.♗xc4 ♖xc4 68.♖xe5 g4! 69.hxg4 ♔f4 70.♖e8 ♔xg4=.

67...♗xd5 68.exd5+. Another drawn position could arise after 68.♖xd5 g4 69.hxg4 ♔xe4! 70.♖h5 (70.♖f5 ♖a3=) 70...♖a1 71.♖xh4 ♔f4 72.g3+ ♔g5=.

68...♔f4 69.♖e8 (69.♖e6 ♖d4 70.d6 ♔f5 71.♖h6 ♔e5 72.♖g6 ♔f5=) 69...♖d4 70.♖d8 ♔e5 71.♖g8 ♔f5= and this is a draw.

Very interesting lines arise after 58...g5!? 59.a6.

(The position is equal after 59.♖xc8 ♖xb5 60.a6 ♖a5 61.♖a8 ♔xe4 62.a7 ♔e3 63.♖e8 ♖xa7 64.♖xe5+ ♔f4=;

59.♔g1 ♖b1+ [59...♔g3? 60.♖xc8 ♖xb5 61.♖c3+ ♔f4 62.♖a3] 60.♔f2 ♖b2+ 61.♔g1 [61.♔e1? ♔e3 62.♔d1 ♗a6] 61...♖b1+= yields nothing;

The advantage also disappears after 59.♖b6 ♖a2 60.a6 ♔xe4 61.♖c6 ♗f5 [61...♗d7? 62.♖c4+ ♔d5 63.♗xd7 ♔xc4 64.♗e6++−] 62.♗c4 ♖a3=.)

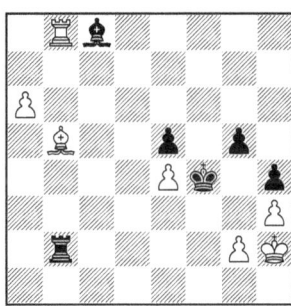

59...♖xb5! A superb exchange sacrifice! Now after 60.♖xb5 ♗xa6 61.♖b6 (61.♖b4 ♗d3 62.♔g1 ♗xe4 63.♔f2 ♔f5=) 61...♗c8 White cannot keep his central pawn alive, and it is a positional draw.

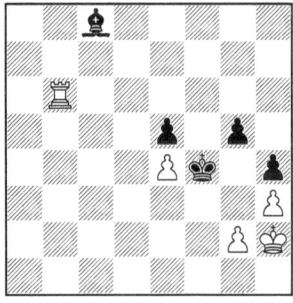

a) 62.♖b8 ♗d7 63.♖g8 (63.♖b4 ♗c6=) 63...♗c6 64.♖f8+ ♔xe4 65.♔g1 (65.g3 hxg3+ 66.♔xg3 ♗d7=) 65...♗d7 66.♔f2 ♗f5. The weakness of his own pawns forces White to exchange them. 67.g4 (67.♖a8 ♔f4=; 67.♖g8 ♔f4=) 67...hxg3+ 68.♔xg3 ♗d7 69.♖f6 (69.

♖g8 ♔f5=) 69...♗c8 70.♖d6 ♔f5! 70...♗f5? loses to 71.♖h6! ♗d7 72.♖h5 ♔f5 73.h4+−.

71.♖d8 ♗e6= and another positional draw.

b) 62.♖f6+ ♔xe4 63.♔g1 ♗f5 64.♔f2 ♔f4=;

c) 62.♖g6 ♗b7 63.♖f6+ ♔xe4 64.♔g1 ♗c8!? 65.♔f2 ♗f5 66.g4 hxg3+ 67.♔xg3 ♗d7=;

d) 62.♖b4 ♗a6 63.♔g1 ♗d3 64.♔f2 ♗xe4 65.♖a4 ♔f5=

59.♖xc8! ♖xb5

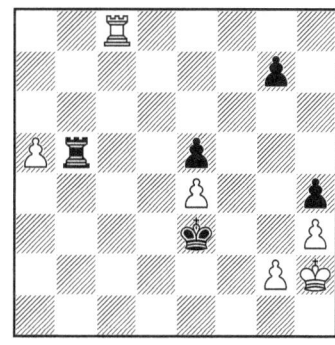

60.♖c3+!

White tucks his rook behind his passed pawn with a tempo not only to support its advance, but also to condemn the black rook to an extremely passive defensive position.

60...♔xe4 61.♖a3 ♖b7

61...♖b8 62.a6 ♔f4 63.a7 ♖a8 64.♔g1+− makes no difference.

62.a6! ♖a7 63.g3!?

It is time to set the king free.

63...hxg3+

63...g5 64.♔g2+− is no better than the text.

There is nothing good from 63...♔d5 64.gxh4 ♔c6 65.♔g3 ♔b6 66.♔g4 e4. Black loses the pawn ending after 66...♖xa6 67.♖xa6+ ♔xa6 68.♔f5 ♔b6 69.♔xe5 ♔c7 70.♔f5 ♔d7 71.♔g6+−, while 66...g6 67.h5 gxh5+ 68.♔xh5+− is hopeless, too.

67.♔f5 e3. The pawn ending is again lost after both 67...♖e7 68.a7 ♖xa7 69.♖xa7 ♔xa7 70.♔xe4 ♔b6 71.♔f5+−, and 67...♖xa6 68.♖xa6+ ♔xa6 69.♔xe4 ♔b6 70.♔f5+−.

68.♖xe3 ♖d7. There is no taking the pawn without an exchange of rooks: 68...♔xa6 69.♖a3+!+− or 68...♖xa6 69.♖e6+!+−, while 68...♖f7+ 69.♔g6 ♖f6+ 70.♔xg7+− leaves no chance to save the game.

69.♖e6+ ♔a7 70.♔g6 ♖d4 71.h5! ♖h4 72.♖e7+ ♔xa6 73.♖xg7+−, and Black is doomed.

64.♔xg3 ♔f5

64...♖a8 65.a7+− only tightens the noose even more.

The alternative king retreat is no better: 64...♔d4 65.♔f3 ♖f7+ (65...e4+ 66.♔e2+−) 66.♔e2 ♖a7

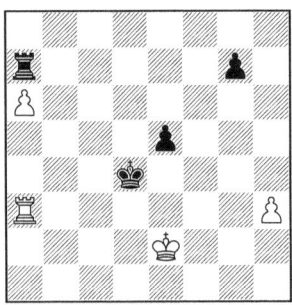

67.♖a5! A precise move. White's sloppy check 67.♖a4+? blows the win following 67...♔c5 68.♔e3 ♔b5! 69.♖a1 ♖xa6 70.♖xa6 ♔xa6 71.♔e4 ♔b5 72.♔xe5 ♔c4! 73.♔f5 (73.h4 ♔d3 74.h5 ♔e3 75.♔f5 ♔f3 76.♔g6 ♔g4=) 73...♔d4 74.♔g6 ♔e5 75.♔xg7 (75.h4 ♔f4 76.♔xg7 ♔g4=) 75...♔f4 76.h4 ♔g4=, and Black does away with the only existing pawn on the board.

67...♔e4. Black is short of a tempo after 67...♔c4 68.♔e3 ♔b4 69.♖a1 ♔b5 70.♔e4 ♖xa6 71.♖xa6 ♔xa6 72.♔xe5+−. After 67...e4 68.♖a1 e3 69.♖a3!+− Black falls victim to a standard zugzwang seen in similar positions.

68.♖a4+ ♔d5 (68...♔f5 69.♔e3+−) 69.♔e3+− with a gradual win.

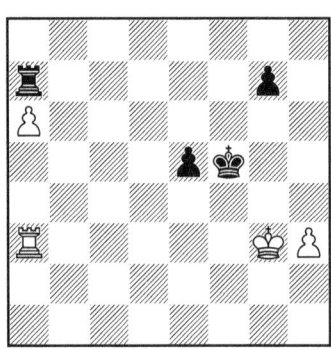

65.♔f3 g6

65...e4+ 66.♔e3 ♔e5 67.♖a5++− is also bad.

66.♖a4 ♔e6 67.♖a5

The youngest grandmaster in history keeps a proper lookout − 67.♔e4 ♖h7!

67...♔f5

White centralizes his king victoriously after 67...♔d6 68.♔e4+−.

68.♖a1 ♔f6

After 68...e4+ 69.♔e3 ♔e5 70.♖a5++− the pawn is doomed, too.

69.♔e4 ♔e6 70.♖a2 ♔f6

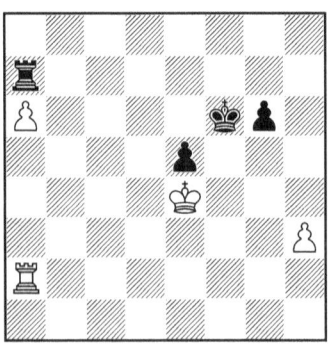

71.♖a5!

And Black is in zugzwang.

71...♔g5

The pawn drops after 71...♔e6 72.♖xe5+ ♔d6 73.♖a5+−.

72.♔xe5 ♔h4 73.♔f6 g5

In case pawns are exchanged with 73...♔xh3 74.♔xg6 ♔g4 75.♔f6+− the white king begins his victorious march towards the black rook.

74.♔g6 ♖a8 75.♖a4+ and Black resigned.

Let us now look at the features of positions with opposite-colored bishops through the eyes of modern grandmasters.

Example No. 40
A. Heimann − V. Malakhov
Germany 2021

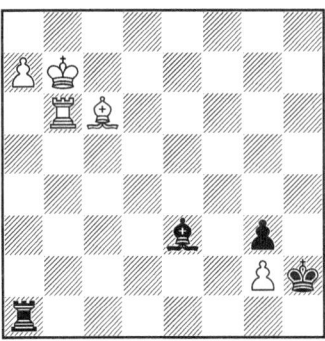

Black to move

White is seemingly close to converting his extra pawn into a win. Meanwhile, the black king's activity is bringing no dividends. The white bishop lends reliable protection to his kingside pawn and simultaneous assistance to the queenside passed pawn.

Despite the above, Black's defensive resources are far from depleted.

66...♖a2?

Unfortunately, Black commits the rook to the wrong square.

66...♗xb6? 67.♔xb6+− is also bad because of the pawn's subsequent promotion.

66...♖a5? 67.♖a6 is also a mistake, as Black has no check from the b-file.

There is no marking time with 66...♔g1? 67.a8=♕ ♖xa8 68.♖b1+!+−, and it turns out that the black king has walked into a check.

Black runs into the same problem with 66...♗f2? 67.♗e4 ♖a4 68.a8=♕ ♖xa8 69.♖h6+!+−.

The correct approach is 66...♖a3! 67.♗e4. Following 67.♖a6 ♖b3+ 68.♔c7 ♗xa7 69.♖xa7 ♖b2! Black captures the g2-pawn on the next move to save the game. White gains nothing either with 67.♗f3 ♗xb6 68.♔xb6 ♖xf3! 69.a8=♕ ♔xg2=, which is a well-known drawn endgame because the black pawn is far too close to the promotion square.

67...♖a4! 67...♖a1? 68.♖a6+− is bad since there is no check from the b-file again. 67...♖a2? fails to 68.♗f3 ♖a3 69.♖a6 ♖b3+ 70.♔c6 ♗xa7 71.♖xa7 ♖b2 72.♔d5! ♖xg2 73.♗xg2 ♔xg2 74.♔e4 ♔g1 75.♔f3 g2 76.♖g7 ♔h1 77.♔f2+−.

68.♗d5 (Black escapes after 68.♗f3 ♖a2! 69.♖a6 ♖b2+ 70.♔c6 ♗xa7 71.♖xa7 ♖xg2!=)

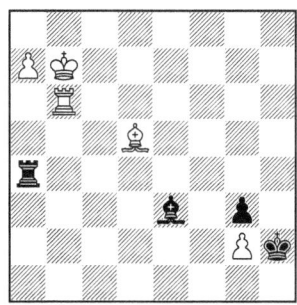

68...♖a1! Yet another precise move. 68...♖a5? fails once again to 69.♖a6 ♖b5+ 70.♔c6 ♗xa7 71.♖xb5+−.

69.♖a6   ♖b1+   70.♔c6   ♗xa7 71.♖xa7

71...♖b2! Black is ready to capture the white pawn with his rook, and the white bishop prevents his own king from getting as close as possible to the potential black passed pawn.

72.♔c5 ♖xg2! 73.♗xg2 (in case of 73.♖h7+ ♔g1 74.♗xg2 ♔xg2 75.♔d4 ♔f2= Black makes a draw, too) 73...♔xg2 74.♔d4 ♔f2 75.♖f7+ (75.♖a2+ ♔f3!= is no better, and after 75.♔e4 g2 76.♖a2+ ♔g3!= the position is also drawn) 75...♔e2!=.

67.♗f3!

67.♗e4? ♖a4 is an error that allows Black to save the game as shown above.

67...♖a3

Black is again lost after 67...♗xb6 68.♔xb6 ♖b2+ 69.♔c5+−.

68.♖a6!   ♖b3+   69.♔c6   ♗xa7 70.♖xa7 and Black resigned in the face of 70...♖b2 71.♔d5! ♖xg2 72.♗xg2 ♔xg2 73.♔e4 ♔f2 74.♖a2+.

Example No. 41
I. Yeletsky − V. Artemiev
Sochi 2017

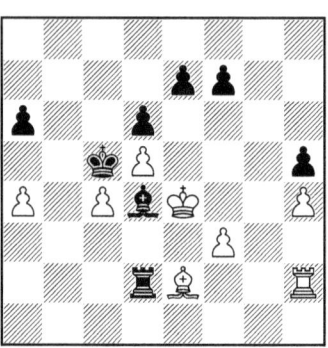

Black to move

Opposite-colored bishops don't make White's life in this endgame any easier. In addition to numerous weak pawns and passive pieces, there are king-related issues to solve.

43...♗g1!

A precisely calculated assault against the white king achieved with a limited number of offensive forces on the board.

44.♖g2   ♖d4+!   45.♔f5   ♗e3! 46.♖h2

White sustains decisive material losses after both 46.♗f1 ♖f4+ 47.♔g5 ♖xf3+−+, and 46.♖g7 ♖f4+ 47.♔g5 ♖g4+ 48.♔xh5 ♖xg7−+.

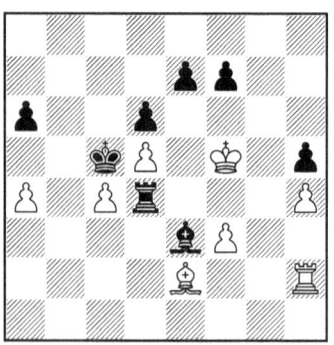

46...♗h6! and nothing can stop the rook from delivering checkmate on the f4-square. Therefore, White resigned.

Example No. 42
K. Lagno – Ju Wenjun
Khanty-Mansiysk 2018

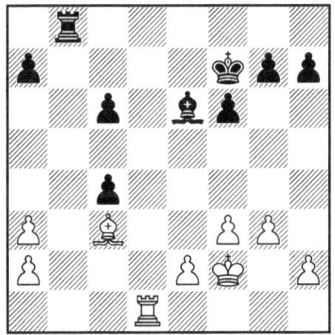

White to move

Black's position might seem fine at first glance. Her rook's open file is as good as that possessed by the white rook, while her doubled pawns compare even better to White's because they are passed ones. However, the key factor for correct evaluation of this position is the difference between the bishops. Besides defensive duties controlling the potential invasion squares of the enemy rook b2 and d2, White's bishop is ready to join the kingside hostilities. In contrast, the black bishop bites on the granite of its own pawn and has no special prospects. Another crucial factor supporting White's superiority is the fact that they are opposite-colored bishops. We keep in mind that opposite-colored bishops in a pure bishop ending favor the defending side more often than not. However, with the addition of a heavy piece the "rook and bishop" or "queen and bishop" tandem significantly increases the attacking potential of the stronger side, which is something to keep in mind when evaluating this type of endgame.

22.g4!

White gears up to develop an initiative on the kingside, where she enjoys pawn superiority. Goal number one is to create new weaknesses in her opponent's position.

22...c5

White also maintains pressure after 22...♔e7 23.h4 ♖d8 24.♖b1!. After 22...♖b6 23.a4! Black does not manage to get at the doubled pawns.

23.h4!

23.♖d6?! ♖b6 24.♖d8 ♖a6! is dubious.

23...h6

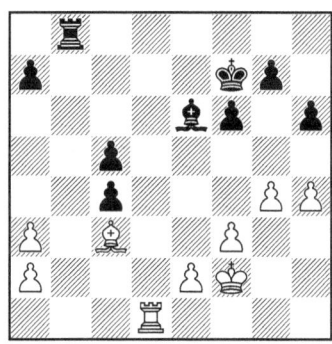

24.a4!

Now White changes the vector of activity and throws forward a pawn on the opposite flank. This should fix a potential weakness – the black a7-pawn, and will also come in handy in future when it comes to taking additional control over the important b7-square. Besides, the pawn is approaching the promotion square, which can be a good plan in positions that feature advancing passed pawns for both sides.

24...♔e7 25.a5! ♖b7

It is obvious that White will avoid the exchange of rooks after 25...♖d8 26.♖g1!

26.♖g1!

It would be premature to go for 26.g5?! hxg5 27.hxg5 fxg5 28.♗xg7 g4!?, and Black either gets rid of all the kingside pawns or drums up enough counterplay thanks to her g-pawn after 29.f4 (29.fxg4 ♗xg4=) 29...♖d7=.

26...♖d7 27.g5! hxg5

After 27...♔f7 28.gxf6 gxf6 29.♖b1 the white rook infiltrates via the b-file.

28.hxg5 ♔f7

28...fxg5? 29.♖xg5 is bad because Black drops a pawn; 28...♗f7!? 29.gxf6+ gxf6 30.♖h1!? ♖d6 31.♖h8 ♗e8 was worth considering.

29.gxf6 gxf6

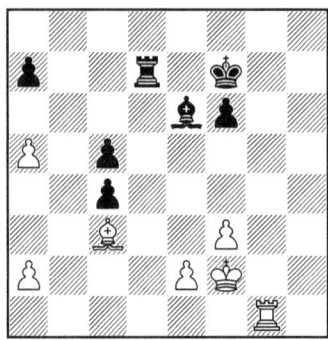

The first part of White's plan is completed. Besides creating a weak pawn on f6, more lines have opened up for the white rook to invade.

30.♖h1! ♔g7

After 30...♔g6 31.♖h8 the white rook is also on a hunt for the black pawns.

31.♖b1!

Black has managed to prevent the white rook's infiltration via the kingside. However, White again changes the vector of her activities and swings the rook to the opposite side of the board.

31...♔f7

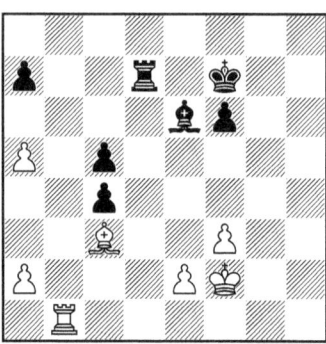

Now White launches part two of her plan by taking turns attacking every weak pawn so as to stretch the few defensive resources that are at Black's disposal.

32.♖b5! ♖c7 33.♖b8 ♖e7

33...♖c8? 34.♖b7+ is bad. It was worth restricting the white rook's scope along the home rank with 33...♗c8!?.

34.♖h8 ♔g6

34...♔g7! 35.♖h5 ♖c7 should have been preferred.

35.♖f8! ♖f7

35...♗f7? 36.♖c8 is bad.

36.♖g8+!

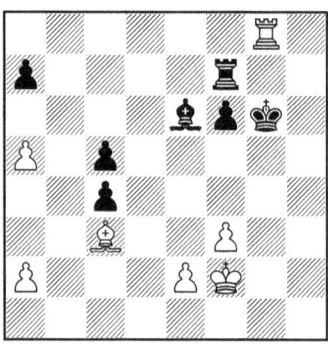

36...♔h7?!

In case of 36...♔g7 37.♖e8!

a) 37...♗f5 38.e4 ♗d7 (38...♗h3 39.♖h8 ♗e6 40.f4!) 39.♖a8 ♗b5

40.♖c8± and Black is in for an uphill battle to make a draw;

b) 37...♗d7 38.♖e4±;

c) 37...♗d5 38.e4 ♗b7 39.♖e6 ♖f7 40.a6 ♗c8 41.♖c6±;

d) 37...♔f7 38.♖d8 ♔e7 (38...♖h7 39.♖d6 ♖h8 40.♖a6 ♖a8 41.♔e3 f5 42.♔f4±) 39.♖a8 ♔d6 40.♗xf6±.

37.♖d8!± ♔g6 38.♖d6 ♖e7

Neither 38...♗f5 39.♖c6±, nor 38...♗c8 39.♖c6± are better than the text.

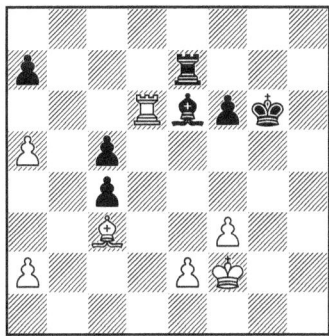

39.♖c6!

Part two of the plan has been completed. It has resulted in winning a pawn. Now the white king can also join in and ramp up the initiative.

39...♔f7 40.♖xc5 ♖d7 41.♖c6 f5 42.♔e3! ♖e7 43.♔f4 ♖d7 44.♖c5!

44.♔e5 ♖d5+! is premature yet.

44...♖d8 45.♖b5 ♖d7?!

45...♗c8! is more resilient.

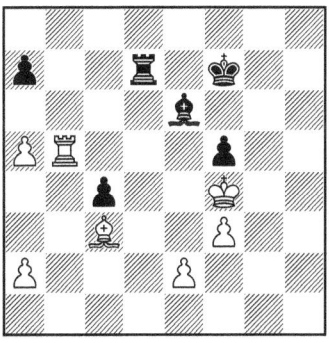

46.a6!

Creating yet more threats. Now Black has to reckon with the potential exchange of rooks on the b7-square and the creation of a dangerous white passer.

46...♔g6

Now, both 46...♗d5 47.♔xf5+− and 46...♖e7 47.♗b4 ♖d7 48.♖b7 ♔e8 49.♔e5 ♗f7 50.♔xf5+− are bad.

47.♔e5! ♖e7

47...♗f7 48.♖b7 ♗e8 49.f4+− leaves Black with no reasonable continuation.

48.♖b7 ♖e8

48...♔f7 49.♔d6+− is an immediate win for White.

49.♖xa7!+− ♗f7+ 50.♔d4 ♖xe2 51.a4

51.♖d7 ♖xa2 52.a7 ♖a3 53.♔e5+− also wins.

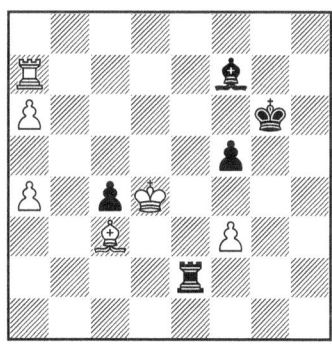

51...♖e6

There is no posting the rook behind the white passed pawn — 51...♖a2 52.a5!+−.

52.♔c5! ♗e8

52...f4 53.♖a8+− is no better than the text.

53.♖g7+ ♔h6 54.a7 ♖a6 55.♖e7! ♖c6+

Black is doomed after both 55...♗xa4 56.♖e6+! ♖xe6 57.a8=♕+−, and

55...♖xa4 56.♖xe8 ♖xa7 57.♔xc4+−. Meanwhile, Black has no means to keep the white passed pawn in check after 55...♗g6 56.♔b5+−.

56.♔b4 ♖c8 57.♖b7! ♖a8 58.♖b8 ♗c6

58...♖xa7 59.♖xe8+− is equally bad.

59.♖b6

and Black resigned.

Example No. 43
A. Rasmussen − A. Brynell
Denmark 2020

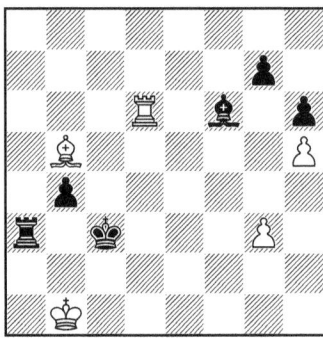

Black to move

Black is up a pawn. Moreover, it is a dangerous passed pawn supported by all pieces remaining on the board. However, with opposite-colored bishops Black should take care not to exchange rooks.

81...b3?

Black is fantasizing about beautiful lines involving a rook sacrifice on a1 and the subsequent weaving of a mating net around the white king.

The immediate rook sacrifice would be a blunder: 81...♖a1+? 82.♔xa1 ♔c2+ 83.♖xf6! (the greedy 83.♔a2? backfires due to 83...b3+ 84.♔a3 ♗e7! 85.♗d3+ [85.♗a4 ♗xd6#] 85...♔c3−+).

83...gxf6 84.♗a4+ b3 (84...♔c3 85.g4+−) 85.g4 ♔c3 86.♔b1+−.

The correct plan was to drive the white king away in order to give the passed pawn an obstacle-free ride to the promotion square: 81...♖b3+! 82.♔c1. Both 82.♔a1? ♔c2+ 83.♔a2 ♖a3# and 82.♔a2? ♖b2+ 83.♔a1 ♔c2 84.♗a4+ b3 85.♗c6+ ♗c3−+ are losing continuations.

82...♗g5+ 83.♔d1 ♖b1+ 84.♔e2 b3 85.♖c6+. White has to give up his rook for a pawn following 85.♗d3 ♖b2+ 86.♔f3 ♖d2 87.♔e4 ♖xd3! 88.♖xd3+ ♔c2 89.♖d7 ♗f6 90.♖c7+ ♗c3−+.

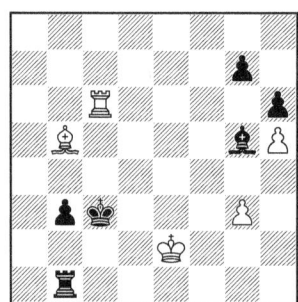

85...♔b2−+ (Black is also winning after 85...♔d4 86.♖c4+ ♔d5 87.♖c7 ♗f6−+) 86.♖c7. The positional evaluation does not change after either 86.♗d3 ♖g1 87.♔f3 ♖c1 88.♖b6 ♖c3 89.♔e2 ♔c1−+, or 86.♖b6 ♖g1!? 87.♔f3 ♖c1 88.♗a4 ♖c3+ 89.♔g2 ♗f6−+.

86...♗f6 87.♖b7 ♖g1!? 88.♔f3 (88.♔f2 ♗d4+−+) 88...♗e5 89.g4. 89.♔e4 ♖e1+ 90.♔f3 ♔c1−+ is also losing since the pawn keeps rolling.

89...♔c1!? 90.♗d3. The game is over after 90.♗e8 b2 91.♗g6 ♖g3+ 92.♔e4 ♗f6−+.

90...♖g3+ 91.♔e4

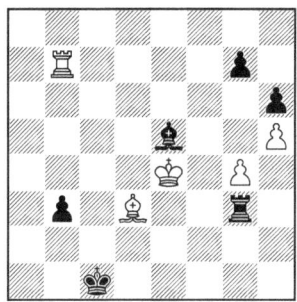

91...♖xd3! This is the most precise way to press home the advantage (of course, 91...b2 is winning, too) 92.♔xd3 b2 93.♔e4 ♗f6 (or 93...♗c3 94.♔d3 ♗a5−+ and the pawn promotes) 94.♖c7+ ♔d2 95.♖b7 ♔c2 96.♖c7+ ♗c3−+ and White is doomed.

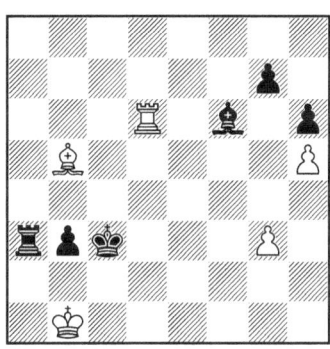

However, there follows a prosaic move

82.♖a6!

and the black rook cannot avoid the exchange with the inevitable draw as a result.

The inclusion of a preliminary check loses the game: 82.♖c6+? ♔b4 83.♖a6 ♖a2! 84.♗f1 (84.♗d3 ♖d2 85.♖b6+ ♔c3−+ is also hopeless) 84...♖d2 85.♔c1 ♗g5−+.

82...♖xa6 83.♗xa6 ♗e5, and Black did not persist further and agreed to a draw. The white king will not be kicked

away from the target square for the passed b-pawn's promotion, while the white bishop defends his kingside pawns easily.

Example No. 44
L. Livaic − M. Vavulin
Croatia 2021

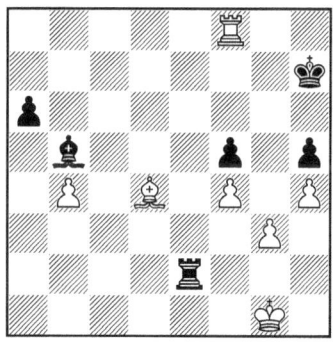

Black to move

Given White's inability to exploit his pawn majority on the kingside by creating a passed pawn, his extra pawn has no particular bearing on the game as yet. Moreover, the exchange of rooks with the opposite-colored bishops on the board leads to an elementary draw even if black drops another kingside pawn. Having said that, Black needs to address his opponent's concrete threats. In making the most natural move Black misses his opponent's latent threat.

46...♗d3?

It was, of course, a bad idea to defend the pawn both with 46...♔g6? 47.♖f6++−, and 46...♗d7? 47.♖f7++−.

The balance was maintained by 46...♖e1+! 47.♔f2 (47.♔g2 ♖e2+ 48.♔h3? ♖d2−+ and now it is the white king who has walked into a mating net) 47...♖e2+ 48.♔f3

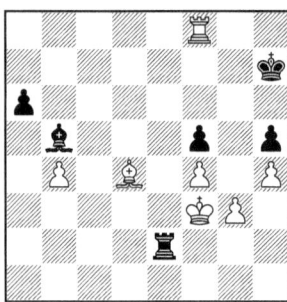

48...♖e4! Having driven the king into a checking position, Black carries out the transfer of his bishop for the purpose of cementing his kingside pawns:

49.♗c3 (49.♖h8+ ♔g6; 49.♗c5 ♗e2+!? 50.♔f2 ♗g4=) 49...♗e2+ 50.♔f2 ♗g4 51.♖h8+ (51.♖f7+ ♔g8 52.♖f6 ♖e2+ 53.♔f1 ♖a2= is also harmless) 51...♔g6 52.♖a8 ♖e2+ 53.♔f1 ♖e6 54.♗e5 ♖b6=.

47.g4!

This excellent pawn break is easy to miss in an over-the-board game. White has weaved a mating net around the black king all of a sudden.

47...♖e4

Both 47...hxg4? 48.h5+−, and 47...fxg4? 48.f5+− are bad, when the black king is trapped.

The white king easily escapes from checks after 47...♖e1+ 48.♔f2 ♖e2+ (48...♖f1+ 49.♔e3+−) 49.♔g3+−.

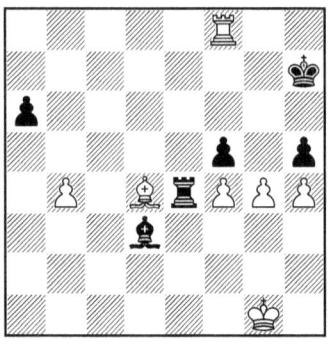

48.♖h8+!

48.♗e5? fxg4 is an error that leaves the bishop hanging and stops the f-pawn dead in its tracks.

48...♔g6 49.gxh5+!

Creating a dangerous passed pawn with check.

49...♔f7 50.♗e5+−

There is no longer keeping that pawn at bay.

50...♖xb4 51.♖h7+

White was also winning nicely after 51.♖d8 ♗b5 52.h6 ♔g6 53.h5+! ♔xh6 (53...♔xh5 54.h7+−) 54.♖h8#.

51...♔e8

51...♔g8 52.♖g7+ ♔f8 53.h6+− is no better, whereas after 51...♔e6 52.♖a7+− the passed pawn cannot be stopped.

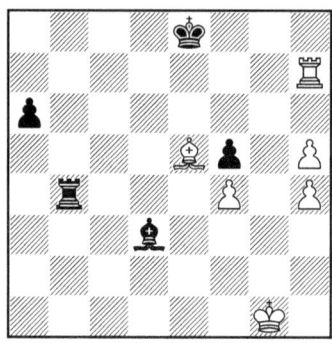

52.h6 ♖b1+

52...♖b6 loses the game along the same lines to 53.♖h8+ ♔f7 (53...♔d7 54.h7 ♖h6 55.♖a8! ♖xh7 56.♖a7++−) 54.♖d8+−.

53.♔f2 ♖b6 54.♖h8+ ♔f7

White wins the rook for his pawn in the following lines: 54...♔d7 55.h7 ♖h6 56.♖a8 ♖xh7 57.♖a7++−, and after 54...♔e7 55.h7 ♖h6 56.♖a8 ♖xh7 57.♖a7++−.

55.♖d8 and, faced with the choice of dropping either the bishop or the rook, Black resigned.

Example No. 45
N. Abdusattorov — A. Puranik
Sitges 2021

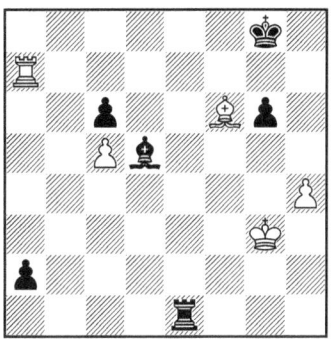

Black to move

Conversion of the extra pawn is fraught with two problems for Black: his king is misplaced and both white pieces control the promotion a1-square. The presence of opposite-colored bishops also plays into White's hands.

50...♖c1?

In attacking the pawn, Black attempts to force White to defend it, thereby trying to disorganize White's pieces.

It was correct to start by first restricting the white king's activity 50...♖f1! 51.♗b2. 51.♖g7+? ♔f8 52.♖xg6 ♔f7–+ is wrong. Implementation of Black's plan cannot be opposed either by 51.♗e5 ♔f8 52.♔g4 ♔e8 53.♔g5? ♖f5+–+, or by 51.♗d4 ♔f8 52.♔g4 ♖f5, followed by the black king heading for the white rook.

51...♔f8! And now Black gradually activates his king.

52.♔g4 (52.♖a4 ♔e7–+) 52...♖f5. Discouraging the white king from approaching the g6-pawn.

53.♗d4

(53.♖g7? ♗f7 54.♖h7 ♖xc5–+ is an error. Black wins after 53.♖a4 ♔e7

54.♖f4 ♖h5! 55.♖a4 ♔d7 56.♖a7+ ♔c8 57.♖g7 ♖f5 58.♖a7 [58.♖xg6 ♖f2 59.♗d4 ♖g2+ 60.♔f5 ♗e4+!–+] 58...♗e6 59.♔g3 ♖xc5–+.)

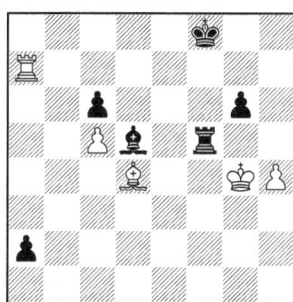

53...♔e8! (53...♗e6 54.♔g3) 54.♖a8+ (54.♖g7 ♗f7 55.♖h7 ♖xc5–+; 54.♗b2 ♗e6 55.♔g3 ♖xc5–+) 54...♔d7 55.♖a7+ ♔c8 56.♖a8+. White is also in bad shape after 56.♖g7 ♗e6 57.♔g3 (57.♖xg6 ♖d5+ 58.♖xe6 ♖xd4+–+) 57...♗f7 58.♖h7 ♔b7 59.♖h8 ♖xc5–+.

56...♔b7 57.♖a5 (57.♖a4 ♗e6 58.♔g3 ♖d5–+) 57...♗e6! Driving the white king away to activate the black rook.

58.♔g3 ♖f1 (58...♖d5 59.♗b2!?) 59.♖a4. 59.♔g2 ♖f4 60.♗f2 ♗d5+ 61.♔g1 ♖g4+ 62.♔f1 ♖b4 63.♔e2 ♖b2+ 64.♔e3 ♖b1–+ loses the game.

59...♖d1

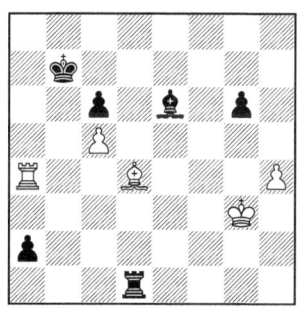

60.♗b2

(60.♗c3? ♖d3+−+; 60.♗e5? ♖d5−+; 60.♗f6 ♖d3+ 61.♔g2 [61. ♔f4 ♖d5] 61...♗d5+ 62.♔h2 ♖f3−+; 60.♗g7 ♖d5 61.♖a5 g5! 62.h5 ♖d3+ 63.♔f2 g4−+)

60...♖d2!? 61.♗a1 (61.♗c3? ♖d3+−+; 61.♗e5? ♖d5−+) 61...♖d5 62.♖a5 (62.♖xa2? ♖d3+−+; 62.♗d4? ♖xd4−+) 62...♖h5 63.♗f6

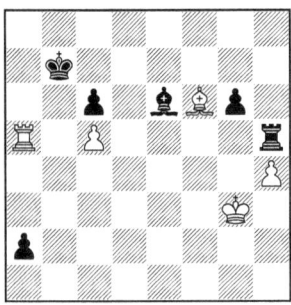

63...♗c4!? Black has finished regrouping his pieces and is at last poised to begin his king's decisive centralization.

64.♗g5 (64.♔g4 ♖f5 65.♗d4 ♔c8−+) 64...♖h8 65.♗f6. 65.♔f4? ♖f8+ 66.♔e3 ♖f1−+ is bad.

65...♖f8

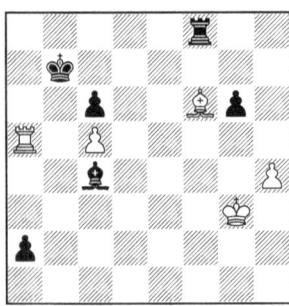

66.♗b2

(66.♗d4 ♖f5 67.♔g4 ♔c8! 68.♖a8+ [68.♖a7 ♖d5−+] 68...♔d7

69.♖a7+ ♔e6 70.♖g7 ♔d5 71.♖d7+ ♔e4−+)

66...♖f5 67.♗d4 ♔c8! 68.♔g4 (68. ♖a4 ♖d5−+) 68...♔d7 69.♖a4 ♗b3 70.♖a5 (70.♖a6 ♖d5−+; 70.♖a3 ♖d5 71.♗b2 ♗c4 72.♖a5 ♔e6−+) 70... ♔e6−+ and the black king's addition to the attack against the c5-pawn is decisive.

51.♔f4! White refuses to defend passively and abandons his pawn en prise for the sake of making his king as active as possible.

Both 51.♖a5? ♔f7 52.♗d4 ♔e6 53.♔f4 ♗b3 54.♔g5 (54.♔e4 ♖h1−+) 54...♔d5 55.♗f6 ♖g1+ 56.♔h6 ♔c4 57.♔g7 ♔b4−+, and 51.♗d4 ♖c4 52.♗e3 ♖b4! 53.♗f2 ♖b7! 54.♖a8+ ♔f7−+ lose the game.

51...♖xc5

51...♖f1+ 52.♔g5! (52.♔e5? ♖f5+−+) 52...♖g1+ 53.♔h6 ♔f8 54.♗g7+ ♔e8 55.♗f6 ♖g2 56.♔g7!= is of no help to win the game either.

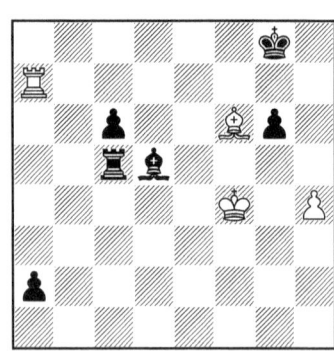

52.♔e5!

Black gets down to converting his two-pawn advantage in the event of the underwhelming 52.♔g5? ♗f7+ 53.♔g4 (53.♔h6 ♖h5#; 53.♔f4 ♖f5+−+) 53...♗e6+ 54.♔g3 ♖f5 55.♗b2 ♔f8!? 56.♖a6 ♗d5−+.

52...♖c1

After 52...♗b3+ 53.♔d6 ♖f5 54.♗e5 ♗d5 55.♖g7+!? ♔f8 56.♖a7 (56.♖xg6? ♖xe5−+) 56...♖f1 (56...♖f7? 57.♖a8#) 57.♖a8+!? ♔f7 58.♖a7+ ♔g8 59.♖g7+ ♔f8 60.♖a7 Black cannot rearrange his pieces profitably.

53.♔d6! ♖d1 54.♗e5!

54.♔e7? is an error that dissipates White's initiative following 54...♖e1+! 55.♔d8 (55.♔d6 ♖e6+−+; 55.♔d7 ♔f7 56.♗c3 ♖e7+−+) 55...♖e4−+ .

54...c5

Black ditches a pawn for the sake of taking control over the a8-square. The line 54...♖b1 55.♖a8+ ♔f7 (55...♔h7? 56.♖h8#) 56.♖a7+ ♔e8 57.♖a8+ ♔f7 58.♖a7+= ends in a perpetual check. Both 54...♗b3+ 55.♔xc6=, and 54...♗e4+ 55.♔e7! c5 56.♖xa2= lead to a draw.

55.♔xc5 ♗b3

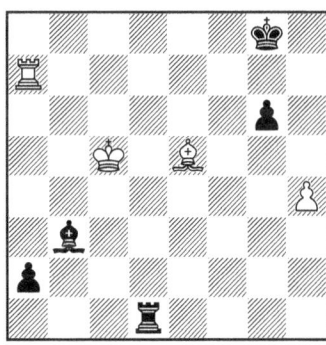

56.♗d4!

Pawn-grabbing is fatal: 56.♖g7+ ♔f8 57.♖xg6? ♖d5+−+.

56...♔f8 57.♗f6 ♖d2 58.♔b4 ♗e6 59.♔c5 ♗d7

Black profits neither from 59...♖d5+ 60.♔c6=, nor from 59...♖d7 60.♖xd7 ♗xd7 61.♔b4=.

60.♗g5!? ♖e2 61.♔d6 ♗e8 62.♗f6

♗f7, and Black abandoned any plans to play for a win. Draw agreed.

We now move on to reviewing positions that feature a rook and knight vs. rook and knight.

Example No. 46
D. Navara − N. Abdusattorov
Belgrade 2022

White to move

Black's only remaining pawn is a dangerous passer. At the same time, White's king and rook cannot by themselves stop the pawn's advance towards the promotion square. The only hope rests with the knight, which is on the opposite flank at the moment. If it is brought to the war theater and given up for the pawn in good time, we reach a drawn ending with a rook and knight vs. rook. Does this idea lend itself to easy implementation, or does it take finding a latent resource to save this position?

54.♘e6?

White is relying on a potential fork along the way, but it is not enough to save the game.

54.♘e8? b3 55.♘f6+ ♔d6 56.♖d4+ ♔c6 57.♘d5 ♖c1 58.♘e7+ (58.♘b4+ ♔c5 59.♘d3+ ♔xd4 60.♘xc1 b2

61.♘e2+ ♚d3−+) 58...♚b5 59.♖d5+
♚a4−+ was losing, too.

The correct approach is 54.♘f5! b3.
White stops the passed pawn after 54...
♖c1 55.♖d4+ ♚c6 56.♖d3=.

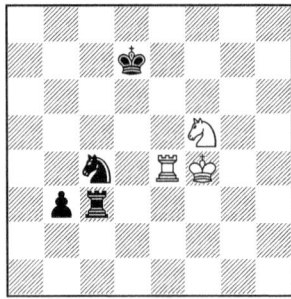

55.♖e7+! 55.♖d4+? ♚c7 56.♘e7
♖c1 57.♘d5+ ♚b7 58.♖d3 b2 59.♖b3+
♚a7 60.♘c3 ♖xc3 61.♖xc3 b1=♕
62.♖xc4 ♕f1+−+ is bad.

55...♚c8. White is up to the task both
after 55...♚c6 56.♘d4+ ♚d6 57.♖b7
b2 58.♖xb2 ♘xb2 59.♘b5+=, and after
55...♚d8 56.♖b7! b2 57.♘d6=.

56.♘d4! b2

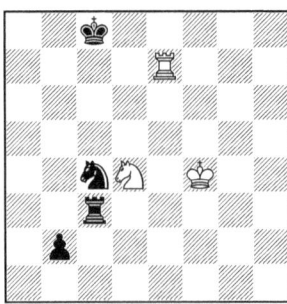

White seems doomed. However,
a drawing mechanism comes to the
rescue: 57.♘b5! b1=♕. It is an easy
draw after 57...♖f3+ 58.♚xf3 ♘e5+
59.♖xe5 b1=♕ 60.♘d6+ ♚d7
61.♘e4=, while the follow-up of 57...
♚d8 58.♘xc3 ♚xe7 59.♘b1 ♚d6

60.♚e4 ♚c5 61.♚d3 ♚b4 62.♚c2=
renders the black passed pawn harmless.

58.♘a7+   ♚d8   59.♘c6+   ♚c8
60.♘a7+ ♚b8 61.♘c6+ ♚c8. Black is
in for checkmate following the sloppy
61...♚a8? 62.♖a7#.

62.♘a7+ and a draw.

54...♚d6!

Naturally, not 54...b3? as it walks
the pawn into a fork: 55.♘c5+ ♚d6
56.♘xb3=.

55.♘d4

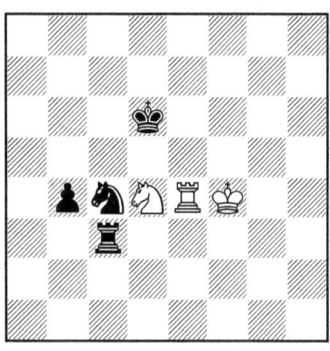

55...♚d5!

The White pieces turn out to
be poorly placed and incapable of
maintaining their knight's key defensive
position.

56.♘b5

White also loses after 56.♘e2 ♖c2!
57.♘d4 (57.♖d4+ ♚c5 58.♖e4 b3−+)
57...♖f2+! 58.♘f3 ♖xf3+! 59.♚xf3
♘d2+−+.

56...♖c1! 57.♘c7+

57.♖e8 b3 58.♖b8 ♚c5 59.♘d4 b2
60.♘b3+ ♚c6 61.♘a5+ ♚c7 62.♖b7+
♚c8−+ is of no help.

White again drops a piece to
57.♘d4 ♖f1+ 58.♘f3 ♖xf3+! 59.♚xf3
♘d2+−+.

57...♚d6! 58.♘b5+

After 58.♘e8+ ♚c5−+ the white

knight can no longer combat the passed pawn.

58...♔c5 59.♘d4

59...♔d5!

Following this yet another precise move White's defensive construction finally crumbles.

60.♘f3

60.♘b3 ♖f1+−+ loses on the spot.

60...b3! 61.♖d4+ ♔c5 62.♘d2

After 62.♖d8 b2−+ White is doomed, too.

62...b2! and White resigned. The blunder 62...♔xd4? 63.♘xb3+ ♔c3 64.♘xc1= would have kept White in the game.

Example No. 47
A. Lugovoi − A. Alavkin
Togliatti 2003

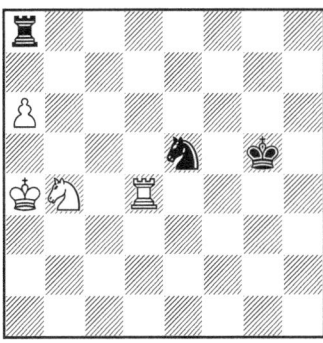

Black to move

The passed pawn has advanced far. Not only is the white king ready to support its progress, but he will also restrict the opponent's pieces that challenge it. This is why Black should calculate as concretely as possible.

71...♘c6!

This knight sacrifice is designed to deflect the white knight from defending the pawn.

71...♔f6? 72.♔a5 ♔e6 73.♔b6 ♘d7+ 74.♔b7 ♖b8+ 75.♔c7 ♖a8 76.♖d6+!+− loses the game.

72.♖d6

A drawn rook and knight vs. rook ending would have arisen after 72.♘xc6 ♖xa6+=.

72...♘b8!

Reinstating the threat of eliminating the only remaining pawn. Of course, 72...♘xb4 73.♔xb4 ♔f5 74.♔b5 ♔e5 75.♖d7 ♔e6 76.♖b7+− is bad.

73.♖d8 ♔f5

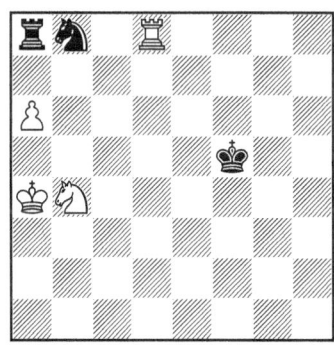

74.♔b3

Both 74.♔b5 ♘xa6! 75.♖xa8 ♘c7+= and 74.♔a5 ♖xa6+! 75.♘xa6 ♘c6+= lead to a draw.

In case of 74.♖e8 ♔f6 75.♔b3 (75.♔a5 ♘c6+ 76.♘xc6 ♖xe8 77.a7 ♖a8=; 75.♔b5 ♔f7! [75...♘xa6? 76.♘d5++−] 76.♖h8 ♘xa6! 77.♖xa8

♘c7+=) 75...♖xa6 76.♘xa6 ♘xa6 77.♖c8 ♚e7!= Black is in time to evacuate the knight from the dangerous territory.

74...♚e6

It was also fine to play 74...♖xa6!? 75.♘xa6 ♘xa6 76.♖c8 (76.♚c4 ♘c7=) 76...♚e5! 77.♚c4 ♚d6!=, with a drawn endgame.

75.♚c4

Black also keeps his position together after 75.♖h8 ♚d7 76.♚c4 ♖xa6=.

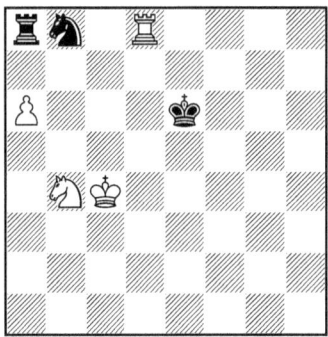

75...♖xa6!

There is no time to spare. In case of 75...♚e7? 76.♖xb8 ♖xb8 77.♘c6+ ♚d6 78.♘xb8 ♚c7 79.♘d7! (the wrong 79.a7? ♚b7 80.♘c6 ♚a8= leads to a draw despite huge material superiority) White gets the upper hand.

76.♘xa6 ♘xa6 77.♚b5 ♚e7!

A crucial intermezzo.

The natural 77...♘c7+? loses to 78.♚c6 ♘a6 79.♖d6+! ♚e7 (79...♚e5 80.♖d5+ ♚e4 81.♖b5+−) 80.♖d7+ ♚e6 81.♖b7+−, and the knight falls into a fatal trap.

78.♖d1

78.♖c8 ♚d7!= is a draw, too.

78...♘c7+ 79.♚c6 ♘e8 80.♖e1+ ♚f7 81.♚d5 ♘f6+ 82.♚e5 ♘e8 and the players agreed to a draw.

Example No. 48
N. Abasov – C. Balogh
Austria 2020

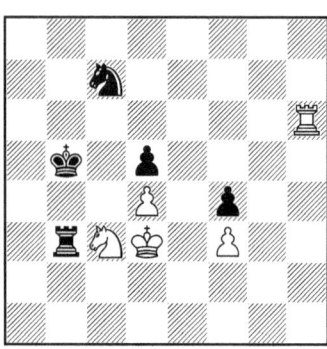

Black to move

Material is equal and Black seems to have nothing to worry about at first glance. He only needs to find a good retreat for his king who is currently in check, in order to defend his position. Of the two available moves, Black opts for the more active one.

77...♚b4?

The correct approach is 77...♚a5! 78.♚c2! White even loses after 78.♖c6? ♘b5 79.♖c5 ♖xc3+! 80.♖xc3 ♘xc3 81.♚xc3 ♚a4−+.

78...♖b4 79.♖c6 ♖c4!? 80.♖xc4 dxc4 81.d5 (81.♘e2 ♘d5= gives equality, too) 81...♚b6 82.d6 ♘e6 83.♘e2 (83.♘e4 ♘d4+ 84.♚c3 ♘xf3 85.♚xc4 ♚c6= leads to the exchange of a different pair of pawns) 83...♚c6 84.♚c3 ♚xd6 85.♚xc4 ♚e5=.

78.♖b6+!

A powerful check!

78...♚a3

Black drops the rook after 78...♚a5 79.♖xb3+−.

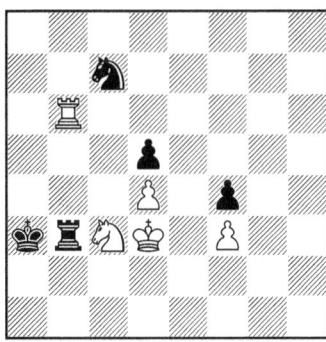

79.♖c6!
and Black resigned prior to getting forcibly checkmated after 79...♘b5 (Black drops a piece in the line 79...♖b7 80.♖xc7 ♖xc7 81.♘b5++−) 80.♖a6+ ♔b2 (80...♔b4 81.♖a4#) 81.♖a2+ ♔c1 82.♖c2#.

Example No. 49
T. Stoyanov – S. Nihal
Sitges 2021

White to move

Only one pawn remains on the board. Therefore, White is only a stone's throw away from making a draw. He just needs to see all of his opponent's threats and deal with them accordingly.

79.♖d4?
This is a blunder that allows his opponent to forcibly exploit White's misplaced king and knight.

79.♘f2? ♖e1+ 80.♔h2 g3# was an immediate disaster, too.

It is also bad to go for 79.♖h2+? ♘h3+ 80.♔f1 (80.♔g2 ♖e2+−+) 80...♖f3+ 81.♔e1 (81.♔e2 ♖a3−+; 81.♔g2 ♖a3 82.♘f2 ♖a2 83.♔f1 ♖xf2+ 84.♖xf2 ♘xf2 85.♔xf2 ♔h3−+) 81...♖a3! 82.♖d2 (82. ♘f2 ♖a1+ 83.♘d1 g3 84.♖d2 ♘f2−+; 82.♔f1 ♖a1+ 83.♔g2 ♖a2+−+) 82... ♖a1+ 83.♖d1 ♖xd1+ 84.♔xd1

84...♘f2+! This is a superb deflecting move!

85.♘xf2 g3 86.♘d3 (86.♔e2 g2−+) 86...g2 87.♘e1 g1=♕−+ and there is no fork because the knight is pinned. This is a manifestation of study-like ideas in an over-the-board game.

79.♖a2 g3 (79...♖e1+? 80.♔h2 ♖b1 81.♘g3=) 80.♘xg3 (80.♖a1? g2 81.♘f2 ♔g3 82.♘h1+ ♔f3−+) 80... ♔xg3 81.♔f1 is a theoretically drawn ending (see the following diagram)

but fighting against a rook and a knight in an over-the-board game with the weaker side's king already cut off on the bottom rank does not lend itself to easier defending than fighting in the same situation against a rook and bishop. The probability of making a mistake and losing the game is very high.

Therefore, a good choice was 79.♖d8!? ♖e1+. Carelessness could even lead Black to a defeat: 79...♔h3? 80.♖h8+ ♘h5 81.♖xh5#. 79...g3 also peters out to a draw: 80.♖h8+ ♘h5 81.♔g2 ♖e2+ 82.♔f3 g2 83.♖xh5+! ♔xh5 84.♘g3+ ♔h4 85.♘xe2=.

80.♔h2 (80.♔f2? ♖xh1 81.♖h8+ ♘h5−+) 80...♖e2+ 81.♔g1 ♖a2 (81...♘h3+ 82.♔f1 ♖a2 83.♖h8+ ♔g5 84.♘g3=) 82.♖h8+ ♘h5 (82...♔g5 83.♖g8+ ♘g6 84.♘g3=) 83.♘f2= and holding this position together is easy for White.

In fact, 79.♔h2!? was equally good: 79...♖h3+ 80.♔g1 ♖a3 81.♔h2 g3+ 82.♘xg3 (82.♔g1? ♖a1+) 82...♖xg3 83.♖d8 ♖g2+ 84.♔h1 ♖g7 (84...♖a2 85.♖g8! ♔h3 86.♔g1!) 85.♖a8, and forcing the white king into a mating net is far from easy.

79...♖e1+!

79...♘e2+? 80.♔f2 ♖h3 81.♖d8!= is an error that allows White to bail out.

80.♔h2

A lost rook ending occurs after 80.♔f2 ♖xh1 81.♖xf4 ♔h3 82.♖f8 g3+ 83.♔e2 (83.♔f3 ♖f1+−+) 83...g2 84.♖h8+ ♔g3 85.♖g8+ ♔h2 86.♖h8+ ♔g1 87.♖g8 ♖h2−+, and the pawn cannot be stopped.

80...♖e2+! 81.♔g1 ♘h3+! 82.♔f1 ♖h2! and White resigned faced with losing his knight.

Example No. 50
D. Andreikin – A. Goganov
Tbilisi 2017

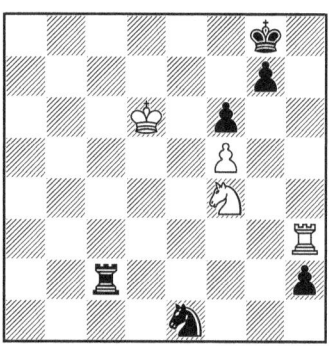

Black to move

Black is two pawns up, one of them being on the verge of promotion. However, White's active pieces are weaving deadly nets around the black monarch. Black needs to take the correct decision to win this.

56...♔f7?

This natural move turns out to be a mistake.

56...♘f3? 57.♘g6 ♖d2+ 58.♔e7 ♖e2+ 59.♔d8 (59.♔d6? ♖e8; 59.♔d7? ♘e5+) 59...h1=♕ 60.♖xh1 ♖h2

61.♖xh2 ♘xh2 62.♔e8 ♘f3 63.♘e7+ ♔h7 64.♘d5 ♔h6 65.♔f7= would have blown the win.

A pretty draw results after 56...♖d2+? 57.♔e7 g5 58.fxg6 ♘f3 59.♔xf6 ♖d1 (59...♖d6+ 60.♔f5 ♖d1 61.♔g4=) 60.♖h5! h1=♕

61.♘d5! What a picturesque position! Despite being a queen up in the endgame, Black cannot win.

61...♖xd5 (61...♕xh5? 62.♘e7+ ♔f8 63.g7+ ♔e8 64.g8=♕+ ♔d7 65.♕c8+ ♔d6 66.♕c6#) 62.♖xh1=.

Winning the game took vacating some squares for the black king with 56...g5!

a) 57.fxg6 ♘f3!

a1) 58.♘d5 ♔g7! The hasty 58...♖c1? 59.♘e7+! ♔f8 60.♖h8+ ♔g7 61.♖h7+ ♔f8 62.g7+ ♔f7 63.g8=♕# is a blunder.

59.♘e7 ♖d2+! 60.♔c5 (60.♔e6 ♘g5+−+; 60.♔c6 ♘e5+ 61.♔c5 ♘xg6 62.♘f5+ ♔f8−+) 60...♘g5! 61.♖h4 ♖d7 (61...♘e6+ 62.♔c6 ♘f8−+) 62.♘d5 (62.♘f5+ ♔xg6 63.♘g3 ♘f3−+) 62...♘e4+ 63.♔c4 ♘d2+ 64.♔c5 ♘f3 65.♖h3 ♔xg6 66.♘xf6 ♖d1−+ and Black grabs the white rook for his pawn.

a2) 58.♔e6 ♘g5+−+;
a3) 58.♘e6 ♖c1−+;

a4) 58.♘h5 ♖c1 59.♘xf6+ ♔g7 60.♘h5+ ♔xg6 61.♘g3 ♔g5−+.

b) 57.♘g6 g4−+;

c) 57.♘e6 ♘f3−+ 58.♖h6 ♘h4!−+;

d) 57.♘h5 ♔f7 58.♘g3 ♖d2+ 59.♔c6 ♘f3−+;

e) 57.♘d5 ♔g7 58.♘e3 (58.♘c7 ♘f3) 58...♖d2+ 59.♔e7 (59.♔c6 ♖d3−+) 59...♖e2−+.

57.♘g6! ♖d2+

The careless 57...♘f3? 58.♖h8+− even turns the tables against Black.

Following 57...♖f2 58.♘h8+! ♔g8 (58...♔e8 59.♘g6 ♖xf5? 60.♔e6+−) 59.♘g6 ♔f7 (59...♖xf5? 60.♘e7+) 60.♘h8+= Black has to put up with a draw.

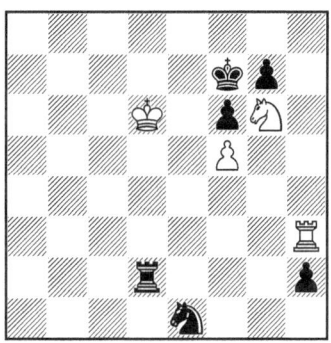

58.♔c7!

A precise move. Black wins following the erroneous 58.♔c6? ♘f3 59.♖h8 ♘e5+−+.

58...♖d5

58...♘f3? 59.♖h8+− is bad again.

The following line leads to a draw again: 58...♖f2 59.♘h8+ ♔g8 (59...♔e7 60.♘g6+!; 59...♔e8? 60.♖e3+ ♔f8 61.♘g6+ ♔f7 62.♖e7+ ♔g8 63.♖e8+ ♔h7 64.♖h8#) 60.♘g6 ♔f7 61.♘h8+=.

59.♘h8+!

The exchange of pawns is obviously

disadvantageous for White: 59.♖xh2? ♖xf5−+.

59...♔e8

There is a repetition after both 59...♔e7 60.♘g6+= and 59...♔g8 60.♘g6 ♔f7 (60...♖xf5? 61.♘e7+) 61.♘h8+=.

60.♖xh2

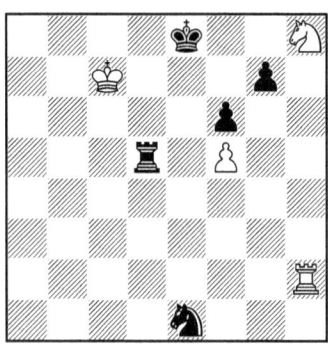

60...♘f3

Black cannot throw in the check first and then grab the pawn with impunity: 60...♖c5+? 61.♔d6 ♖xf5? 62.♖a2+−.

The following lines arise after 60...♖xf5 61.♖e2+! (61.♖a2 ♔f8! 62.♔d6 ♔g8!) 61...♖e5 62.♖a2!

a) 62...♖e4!

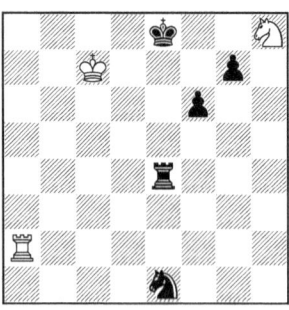

63.♔d6! The black king escapes after 63.♖a8+? ♔e7 64.♘g6+ ♔f7 65.♘h8+ ♔e6 66.♖e8+ ♔f5−+.

63...♖d4+. The continuation 63... ♔f8 64.♖a8+ ♖e8 65.♘g6+ ♔f7 66.♘h8+= results in a repetition of moves.

64.♔e6

a1) 64...♘f3

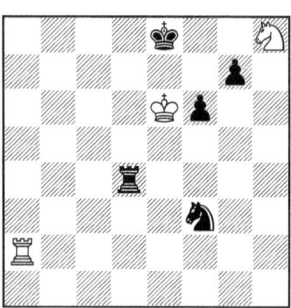

65.♘f7! White goes down after 65.♖a8+ ♖d8 66.♖xd8+ ♔xd8 67.♘f7+ ♔c7 68.♘h6? ♘g5+! 69.♔f5 gxh6 70.♔xf6 ♔d6 71.♔g6 ♘f7−+.

65...♖e4+ (65...♘g5+ 66.♘xg5 fxg5 67.♖a8+ ♖d8 68.♖xd8+ ♔xd8 69.♔f5=) 66.♔d5

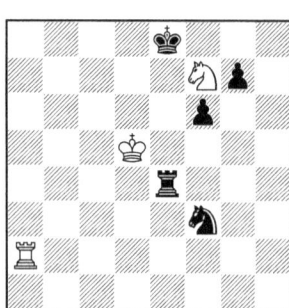

a1.1) 66...♖g4 67.♘d6+ ♔d8 (67... ♔f8 68.♖a8+ ♔e7 69.♖a7+ ♔d8 70.♘f7+ ♔c8 71.♘d6+ ♔b8 72.♖b7+ ♔a8 73.♖e7= and White's initiative compensates for the pawn deficit) 68.♘f5! (68.♖a8+?! ♔c7 69.♖a7+ ♔b6 70.♘c8+ ♔b5 71.♘d6+ ♔b4)

68...g6 (68...♞e5 69.♚e6=; 68...♜g5 69.♚e6=)

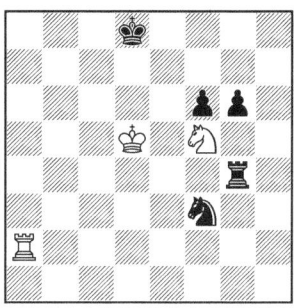

69.♚d6! White does not pause the black king chase even for a moment.

69...♚c8 (69...♚e8? 70.♜a8+ ♚f7 71.♞h6++−) 70.♞e7+ ♚b7 71.♜f2 ♞g5 (71...♞d4 72.♜xf6=)

72.♜b2+. A drawn position also results after 72.♜xf6 ♞e4+ 73.♚e5 ♞xf6 74.♚xf6 g5 75.♚f5 ♜g1 76.♞g6 g4 77.♞f4 ♚c6 78.♞e2 ♜e1 79.♞g3=.

72...♚a6 73.♞xg6 ♞e4+ 74.♚e6 ♜xg6 75.♚f5!= and White has saved the endgame;

a1.2) 66...♜b4 67.♞d6+=;

a1.3) 66...♜e7 67.♞d6+ ♚d7 68.♜a7+ ♚d8 69.♜a8+ ♚c7 70.♜a7+=;

a1.4) 66...♜e3 67.♞d6+ ♚d8 68.♜a8+ ♚c7 69.♜a7+=

a2) The game ends in a draw after both 64...♚d8 65.♜a8+ ♚c7 66.♜a7+ ♚c6 67.♜xg7=;

a3) and 64...♜d8 65.♞f7 ♜b8 66.♜h2 ♜b6+ 67.♞d6+ ♜xd6+ 68.♚xd6 ♚f7=;

a4) interesting lines arise after 64... ♞d3 65.♜a8+ (65.♞g6? ♞c5+ 66.♚f5 ♜d5+−+) 65...♜d8 66.♜xd8+ ♚xd8 67.♞f7+ (67.♚f7? ♞e5+ 68.♚xg7 ♚e7! 69.♚h6 ♞f7+ 70.♞xf7 ♚xf7 71.♚h5 ♚e6 72.♚g4 ♚e5−+)

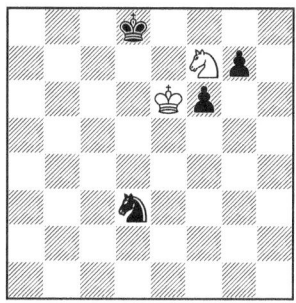

67...♚e8

(67...♚c7 68.♞h6! ♞f4+ [68...♞e5 69.♞f5=; 68...♞c5+ 69.♚f7 gxh6 70.♚xf6=; 68...gxh6 69.♚xf6 ♞f4 70.♚f5=] 69.♚f7 gxh6 70.♚xf6 ♚d6 [70...h5 71.♚g5=] 71.♚f5 ♞d5 72.♚g6=)

68.♞d6+! ♚f8 69.♞e4! ♞f4+ 70.♚f5 ♞d5 (70...♞h5 71.♚g6=) 71.♚e6 ♞c7+ 72.♚d7

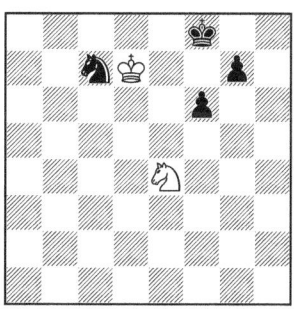

However, the positional evaluation is never subject to change – White escapes:

a4.1) 72...♘e8 73.♔e6! ♔g8 (73...g6 74.♘xf6=; 73...g5 74.♘xg5 fxg5 75.♔f5=) 74.♔e7 f5 (74...♘c7 75.♘xf6+=) 75.♔g5 ♘f6 (75...♘c7 76.♔d6 ♘b5+ 77.♔e5 g6 78.♔f6=) 76.♔e6 f4 77.♔e5 ♘h5 78.♔f5 ♔f8 79.♔g6 ♘g3 80.♘e6+=;

a4.2) 72...f5 73.♘d6 f4 74.♔xc7 ♔e7 75.♘e4 ♔e6 76.♔c6 ♔e5 77.♘d2=;

a4.3) 72...♘b5 73.♔e6 ♘d4+ 74.♔d5=;

b) 62...♖c5+ 63.♔d6 ♖c8 64.♖e2+ ♔f8 65.♖xe1=;

c) 62...♖e7+ 63.♔c6! ♖e6+ (63...♖e4 64.♔d5! f5 65.♔d6 ♖d4+ 66.♔e6=) 64.♔d5 ♖e5+ 65.♔d6=;

d) 62...♖e6 63.♖a8+ ♔e7 64.♘g6+ ♔f7 65.♘h8+ ♔e7 66.♘g6+=;

e) 62...♖e3 63.♖a8+ ♔e7 64.♘g6+ ♔f7 (64...♔e6? 65.♖e8+) 65.♘h8+=;

f) 62...♔f8 63.♘g6+=

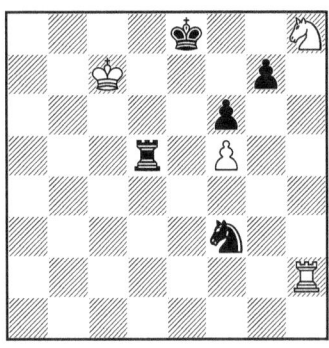

61.♖e2+!

61.♖g2? loses to 61...♖d7+ 62.♔c8 ♘d4−+.

61...♖e5?

Taking the wrong decision once again. Black gets checkmated following 61...♔f8? 62.♘g6+ ♔f7 63.♖e7+ ♔g8

64.♖e8+ ♔h7 (64...♔f7 65.♖f8#) 65.♖h8#.

However, 61...♘e5! is stronger: 62.♘g6 ♔f7 63.♘f4 (63.♘xe5+ fxe5−+; 63.♘h8+ ♔g8 64.♘g6 ♘xg6 65.fxg6 ♔f8−+) 63...♖d7+ 64.♔b6 ♖d4, and White is in for an uphill battle to make a draw.

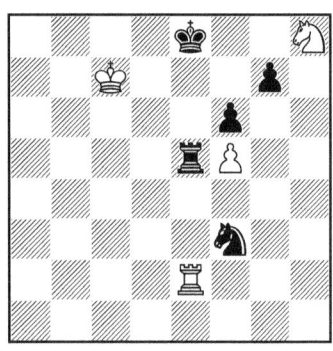

62.♖a2!

Setting up serious threats against the black king yet again.

62...♘h4

Both 62...♖xf5? 63.♔d6+− and 62...♘d4? 63.♖a8+ ♔e7 64.♘g6+ ♔f7 65.♖f8# are bad.

White equalizes after 62...♖e7+ 63.♔b6 (it's not too late for White to blunder into a loss: 63.♔d6? ♖d7+ 64.♔e6? ♘d4#) 63...♘e5 (63...♘d4 64.♖a8+ ♔d7 65.♖a7+ ♔d6 66.♘f7+ ♖xf7 67.♖xf7 ♘xf5 68.♖f8=) 64.♖a8+ ♔d7 65.♔c5! ♘c6 (65...♘d3+ 66.♔d4=) 66.♘g6 ♖e1 67.♘f8+ ♔c7 68.♘e6+ ♔b7 69.♖g8=.

63.♖a4!?

63.♖a8+ ♔e7 64.♖a4!?= was also fine.

63...♘xf5

The black king falls to checkmate again in the line 63...♖e7+ 64.♔c6! ♘xf5? 65.♖a8#.

64.♖a8+ ♔e7 65.♘g6+ and the opponents agreed a draw.

Example No. 51
D. Bocharov – M. Oganian
Sochi 2017

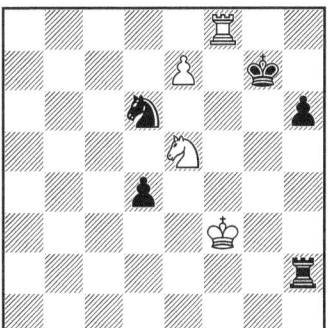

White to move

The only remaining white pawn is on the verge of promotion. All that is left to do is to eliminate the last defender – the black knight.

61.♖f7+?!

This is the first step towards a point of no return.

61.♘c4? ♖h1 62.♔e2 (62.♘xd6? ♖f1+=; 62.♔g2? ♖e1=; 62.♔f2 ♖h2+!) 62...♖h3! 63.♘xd6 (63.♔f1 ♖h1+!; 63.♔d1 ♖d3+!) 63...♖e3+= also fails to win.

White gets the upper hand with the correct 61.♖d8! ♖h3+ (61...♖h5 62.♘c6+−) 62.♔g2 ♖e3 63.♘c6 ♘c4 64.e8=♕ ♖xe8 65.♖xe8 d3 66.♔f3+−.

61...♔g8

Of course, 61...♘xf7? 62.e8=♕+− is bad.

62.♖f6?

Letting the win go once and for all. It was not too late to get back on track with 62.♖f8+! ♔g7 (62...♔h7 63.♘c4+−) 63.♖d8!+−.

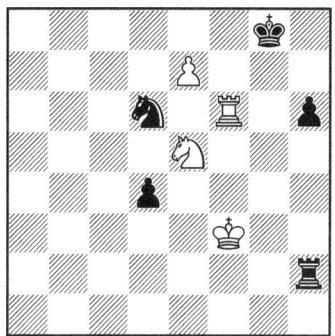

62...♖f2+!

Here comes a life-saving resource missed by White!

63.♔xf2 ♘e4+ 64.♔e2 ♘xf6 65.♔d3 ♔g7 66.♔xd4 ♘e8 67.♔e4 and the opponents agreed to a draw.

Lessons from my Career

Example No. 52
S. Sjugirov – A. Galkin
Novokuznetsk 2008

White to move

Black is a pawn up and enjoys active pieces. That said, White is not without trump cards of his own.

68.e7!

White resorts to this minor dynamic resource in an attempt to exchange pawns, which will reduce Black's already insignificant chances of winning this position even further.

68...♖f3+!

This is an attempt to introduce complications and provoke White into making mistakes. 68...♖e3 69.♘f6! yielded nothing. Meanwhile, following 68...♘xe7 69.♖xd4+ a draw becomes evident.

69.♔g2

Both 69.♔e2? ♖e3+−+ and 69.♔e1? ♖e3+−+ are ill-advised.

69...♖e3

70.♖xd4+!

White opts for a more attractive line. 70.♘b6!? ♖e5 (70...♘xe7 71.♖xd4+=) 71.♘d5+ ♔g5 72.♔f3 also looked good, when Black will have to agree to the exchange of pawns anyway.

70...♘xd4 71.♘f6! ♖e2+!

Yet another intermediate check. Giving back the rook with 71...♖xe7 72.♘d5+ would immediately shut the door on Black's attempt to outplay his opponent.

72.♔f1!

The alternative king retreats throw the game away:

a) 72.♔h1? ♘f3 73.e8=♕ ♖h2#;

b) 72.♔h3? ♘f3 73.e8=♕ ♖h2#;

c) 72.♔g1? ♔g3 73.e8=♕ ♘f3+ 74.♔f1 ♖f2#.

72...♔g5!

Black is virtually conjuring his chances out of thin air. 72...♖xe7 73.♘d5+= is harmless again.

72...♔f3 73.e8=♕ ♖xe8 74.♘xe8 h5 75.♘f6 h4 76.♔g1= yields nothing, too.

73.e8=♕ ♖xe8 74.♘xe8 ♘b5!

Trying to keep the white knight at bay.

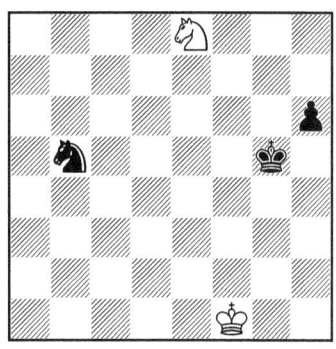

75.♘g7?

Exhausted by a lengthy defense, White quickly produced the most obvious move, sending a clear message that a draw in this position was a matter of fact.

However, if he were to take his time and think more deeply, he would have probably found a simple continuation: 75.♔g2! ♔g6 (75...h5 76.♔h3=) 76.♔h3 ♔f7 77.♔g4 ♔xe8 78.♔h5!= and the last pawn leaves the board, rendering Black's extra knight superiority of no use.

There followed

75...♘c7!

and the white knight turned out to be trapped. White resigned since there is no escape from the black king's journey to g6.

Example No. 53
M. Sebenik – K. Shevchenko
Catez (SLO) 2022

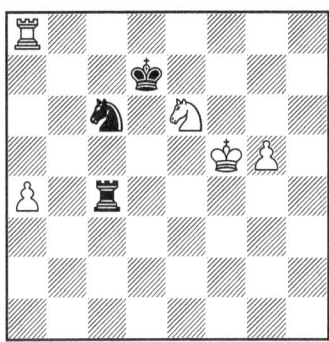

White to move

This game underlines the axiom "more haste less speed".

White is two pawns up. Conversion of his advantage requires no more than exercising diligence.

67.g6?

In his desire to finish the game as soon as possible White misses his opponent's saving opportunity.

There is more than one way to succeed in this position. For example, 67.♖a6!? ♖c1 was one option. Black goes down after both 67...♘e7+ 68.♔f6 ♘d5+ 69.♔e5 ♘e7 70.♖d6+ ♔e8 71.♔f6 ♘g8+ 72.♔g7+− and 67...♔c8 68.♖xc6+! ♖xc6 69.g6 ♔d7 70.g7 ♖c8 71.♘f8++−.

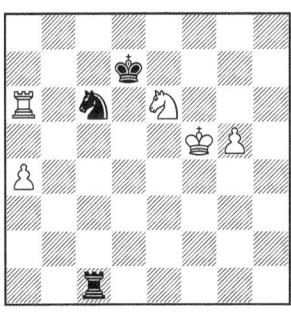

68.g6 ♘e7+. The rook checks lead nowhere: 68...♖f1+ 69.♔g5 ♖g1+ 70.♔f6 ♖f1+ 71.♔g7+−.

69.♔f6 ♖f1+. Black is checkmated following 69...♘d5+ 70.♔e5 ♘e7 71.♖d6+ ♔e8 72.♖d8#.

70.♔g7 ♘f5+ 71.♔g8 ♘e7+. White also prevails after 71...♘h6+ 72.♔h7 ♘f5 73.♘c5+ ♔c7 74.♖e6+−.

72.♔h7 ♖g1 (72...♖h1+ 73.♔g7+−) 73.♘c5+. It's not too late for White to lose: 73.g7? ♖h1#.

73...♔c7 (73...♔e8? 74.♖a8++−) 74.g7 ♘f5 (74...♖h1+ 75.♖h6 ♖xh6+ 76.♔xh6 ♘f5+ 77.♔h7 ♘xg7 78.♔xg7 ♔b6 79.♘b3+−) 75.g8=♕ ♖h1+ 76.♔g6 ♘e7+ 77.♔f7 ♘xg8 78.♔xg8+− and the subsequent conversion of White's overwhelming material advantage is only a question of time.

67...♘e7+! 68.♔f6 ♘xg6! 69.♖a7+

It is this intermediate check that White pinned his hopes on when moving his pawn forward.

Nor is White winning after 69.♖d8+ ♔c6 70.♖c8+ (70.♔xg6 ♖xa4) 70...♔d5 71.♖xc4 ♔xc4 72.♔xg6 ♔b4=. Meanwhile, the rook ending arising after 69.♔xg6 ♔xe6= is a relatively easy draw.

69...♔d6

There existed an alternative way to secure a draw: 69...♔c6 70.♔xg6 ♔b6! 71.♖a8 ♔b7! 72.♖a5 (72.♖d8 ♖xa4! 73.♘c5+ ♔c7 74.♖d7+ ♔c6=; 72.♖e8 ♔b6=) 72...♔b6! 73.♖b5+ ♔c6= and White cannot hold on to his only remaining pawn.

70.♖a6+

Nor does White have winning chances after 70.a5 ♘f4=.

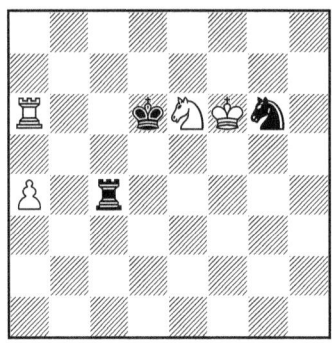

70...♖c6! 71.♖xc6+ ♔xc6 72.♔xg6 ♔b6!

and it turns out that the knight cannot keep his pawn alive.

There followed:

73.♔f5 ♔a5 74.♘c5 ♔b4! and the opponents agreed to a draw.

Example No. 54
D. Navara – M. Carlsen
Biel 2018

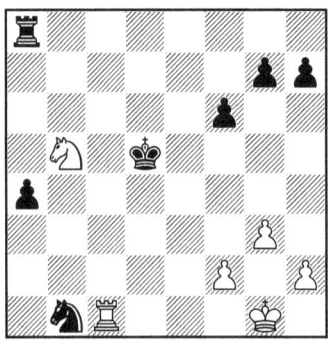

Black to move

Despite being a pawn up Black is experiencing some obvious problems: his knight is hanging and the rook stands on a forkable square. Will he manage to bail out?

35...a3!

Magnus comes up with the precise order of moves that allows him to hold this endgame.

35...♘d2? fails to 36.♘c7++−.

35...♖b8? 36.♖xb1 ♔c5 37.♖c1+ ♔b4 (37...♔xb5? 38.♖b1+) 38.♘d4 ♖a8 39.♖c7 is equally bad.

36.♖xb1

36.♘c7+! ♔d6! 37.♘b5+ (37.♘xa8? a2−+) 37...♔d5 results in a repetition of moves.

36...a2 37.♘c3+

White has to give up his rook for the black pawn following the erroneous 37.♖a1? ♔c4 38.♘c7 ♖a7 39.♘e6 ♔b3.

37...♔d4 38.♘xa2

A drawn pawn ending results after 38.♘e2+ ♔d3 39.♘c1+ ♔c2 40.♖a1 ♔b2 41.♖xa2+ ♖xa2 42.♘xa2 ♔xa2 43.♔g2 ♔b3 44.♔f3 ♔c4 45.♔e4 ♔c5=.

38...♖xa2 39.♖b7

Likewise, 39.♖e1 ♖a7 40.♔g2 ♔d5= promises White nothing.

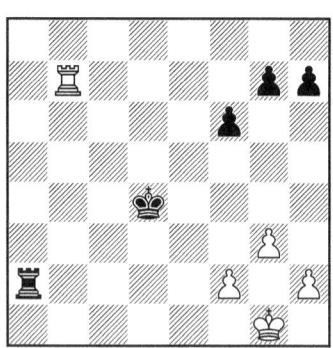

39...♔e4! 40.♔g2

Active counterplay allows Black to maintain the balance following 40.♖xg7 ♔f3! 41.h4 ♖xf2.

40...g5!

Yet another precise move. Black is clearly unwilling to find himself with a compromised pawn structure on the kingside.

41.♖xh7 ♔f5=

This is a drawn rook ending with pawns on the same flank.

42.♖g7 g4 43.♖h7 ♔g6 44.♖h4 f5 45.h3 and White offered a draw without testing the world champion's mastery of basic defensive technique.

We now turn to examples of endings with rook and bishop versus rook and knight.

Example No. 55
S. Drygalov – A. Gabrielian
Chelyabinsk 2022

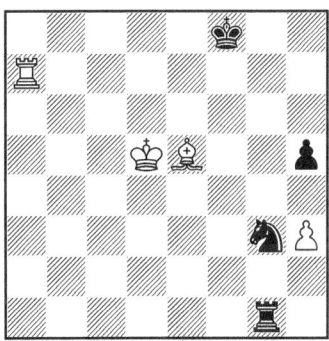

Black to move

Black is up against serious problems despite material equality. His king is in danger. White is ready to shut the mating trap by moving his king to e6. The black knight is hanging, which prevents the black rook from becoming active and coming to his king's rescue. Moreover, White also has a rook's pawn on the board, whose promotion square's color matches that of the bishop. It takes extremely precise play to stay in the game.

58...h4?

As a result, the black pieces will no longer be in time to help their king escape from the mating trap.

Both 58...♘f5? 59.♔e6 ♘g7+ 60.♗xg7+ ♖xg7 61.♖a8# and 58...♖d1+? 59.♔e6+− are bad.

The correct approach is 58...♘e2! 59.♔e6. 59.♖h7 ♘f1!? 60.♖xh5 (60.♔e6 ♘f4+=; 60.♔e4 ♖g1 61.♔f5 ♔g8 62.♖h8+ ♔f7=) 60...♘f4+ 61.♗xf4 ♖xf4= leads to a drawn rook ending.

59...♖g6+ 60.♔f5 (60.♗f6 ♘d4+=) 60...♖c6 61.♖a2 (61.♗f6 ♖c5+ 62.♔g6 ♘f4+ 63.♔h7 ♖f5=) 61...♘c3 62.♖c2 (62.♖d2 ♘b5!?) 62...♘d5! 63.♖xc6 ♘e7+= and the exchange of rooks makes a draw inevitable.

59.♔e6! ♔g8 60.♖g7+!

60.♖a8+ ♔h7 61.♔f7 ♖f1+ 62.♗f6 ♖xf6+ 63.♔xf6 ♘e4+ 64.♔f5+− was also decisive.

60...♔f8

60...♔h8 loses on the spot to 61.♖xg3++−.

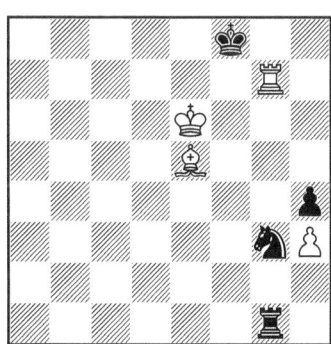

61.♖g4!

White keeps weaving mating threats around the black king.

61...♘e2

Black is checkmated after 61...♖f1 62.♗d6+ ♔e8 63.♖g8++−. 61...♖e1 62.♖xh4+− is no better than the text.

62.♖a4! ♔g8

62...♖g6+ 63.♗f6+− is bad, too.

63.♖xh4 ♔f8

63...♖g6+ 64.♗f6 ♔f8 65.♖a4+− fails again.

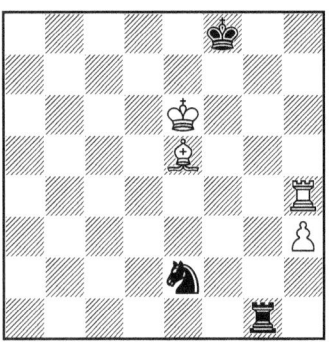

64.♖e4!

Delivering the final blow to the last of Black's defensive formations.

64...♘g3

Black drops the rook after both 64...♖g2 65.♖a4 ♔g8 66.♖a8+ ♔h7 67.♖h8+ ♔g6 68.♖g8++− and 64...♘c1 65.♖c4 ♔g8 66.♖c8+ ♔h7 67.♖h8+ ♔g6 68.♖g8++−.

In case of 64...♖e1 65.♖a4 ♔g8 66.♖h4+− Black can bribe his way out of checkmate only at the cost of a knight.

65.♖f4+ ♔e8

65...♔g8 66.♖g4++− is also game over.

66.♖a4 and Black resigned. It is worth highlighting that had there been no pawns and no black knight in the initial position it would have been a draw with correct play. By contrast, the course of the game showed that Black's knight was the culprit of his going wrong and failing to set up proper defense for the king.

Example No. 56
P. Nguyen – M. Krasenkow
Poland 2020

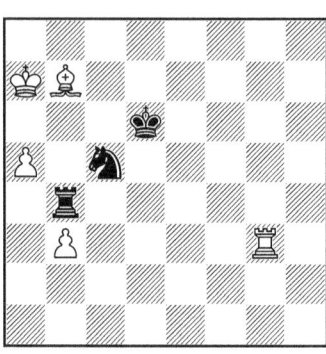

White to move

White is up two pawns.

His main task in this position is either to keep them alive, or to prevent the black knight's sacrifice for both at once.

77.♖g6+?

This erroneous check allows black to escape.

The winning move is 77.a6!

a) 77...♘d7 78.♖d3+ ♔c7 (78...♔e7 79.♖c3+−) 79.♖c3+ ♔d8. 79...♔d6 doesn't saves the game either: 80.♖c6+ ♔e5 (80...♔e7 81.♗c8! ♖xb3 82.♖c7 ♔d8 83.♖b7!♖xb7+ 84.axb7 ♘e5 85.♔b6+−) 81.♗c8+− ♘f8 (81...♘f6 82.♖e6++−) 82.♖b6.

80.♗d5+− and both pawns have survived.

b) Following 77...♖xb3 78.♗xb3 ♘xb3 79.♔b6+−, the pawn inevitably becomes a queen;

c) Capturing with the knight forces the exchange of rooks after 77...♘xb3 78.♖g6+ ♔c7 (78...♔c5 79.♖c6+ ♔d4 80.♖b6+− is bad) 79.♖c6+ ♔d7 80.♖b6+−, and the pawn inevitably queens.

d) 77...♔c7 is not a saving move due to 78.♖g7+ ♘d7 (78...♔d6 79.♖g6+ ♔e7 80.♖b6+−; 78...♔d8 79.♗d5 ♘xb3 80.♖b7+−)

79.♗f3. 79.♗d5 ♔d6 80.♗c4 ♔c6 81.♗f7 ♔d6 82.♗e8 ♘c5 83.♖g6+ ♔e7 84.♖b6+− wins, too.

79...♔d6 (79...♖xb3 80.♗g4 ♖d3 81.♖xd7+ ♖xd7 82.♗xd7 ♔xd7 83.♔b7+− is bad) 80.♖g6+ ♔e5 (80... ♔c7 81.♖c6+ ♔d8 82.♗d5+− is no better) 81.♗d1+−.

77...♔e7

77...♔c7? 78.♖c6+ drops the knight.

Black also emerges a piece down after 77...♔e5? 78.♖g5+ ♔d6 (78... ♔d4 79.♖d5+) 79.♖d5++−.

However, 77...♔d7! is stronger

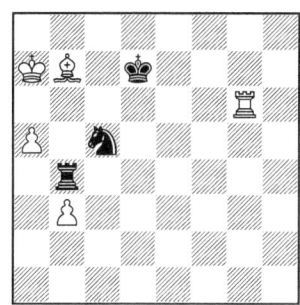

78.♗d5. None of 78.♖g7+ ♔d6, 78.♗c6+ ♔c7 79.♗d5 ♘xb3 80.♖c6+ ♔d7 81.♖b6 ♖xb6 82.axb6 ♘c5= or 78.♖b6 ♖xb3 79.♗c6+ ♔d8!? carries any danger for Black.

78...♘xb3 79.♗xb3. The knight stops the pawn after both 79.♖b6 ♖xb6 80.axb6 ♘c5= and 79.a6 ♘c5!

79...♖xb3 80.♖b6 ♖a3 (or 80...♖c3=) 81.a6 ♔c7= with an easy draw.

78.♗d5

78.♖b6? ♖xb3! 79.♖xb3 ♘xb3 80.a6 ♘c5= yields nothing.

78...♘xb3 79.♗xb3 ♖xb3 80.♖b6 (80.a6 ♔d7 81.♖b6 ♖c3! leads to a draw) **80...♖c3!**

A precise move!

81.♔b7

81.a6 ♔d7= is also a draw.

81.♔b8 ♔d7 (81...♔d8? 82.♖d6+ ♔e7 83.♖h6 ♔d7 84.♖h7+! ♔d6 85.a6+− is a blunder) 82.♖b7+ ♔d8= results in a theoretically drawn ending.

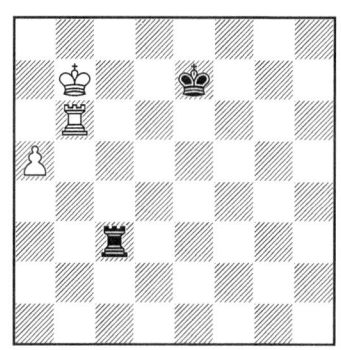

81...♔d7!

Yet another precise move! 81...♔d8? would have failed to 82.♖d6+ ♔e7 83.♖c6 ♖b3+ 84.♔b6+−.

82.♖b1

In case of 82.a6 ♖c7+ 83.♔b8 ♖c8+ the white king is forced to block his pawn's progress.

82...♖c7+ 83.♔b8 ♖c8+ 84.♔b7 ♖c7+ 85.♔b6 ♖c6+ 86.♔b7 and the opponents agreed to a draw.

Example No. 57
J. Stocek − J. Votava
Czech Republic 2020

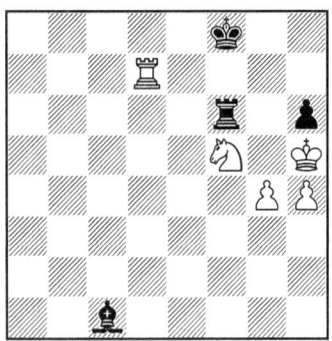

Black to move

Black is down a pawn. However, the good news is that there are only a few pawns on the board and located on the same flank at that. Black's aim is to give up his bishop for both pawns and transpose into a drawn rook and knight vs. rook ending. However, it is not as simple as that. The h6-pawn is extremely weak, and White will try to appropriate it.

79...♔g8?

Black wants to take control over the h7-square, which the white rook could use to get to the black pawn. However, Black underestimates White's follow-up.

79...♖a6? was also losing, to 80.♖c7

♗f4 (80...♗d2 81.♖c8+ ♔f7 82.♖c2 ♗f4 83.♖f2+− makes no difference) 81.♖c4! ♗d2 82.♖c8+ ♔f7 83.♖c2 ♗f4 84.♖f2 ♗c1 85.♘xh6++−.

The most resilient defense, albeit insufficient to save the game, was 79...♖c6! 80.♖g7! There is no more winning after 80.♖d6? ♖xd6 81.♘xd6 ♔g7 82.♘f5+ ♔h7=, and Black also holds after 80.♖h7 ♖c5!, but not 80...♔g8? 81.♖xh6 ♗xh6 82.♘e7++−.

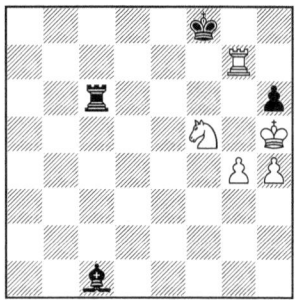

80...♔e8. 80...♗f4 81.♖g6 ♖c5 82.♖f6+ ♔e8 (82...♔g8 83.♔g6+−) 83.♔g6 ♖c4 84.♔h7♗c1 85.♖g6 ♖c7+ (85...h5 86.♘d6++−) 86.♔g8+− is no better and the pawn drops.

81.♖g6 ♖c5

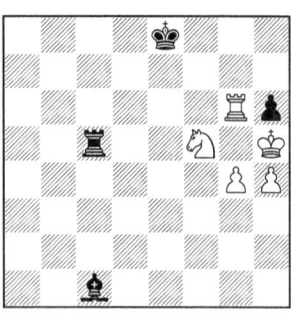

82.♖f6! Paving the road for the white king.

82...♖a5. Black loses after both 82...♔d7 83.♔g6 ♖c4 84.♘xh6 ♗xh6 85.g5!

♖xh4 86.gxh6 ♔e7 87.♔g7+− and 82...
♗d2 83.♔g6 ♖c4 84.♘d6++−.

83.♖c6. The time for the king to
move forward is not yet right: 83.♔g6
♖a4 84.♘xh6 ♗xh6 85.g5 ♗f8 86.h5
♗e7 87.♖f5 ♖g4 88.h6 ♗xg5! 89.♖xg5
♖xg5+ 90.♔xg5 ♔f7 and Black is out
of the woods.

83...♗d2. Black goes down after
83...♗f4 84.♖c4 ♗d2 85.♔g6 ♖a6+
86.♔h7 ♖a7+ 87.♔g8+−.

84.♖c2 ♗f4. 84...♗d5 is of no help:
85.♔g6 ♗f4 86.♖c4 ♗d2 87.♖d4+−.

85.♖c4 ♗d2 86.♔g6 ♖a6+ 87.♔h7

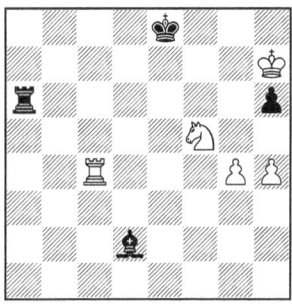

87...♖a7+. Black does not hold
the pawn either after 87...♖f6
88.♖c8+ (88.♔g8 ♖g6+ 89.♘g7+
♔e7 90.♖e4+ ♔f6 91.♖e6# is also
decisive) 88...♔f7 89.♖c2 ♗f4 90.♖f2
♗c1 91.♘xh6+ ♗xh6 92.♖xf6+ ♔xf6
93.♔xh6+−.

88.♔g8 ♖a8 (88...♖d7 89.♖c8++−)
89.♖e4+ ♔d7+ 90.♔f7 (90.♔g7+−
is equally good) 90...♔c6 (90...♗c1
91.♖d4+ ♔c6 92.♖c4++− drops the
bishop) 91.♖d4 ♖a2 92.♔g6 ♔c5
93.♔h5 ♖b2 94.♖d8+−, and the pawn
is doomed. It is worth noting that the
winning plan in this type of position is to
drive the black king away from the weak
pawn and create alternative threats to
each enemy piece, including the idea of

exchanging rooks and transposing into a
winning minor-piece ending.

80.♖g7+! ♔f8
80...♔h8 81.♖g6+− makes no
difference.

81.♖g6
It turns out that the besieged pawn
will not survive.

81...♔f7
The pawn also perishes after 81...
♖xg6 82.♔xg6+−.

82.♘xh6+ and Black threw in the
towel.

Example No. 58
V. Ivic − L.D. Nisipeanu
Catez 2022

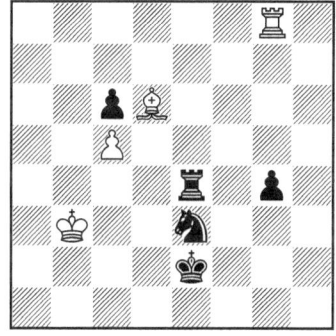

Black to move

Black is a pawn up. White's drawing
plan envisages attacking the c6-pawn
with the rook and giving up the bishop
for the passed g-pawn, if the need arises.
Does Black have anything to counter
that?

53...♘f5?
The Romanian grandmaster only
finds a way to address the issue of
defending his weak pawn, missing
another vital factor in this position.

The correct plan was a combination
of threats of advancing the passed pawn

and checkmating the white king via 53... ♔d3! 54.♖d8. White after loses also 54.♖c8 ♘c2 55.♖b8 ♖c4 56.♖b7 ♘d4+ 57.♔a3 ♔c3! 58.♗e5 ♖xc5 59.♖b3+ ♔c2 60.♗xd4 ♖a5+ 61.♔b4 ♖b5+−+. No better than that is 54.♖g6 ♘d5 55.♖g8 ♖b4+ 56.♔a3 ♔c3! 57.♗e5+ ♔c2 58.♖g6 ♖e4 59.♖g5 g3! 60.♗xg3 ♘c3−+, followed by checkmate.

54...♘d5! 55.♔b2. In case of 55.♖b8 ♖e1 56.♔b2 ♘c3 57.♖f8 ♔c4 58.♖f4+ ♖e4 59.♖f1 (59.♖xe4+ ♘xe4−+) 59...♖e2+ 60.♔c1 ♔b3−+ the white king again finds himself in a mating net.

55...♖e2+ 56.♔b3. White is checkmated in the line 56.♔c1 ♖c2+ 57.♔b1 (57.♔d1 ♘e3+ 58.♔e1 ♖e2#) 57...♘c3+ 58.♔a1 ♖a2#, while after 56.♔a3 ♔c3 57.♖b8 ♖e3 58.♔a4 ♖e1 59.♖b3+ ♔c4 60.♔a3 ♖e3−+ Black manages to exchange off the rooks.

56...♖e1! Pressing the white king further.

57.♔b2 ♖e4! 58.♖c8. The exchange of rooks occurs again after 58.♖b8 ♖b4+−+. 58.♖h8 ♖b4+ 59.♔a3 ♖b1 60.♖h2 ♖g1 61.♔b2 ♘c3−+ is of no help.

58...♖b4+ 59.♔a3 (59.♔c1 ♘c3 60.♖b8 ♖xb8 61.♗xb8 g3 62.♗xg3 ♘e2+−+) 59...♔c4 60.♖g8 (the checkmating trap shuts again following 60.♖xc6 ♘c3−+) 60... ♔c3 61.♗e5+ ♔c2 62.♖h8 ♖b3+ 63.♔a4. White is checkmated one more time in the line 63.♔a2 ♘b4+ 64.♔a1 ♖a3#.

63...♖b5 64.♖h2+. Black wins a piece after 64.♖g8 ♖xc5 65.♖xg4 ♘b6+−+.

64...♔d3 65.♗d6 (65.♖g2 ♖xc5 66.♖g3+ ♘e3 67.♗f4 ♖c4+−+) 65... ♘c3+ 66.♔a3 ♔c4−+ and checkmate is inevitable.

Also, 53...♔d2! 54.♖c8 ♘c2 looks good and carried the same ideas.

54.♔c3!

Not only does White remove his king from the forkable square, but gives it more freedom of action at that.

54.♖c8? was wrong: 54...♖e6 55.♖g8 (55.♖xc6? ♘d4+−+; 55.♗f8 g3−+; 55.♗b8 g3 56.♖g8 ♔f2 57.♖f8 ♖e3+ 58.♔b4 ♖f3−+) 55...g3 56.♔b4 (56.♗xg3 ♖e3+ 57.♔b4 ♖xg3 58.♖xg3 ♘xg3 59.♔a5 ♘f5 60.♔b6 ♘d4−+) 56...♔f3 57.♖f8

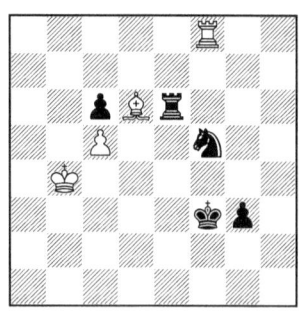

57...♔g4 (57...♔g2? 58.♖xf5+ ♔g4 59.♖f8) 58.♖g8+ ♔h3 59.♖h8+ ♖h6−+ and White is doomed.

54...♘d4

There is no rolling back to the

previous position with 54...♘e3 55.♖c8! ♘d5+ 56.♔b3

a) 56...♖e6 57.♖xc6 g3 58.♖c8 g2 59.♖g8 ♔f1 (59...♔f2 60.♖f8+ ♖f6 61.♖xf6+ ♘xf6 62.c6!=) 60.♗h2 ♖h6 61.♖f8+ ♘f6 (61...♔e2 62.♗g1=) 62.c6!= and the passed pawn ensures White a draw;

b) 56...♘b4 57.♔a4! ♔f3 58.♔a5=;

c) 56...♖b4+ 57.♔a3 ♔d3 58.♖xc6 ♔c4 59.♗e5! ♖b3+ 60.♔a4 ♖b7 61.♔a5! ♖a7+ 62.♗a6 ♖xa6+ 63.♔xa6 ♔xc5 64.♔b7=.

54...♖d4 55.♖g5 ♖d3+ 56.♔b4 ♘e3 57.♖g8 ♔f3 58.♖c8= yields nothing, too.

55.♔b4!

White exploits the first opportunity that presents itself to evacuate his king from dangerous territory.

55...♘c2+ 56.♔a5 ♖b4

It is unclear how Black would improve his position after 56...♔f3 57.♔b6 ♘b4 58.♖f8+=.

57.♖c8 ♖b5+ 58.♔a4 ♖b7

The line 58...♖b1 59.♖xc6 ♖a1+ 60.♔b3! ♘d4+ 61.♔b2 ♘xc6 62.♔xa1 ♔f3 63.♔b2 ♔e4 64.♔c3 ♘e5 65.♗xe5 ♔xe5 66.c6 ♔d6 67.♔d4 g3 68.♔e3 g2 69.♔f2 ♔xc6 70.♔xg2 leads to complete liquidation of material.

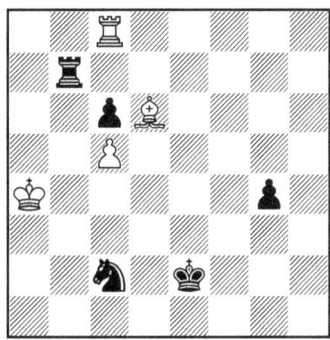

59.♖xc6!

White is not afraid of sacrificing the exchange because he gets a dangerous passed pawn in return.

59...♖a7+ 60.♔b5

Naturally, 60.♔b3? ♘d4+−+ is bad.

60...♘d4+ 61.♔b6 ♘xc6 62.♔xc6 ♔f3 63.♔d5 ♖a5

In case of 63...g3 64.♗xg3 ♔xg3 65.c6= White forces Black to part with his rook.

64.♔e6 ♖a6

64...♔e4 65.c6= makes no difference.

65.♔d5 ♖a5 66.♔e6 g3 67.♗xg3 ♖xc5

There is no avoiding a draw after 67...♔xg3 68.c6=.

68.♗d6 and the players agreed to a draw.

Example No. 59
D. Gordievsky – E. Romanov
Moscow 2018

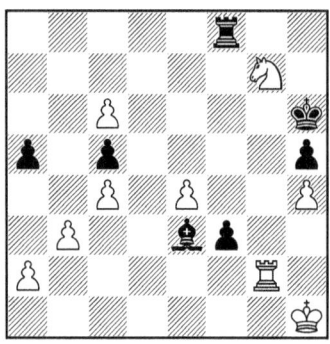

White to move

Black has a dangerous passed pawn, supported by his rook and bishop. White seems to be in for many problems.

43.♘f5+! ♖xf5 44.♖g6+!

A brilliant decision! And Black resigned in the face of 44...♔xg6 45.exf5+ ♔f6 46.c7 f2 47.♔g2.

A most interesting endgame results after 44.exf5 fxg2+ 45.♔xg2 ♗f4 46.♔f3 ♗c7 47.♔e4 ♔g7 48.♔d5 ♔f6 49.♔xc5 ♔xf5 50.♔b5! 50.a3 blows the win after 50...♔e6 51.b4 (51.♔b5? ♔d6) 51...axb4 52.axb4 ♔e7 53.b5 ♔d8 54.b6 ♗g3 55.♔b5 (it is a stalemate after 55.c7+ ♔c8 56.♔c6 ♗xc7! 57.bxc7) 55...♔c8! 56.♔a6 ♗f2! (56...♗xh4? 57.b7+ ♔b8 58.c7+! ♔xc7 59.♔a7+–) 57.♔a7 ♗e3=.

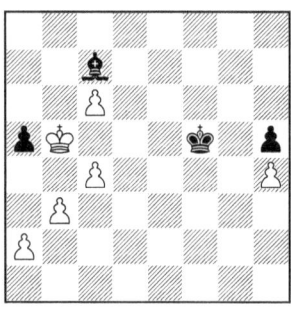

50...♔g4. In case of 50...♔e6 51.♔a6 ♔d6 52.♔b7 ♗d8 53.a3+– the avalanche of white pawns decides the outcome.

51.♔a6 ♔xh4 52.♔b7 ♗e5 53.c7 ♗xc7 54.♔xc7 ♔g3 55.c5 h4 56.c6 h3 57.♔b6 h2 58.c7 h1=♕ 59.c8=♕+– ♕h6+ 60.♕c6 (60.♔xa5? ♕d2+) 60...♕e3+ (60...♕d2 61.♕g6+! ♔h4 62.♕e4+ ♔g5 63.♕e5+ ♔g6 64.♕xa5+–) 61.♕c5 ♕h6+ 62.♔b5 (62.♔xa5? ♕d2+) 62...♕d2

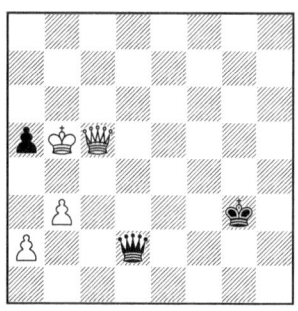

63.a3! (63.♕a3? ♕d5+ 64.♔a6 ♕c6+! 65.♔xa5 ♕a8+ 66.♔b4 ♕f8+ 67.♔a4 ♕a8+=) 63...♔g2 (63...♔f3 64.♔a4 ♔g2 65.♕xa5+–; 63...♕d3+ 64.♔a4+–) 64.♔a4 (64.♔a6? ♕d3+ 65.♕b5 ♕d6+=) 64...♔h2! Black seeks the most convenient square for his king.

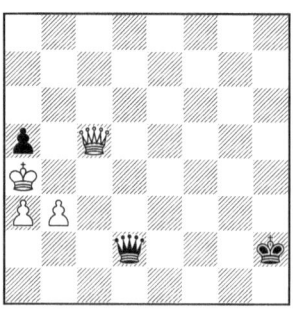

65.♕e5+! 65.♕xa5? is an error that leads to a theoretical draw after 65...

♕d7+ 66.♔b5 ♕a7+ 67.♔b4 ♕d4+ 68.♔c4 ♕d2+ 69.♔b5 ♕d7+.

65...♔g1 (65...♔h3 66.♕xa5+−; 65...♔h1 66.♕xa5+−) 66.♕xa5. This endgame is winning thanks to the king being placed on g1. For example, 66...♕d4+ (66...♕d7+ 67.♕b5 ♕a7+ 68.♔b4 ♕d4+ 69.♕c4 ♕b6+ 70.♔c3+−) 67.♕b4 ♕a7+ 68.♔b5 ♕b7+ 69.♔c5 ♕c7+ 70.♔d5 ♕d7+ 71.♕d6+−.

The following example highlights the skill of correct evaluation when it comes to transposition from a more to a less complex endgame.

Example No. 60
P. Ponkratov − R. Hasangatin
Sochi 2022

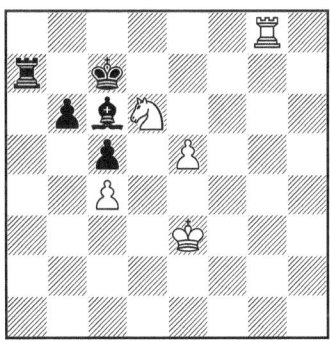

White to move

White's pieces are more active and he has a dangerous passed pawn. However, the limited number of pawns definitely plays into the defending side's hands. White wants to come up with a precise continuation and exploit the black rook's having not yet joined the fray. This is a natural but erroneous decision.

40.♔f4?

He needed to transpose into a minor-piece endgame with 40.♖g7+! ♔b8 (40...♗d7? 41.♘b5++− loses on the spot) 41.♖xa7! ♔xa7 42.e6!

(42.♔f4? is bad because of 42... ♗d7! 43.♔g5 ♔b8 44.♔f6 ♔c7 45.♔f7 [45.♘b5+ ♗xb5 46.cxb5 c4 47.e6 c3 48.e7 c2 49.e8=♕ c1=♕=; 45.♔e7 ♗c6! 46.e6 b5 47.cxb5 ♗d5=] 45...b5! 46.cxb5 [46.♘xb5+ ♗xb5 47.cxb5 c4 48.e6 c3 49.e7 c2 50.e8=♕ c1=♕=] 46...♔b6 47.♔e7 ♗h3=)

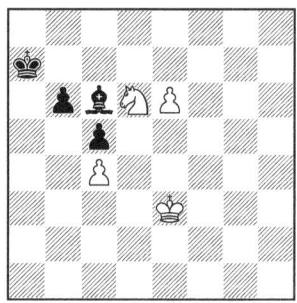

42...♔a6

(In case of 42...♔b8 43.♔f4! [43.e7? ♔c7 44.e8=♕ ♗xe8 45.♘xe8+ ♔c6 46.♔e4 b5=] 43...♔c7 44.♔e5 ♕d8 45.♔f6 ♔c7 [45...♗e8 46.e7+ ♔d7 47.♘xe8 ♔xe8 48.♔e6 b5 49.cxb5 c4 50.b6 c3 51.b7 c2 52.b8=♕#] 46.♘b5+ ♔b7 [after 46...♗xb5 47.cxb5 c4 48.e7 ♔d7 49.♔f7+−] 47.e7 ♔a6 48.♔e5 ♔a5 49.♘c7 ♔b4 50.♔d6 ♗a4 51.♘b5+− the white pawn queens.)

43.♔f4! The white king heads off on a victory march. It is premature to grab the bishop: 43.e7 ♔a5 44.e8=♕? ♗xe8 45.♘xe8 b5!= and the only white pawn leaves the board.

43...♔a5 44.♔e5 ♔b4 (assigning the bishop to a different diagonal is of no help either: 44...♗f3 45.e7 ♗h5 46.♔f6 ♔b4 47.♘f7+−) 45.♔f6!?

♔c3 (45...♗a4 46.♔e7+−) 46.♔e7!?
♔d4. In case of 46...♗f3 47.♔d8
♔b4 48.e7 ♗h5 49.♔c7 ♔a5 50.♔c6
♗g6 51.e8=♕ ♗xe8+ 52.♘xe8 ♔b4
53.♘d6 ♔a5 54.♘c8 b5 55.cxb5 c4
56.♘b6 c3 57.♘c4+ ♔b4 58.♘e3+−
the white knight copes with the black
passed pawn, whereas the white passed
pawn heads for the queening square.

47.♔d8! ♔e5 48.♔c7 ♗a4. 48...
♗f3 is of no help either: 49.e7 ♗h5
50.♔c6 b5 51.cxb5 c4 52.b6 c3
53.b7 c2 54.♘c4+! ♔d4 55.b8=♕
c1=♕ 56.♕e5+ ♔d3 (56...♔xc4
57.♕c5++−) 57.♕d5+ ♔c3 (57...♔e2
58.♕xh5++−) 58.♕xh5+−.

49.e7 ♔e6. The white pawn
inevitably queens in case of 49...♔d4
50.♘b5++−.

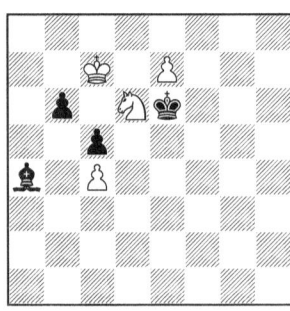

50.♘c8! 50.e8=♕+? is premature
yet again: 50...♗xe8 51.♘xe8 b5!

52.cxb5 c4 53.♘g7+ ♔e5! 54.b6 c3
55.b7 c2 56.b8=♕ c1=♕+ 57.♔d7+
♔e4= and White's extra piece does not
change this endgame's evaluation.

50...♗e8. 50...♔f7 is no better:
51.♘xb6 ♗e8 52.♔d8 ♗c6 53.♘d7+−.

51.♔d8 ♗h5 (51...♗c6 52.♘xb6+−)
52.♘xb6+− and Black is doomed.

40...♖a1!

Now Black generates sufficient
counterplay thanks to his rook's activity.

41.♖g7+ ♗d7! 42.♖h7

Neither 42.e6 ♔xd6 43.exd7 ♖a8=
nor 42.♘b5+ ♔d8= promise White
anything.

42...♖g1

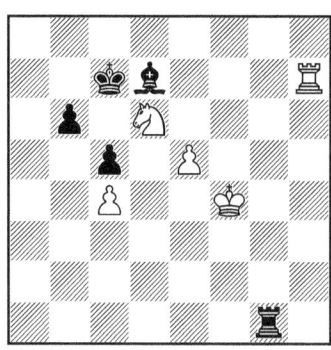

43.♘e4

White's advantage also dissipates
after 43.♘f5 ♖f1+ 44.♔e4 ♖e1+
45.♔d5 ♖d1+ 46.♔e4 ♖e1+ 47.♘e3
♔d8 48.♖h6 b5 49.♖d6 ♔c7=.

43...♔d8 44.♖h6

44.♘f6 ♗e6 45.♖h8+ ♔e7
46.♘d5+ ♔f7 47.♘xb6 ♖f1+ 48.♔g3
(48.♔e3 ♖e1+=) 48...♔f5 49.♖h7+
♔e8= is no better: Black wins the pawn
back.

**44...♖f1+ 45.♔e3 ♖e1+ 46.♔f3
♖f1+ 47.♔e3**

After 47.♔e2 ♖f5 48.e6 ♖e5! 49.exd7
♖xe4+ 50.♔d3 ♖d4+ 51.♔c3 ♔c7! it

is now White who needs to come up with precise play to make a draw.

47...♖e1+ 48.♔f4 ♖f1+ 49.♔e3 ♖e1+ 50.♔f4 ♖f1+ 51.♔e3 and, having repeated the position more than once, the opponents agreed to a draw.

Example No. 61
A. Mikaelyan − S. TerSahakyan
Yerevan 2022

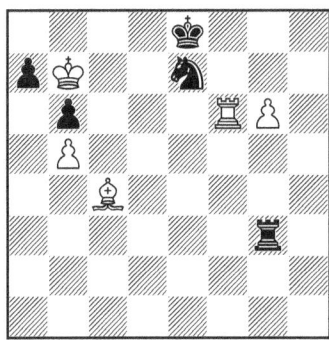

White to move

White has a decisive advantage. Black's pawns are doomed, and his pieces are somewhat misplaced. However, this type of position always comes with the idea of annihilating all of your opponent's pawns even at the cost of a knight so as to make a draw in a rook and bishop versus rook ending.

78.♔xa7?

It is hard to refuse winning a pawn while maintaining a trap for Black at that. However, White underestimates his opponent's counterplay.

78.♗f7+?! and its apparently logical continuation is a pointless idea due to 78...♔d7 (78...♔d8? 79.♖d6#) 79.♖f1 (it is not too late for White to lose: 79.♔xa7? ♔c7 and the white king is caught in a checkmating net) 79...♔d6!

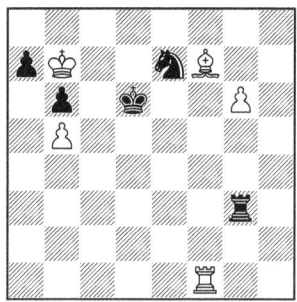

80.♖c1. Black equalizes after 80.♔xa7 ♔c5 81.♔a6 ♖a3+ 82.♔b7 ♔xb5 83.g7 ♖g3.

80...♖g5 81.♗e8?! (the logical continuation of his approach starting from move 78. 81.♖c6+? ♔d7! 82.♖c7+ ♔d8!; 81.♖d1+! returns white to winning ways) 81...♘f5 82.♔xa7 ♔e7 83.♖e1+ (83.♗f7 ♘d6=) 83...♔f6 84.♔xb6 ♘d6 and a drawn rook and bishop vs. rook ending looms ahead.

One winning approach is 78.♖f1!?

a) 78...♘xg6 79.♗f7+! ♔e7. Likewise, 79...♔d7 80.♖d1+! ♔e7 81.♗xg6 ♖xg6 82.♔xa7 ♖f6 83.♔b7! ♖h6 84.♔c7! ♖g6 85.♖d7+! ♔e8 86.♖d6+− is not a game changer.

80.♗xg6 ♖xg6 81.♔xa7 ♔d7 82.♖d1+!? ♔c7 (82...♖d6 83.♖xd6+ ♔xd6 84.♔xb6+−) 83.♖c1+! ♔d7 (83...♔d8 84.♔b7+−) 84.♔b7 ♖d6 85.♖c6 ♖d1 86.♔xb6+− with a winning rook ending;

b) 78...♖xg6? 79.♗f7+ ♔d7 80.♗xg6 ♘xg6 81.♖d1+ ♔e6 82.♔xa7+− fails on the spot;

c) 78...♔d7 79.♖d1+ ♔e8 80.♗f7+ ♔f8 81.♖d8+ ♔g7 82.♔xa7 ♘xg6 83.♗xg6 ♖xg6 84.♖b8+− results in a winning rook ending for White;

d) 78...♖g4 79.♗f7+ ♔d7 80.♖d1++− finds the black king in a mating net.

In fact, it was fine to play 78.♖f2!? with the same ideas.

78...♔d7!

Creating a real threat to the g6-pawn and gearing up for a hunt after the white king. 78...♘xg6? is bad: 79.♗f7+ ♔e7 80.♖xg6 ♖a3+ 81.♔xb6 ♔xf7 82.♖d6 ♔e7 83.♖d1+−.

79.♔xb6

79.♗f7? fails due to 79...♔c7−+. White walks into a fork after 79.♖xb6? ♘c8+=.

79...♘xg6?

A strange decision. Why did Black leave the rooks on the board?! 79...♖xg6! is way stronger: 80.♖xg6 ♘xg6 81.♔b7 ♘e5 82.♗f1 ♔d6 83.b6 ♘d7= eliminating the last pawn.

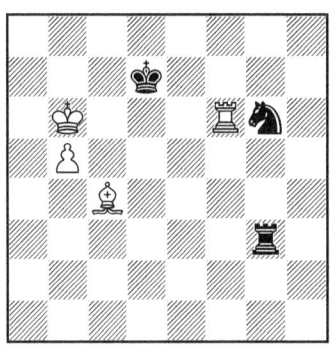

80.♗d5?

White returns the favor. 80.♗d3! ♘e7 was nearing a victory yet again. 80...♖xd3? fails to 81.♖xg6+.

Following 80...♘e5? 81.♗f5+ ♔d8 82.♖d6+ ♔e7 83.♖e6+ ♔d8 84.♖xe5 ♖e3 White will not fall into a stalemate trap with 85.♖c5+−.

The continuation 80...♘h4? 81.♗e4+− clearly highlights the difference between the power of two minor pieces.

81.♗f5+! Activity of the white pieces

makes it possible to harass the opponent's king even with limited material on the board. The degree of coordination that a rook and minor piece can generate manifests itself clearly in this position.

81...♔e8 (81...♔d8? 82.♖f8#; 81...♘xf5 82.♖xf5+− with a winning rook ending)

82.♗e4! Restricting the black knight to the maximum one more time. 82.♔b7? ♖b3 83.b6 ♘d5= is an error.

82...♔d7. Neither 82...♔d8 83.♖d6+ ♔e8 84.♔c7+− nor 82...♖g8 83.♔c7 ♖g7 84.♗c6+ ♘xc6+ 85.♔xc6+− is of any help.

83.♗c6+! ♘xc6 (83...♔d8 84.♖f8#) 84.bxc6+ ♔e7 (84...♔c8 85.♖f8#; 84...♔d8 85.c7+ ♔d7 86.♖f7+ ♔e6 87.c8=♕+ ♔xf7 88.♕c7++−) 85.♖h6. The premature 85.c7? ♖b3+= gives the win away.

85...♖b3+ 86.♔c7 with an easy victory.

80...♘e5 81.♗c6+?!

Yet another slip. White could still fight for a win with 81.♔c5! ♘d3+ (81...♔c7? 82.b6+ ♔d7 83.♖d6++−; 81...♖c3+? 82.♔d4 ♘g4 83.♖f7++−) 82.♔d4 ♔e7 (82...♘b4 83.♗e4! ♖b3 84.♔c4! ♖b2 85.♔c5) 83.♖e6+ ♔d7 84.♖h6 ♘f4 (84...♘b4 85.♗e6+ ♔c7 86.♗f5+−) 85.♗c6+ ♔c7 86.♗e4!

♖b3 87.♔c4 ♖b2 88.♔c5, and the cut off knight makes it extremely hard for Black to deal with the white passed pawn.

81...♔e7 82.♖h6 ♖b3 83.♔c7 ♘c4 84.♖h4 ♖c3 85.♖d4! ♘a3! 86.♖e4+

White does not blunder the fork 86.b6? ♘b5+−+.

86...♔f6 87.♔d6

Black equalizes following 87.b6 ♘b5+ 88.♔d7 (88.♔b7 ♘d6+) 88...♖d3+! 89.♗d5 ♘c3!.

87...♖d3+ 88.♔c5 ♖c3+ 89.♔b4 ♘xb5 90.♗xb5 ♖c7 and Black reached a draw in this endgame.

Example No. 62
P. Pultinevicius – M. Dziuba
Poland 2020

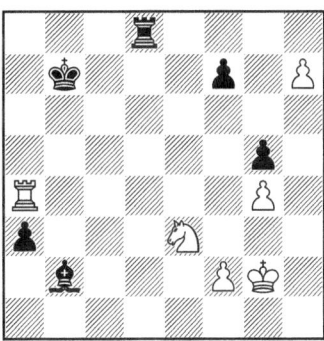

Black to move

Each side has a far-advanced passed pawn of its own. At the same time, these passed pawns are controlled by the opponent's pieces, which implies we might witness their mutual annihilation and a subsequent draw.

48...♖a8?

However, it was an error of judgement for black to believe that the bishop in this position is superior to the knight due to its capability of both controlling

the promotion square of the opponent's pawn and supporting his own passer.

An attempt to cut the knight off from the action runs into a refutation: 48...♖c8 49.♘c4 ♖xc4? 50.♖xc4 a2 51.♖b4+! ♔c6 52.♖xb2 a1=♕ 53.h8=♕+−.

Both 48...♔c6!? 49.♘c2 (49. ♘c4? ♔b5) 49...♖h8= and 48...♔b6!? 49.♘c2 ♔b5 50.♖a7 ♔b6 51.♖a4 (51. ♖xf7 a2=) 51...♔b5= result in drawn positions.

Alternatively, the sides could exchange off the pawns immediately with 48...♖h8 49.♘c4 ♖xh7=.

49.♖xa8 ♔xa8 50.♘c4!

This was a clearly overlooked resource. Neither the pawn nor the bishop have any freedom of movement now.

50...♔b7

50...a2 loses the game to 51.♘xb2 a1=♕ 52.h8=♕++−.

51.♔f3! White should not rush to grab the pawn with 51.♘xa3 ♔c6 52.♘c4 ♗h8 53.♔f3 ♔d5 54.♘e3+ ♔e5, and the h7-pawn is doomed.

51...♔c6

51...♔c7 52.♔e4! ♔d7 is a transposition to the lines analyzed below.

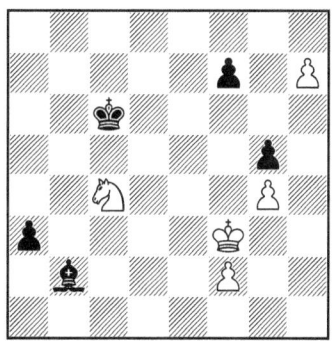

52.♘xb2!

The most precise move. In transposing from a pawn to a queen ending, White exploits the misplaced position of the black king.

52.♔e4!? ♔d7 53.♔f5 ♔e7 54.♘xa3 was winning, too (it was not too late to throw the game away with 54.♔xg5? ♗f6+ 55.♔f5 a2–+) 54...♔f8 55.♘c4 ♗d4 56.♔e4! ♗h8 (56...♗f6 57.♘d6 ♔g7 58.♘e8++– is bad) 57.♘e5 ♔g7 (57...f6 58.♘g6+ ♔g7 59.♘xh8 ♔xh8 60.♔f5+– also gives White a winning pawn ending) 58.♔f5 ♔f8 (white grabs the second pawn after 58...♔xh7 59.♘xf7) 59.♘f3 f6 60.♔g6+–.

52...axb2 53.h8=♕ b1=♕

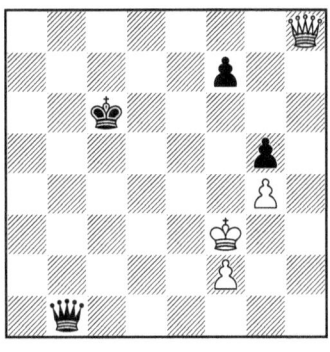

54.♕f6+!

White captures all his opponent's pawns with tempo.

54...♔d7

Both pawns also drop after 54...♔d5 55.♕xf7+ ♔e5 56.♕e7++– or 54...♔c5 55.♕xg5+ ♔d6 56.♕f6++–.

55.♕xf7+ ♔d6 56.♕f6+ ♔c7 57.♕e7+ ♔b8 58.♕d8+ ♔a7 59.♕xg5+–

This is a technically winning queen ending. White only needs to be precise in steering away from the black queen's checks and setting his extra pawns in motion.

59...♕h1+ 60.♔e2 ♔b7 61.♕g6 ♔c7 62.♕d3 ♔c8 63.♕d4 ♕h4 64.♔f3 ♕h3+ 65.♔f4 ♕h6+ 66.♔g3 ♕h1 67.g5 ♕g1+ 68.♔f4 ♕h2+ 69.♔f5 ♕h3+ 70.♕g4 ♕h8 71.♔g6+ ♔b8 72.♕f4+ ♔a8 73.♕e4+ ♔a7 74.♕e7+ ♔a8 75.♕f7 ♕d4 76.♕f8+ and Black resigned in the face of the inevitable exchange of queens.

Example No. 63
G. Kjartansson – R. Svane
Catez 2022

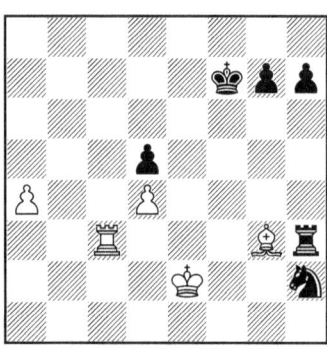

Black to move

Despite being a pawn up it is obviously Black who is fighting for a draw. His knight is stuck in the enemy rear, and the problem of fighting the white passed a-pawn is very much on the agenda.

37...h5?

To counter the opponent's passed pawn with his own one is an error of judgement from the German grandmaster.

To move its fellow pawn 37...g5?! was still dubious: 38.a5 (38.♗e1? ♖xc3 39.♗xc3 ♔e6 is wrong because the black king is in the square of the pawn: 40.a5 ♔d7 41.a6 ♔c6) 38...♖h6 39.♖c7+ (39.a6? ♖xa6 40.♗xh2 ♖a2+) 39...♔e8

40.♖b7 (40.♖a7 ♖e6+ 41.♔d3 ♘g4 42.♗e5 ♘f6 43.a6 ♘d7 44.♔c3 g4=)

a) 40...♔d8

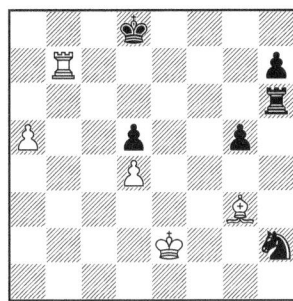

41.♖b5! Switching to attacking the weak black pawns. 41.♖g7?! ♖e6+ 42.♔f2 ♖f6+ 43.♔g2 ♘g4 44.♖xg5 ♘e3+= is dubious.

41...♖e6+ (41...♘g4?! 42.♖xd5+ ♔c8 43.♖xg5) 42.♔d3 ♘f3 (42...♘f1?! 43.♗e5 g4 44.♖b1; 42...♘g4 43.♖xd5+ ♔e7 44.♗c7 h6 45.♗d8+ ♔f7 46.♗b6 ♘f6 47.♖d8 ♔e7 48.♖h8±) 43.♖xd5+

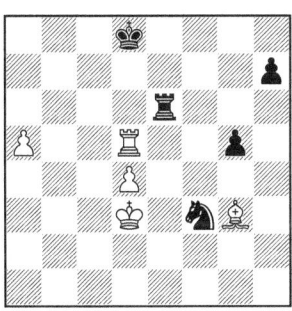

and Black is in dire straits. For example:

a1) 43...♔c8 44.♖f5 g4 45.♖f8+ (45.♖f7 h5!?; 45.d5 ♖a6 46.d6 ♔d7 47.♔c4) 45...♖b7 (45...♔d7 46.♖f7+!) 46.d5! ♖a6 (46...♖h6 47.♖f7+ ♔a6 48.d6+−; 46...♖e7 47.d6 ♖d7 48.♖e8! ♔c6 49.♖e7) 47.♖f7+ ♔c8 (47...♔a8 48.d6+−) 48.♖c7+ ♔d8 49.♖xh7+−;

a2) 43...♔e7 44.♖f5 g4 45.d5 ♖a6 46.♔c4 ♖xa5? 47.d6++−;

a3) 43...♔e8 44.♔c4 h5 45.♖f5 ♘d2+ 46.♔d3 ♘e4 47.♗e5+−;

b) It is bad to play both 40...♘g4? 41.♔f3;

c) and 40...g4 41.♖b6! ♖h3 42.♗d6 ♘f3 43.a6 ♘xd4+ 44.♔f2+−;

d) Meanwhile, White is winning in the case of 40...♖e6+ 41.♗e5 ♘g4 42.♖b6! ♔e7 43.a6 ♘xe5 44.dxe5+−.

To fight the white passed pawn it was worth the rook retreating immediately with 37...♖h6! 38.♖c7+

(In case of 38.a5 ♖e6+ 39.♖e3 [39.♔d3 ♘g4 40.♖c7+ ♔g6=] 39...♖c6 40.♖a3 [40.♗xh2 ♖c2+ 41.♔d1 ♖xh2 42.♖a3 ♖b2 43.a6 ♖b8 44.a7 ♖a8 45.♔c2 ♔e6 46.♔c3 ♔d6=] 40...♖e6+

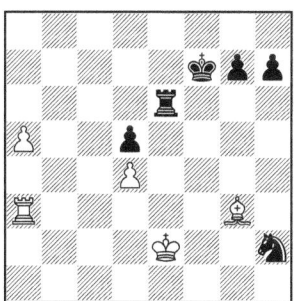

a) 41.♔d1 ♘g4 42.a6 ♘e3+ 43.♔c1 ♖c6+ 44.♔b1 ♘c4 45.♖a2 ♖c8 46.a7 ♖a8 47.♔c2 h5!?=;

b) 41.♔f2 ♘g4+ 42.♔f3 ♘f6 43.a6 ♖e8 44.a7 ♖a8=;

c) 41.♗e5 ♘g4= and Black maintains equality.)

38...♔f8 39.♗e5 (39.a5 ♖e6+ 40.♔d3 ♘g4= is harmless) 39...♖g6!

a) 40.a5 ♘g4 41.♗xg7+ (41.♖xg7? ♘xe5 42.♖xg6 ♘xg6 43.a6 ♘f4+ 44.♔f3 ♘e6 45.a7 ♘c7−+) 41...♔g8 (Of course, 41...♖xg7? is bad since the pawn queens after 42.♖xg7 ♔xg7 43.a6+−)

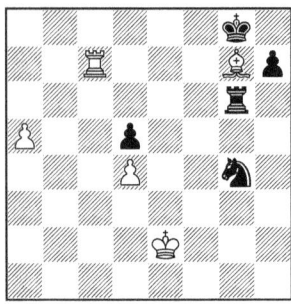

42.♔f3

(42.♗e5 ♘xe5 43.dxe5 h5 44.♖d7 h4 45.♖d6 ♖g2+ 46.♔f3 ♖a2= is harmless.

Active counterplay comes to Black's rescue in the case of 42.♖a7 h5 43.a6 h4 44.♗e5 ♘xe5 45.dxe5 [45.♖a8+ ♔g7 46.a7 ♖a6 47.dxe5 d4!] 45... h3 [45...d4=] 46.♖a8+ ♔h7 47.a7 h2 48.♖h8+ ♔xh8 49.a8=♕+ ♖g8! 50.♕xd5 ♖g1 51.♕d8+ ♔g7 52.♕e7+ ♔g8 53.♕e6+ ♔g7 54.♕f6+ ♔g8= and White has nothing better than perpetual check.)

42...h5   43.♔f4   ♖a6   (43...h4? 44.♔f5) 44.♔g5

44...♘f2! Rerouting the knight to the central outpost. 44...♖xa5? fails to 45.♔xh5 ♘f2 46.♔g6! ♖a8 47.♗f6

♘e4 48.♖g7+ ♔f8 49.♗e7+ ♔e8 50.♖g8++−.

45.♔xh5 (45.♗e5 ♔f8!? 46.♔xh5 ♖xa5 47.♔g6 ♔e8=) 45...♘e4. 45... ♖xa5? 46.♔g6 ♖a6+ 47.♗f6+− is bad again.

46.♗e5 (46.♔g4 ♖xa5 47.♔f5 ♖a6=) 46...♖xa5 47.♔g6 ♔f8 48.♔f5 ♔e8= and Black is out of the woods;

b) Black gets back the sacrificed piece in the case of 40.♗xh2 ♖g2+ 41.♔e3 ♖xh2=;

c) Neither does he have any problems following 40.♖xg7 ♖xg7 41.♗xg7+ ♔e8 42.♔e3 ♔d7 43.♔f4 ♘f1=;

d) Meanwhile, a draw becomes evident in the case of 40.♗xg7+ ♔g8! 41.♗e5 ♘g4 42.♗f4 ♖a6 43.♔f3 h5=.

Back to the starting position, it also looked good to free up the knight and vacate the h1-square for the black rook to reposition itself to the opposite flank in order to challenge his opponent's passed pawn:

37...♘g4!? 38.a5

(38.♖c7+   ♔g6   39.♔f3   ♘e3! yields nothing; following 38.♔f3 ♘f6 39.♖c7+

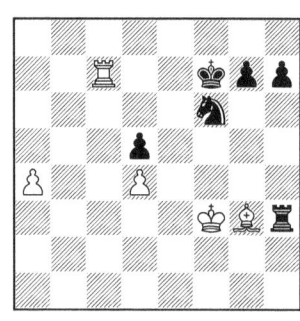

39...♔e8 [39...♔g6 40.♔g2 ♖h5 41.a5 ♘e4 42.♗e5 ♖g5+ 43.♔f3 ♖h5 44.♖xg7+ ♔f5 45.a6 ♖h3+ 46.♔e2 ♖a3 47.a7 ♘c3+ 48.♔d2 ♘b5=] 40.♔g2

♖h6 41.♖xg7 [41.a5 ♘d7!?] 41...♘h5 42.♖g5 ♘xg3 43.♔xg3 ♖a6=)

38...♖h1! 39.♖a3 ♖c1! 40.a6 ♖c8 41.a7 ♖a8

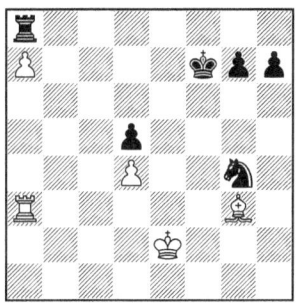

42.♔d3

(42.♗b8 h5 43.♔d3 h4 44.♔c3 ♘e3= is a transposition of moves back to the same 42.♔d3 line; 42.♔f3 ♘f6 43.♗e5 g5!? 44.♖a6 ♘d7 45.♔g4 ♘xe5+ 46.dxe5 d4 47.♔f5 [47.♔f3 h5 48.♔e4 h4 49.♔xd4 h3=; 47.♔xg5 d3 48.♔f5 d2=] 47...d3 48.♖a2 [48.♖h6 ♔g7!] 48...d2= is also harmless for Black)

42.g5!? 43.♔c3 (43.♖a6 h5 44.♗b8 ♘f6=; 43.♗b8 h5!?) 43...♘e3!? 44.♗b8 (44.♔b4? ♘c2+)

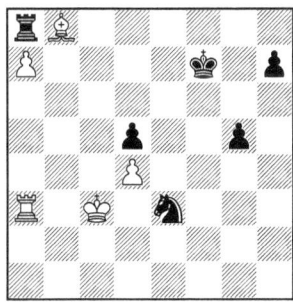

44...h5! Having stopped the white passed pawn, Black sets in motion his connected pair on the kingside.

45.♖a5 h4. 45...♔e6 46.♖a6+ ♔f5 47.♖h6 h4 48.♔b4 ♘g2 49.♔c5 ♘f4

50.♔c6 ♔g4 51.♔b7 ♖xa7+ 52.♔xa7 h3 53.♔b6 ♔g3 54.♔c5 h2= also leads to a draw.

46.♔d3 ♘g4!? 47.♖xd5 h3 48.♔e2 (48.♖f5+ ♔e6 49.♖f1 ♔d5=; 48.♖xg5 h2 49.♖h5 h1=♕ 50.♖xh1 ♘f2+ 51.♔c4 ♘xh1 52.♔d5 ♘f2 53.♔c6 ♔e7 54.♔b7 ♖xa7+=) 48...h2 49.♖f5+ ♔e6 (49...♘f6 50.♖f1 g4 51.♖a1 g3 52.♗xg3 h1=♕ 53.♖xh1 ♖xa7 54.♗e5 leaves White with some practical chances.)

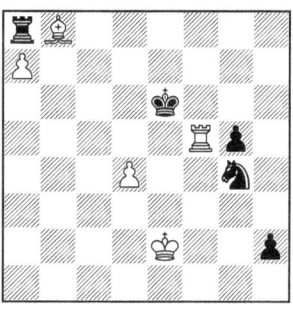

50.♖f1 ♘h6! 51.♖a1 (51.♖h1 ♘f5 52.♔d3 ♔d5 53.♖xh2 ♘xd4=; 51.♔f3 ♘f5=) 51...♘f5 52.♔d3 ♘d6 53.♖e1+. 53.♖h1 ♘b5 54.♖xh2 ♘xa7 55.♖h6+ ♔f5= leads to equality, too.

53...♔d5! 54.♖e5+ ♔c6 55.♖c5+ ♔d7 56.♖c7+ ♔e6 57.♖h7 ♘b5

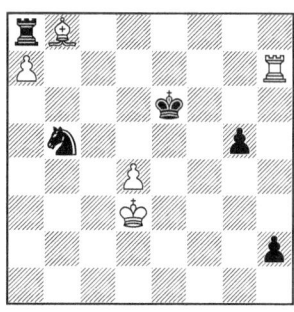

58.♔e4. Neither 58.♔c4 ♘xa7 59.d5+ ♔f5 60.♗xh2 ♘c8 61.♔c5

♖a5+= nor 58.♖xh2 ♘xa7= promise White any real winning chances.

58...♘d6+ 59.♔e3 ♘b5= and Black is fine.

38.a5! h4

38...♘g4 39.a6 ♖h1 40.♖a3+− is losing as well.

39.♗e1

39.a6? hxg3 40.a7 ♖h8! 41.♖xg3 ♖a8 42.♖g2 ♖xa7 43.♖xh2 ♖a2+−+ is bad of course.

39...♖xc3 40.♗xc3 h3 41.a6! ♘g4 42.♔f3!

Unlike his counterpart, the white king is in the square of the opponent's passed pawn.

Promotion of both pawns within one move plunges White into disaster 42.a7? h2 43.a8=♕ h1=♕ 44.♕b7+ ♔g6 45.♕a6+ ♔h5−+.

42...♘e3

42...h2 43.♔g2 ♘e3+ 44.♔xh2 ♘c4 45.♗a5!+− makes no difference either.

43.♔g3! ♘c4

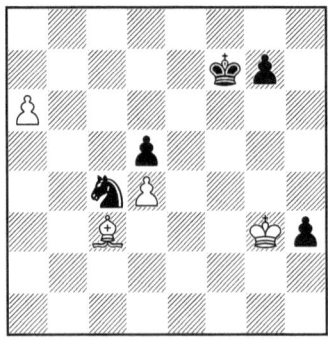

44.♗a5!

The last finesse. The white bishop, albeit by sacrificing itself, cuts off the squares from which the opponent's knight could catch up with the passed pawn. Black resigned without waiting for his opponent to queen his pawn.

Example No. 64
J. Song − R. Sadhwani
Reykjavik 2022

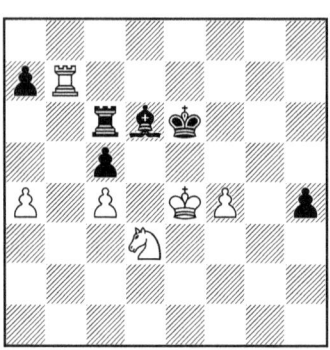

Black to move

White's pieces are considerably more active. Besides, Black has some issues with his king.

46...♖a6?

This natural move that defends a pawn and attacks his opponent's one turns out to be a blunder. It was correct to exchange off White's active rook even at the cost of a pawn: 46...♖c7! 47.♖xc7 (47.♖b8?! ♖h7 48.f5+ ♔f6∓) 47...♗xc7 48.♘xc5+ ♔d6

a) 49.♘d3 h3 50.♔f3 ♔e6 51.♔g3 (51.c5 ♔d5=) 51...♔f5! 52.♔xh3 ♗xf4 53.♔g2 (53.♘xf4 ♔xf4 54.c5 ♔e5=) 53...♔e4! 54.♘c5+ ♔d4 55.♘e6+ ♔xc4 56.♘xf4 ♔b4=, eliminating the only remaining white pawn;

b) 49.♘a6 ♗a5 50.♔f3 ♔c6 51.♔g4 ♔b6 52.♘b8 ♔c7 53.♘a6+ ♔b6= is a relatively easy draw;

c) in case of 49.♘b3 h3 50.♔f3 ♔e6 51.♘d4+ ♔f6 52.♘e2 (52.♘b5 ♗b8 53.♔g3 ♗xf4+! 54.♔xh3 a6 55.♘c3 ♔e5=) 52...♔f5 53.c5 ♔e6 54.♔g3 ♔d5= Black is in time to cope with the white pawns.

47.♖h7! ♖xa4

In winning the pawn, the black rook has departed from the theater of operations.

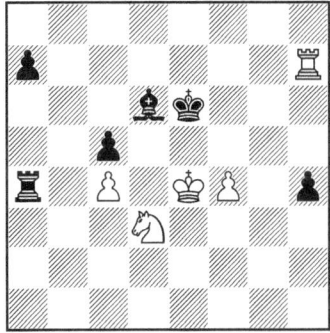

48.♖h6+?

A failure to prosecute his advantage. White overlooks his opponent's counterplay.

The winning move is 48.f5+! ♔f6 49.♖h6+ ♔e7 50.♖e6+! ♔d7 51.♔d5! ♗f8 (51...♗e7 52.♘e5+ ♔d8 53.♘c6++− is bad, too) 52.♘e5+ ♔d8 (52...♔c7 53.♖f6 ♗e7 54.♖f7 ♔d8 55.♘c6++− is also losing) 53.♘g6! ♗g7 (53...♗h6 54.♘xh4 ♗g5 55.♘f3 ♗e7 56.f6+−) 54.f6 ♗h6 55.♘xh4+−.

48...♔e7! 49.♔d5

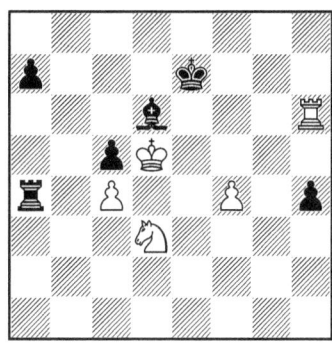

49...♖a3!

This is a dynamic saving resource. 49...♗b8? fails to 50.♖h7+ ♔f6 (50...♔d8 51.♘xc5+−) 51.♘e5 ♗xe5 52.fxe5+ ♔g6 (52...♔f5 53.e6+−) 53.♖xh4+− with a winning rook ending.

50.♘xc5

Throwing in a check is of no help for White: 50.♖e6+ ♔f8=.

50...♗xc5 51.♔xc5 h3 52.♔b4 ♖f3 53.♔b5 ♖b3+ 54.♔a4 ♖f3 55.♔b5 ♖b3+ 56.♔a4 ♖f3 57.♔b5 and White had to make do with a draw by repeating the position.

Example No. 65
S. Tiviakov − E. L'Ami
Netherlands 2020

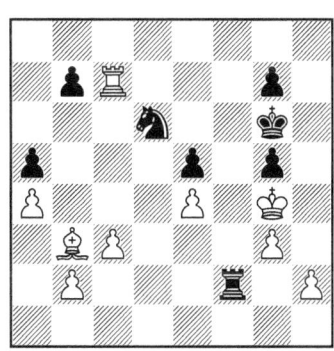

White to move

Despite his extra pawn and seemingly active pieces, it is White who has to be careful to hold this endgame. Numerous weak pawns and the vulnerable king necessitate coming up with exact moves in this position.

31.h4?

Appearing to solve the problem of the hanging h2-pawn and potentially providing more options for his king. However, this move is an error.

An attempt to defend the central pawn backfires with checkmate after 31.♗d5? ♘e8! 32.♖e7 ♘f6+ 33.♔h3 g4+ 34.♔h4 ♖xh2#.

It was correct to evacuate the king preemptively from the dangerous position with 31.♔h3! ♘xe4 (after 31... ♖xb2 32.♗d5 ♖e2 33.c4 ♘xe4 34.♗xb7 ♘f6 35.♗c8 the position is equal) 32.♖xb7 ♔f5. There is no snapping shut the mating trap with either 32... ♘f6 33.♗e6!? e4 34.g4 or 32...♔h5 33.♗e6±.

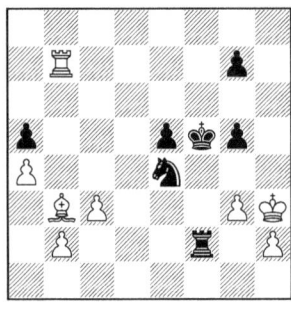

33.♗d1! (both 33.♖xg7? g4+ 34.♖xg4 ♘g5+ 35.♖xg5+ ♔xg5−+ and 33.g4+?! ♔f4 34.♖f7+ ♘f6 are bad) 33...♘f6 34.♖f7! (34.g4+?! ♔f4 35.♖xg7 e4; 34.♖xg7?! e4 35.♗f7 e3 36.g4+ ♔e4) 34...♔g6. White is fine following 34...♖xb2 35.♗g4+ ♔e4 36.♖xg7, while 34...e4 35.♗g4+ ♔g6 36.♖b7!? e3 37.b4!? ♖b2 38.♖e7 axb4 39.cxb4 ♖xb4 40.♗e2 g4+ 41.♔g2 ♘d5

42.♖e5 ♖b2 43.♔f1 ♖b1+ 44.♔g2 ♖b2 45.♔f1 results in a draw.

35.♖a7 ♔f5. 35...♖d2 36.♗g4 is harmless. White is also fine after 35... ♖xb2 36.♗g4!? ♘e4 37.♖a6+ ♔f7 38.♗h5+ ♔e7 39.♖xa5.

36.♖f7 ♔g6 37.♖a7 with an equal position.

White could also play 31.♗e6 ♘xe4 32.♖xb7 ♖f6, creating a double threat of capturing the bishop and delivering a knight checkmate from f2.

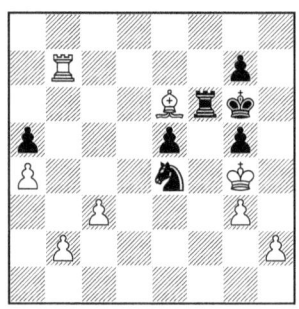

33.♗f5+!

This strong rejoinder throws a wrench in Black's plans: 33...♖xf5 34.♖xg7+! ♔f6 (34...♔xg7 35.♔xf5=) 35.♖f7+! ♔xf7 36.♔xf5 ♘c5. 36...♘f2 37.♔xg5= also leads to equality.

37.♔xg5. 37.b4? axb4 38.cxb4 e4! 39.bxc5 e3 40.c6 ♔e7−+ would be a blunder.

37...e4 (37...♘xa4 38.b4!=) 38.♔f4 ♘xa4 39.b4=, eliminating every remaining black pawn.

31...gxh4?

Black fails to exploit the opportunity presented by his opponent. The winning continuation is 31...♘e8! 32.h5+. White is checkmated after 32.♖xb7 ♘f6+ 33.♔h3 g4#; 32.♗f7+ ♖xf7 33.h5+ ♔f6 34.♖xf7+ ♔xf7 35.♔xg5 ♘d6 36.g4 ♘xe4+ 37.♔f5 ♘d6+ 38.♔xe5 ♘c4+−+ is also losing.

32...♔h6 33.♖f7 (the pawn capture is again followed by checkmate: 33.♖xb7 ♘f6+ 34.♔h3 g4+ 35.♔h4 ♖h2#) 33...♘f6+ 34.♖xf6+ gxf6−+ and Black converts his extra exchange.

32.gxh4 ♖xb2

Following 32...♘xe4 33.♖xb7 the pawn cannot be touched: 33...♖xb2? 34.♗f7++−.

33.♗d5

The position is also equal after 33.♖d7 ♘xe4 34.♖xb7=.

33...♖f2 34.c4 ♖f4+ 35.♔h3 ♘xe4 36.♗xb7 and the opponents agreed to a draw.

Example No. 66
E. Blomqvist – K. Lie
Norway 2020

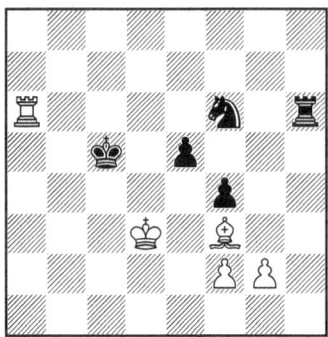

Black to move

Despite the equal material, Black has yet to address the problem of his weak e5 and f4 pawns. His pieces are pinned, and his king is cut off from coming to his pawns' rescue.

51...♘g8?

In an attempt to unpin Black chooses the wrong path, which clears the white king's way to his opponent's weak pawns.

There is no marking time with

51...♖g6? 52.♖e6 (or 52.♖c6+ ♔b5 53.♖e6+−) 52...♖h6 53.♖xe5+ ♔d6 54.♖f5+−, and Black drops both pawns.

The way to go is 51...♘g4! 52.♖a5+. The exchange of rooks leads to a drawn position: 52.♖xh6 ♘xh6 53.♔e4 ♔d6=. White gains nothing with 52.♖a2 ♘f6 53.♖c2+ ♔d6 54.♖c6+ ♔e7= and the black pieces have consolidated.

52...♔b6 53.♖a2 ♘f6 (53...♖g6?! 54.♔e4!) 54.♖c2! cutting the black king off.

(Alternatively, 54.♖e2 ♘d7 55.♗g4 [Black also equalizes after 55.♔e4 ♔c7 56.♗g4 ♘f6+ 57.♔f5 ♘xg4 58.♔xg4 ♔d6=] 55...♔c7!? [In order to save the game after 55...♘c5+ 56.♔c4 ♖g6 57.♗f5 ♖xg2 58.♖b2+ ♔c6 59.♖b5 ♖xf2 60.♖xc5+ ♔d6 61.♖d5+ ♔e7 62.♖xe5+ ♔f6, Black needs to show mastery of the rook vs. rook and bishop ending.]

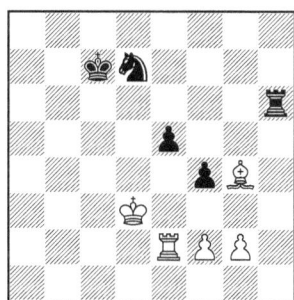

56.♗xd7. White has nothing to write home about after 56.♔e4 ♘f6+ 57.♔f5 ♘xg4 58.♔xg4 ♔d6=.

56...♔xd7 57.♖xe5 ♖g6 58.♔e4 ♖xg2 59.f3 ♖g8!? 60.♔xf4 ♖f8+!? 61.♔e4. A drawn position arises after 61.♖f5 ♖a8 62.♔g5 ♔e7=.

61...♔d6 62.f4 ♖a8 63.♔f5 ♖f8+ 64.♔g4 ♖g8+ 65.♖g5 ♖f8 with a drawn rook ending.)

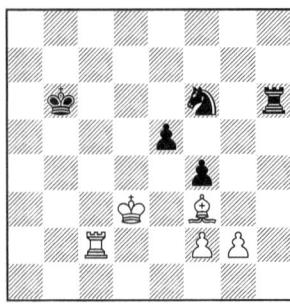

54...♘d7 55.♔e4. It is also a draw after 55.♗g4 ♘c5+ 56.♔c4 ♖d6!? 57.♖b2+ ♔c6 58.♗f3+ e4 59.♖b5 exf3 60.♖xc5+ ♔d7 61.gxf3 ♔e6=.

55...♖c6 56.♖d2. Neither does White win a pawn following 56.♖xc6+ ♔xc6 57.♗g4 ♘f6+! 58.♔f5 ♘xg4 59.♔xg4 ♔d6=.

56...♔c7 57.♗g4 ♘f6 58.♔f5 ♘xg4 59.♔xg4

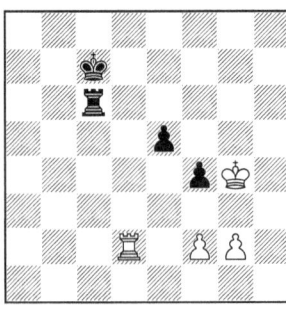

59...♖d6! Offering the exchange of rooks to activate the king and looking for a potential transition to a drawn pawn ending.

60.♖e2 ♖g6+!? (a draw also results after 60...♖d5 61.♔f5 ♔d6 62.♔f6 ♖a5=) 61.♔f5 (61.♔f3♔d6=) 61...♖xg2 62.♔xe5 f3 (following 62...♔d7 63.♔xf4 ♔d6 the rook ending is also drawn) 63.♖d2 ♖g8 64.♔e4 ♖f8 65.♖d3 ♔c6 66.♖xf3 ♖e8+ 67.♔f4 ♔d5!? 68.♖d3+ ♔c4 69.♖d2 ♖f8+

70.♔e3 (70.♔g5 ♔c3 71.♖a2 ♖g8+ 72.♔f6 ♖f8+ 73.♔g7 ♖f4= makes no difference to the evaluation) 70...♖e8+ 71.♔f3 ♖f8+ 72.♔g2 ♖g8+ 73.♔f1 ♖f8 74.♖d7 ♔c5= with a theoretically drawn endgame. The white rook cannot cut off the black king and help promote the white passed pawn at the same time.

52.♖a5+! ♔d6 53.♔e4 ♖h4

53...♖e6 54.♖d5+ ♔c7 55.♖xe5+− is bad, too.

53...♘f6+ fails to 54.♔f5 e4 (54...♘d7 55.♖a6++−) 55.♖a6+ ♔e7 56.♗xe4 ♖h5+ 57.♔g6 ♖e5 58.♖xf6 ♖xe4 59.♔g5+− with a hopeless rook ending.

54.♖d5+

54.♖a6+!? ♔e7 55.♔xe5 ♔f8 56.♖a4+− is also winning for White.

54...♔c7

54...♔e6 is no better than the text: 55.♖xe5+ ♔f6 56.♖f5+ ♔g6 57.♖xf4 ♘f6+ 58.♔e3+−, and White gets down to converting his extra two pawns.

55.♖xe5 ♘f6+ 56.♔f5 ♘d7 57.♖e6 ♔d8 58.♔g5 ♖h1 59.♔xf4+− and White went on to win.

Example No. 67
N. Salimova − A. Kozak
Catez 2022

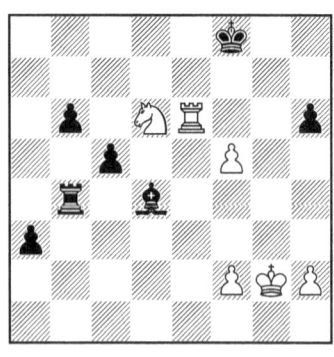

White to move

The black pawn is two squares away from queening. To give up the rook for this pawn is pointless for White. Therefore, it is worth looking for saving counterplay and hoping that her opponent is going to allow it.

45.f4!

In moving the pawn forward White takes control over the g5- and e5-squares, which the black king could use to escape from the checks.

White goes down after both 45.♖e8+ ♔g7 46.♖e7+ ♔f6 47.♖f7+ (47.♖a7 ♗b2–+) 47...♔e5–+ and 45.f6 ♗xf6 46.♖xf6+ ♔e7 47.♖xh6 ♖a4 48.♘c8+ (48.♘f5+ ♔f7 49.♘d6+ ♔f8–+ and the black passed pawn seals the game) 48...♔f7 49.♘xb6 ♖a6–+.

45...a2?

Having prematurely believed in his victory, Black does not exercise diligence. It was necessary to go for 45...♖b2+!

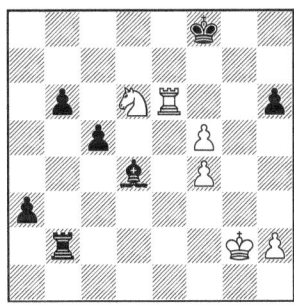

46.♔f3 (46.♔f1? a2 47.♖e8+ ♔g7 48.♖e7+ ♔g8 49.♖e8+ ♔h7 50.♖e7+ ♗g7–+ is bad) 46...♖b3+! 47.♔g4 (47.♔e2 ♖e3+!–+; 47.♔e4 ♖e3+–+) 47...♖e3! 48.♖xh6 ♗g7–+ and the triumphant march of the passed pawn should resume once Black takes care of his king's safety.

46.♖e8+ ♔g7 47.♖e7+ ♔g8

47...♔f6? 48.♖f7#.

48.♖e8+ ♔h7 49.♖e7+

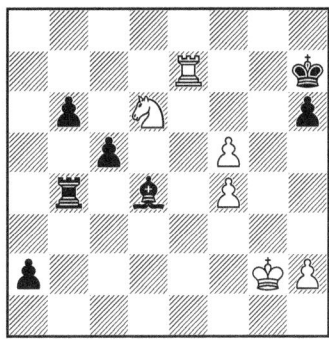

49...♔h8

And so Black has to make do with perpetual check.

Black must have initially calculated that he could use his bishop as a shield from checks. However, he later spotted his king getting checkmated after 49...♗g7? 50.f6 a1=♕ (50...♖b2+ 51.♔g3 ♖b3+ 52.♔g4+–; 50...♔g8 51.♖xg7+ ♔f8 52.♖a7+–; 50...♔g6 51.fxg7 ♔h7 52.♖a7+–) 51.♖xg7+ ♔h8 52.♘f7#.

50.♖e8+ ♔g7 51.♖e7+ and the opponents agreed peace.

Example No. 68
J. Pulpan – R. Kempinski
Czech Republic 2020

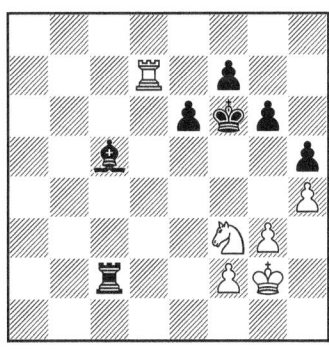

White to move

White is a pawn down and has a weak f2-pawn. However, all pawns are on the same flank, and, for example, if he can get the minor pieces off the board it will be a drawn four pawns vs. three rook ending, which should not be hard to defend. This is especially so given the best possible pawn arrangement that the defending side enjoys. At the same time, if the rooks are exchanged then this also brings substantial drawing chances. Note also the standard factor for this type of position when the promotion h1-square is not of the same color as the bishop. That may play into White's hands in terms of making a draw in some lines.

40.♖d2?

White misses a direct opportunity to equalize with active play: 40.♘g5! ♖xf2+ 41.♔h3 ♖c2. The position is also equal after 41...♔e5 42.♘xf7+ ♔f5 (42...♔e4 43.♘g5+) 43.♘d6+! ♔e5 (43...♗xd6 44.♖f7+) 44.♘f7+. White restores the material balance following 41...♖f5 42.♖xf7+ ♔e5 43.♖g7 ♖f6 44.♘h7=.

42.♖xf7+ ♔e5 43.♖c7. 43.♖g7 saves as well: 43...♗g1 44.g4 (44.♘f3+ ♔f6!) 44...♖c3+ 45.♔g2 ♗c5 (the position is level after 45...♗d4 46.gxh5 gxh5 47.♘f3+ ♔f6 48.♖g5) 46.♖xg6 hxg4 47.♖xe6+ ♔f5 48.♖f6+! ♔xf6 49.♘e4+=.

43...♔d5 (43...♔d6 44.♖g7=) 44.♖g7 e5 (44...♗g1 45.♘f3=) 45.♖xg6= and the position is equal.

40...♖xd2 41.♘xd2 ♔e5

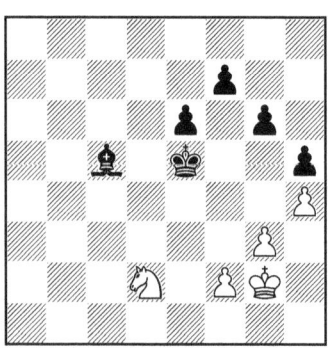

We have already highlighted that pawns on the same flank mean more chances for the defending side to hold ground.

42.♔f1?

White's handling of this ending is overly passive. 42.f4+! ♔d5 (42...♔d4? 43.♘f3+ ♔e3 44.♘e5) 43.♔f3 was stronger.

42...♗b4 43.♘c4+?

And incomprehensible dances begin again, this time with the knight, which drive it into a locked stable. 43.♘f3+ ♔d5 44.♔e2 was a better idea.

43...♔d4 44.♘e3 ♔d3 45.♘g2?

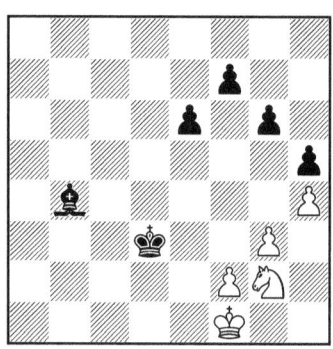

45...♗d2!−+

The knight is completely bereft of moves. Creating a passed pawn and zugzwang ideas ensure Black's victory.

46.f3

White is also lost after 46.♔g1 ♔e2 47.f4 ♔f3 48.♔h2 ♔g4−+.

46...e5 47.g4

Both 47.♔g1 ♔e2 48.f4 e4−+ and 47.♔f2 ♗c3 48.♔f1 ♗d4 49.♘e1+ (49.g4 ♔d2−+) 49...♔e3 50.♔g2 ♔d2 51.♔f1 f5 52.♘g2 ♗c5 53.♘e1 e4 54.fxe4 fxe4 55.♘g2 ♗d6 56.♔f2 ♗e5−+ are hopeless.

47...e4 and White resigned in the face of 48.fxe4 hxg4 49.e5 g3!.

Example No. 69
S. Bogner – E. L'Ami
Germany 2022

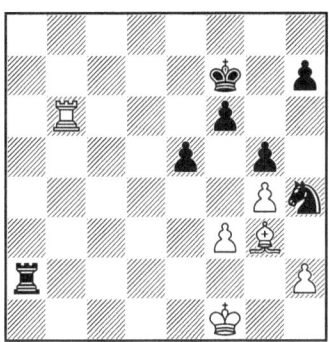

White to move

White is a pawn down, and his king is utterly misplaced. That said, all pawns are on the same flank. Besides, the white bishop can exchange itself for the opponent's knight, transposing into a rook ending known for its drawish tendencies.

52.♖b3?

This is a natural move that defends the pawn. The check 52.♖b7+?! ♔g6 only ends up improving the black king's position.

The immediate exchange of minor pieces looks unsatisfactory for White too: 52.♗xh4?! gxh4 53.♔g1 (53.h3 ♖h2!) 53...h3! 54.♖b3 ♖g2+ 55.♔h1 ♔g6 56.f4 exf4 57.♖xh3 ♖xg4.

It was necessary to take advantage of this particular moment to transpose into a rook ending with the desired pawn structure: 52.f4! exf4 (the black king runs into problems following the underwhelming 52...e4?! 53.♖b7+ ♔g6? 54.f5+ ♔h6 55.♗d6 ♖a8 56.♖f7) 53.♗xh4 gxh4 54.♖b4! ♖xh2 (54...♔g6 55.♖xf4 ♔g5 56.♖f5+!

♔xg4 57.♖xf6= is an easy draw) 55.♖xf4 ♔g6.

(It would be an error to go for the early 55...h3? 56.g5!=. An attempt to pass the turn brings no success: 55...♔g7 56.♖f5 ♔g6 57.♖h5 h3 58.♔g1 ♖g2+ 59.♔h1 [White also holds a draw in case of 59.♔f1 ♖xg4 60.♖xh3 ♖a4 61.♖b3 ♖a2 62.♖g3+!=]

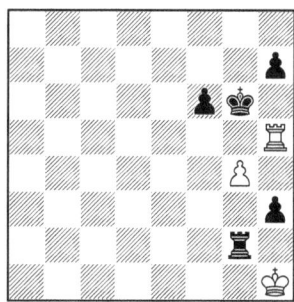

59...♖g3. It is a theoretical draw after 59...♖xg4 60.♖xh3 ♖a4 61.♖g3+ ♔f5 62.♖f3+ ♖f4 63.♖h3=.

60.♔h2 ♖a3 61.♖xh3! ♖xh3+ 62.♔xh3 ♔g5 [62...h5 63.♔h4! hxg4 64.♔xg4= does not work] 63.♔g3 h6 64.♔f3! [64.♔h3? h5−+] 64...♔h4 65.♔f4 ♔h3 66.♔f3= with a drawn pawn ending.)

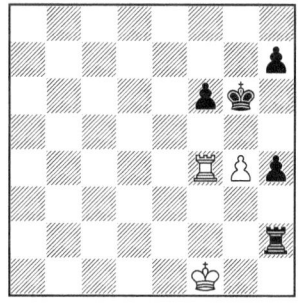

56.♖f5! Activating the rook.

56...h3 57.♖h5 h6. The essence of the position changes neither with 57...

♖g2 58.♖xh3 ♖xg4 59.♔f2=, nor with
57...♖h1+ 58.♔f2 h2 59.♔g2 ♖g1+
60.♔xh2 ♖xg4 61.♖a5=.

58.♔g1 ♖g2+ 59.♔h1 ♖xg4 (59...
♖g3 60.♔h2 ♖a3 61.♖xh3 ♖xh3+
62.♔xh3 ♔g5 63.♔g3=) 60.♖xh3=
and we reach a classical rook and h-
and f- pawns vs. rook ending that is a
draw with precise play from the weaker
side.

52...♔g6! 53.h3?!

Here the white pawn is also subject
to attack from the black pieces. Such
positions do not lend themselves to easy
defense. Therefore, White's committing
such inaccuracies should come as no
surprise.

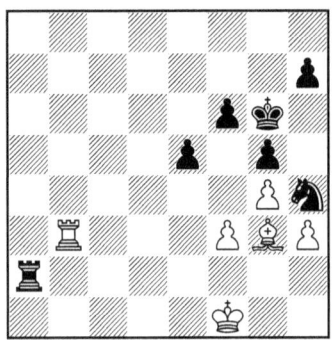

53...♘g2! 54.♔g1 White is also in
bad shape after 54.♖c3 ♘f4 55.♗xf4
gxf4 56.♔g1 (56.h4 h5−+) 56...
♔g5−+.

54...♘f4 55.♗xf4 gxf4! 56.h4
56.♖b8 ♔g5−+ fails on the spot.

In case of 56.♖b7 h6!? 57.h4 (57.
♖b8 ♔g5−+) 57...h5! 58.gxh5+ ♔xh5
59.♖h7+ ♔g6 60.♖h8 ♖a7! 61.h5+ (61.
♔g2 ♖h7 62.♖g8+ ♔f7 63.♖g4 ♖g7
64.h5 f5−+) 61...♔g7 62.♖b8 ♔h6!
63.♖h8+ (63.♖f8 ♔g5 64.h6 ♖h7−+)
63...♖h7 64.♖f8 ♔g5−+ the second
pawn falls and the game is over.

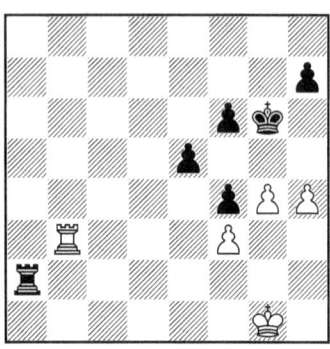

56...h5!

Chipping at the white pawn
formation in order to clear the way for
the decisive inroad of the black king into
the enemy camp.

57.g5

White is also lost after 57.gxh5+
♔xh5 58.♖b6 ♔xh4 59.♖xf6 ♔g3−+.

57.♖b6 hxg4 58.fxg4 e4 59.g5 ♖a1+
is of no help either.

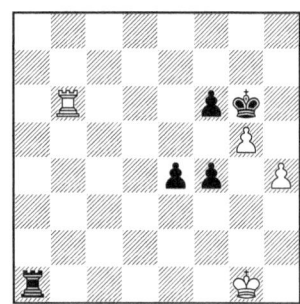

60.♔g2 (60.♔h2 e3 61.♖xf6+
♔h5 62.♔h3 [62.♖xf4 e2−+] 62...
♖h1+−+)

60...e3 61.♔f3 ♔h5 62.gxf6 (62.
♖xf6 ♖f1+ 63.♔e2 ♖f2+ 64.♔e1
♔g4! 65.g6 ♔f3−+) 62...♖f1+ 63.♔e2
♖f2+ 64.♔e1 ♔g6 65.h5+ ♔f7 66.h6
♖h2−+ and now that Black has coped
with White's passed pawns the turn has
come for the pair of black passers to
begin their triumphant march.

57...fxg5 58.♖b6+ ♔f5 59.♖h6

59.hxg5 ♔xg5 60.♖e6 ♖a5 61.♔g2 ♔h4−+ is hopeless as well.

59...g4

59...e4!? 60.fxe4+ ♔g4 61.hxg5 ♔g3! 62.♔f1 f3−+ was the alternative way to succeed.

60.♖xh5+ ♔e6 61.fxg4 e4! 62.♖h6+ ♔e5 63.g5

To throw in one more check 63.♖h5+ ♔d4−+ makes no sense.

63...e3 64.♖h8 f3 65.g6 ♖g2+ and White resigned.

Example No. 70
M. Vachier-Lagrave — V. Anand
Stavanger 2018

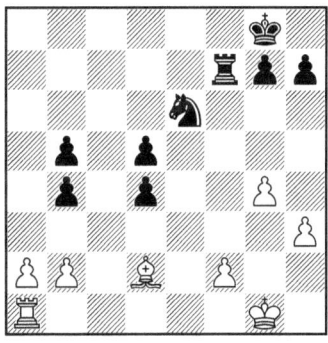

Black to move

Black is a pawn up, but with a pair of doubled pawns. Moreover, he is now facing issues with the b4-pawn. He wants to win. What should he play?

30...b3!

The pawn is doomed anyway. However, now Black creates an additional white weakness.

White recaptures the pawn in case of 30...♖f3?! 31.♗xb4 ♖xh3 (31... ♘f4 32.♗d6=) 32.♖e1 ♔f7 (32... ♘f4? 33.♖e8+ ♔f7 34.♖f8++−) 33.♖e5=.

The rook ending arising after 30... ♘f4 31.♗xf4 ♖xf4 32.♔f1= brings no real prospects.

31.axb3

31.a3? ♖c7−+ is utterly bad. 31.♔g2?! ♖a7 32.a3 ♖c7 33.♖c1 ♖xc1 34.♗xc1 ♘c5 35.♔f3 ♘d3−+ is also poor.

31...♖f3 32.b4

White gains nothing from the rook checks 32.♖a8+ ♔f7 33.♖a7+ ♔f6 34.h4 ♖xb3 35.♗c1 ♖b4−+.

White also loses after 32.♖a3 ♖xh3 33.b4 ♖xa3 34.bxa3 ♔f7 35.♔f1 g6 36.♔e2 (36.g5 d3−+; 36.f4 ♘g7 37.♔e2 h5 38.gxh5 gxh5−+) 36... h5−+.

White's position is totally grim after 32.♔g2 ♖xb3 33.♗c1 ♘c5−+.

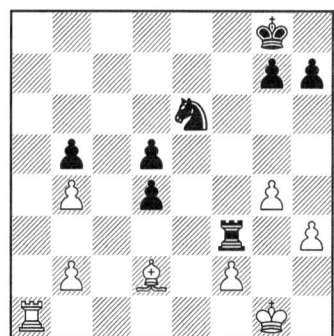

32...♖d3!

This attacking move aims at disorganizing White's defensive formations.

33.♖e1

33.♗c1? ♖d1+ 34.♔g2 d3−+ fails on the spot.

33...♔f7 34.♗c1

34.♖e2 ♖b3!? 35. ♗c1 (35.♗e1 ♘g5−+) 35...♖xb4−+ is as good as the text.

34...♖xh3 35.♖e5

Black is also winning subsequent to 35.♔g2 ♖b3 36.♖e5 ♖xb4 37.♖xd5 ♖c4 38.♗d2 ♖c2−+.

35...♖d3! 36.♔f1

White is also in trouble after 36.♔g2 ♖d1!? 37.♗g5 d3 38.♖xd5 (38.♖f5+ ♔g6 39.♗e3 d4−+; 38.♔f3 d4 39.♖xb5 ♘xg5+ 40.♖xg5 ♖e1−+) 38...♘xg5 39.♖xg5 ♔e6! 40.♔f3 (40.♖xg7 d2) 40...♖e1−+, and the black pawn is unstoppable.

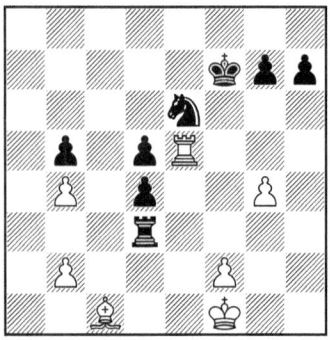

36...♖d1+!

Exchanging the rooks and transitioning into a technically winning minor-piece ending.

37.♖e1 ♖xe1+ 38.♔xe1 g6 39.f4

The creation of a second passed pawn after 39.♔e2 h5−+ is decisive. White is also doomed in case of 39.g5 d3 40.f4 (40.♗e3 d4 41.♗c1 ♔e7−+) 40...♘d4−+.

39...♘d8 40.g5

40.♔e2 h5 41.gxh5 gxh5 42.♔d3 (42. ♔f3 ♔f6−+) 42...h4−+ fails as well.

40...♔e6, and White resigned in the face of 41.♔e2 ♔f5 42.♔d3 ♘e6 43.♗d2 ♔g4! 44.♗c1 (44.b3 ♔f5!) 44... ♘xf4+ 45.♔xd4 ♘e2+.

The next part of this topic analyzes examples in which a rook and a minor

piece are fighting against a rook. There are cases where both sides have pawns and where the side a piece up has none. We will see that the side having the extra piece is not always in the driver's seat.

Example No. 71
J. Leon Valdes − C. Albornoz Cabrera
Mexico 2022

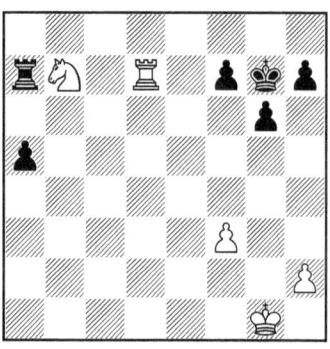

White to move

White is up a piece for two pawns, but he is facing problems with the pinned knight. Besides, the a-pawn is supported by the rook, which means that measures should be taken to confront its progress towards the queening square. White is fighting for a draw. Taking the right decision in this position requires correct evaluation of the aftermath of exchanging rooks.

33.♘c5?

And White is not up to the task.

The immediate 33.♖d5 ♖xb7 34.♖xa5 ♖b2! results in having the king cut off along the home rank.

Therefore, it was correct to play 33.♔g2!? a4 34.♖d4! a3. White holds the ending after 34...♖xb7 35.♖xa4=.

35.♘c5 a2 36.♘b3 ♖b7 37.♖a4 (37. ♖d2 ♖xb3 38.♖xa2 leads to the same line via transposition; 37.♘a1? ♖b1 38.♘c2 ♖b2−+ is an error as the white knight perishes and the pawn survives) 37...♖xb3 38.♖xa2= with a well-known drawn rook ending with three pawns vs. two on the same flank.

33...♖xd7 34.♘xd7 a4!

The nearer the passed pawn gets to the promotion square, the more it ties down the white knight guarding it.

35.♘c5 a3 36.♔f2

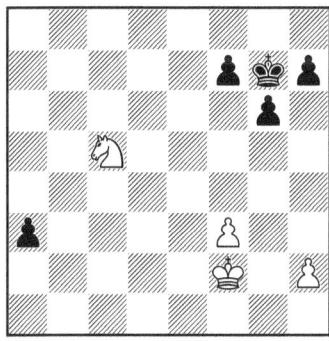

36...a2!

36...♔f6? 37.♘e4+! ♔e5 38.♘c3 ♔d4? 39.♘b5+ is premature.

37.♘b3 ♔f6! Black is winning. The a2-pawn is not just equal to the white knight, but even superior to it, because the latter is ill-suited to fighting rook pawns. When it comes to a pawn that has reached the penultimate rank, the knight will never cope with it alone if the black king comes to support its pawn. At the same time, Black has an extra pawn on the kingside and every opportunity to create yet another passed pawn.

38.♔e3

The black king battles through to the knight after 38.♔g3 ♔e5 39.♔f2 ♔d5 40.♔e2 ♔c4 41.♘a1 ♔c3 42.♔d1 ♔b2 43.♘c2 g5, and now White's defense

is overstretched by the opening of a second front via the creation of a passed pawn: 44.♔d2 f5 45.♔d3 h5 46.♔d2 g4 47.fxg4 fxg4 48.♔d3 h4−+.

38...♔f5 39.♘d4+

White uses the check to redeploy the knight.

39.f4 ♔g4−+ is bad.

There is no holding the position with 39.♔f2 ♔f4 40.♘a1 g5 41.♘c2 h6 (the careless 41...f5? fails to 42.♘b4! a1=♕ 43.♘d3#) 42.♘a1 h5 43.♘c2. In case of 43.h3 h4 44.♘c2 f6! 45.♘a1 f5 46.♘c2 g4 47.fxg4 fxg4 48.hxg4 ♔xg4 49.♔g2 h3+ 50.♔h2 (50.♔f2 ♔f4 51.♔g1 ♔f3−+) 50...♔f3 51.♔xh3 ♔e2 52.♔g2 ♔d2 53.♘a1 ♔c3 54.♔f2 ♔b2−+ the knight perishes and the black pawn queens.

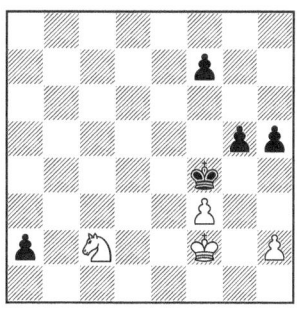

43...g4 44.fxg4. There is no marking time with 44.♘a1 gxf3 45.♘c2 ♔e4 46.♔f1 ♔e5 47.♔f2 ♔d6 48.♔xf3 ♔c5 49.♔e3 ♔c4 50.♔d2 ♔b3 51.♔c1 ♔c3 52.♘a1 f5−+, and Black again overstretches White's defense with his passed pawns on opposite flanks.

44...hxg4 45.♔g2 f5 46.♔f2 ♔e4 47.♔g3 ♔e5! (47...♔d3? blunders to the 48.♘b4+ fork) 48.♔h4 (48.♘a1 ♔d4−+; 48.♔f2 ♔d6 49.♔e3 ♔c5 50.♔d3 f4−+; 48.h3 gxh3 49.♔xh3 ♔d6 50.♔g3 ♔c5 51.♔f4 ♔c4 52.♔xf5

♔c3 53.♘a1 ♔b2−+) 48...♔f4 49.♔h5 (49.♘a1 ♔f3 50.♘c2 ♔g2−+) 49...♔f3 50.♔g5 f4−+ and one of the black pawns becomes a queen.

39...♔g5 40.♘c2 ♔h4! 41.♔f2 ♔h3 42.♔g1 g5 43.♘a1 f5 44.♘c2 f4 45.♘a1 h5 46.♘c2

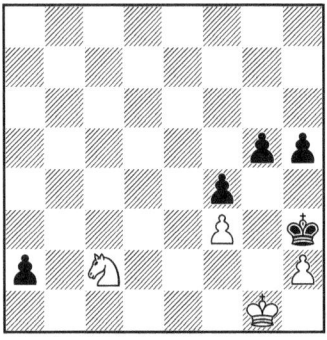

46...g4

Black has prepared everything to the max and creates yet another passed pawn with a decisive effect.

47.fxg4

In case of 47.♘a1 g3! (47...gxf3? 48.♘b3 f2+ 49.♔xf2 ♔xh2 50.♘a1! f3 [50...♔h3 51.♔f3!] 51.♘c2 h4 52.♘a1 h3 53.♘c2!= throws the win away) 48.hxg3 (48.♘c2 gxh2+ 49.♔h1 ♔g3−+) 48...♔xg3 49.♘c2 ♔xf3−+ White is also helpless.

47...hxg4 48.♘a1

48...f3!

The careless 48...g3? 49.hxg3 ♔xg3 (49...fxg3 50.♘c2 g2 51.♘a1 ♔g3 52.♘c2 ♔f3 53.♘a1 ♔e2 54.♔xg2 ♔d1 55.♔f2 ♔c1 56.♔e2 ♔b1 57.♔d2 ♔xa1 58.♔c2= also leads to a well-known draw) 50.♔f1 ♔f3 51.♘c2! ♔e4 52.♔e2 ♔d5 53.♘b4+!= would have missed the win.

49.♘c2 f2+! 50.♔xf2 ♔xh2 and the g-pawn cannot be stopped. Therefore, White resigned.

Example No. 72
M. Richter − G. Kamsky
Germany 2022

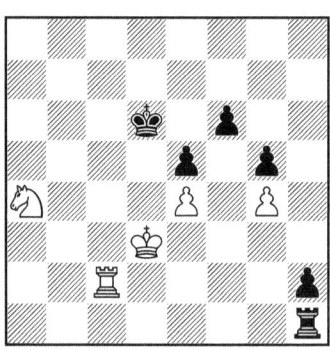

White to move

Despite being a piece up, it is White who needs to come up with precise play not to go down in this endgame. Black's passer is one square away from queening, and the supporting rook is geared up to make room for its pawn with a check or attack.

61.♔c3?

This is an ill-advised decision. 61.♔c4? is also bad due to 61...♖a1! 62.♖d2+ ♔e7 63.♖xh2 ♖xa4+ 64.♔d3 (64.♔d5 ♖d4+−+ is no better) 64...♖a3+! 65.♔c4 (65.♔e2 ♖a2+−+) 65...♖e3 66.♔d5 ♖d3+ 67.♔c5 ♔e6

68.♖g2 (68.♖e2 ♖c3+ 69.♔b4 ♖g3−+)
68...♖c3+ 69.♔b5 ♖e3−+ winning the
second pawn.

It was better for White to shield
himself from a potential rook check in
such a way that the white king gets closer
to his pawns: 61.♖d2! ♖a1 62.♔e3+!
♔e7 63.♖xh2

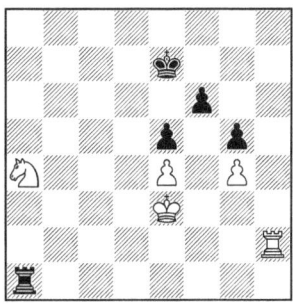

63...♖xa4. 63...♖a3+ makes no
difference: 64.♔f2! ♖xa4 (64...♖a2+
65.♔g3 ♖xa4 66.♖h7+! ♔d6 67.♔f3
♖a1 68.♔f2!=) 65.♖h7+! (65.♔f3?
♖a3+ 66.♔f2 ♖a2+−+) 65...♔d6 (65...
♔e6 66.♔f3 ♖a1 67.♔f2!=) 66.♔f3
♖a1 (66...♖a3+ 67.♔f2! ♔c5 68.♖f7
♔d4 69.♖xf6 ♔xe4 70.♖f5=) 67.♔f2!
♖a3 68.♖f7 ♔e6 69.♖b7= with an easy
draw in this rook ending.

64.♖h7+!? ♔e6 (64...♔d6 65.♖f7
♔c5 66.♖xf6 ♖a3+ 67.♔f2 ♔d4
68.♖f5 ♔xe4 69.♖xg5=) 65.♖b7 ♖a3+
(65...♖a1 66.♔f2!) 66.♔f2 ♖a4 67.♔f3
♖a1 68.♔f2!= and the white king can
take care of his own pawns and restrict
the black rook all by himself.

61.♘c3 ♖d1+ 62.♘xd1 h1=♕
63.♘e3 looked interesting. At first
glance the position seems drawn. The
black king is kept at bay by the white
pieces and cannot break through to the
action for now, and such a structure
renders the extra pawn of little value.

Further, the white pieces are well-
coordinated. The only real opportunity
for Black to play for a win involves
finding an opportune moment to break
through with f5 so as to create a passer
or deflect the white knight and then
immediately pile up on the unprotected
white g4-pawn. However, the way to
implement this is not entirely clear.

For example, 63...♕a1 (63...♕f3
64.♖c1!?) 64.♖c4 ♔d7 65.♖c3!? ♕b1+
(65...f5 66.exf5 e4+ 67.♔d4!) 66.♖c2
♔d8 (66...♕b4 67.♖c4!) 67.♔e2
♕b4 68.♖c4 (68.♔d3? ♕d4+) 68...
♕b3 69.♔d2 ♕b2+ (69...f5 70.exf5!)
70.♔d3! ♔d7

71.♘d5!? Here, White has no
shortage of spare moves, which
safeguards him from his opponent's
pawn break in the least favorable
situation.

71...♔d6 (71...♕b1+ 72.♔d2 ♕f1
73.♘e3 is also harmless) 72.♘e3!
(There is no capturing the pawn:
72.♘xf6? ♕b3+ 73.♖c3 ♕d1+
74.♔c4 ♕a4+ 75.♔d3 ♕d4+ 76.♔c2
♕f2+−+ and the knight falls.) 72...
♕b1+ 73.♔d2 and it is unclear how to
go about undermining White's defensive
ramparts.

61.♘b2 ♖d1+ 62.♘xd1 h1=♕
63.♘e3 serves the same purpose and

transposes to the lines reviewed earlier after 61.♘c3.

61...♖a1! 62.♖d2+

In case of 62.♖xh2 ♖xa4 63.♖e2 (63.♔d3 ♖a3+ 64.♔c4 ♖e3−+) 63...♖a3+ 64.♔c4 ♔e6!? 65.♖e1 ♖g3−+ yet another white pawn falls.

62...♔e7

62...♔e6? fails to 63.♘c5+.

62...♔c6 63.♖xh2 ♖xa4 64.♔d3 (64.♖h6 ♖xe4 65.♖xf6+ ♔d5−+) 64...♖a3+ 65.♔c4 (65.♔e2 ♖a2+−+) 65...♖e3−+ was also a winner.

63.♖xh2 ♖xa4 64.♖h7+

Both 64.♔d3 ♖a3+−+ and 64.♖e2 ♖a3+ 65.♔c4 ♔e6!?−+ lose the game.

64...♔e6 65.♔d3 ♖a3+

Black could also succeed via 65...♖a1 66.♔e2 ♖g1 67.♔f3 ♖f1+! 68.♔g3 (68.♔e3 ♖f4−+) 68...♖f4−+, and the white pawn is doomed.

66.♔e2 ♖g3 and White threw in the towel.

The following example demonstrates how easy it is to blow winning chances with sloppy play.

Example No. 73
D. Kadric − T. Injac
Catez 2022

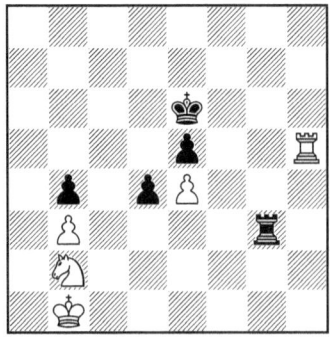

White to move

Black has only a pawn for a piece. At first glance, any continuation seems winning for White. This was probably White's mindset during the game as well.

36.♘c4? The Bosnian grandmaster was of the mistaken opinion that the only remaining pawn would suffice to secure him a win.

White could have tried 36.♔c2!? ♖c3+. 36...♖e3? fails to 37.♘d3! ♖xe4 (37...♖e2+ 38.♔d1+−) 38.♘c5++−, and in case of 36...♖g2+ 37.♔c1 ♖g1+ (37...♖g3 38.♘c4 ♖xb3 39.♖xe5+ ♔f6 40.♖f5+ ♔e6 41.♘d2+−) 38.♘d1 ♖g2 (38...♖g3 39.♔c2 ♖g2+ 40.♔d3 ♖g3+ 41.♔c4+−) 39.♖h6+ ♔e7 40.♖b6 ♖e2 (40...♖g4 41.♘f2+−) 41.♘b2 ♖xe4 42.♘c4 ♖e1+ 43.♔d2 ♖b1 44.♔c2!? ♖e1 45.♔d3! ♖b1 46.♖xb4+− the black pawns will gradually perish.

37.♔d2 ♖xb3 (37...♖e3 38.♘d3 ♖xe4 39.♘c5++−) 38.♘d3+− with an easy win.

36.♔a2!? ♖e3 37.♖h6+ ♔e7 38.♖b6 ♖xe4 (38...d3 39.♖xb4 d2 40.♖b5 ♖xe4 41.♔b1 ♖d4 42.♔c2 e4 43.♖c5 ♔d6 44.♖c4+−) 39.♖xb4 ♖e2 (39...♔d6 40.♔a3 ♖e1 41.♖b8+−; 39...♔e6 40.♘c4+−) 40.♔a3 ♖e1 (40...♔e6 41.♖b6+ ♔d5 42.♘c4 e4 43.♔b4 e3 44.♖d6+ ♔e4 45.♔c5 d3 46.♖d4++−) 41.♖c4 ♔e6 (41...♖a1+ 42.♔b4+−) 42.b4!+− also looked good, and the combination of ardent struggle against black pawns and promotion of his own passer should guarantee White success.

36...♖xb3+ 37.♔a2

White has to dispatch his king to the rim of the board. 37.♔c2? fails to 37...♖c3+.

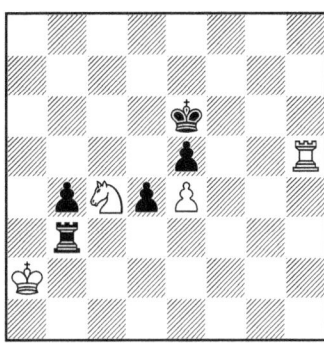

37...♖c3!

However, it turns out that Black develops sufficient counterplay to ensure a draw. This entails both the attack on the e4-pawn and the timely advance of his passed pawns.

38.♖xe5+

38.♘xe5 ♖c5!= renders the position drawn at once.

Meanwhile, in case of 38.♖h6+ ♔e7 39.♘b6 (nor does White get the upper hand with 39.♘xe5 d3 40.♖h2 ♔e6 41.♘f3 ♖c2+! 42.♖xc2 dxc2 43.♔b2 b3 44.♘d2 ♔e5 45.♔c1 ♔d4=) 39...♖c1!? 40.♔b2 ♖e1 41.♖h4 (41.♘d5+ ♔f7 42.♖h4 d3!=) 41...♔f6 42.♖g4 (42.♘c4 ♔g5=) 42...d3 43.♘c4 ♔e7!? it is unclear how White is supposed to untangle and coordinate his pieces properly:

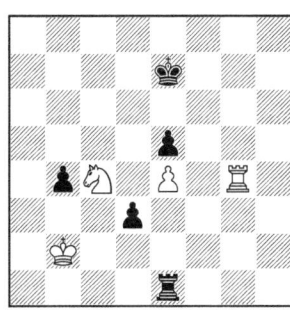

44.♔b3 (44.♘d2 ♖e2 45.♔c1 ♖e1+ 46.♔b2 ♖e2=; 44.♖h4 ♔f6=) 44...

♖b1+ 45.♔a4 b3 46.♔b4 (46.♖g7+ ♔f6 47.♖b7 ♔g5 48.♖xb3 ♖a1+! 49.♔b5 ♔f4 50.♖xd3 ♔xe4=; 46.♖g5 b2 47.♔b3 d2 48.♖xe5+ ♔f6 49.♖f5+ ♔e6 50.♘xd2 ♖d1=) 46...b2 47.♖g2 ♖e1= and Black eliminates White's only remaining pawn.

38...♔f6! 39.♖c5

A drawn position also arises after 39.♖f5+ ♔e6 40.♘b6 (40.♖c5 d3!? 41.♔b1 ♖c2 42.♖e5+ ♔f6 43.♖f5+ ♔e6 44.♘b2 ♖e2=) 40...♖e3=.

39...d3

39...♔g7!? was also fine: 40.♖c7+ (40.e5 d3!=; 40.♔b2 d3=) 40...♔f6 41.e5+ ♔e6=.

40.♖f5+

The alternative check 40.e5+ ♔e6= is as good as the text.

40...♔e6 and White had to make do with a draw without even waiting for 41.♘b2 d2 42.♖d5 ♖a3+ 43.♔b1 ♖e3 44.♖d4 ♔e5=.

Example No. 74
D. Dubov – N. Grandelius
Wijk aan Zee 2022

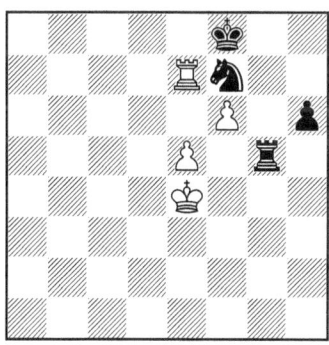

White to move

White is a piece down. That said, he has a pair of far-advanced pawns and an active rook, allowing him to fight for a draw. Besides, Black is down to only one pawn, whose elimination could bring White to a drawn rook and knight vs. rook ending.

76.♔f4?

This is an erroneous decision. 76.♔d5? also fails, to 76...♖f5! 77.♔e4 (77.♔e6? ♖xe5+ 78.♔d7 h5−+) 77...♖f1, and Black deals with the white pawns:

a) 78.e6 ♘d6+ 79.♔e5 (79.♔d5 ♘e8 80.♖f7+ ♔g8 81.♔e5 ♖e1+ 82.♔d5 h5−+) 79...♘c4+ 80.♔d5 (80. ♔d4 ♖f4+ 81.♔c5 ♖xf6 82.♖h7 ♘e3 83.♔d6 ♔g8 84.♖a7 ♖f1−+) 80... ♘e3+ 81.♔e4 (81.♔e5 ♘g4+ 82.♔d6 ♘xf6 83.♖f7+ ♔e8 84.♖e7+ ♔d8 85.♖a7 ♘e4+ 86.♔e5 ♘g5−+) 81... ♖xf6! 82.♖f7+ ♖xf7 83.exf7 ♘c2−+;

b) 78.♖a7 ♘g5+! 79.♔d5 h5 80.♖a8+ ♔f7 81.♖h8 ♖h1−+;

c) 78.♔d5 ♘g5 79.♖g7 ♖d1+ 80.♔c4 ♖e1 81.♔d5 ♘f7 82.e6 ♖e5+−+.

76.e6! is best: 76...♘d6+ (76...♘d8 77.♖h7 ♘xe6 78.♖xh6=) 77.♔d3! (77. ♔f4? ♘f5+−+; 77.♔d4? ♘f5+−+; 77.♔e3? ♘f5+−+) 77...♖g3+ (77... ♖g6 78.♖d7 ♘e8 79.f7=; 77...♖d5+ 78.♔c2! ♘f5 79.♖h7 ♘d4+ 80.♔c3 ♘xe6 81.♖xh6=)

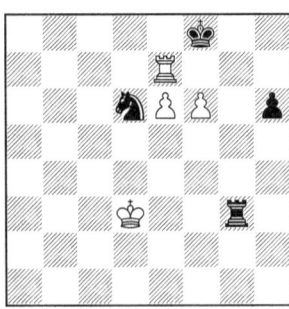

78.♔c2! This way only! Both 78.♔e2? ♖g6 79.♖d7 ♘e8 80.f7 ♖xe6+−+ and 78.♔d4? ♘f5+−+ are bad.

78...♖e3 (78...♘f5? 79.♖d7+−; 78... ♘e8 79.♖h7=; 78...♖f3 79.♖d7 ♘e8 80.f7 ♘g7 81.e7+ ♔xf7 82.e8=♕+ ♔xe8 83.♖xg7=) 79.♖h7 ♖xe6 (79... ♔g8 80.f7+ ♘xf7 81.exf7+ ♔f8 82.♖xh6 ♔xf7=) 80.♖xh6= with a drawn endgame.

76...♘h8! 77.♔e4 ♘g6 78.♖h7

Neither 78.♖e6 ♔f7 79.♔d5 ♘f4+−+ nor 78.♖g7 ♖xe5+ 79.♔d4 ♖g5−+ help any longer.

78...♖xe5+ 79.♔d4 h5 80.♖g7

80.♖h6 ♖g5!−+ makes no difference either.

80...♖g5 81.♖h7 ♘e5 82.♖g7

White also fails after 82.♔e4 ♘f7 83.♔f4 ♔g8 84.♖xf7 ♖g4+!−+.

82...♘f7 and White resigned.

Example No. 75
J. Santos Latasa − B. Gledura
Catez 2021

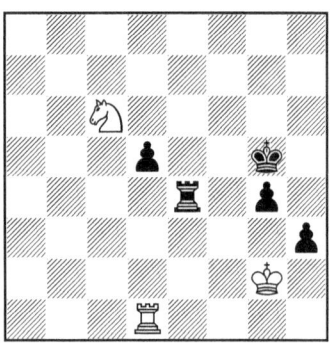

White to move

Black has three pawns for the knight. Not only do the connected passed pawns on the kingside seek to become queens, but they also create dangerous threats to the white king as well. White needs precise play to avoid the worst.

51.♔f1?

A wrong decision. The king is misplaced here.

51.♔g3? also fails to 51...♖e3+ 52.♔f2 ♖c3! 53.♖xd5+ (53.♘d4 g3+ 54.♔g1 ♔g4−+) 53...♔h4−+ and White has nothing to say to the advance of the black passed pawns: 54.♘e5 (54.♘d4 g3+ 55.♔f1 ♔g4 56.♘e2 ♖f3+ 57.♔e1 h2−+; 54.♘e7 g3+ 55.♔e2 g2−+) 54...g3+ 55.♔e2 h2 56.♘g6+ (56.♖d1 g2−+) 56...♔g4 57.♘e5+ ♔h3−+.

Likewise, 51.♔f2? loses to 51...♔h4! 52.♖xd5 (52.♘d4 ♖f4+! 53.♔e3 ♖xd4! 54.♖xd4 h2 55.♖d1 g3 56.♔f3 ♔h3 57.♖a1 d4! 58.♖b1 d3 59.♖a1 d2 60.♖b1 g2−+) 52...g3+ 53.♔f3 (53.♔g1 ♖e1#) 53...h2 54.♖d1 ♖e6! 55.♘d4 ♖f6+ 56.♔g2 (56.♔e3 g2−+) 56...♖f2+ 57.♔h1 ♔h3−+ and the white king has walked into a deadly trap.

White can draw with both 51.♔g1! ♔f4

(A draw results both after 51...g3 52.♖xd5+ ♔h4 53.♖d4=,

and after 51...♖c4 52.♘e5 ♖a4 53.♖xd5 g3 54.♘f3+ ♔f6 [54...♔f4 55.♖d4+=] 55.♖d1=;

In case of 51...♔h4 52.♘d4 ♖e5 [52...g3 53.♘f5+ ♔g4 54.♘xg3! ♔xg3 55.♖d3+! ♔h4 56.♖xd5; 52...♔g3 53.♘f5+ ♔f4 54.♖xd5 ♖e1+ 55.♔h2 ♖e2+ 56.♔g1] 53.♘c6!? [53.♖f1=] 53...♖e2 [53...♖f5 54.♘e7=] 54.♘b4 g3 55.♘xd5 h2+ 56.♔h1= the knight is poised to deliver a fork and thus prevents Black from snapping the mating trap shut.)

52.♖xd5 ♖e1+ 53.♔h2 (53.♔f2? h2−+) 53...♖e2+ (53...g3+ 54.♔xh3 ♖e2 55.♖d4+ ♔f3 56.♖d3+=) 54.♔h1 (54.♔g1? h2+ 55.♔h1 g3 56.♖d1 ♔g4−+) 54...g3 (54...♔g3 55.♖d1=) 55.♖d1 ♔g4 56.♘b4 h2 57.♘d5=.

And with 51.♔h1! ♔h4 (51...♔f4 52.♖xd5!; 51...g3 52.♖xd5+! ♔f6 53.♖d6+ ♔f5 54.♖d5+ ♔e6 55.♖d1=) 52.♘d4!= ♔g3 (52...g3 53.♘f5+ ♔g4 54.♘xg3 ♔xg3 55.♖d3+!=) 53.♘f5+ ♔f4 54.♖xd5 ♖e1+ 55.♔h2 ♖e2+ 56.♔h1, and White is out of the woods.

51...♔h4!−+ 52.♘d4

White also loses with 52.♖xd5 h2 53.♔g2 ♖e2+ 54.♔h1 g3 55.♖e5 (55.♖d1 ♔h3−+; 55.♖d4+ ♔h3−+) 55...♖xe5 56.♘xe5 ♔h3−+. Meanwhile, in case of 52.♔g1 g3 53.♖d4 (53.♖xd5 ♖e1#; 53.♘d4 ♔g4−+)

the winning move is 53...♔g4!

a) 54.♖xe4+ dxe4 55.♘d4 (55.♘e5+ ♔f4 56.♘g6+ ♔g5 57.♘e5 e3−+) 55...e3 56.♔h1 ♔f4 57.♔g1 ♔e4 58.♘e2 g2! 59.♔h2 ♔d3 60.♘f4+ ♔c2! (60...♔d2? 61.♘xh3 e2 62.♘g1!=; 60...♔c4? 61.♘e2!), and White cannot cope with the black passed pawns: 61.♔g1 (61.♘xh3 e2−+; 61.♘e2 ♔d2−+) 61...♔d2 62.♘xh3 e2−+;

b) 54.♔h1 ♔f3 55.♖d3+ ♔f2 56.♖d2+ ♔f1 57.♖d1+ ♖e1 58.♖xe1+

♔xe1 59.♘e5 ♔f2 60.♘g4+ ♔e2 61.♔g1 d4–+;

c) 54.♔f1 ♔f3 55.♖d3+ ♔f4 56.♘d4 g2+ 57.♔f2 ♖e1–+;

d) 54.♘e5+ ♔f4 55.♘g6+ ♔f3 56.♖d1 d4–+.

52...g3! 53.♔g1

There is no stopping the black pawn after 53.♘f5+ ♔g4 54.♘xg3 (54.♘h6+ ♔h5 55.♘g8 ♔h4 56.♘h6 ♖f4+ 57.♔g1 h2+ 58.♔g2 ♖f2+ 59.♔h1 ♔h3–+) 54...♖f4+! (54...♔xg3? 55.♖d3+!=) 55.♔e2 (55.♔g1 ♔xg3 56.♖d3+ ♔f3 57.♖xd5 h2+ 58.♔h1 ♖f1#) 55...♔xg3 56.♖xd5 h2–+.

53...♔g4 54.♔h1 ♖e3

54...h2!? 55.♔g2 ♖f4 56.♘e6 (56. ♖d2 ♖f1–+) 56...♖f2+ 57.♔h1 would have been a transposition to 54...♖e3.

55.♔g1

55.♘c2 ♖b3 56.♘d4 (56.♖xd5 ♖b1+–+; 56.♖d4+ ♔f3 57.♘e1+ ♔e2–+) 56...♖b2–+ is also bad.

55...♔f4

Without committing to any pawn structure as yet, Black is seeking to figure out the right sequence of moves.

56.♔f1 ♔e5 57.♔g1 ♔f4 58.♔f1

58.♖f1+ ♔g5 59.♘f5 ♖c3!?–+ is not going to make life any easier.

58...♔g4 59.♔g1 ♖e5 60.♔f1 ♖e4 61.♔g1

61...h2+!?

Settling on the winning plan, at last.

62.♔g2

62.♔h1? ♔h3–+ is bad.

62...♖f4 63.♘e6 ♖f2+ 64.♔h1 ♖f6

64...g2+? blunders to 65.♔xh2 ♖f1 66.♖d4+!. 64...♖e2 was winning as well: 65.♘g5 (65.♖d4+ ♔f3 66.♘g5+ ♔e3 67.♖d1 d4–+) 65...♖e5 (65...♔xg5? fails to 66.♖xd5+ ♔g4 67.♖g5+!=, with a furious rook) 66.♘f7 ♔h3 67.♘xe5 g2#.

65.♖e1

There is no saving the day with 65.♖d4+ ♔f3 (65...♔h3? 66.♘g5#) 66.♖d3+ (66.♘g5+ ♔e2–+) 66...♔e2 67.♖xg3 ♖xe6 68.♔xh2 d4–+ with a winning rook ending.

65...♖f5 66.♔g2

Yet another pawn checkmate results after 66.♘d4 ♔h3 67.♘xf5 g2#.

66...♖f2+ 67.♔h1 g2+ 68.♔xh2 ♖f1 and White resigned.

Example No. 76
A. Belozerov – I. Duzhakov
Sochi 2017

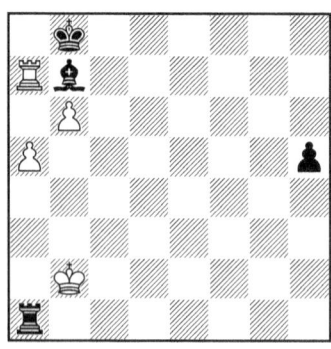

Black to move

Black is a piece up and with a remote passed pawn, whose queening square is the same as the bishop's color. However, White enjoys a pair of far-advanced passed pawns, which, besides being dangerous in themselves, can also collaborate with the rook to create a mating net for the black king.

88...♖a4

Looking to keep the white pawns' advance at bay.

In case of 88...♖g1 89.a6 ♗c8 (89...♗e4 90.♖e7 ♖b1+ 91.♔c3=) 90.♖h7= the last black pawn abandons the board.

88...♖h1 looked interesting: 89.a6 (89.♔c3? ♖b1 90.a6 ♖xb6 91.♖xb7+ ♖xb7 92.axb7 h4−+) 89...♗c8 (89...♗xa6 90.♖xa6 ♔b7 91.♖a3 with a drawn rook ending; 89...♗e4 90.♖e7!)

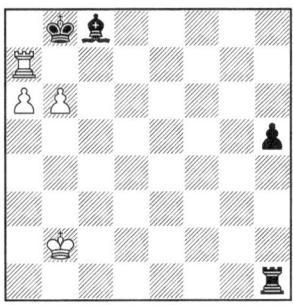

90.♔c3! 90.♖h7? ♗xa6−+ is bad, while 90.b7? also fails to 90...♖b1+! 91.♔xb1 (91.♔a3 ♗xb7 92.♖xb7+ ♖xb7 93.axb7 h4−+) 91...♗f5+ 92.♔c1 ♔xa7 93.♔d2 ♗d7 94.♔e3 ♗b5 95.♔f4 ♗xa6 96.♔g5 ♗e2−+.

90...h4 (a lack of caution is a deadly risk for Black: 90...♖h4?! 91.b7 ♖c4+? 92.♔xc4 ♗e6+ 93.♔c5 ♔xa7 94.♔d6 ♔b8 95.♔xe6 h4 96.♔d6 h3 97.♔c6 h2 98.♔b6 h1=♕ 99.a7#)

91.♔d4! 91.b7? ♔xa7 92.bxc8=♕ ♖c1+−+ is premature again, while 91.♔d2 h3 92.b7 ♗xb7 93.♖xb7+ ♔a8 94.♖h7 h2 95.♔e2 ♖a1−+ was also losing.

91...♖d1+. Both 91...h3 92.b7 ♗xb7 93.♖xb7+ ♔a8 94.♖b2! h2 95.♖d2=, and 91...♖xa6 92.♖xa6 h3 93.♖a2! h2 94.♖d2 ♔b7 95.♔d5 ♔xb6 96.♔d6 ♔a7 97.♖a2+ ♔b8 98.♖b2+ ♔c8 99.♖c2+ ♔d8 100.♔c6 ♔e7 101.♖e2+ ♔f6 102.♖c2 ♔f5 103.♔c5 ♔e4 104.♔c4 ♔f4 105.♔c5 ♔g3 106.♖c3+ ♔f2 107.♖c2+ ♔e3 108.♔c4= lead to a drawn rook ending.

92.♔e3 (92.♔c5? fails to 92...♖d7!−+) 92...♖d8 (both 92...h3 93.b7 ♖d3+ 94.♔f4!= and 92...♖d7 93.b7 ♗xb7 94.♖xb7+ ♖xb7 95.axb7 h3 96.♔f2= result in a draw) 93.♖h7 (93.♔f4? ♖h8−+) 93...h3 94.a7+ ♔a8 95.b7+ ♗xb7 96.♖xh3=, and Black has nothing more than a drawn rook and bishop vs. rook ending.

89.♔b3!

But White does not allow Black to keep his rook on the a-file.

89...♖f4

89...♖a1 90.♔b2! leads to a repetition of moves

90.a6 ♗d5+

The line 90...♗c8 91.♖h7 ♗xa6 (91...h4?! 92.♖h8 ♖f6! 93.b7 ♖b6+ 94.♔c4

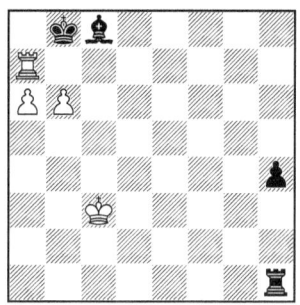

♖xb7 95.axb7 ♔xb7=) 92.♖xh5= could
have again seen a drawn rook and bishop
vs. rook ending.

Meanwhile, following 90...♗f3
91.♖h7 ♖f8 92.♔b4= Black cannot set
his passed pawn in motion.

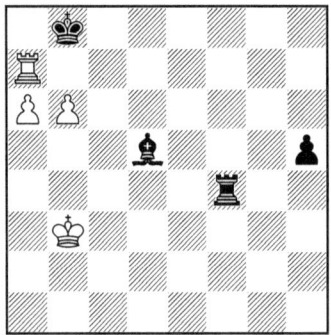

91.♔c3!

The careless 91.♔c2? fails to 91...
♖f6! 92.♖d7 (92.♖h7 ♗e4+−+) 92...
♗e4+ 93.♔d2 ♖xb6−+.

91...♖f7

91...♖a4 92.♖d7= is no better.

In the meantime, in case of 91...
♖c4+ 92.♔d2! ♖c8

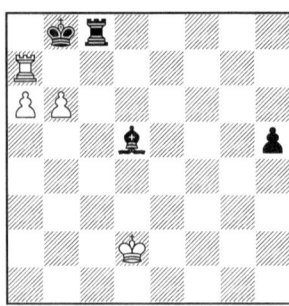

93.♖h7! (93.b7? ♖c2+! 94.♔xc2
♔xa7 95.♔d2 h4 96.♔e3 h3 97.♔f2
h2−+) 93...♖d8 (93...♗f3 94.♔e3 ♖f8
95.♖d7 h4 96.♖h7 draws) 94.♔e3=
White's active counterplay compensates
for his material deficit.

92.♖xf7 ♗xf7 93.♔d4

Now Black's bishop does not make
it in time to help his king eliminate
the white pawns and defend his only
remaining one.

93...♗e8

93...h4 94.♔e3 ♗c4 95.a7+ ♔b7
96.♔f3= gives a draw, too.

**94.♔e3 ♗b5 95.a7+! ♔b7 96.♔f4
♗c6 97.♔g5 ♔xb6**

White also exploits the
overworked bishop after 97...♗f3
98.♔h4 ♔xb6 99.a8=♕ ♗xa8 100.
♔xh5=.

98.♔xh5 ♔xa7 and a draw.

Example No. 77
V. Kramnik − S. Shankland
Wijk aan Zee 2019

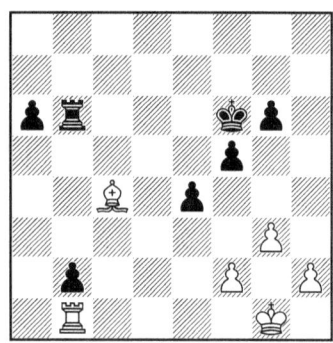

White to move

50.♗a2?

White overestimates his material
superiority and misevaluates his bishop's
capability of neutralizing Black's pair of
dangerous connected passed pawns. It
was correct to eliminate the dangerous
passed pawns and transpose into a
drawn rook ending via 50.♗xa6! ♖xa6
51.♖xb2=.

**50...a5! 51.♔f1 a4 52.♔e2 a3
53.♔d2 ♖c6**

It turns out that all white pieces are stymied by the black passed pawns, while Black has a powerful additional resource to fuel his threats − his king.

54.h4   ♔e5!   55.♖e1   ♔d4!−+ 56.♗b1

56.♖b1 is also bad: 56...♖c3! 57.♖e1 ♖f3 58.♔e2 (58.♖e2 ♖xf2 59.♖xf2 e3+ 60.♔e1 exf2+ 61.♔xf2 ♔c3−+) 58...♖d3 59.♖h1 (59.♗b1 ♔c3!−+) 59...♔c3 60.h5 gxh5 61.♖xh5 ♖d2+ 62.♔e1 ♖c2 63.♖xf5 ♖c1+ 64.♔e2 ♖a1−+.

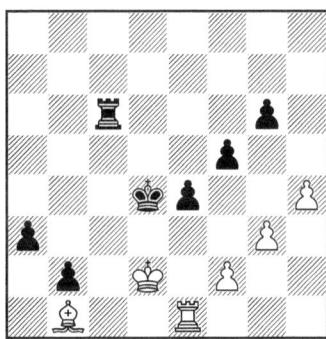

56...♖c3!

Assisted by the king, the black rook takes up a strike position.

57.♖h1   ♖d3+!?

57...♔c4!? was also a winner: 58.♗a2+ (58.h5 gxh5 59.♖xh5 ♖c1−+) 58...♔b4 59.♖e1 ♖d3+ 60.♔c2 (60. ♔e2 ♔c3−+) 60...♖f3 61.♖f1 (61. ♖e2 ♖c3+ 62.♔d2 ♖c1 63.♖e1 ♖a1 64.♗b1 ♖xb1 65.♖xb1 ♔b3−+) 61... e3−+.

58.♔c2

It is curtains after both 58.♗xd3 exd3−+ when there is no stopping the a-pawn, and 58.♔e2 ♔c3−+.

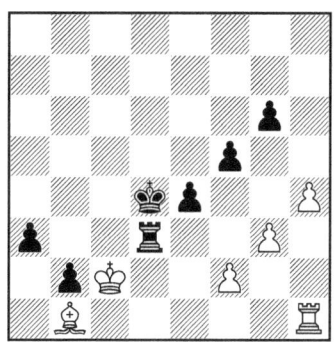

58...♖c3+!

58...♖f3?! is premature: 59.♖d1+ ♔e5 60.♖d2.

59.♔d2   ♖f3!   60.♔e2

60.♖f1 ♖xf2+! 61.♖xf2 e3+−+ is bad, too.

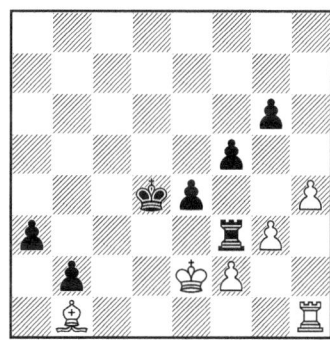

60...♖d3!

A beautiful rook dance! The road for the black king to help his passed pawns is now free.

61.h5

61.♗xd3 fails on the spot to 61... exd3+ 62.♔d2 a2−+.

In the case of 61.♖d1 ♔c3! 62.♗xd3 exd3+ 63.♖xd3+ ♔b4!? 64.♖d8 (64. ♖d1 a2−+) 64...a2−+ there is no stopping the pawn from queening.

61...gxh5 62.♔e1

62.♖xh5 ♖c3 63.♖h1 ♖c1 64.♖d1+ ♔c3−+ makes no difference.

62...♖c3 63.♔d2 f4!?

Black creates another passed pawn.

64.♗a2

Black wins easily after 64.gxf4 h4 (or 64...♖c1 65.♖xc1 bxc1=♕+ 66.♔xc1 h4–+) 65.f5 (65.♖xh4 ♖c1–+) 65...♖c1 66.f6 (66.♖xc1 bxc1=♕+ 67.♔xc1 h3–+) 66...♖xh1 67.f7 ♖xb1 68.f8=♕ ♖d1+! 69.♔xd1 b1=♕+ 70.♔d2 ♕d3+ 71.♔e1 a2.

64...e3+ 65.fxe3+ fxe3+ 66.♔e2 ♖c2+ and White resigned in the face of 67.♔f3 ♖f2#.

Example No. 78
F. Vallejo Pons – I. Kovalenko
Spain 2020

White to move

To win this game White needs to deal with the black passed pawns, which are supported by the king and rook. Which continuation to choose?

56.♔d5?

This is a natural but erroneous move. 56.♔d6? also blows the win: 56...h3 57.c5 (57.♗e5 ♖d3+ 58.♔e6 ♔g2!? 59.♗xf4 ♖d4!=) 57...♖d3! 58.♔e5 (a draw also results after 58.♔d5 f3 59.c6 f2 60.c7 f1=♕ 61.c8=♕ ♖xd4+!? 62.♔xd4 ♕f4+ 63.♔d3 ♕f3+ 64.♔c4

♕e2+) 58...h2 59.c6 ♖d1 60.c7 ♖c1 61.♗b6 ♔g2=.

Throwing in the check brings no benefits 56.♖g8+ ♔f3!.

The correct continuation is 56.♗e5! h3 (56...♖f3 57.♔d4 ♖f2 58.c5 h3 59.♔d3! h2 60.c6 ♖f1 61.c7 ♖c1 62.♗c3+–)

57.♔d4! It is from this square that the white king performs to his full potential.

57...♖b2. Black is in bad shape after both 57...h2 58.♗xf4+! ♔xf4 59.♖xh2 ♔f5 60.♖e2 ♖b8 61.c5+–, and 57...♖b7 58.♖f8+–.

58.♖g8+!? Transposition into a rook ending is also an immediate winner: 58.♗xf4+ ♔xf4 59.♖xh3+–.

58...♔f3 59.♖f8 h2 60.♖xf4+ ♔g2 (60...♔e2 61.♖h4+–; 60...♔g3 61.♖f8+ ♔g2 62.♖g8+ ♔f1 63.♖h8 ♔g1 64.♗xh2++–) 61.♖g4+ ♔h3 (61...♔f3 62.♖h4+–) 62.♖g3+ ♔h4 63.♖g8 h1=♕ (63...♖d2+ 64.♔c3+–) 64.♗h8++– and White has successfully dealt with both the black passed pawns and the newly-promoted black queen that has come to replace one of the pawns.

56...h3! 57.c5

There is no win either after 57.♗e5 ♖d3+! (57...h2? 58.♗xf4+ ♔xf4 59.♖xh2+–) 58.♔e6

(58.♔e4 ♖e3+! 59.♔d4 [59.♔f5 ♖xe5+!] 59...♖xe5! 60.♔xe5 [60.♖g8+ ♔h2 61.♔xe5 f3=] 60...f3=; 58.♔c5 ♖e3! 59.♗b8 ♖f3 60.♔d5 h2 61.♔e4 ♖f1=)

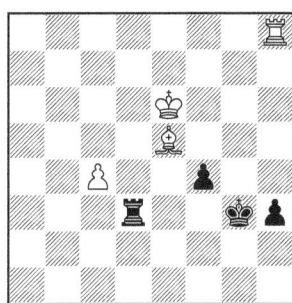

58...♖e3. 58...h2? 59.♗xf4+ ♔xf4 60.♖xh2+− is bad.

A drawn ending results also after 58...♔g2 59.♗xf4 ♖d4 60.♖g8+ ♔h1 61.♔f5 ♖xc4=.

59.c5 (59.♔f5 ♖xe5+! 60.♔xe5 f3=) 59...h2. And now the sacrifice 59...♖xe5+? fails to 60.♔xe5 f3 61.c6 f2 62.♖g8+ ♔h2 63.♖f8 ♔g1 64.c7 f1=♕ 65.♖xf1+ ♔xf1 66.c8=♕ h2 67.♕h3+ ♔g1 68.♕g3+ ♔h1 69.♕e1+ ♔g2 70.♕e2+ ♔g1 71.♔f4! h1=♕ 72.♔g3+−.

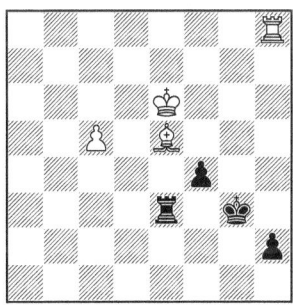

60.c6 ♖e2! 61.c7 (61.♔f5 ♔g2=) 61...♖c2 62.♗xf4+ (62.♔f5 ♔g2=; 62.♔d7 ♔g2=) 62...♔xf4 63.♖xh2 ♖xc7=.

57...h2 58.♗e5

Following 58.c6 ♖b8! 59.♖h7 ♔g2 Black is going to take the white rook in exchange for his passed rook pawn.

58...♔g2 59.♗xf4 h1=♕ 60.♖xh1 ♔xh1 61.c6 ♖c3 62.c7 ♖xc7 63.♗xc7 and the opponents shook hands on a draw.

Lessons from my Career

Example No. 79
I. Nepomniachtchi − A. Galkin
Moscow 2011

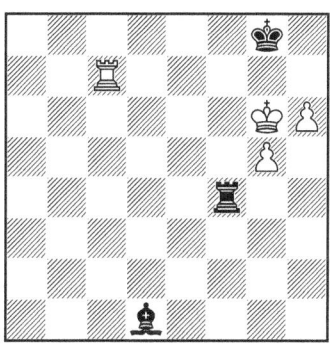

Black to move

Despite his nominal material advantage, it is Black who needs to fight back in this endgame. White's pair of far-advanced passed pawns, poised to reach the promotion squares, and the black king, pressed in the bottom rank and running a high risk of getting checkmated, prompt Black to look for a precise sequence of moves to save this endgame.

68...♗g4!?

There was an alternative way to bail out: 68...♖f8!? 69.h7+ (69.♖g7+ ♔h8 yields nothing) 69...♔h8 70.♔h6 ♗c2!? 71.♖xc2 ♖f6+! 72.♔h5 (both 72.gxf6 and 72.g6 ♖xg6+ 73.♔xg6 result in stalemate) 72...♖a6 (there is no stalemate following the erroneous 72... ♖h6+? 73.gxh6!)

and it turns out that White cannot win this rook ending: 73.g6 (73.♖c7 ♖h6+!=) 73...♖xg6! 74.♖c8+ ♔xh7 75.♖c7+ ♔g7=.

69.h7+

69.♖b7 ♗f5+ or 69.♖g7+ ♔h8 lead to a draw, too.

69...♔h8 70.♔h6 ♗f5 71.g6

The white king is not even exempt from getting checkmated: 71.♖f7? ♖h4#.

71...♖h4+ 72.♔g5

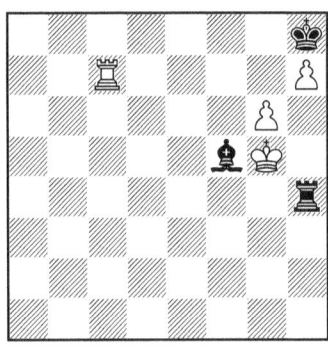

72...♖g4+!

Ditching his own pieces. **73.♔xf5 ♖xg6 74.♔xg6** and stalemate.

To wrap up this part of the topic we delve in detail into pawnless or near pawnless rook and bishop versus rook endgame examples, and then follow those up with slightly less common rook and knight versus rook examples. In both cases, the side with the material advantage has the initiative. We will try to single out both the optimum defensive strategy for the weaker side to be employed in an over-the-board game and the winning one for the stronger side.

Example No. 80
H. Raja – S. Khanin
Saint Louis 2022

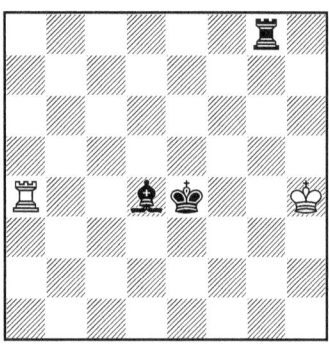

Black to move

It is with this game's diagram that we begin our study of pawnless or near pawnless rook and bishop versus rook endings so as to highlight immediately the key drawn position and its main features. There are two files between the opposite-placed kings of the stronger and the weaker sides. The weaker side's rook pins the bishop, which shields the king from potential checks from the rear. Meanwhile, the stronger side's rook cuts off the weaker side's king on the edge.

94...♔e5

There are two ways for the attacker to succeed in such positions: either White loses his rook, or Black drives the white king into a mating net. The second way is more realistic. Therefore, Black's task is to regroup in such a way that there remains only one file between the kings of the stronger and weaker sides, the latter being cut off on the edge file. That will contribute to creating checkmating threats.

If Black does not commit the position of his king, White can also just mark time with 94...♖g1 95.♖b4!?.

Accordingly, if instead of moving up the black king moves down, the white king proceeds in the opposite direction as well: 94...♔e3 95.♔h5! ♗e5 96.♖g4!?

95.♔h3!

The white king immediately shifts in the direction opposite to that of the black king.

95...♗e3 96.♖g4!

Yet another key move. White threatens a rook exchange to lift his king's cutoff from the edge file.

96...♖a8 97.♖b4 ♗f4 98.♔g4

The white king has broken free, making Black look for ways of edging it back to the rook file or home rank yet again.

98...♖g8+

99.♔f3!

Now let us digress and show you, by way of example, how the stronger side prevails if only one file remains between its king and his weaker counterpart cut off to the board rim: 99.♔h5? ♔f5! 100.♖b5+ ♗e5. The first checkmate threat is in the air.

101.♖b6 ♖g1! The second checkmate threat appears.

102.♖b4 ♖g2! Importantly handing his opponent the move to worsen the location of the white rook that is busy defending against checkmate.

103.♖a4 ♖g7! The third checkmate threat is on the agenda.

104.♖a6

104...♗c7! Yet another crucial move of a restrictive nature. Black takes control of both the d8-square, from which White could disturb the black king with a check, and the c7-square to discourage the white rook from showing up there.

105.♖c6. 105.♔h6 loses to 105...♖d7! 106.♔h5 ♖d1 107.♖a4 ♗d8 108.♔h6 ♖d7–+ and White is defenseless.

105...♗f4! Threatening checkmate, Black will return the bishop to e5 while winning an important tempo.

106.♖c5+ ♗e5. This is now the fifth checkmating threat on its way.

107.♖c6 ♖g5+! It is necessary to

force the white king to commit to a route.

108.♔h6. 108.♔h4 fails immediately to 108...♖g2−+, and the white rook is unable to prevent his king from getting checkmated from the f6-square.

108...♖g1. This is the sixth checkmate threat. 109.♔h7 ♖g7+! 110. ♔h6 ♖d7! The seventh checkmating threat is on the horizon.

111.♔h5 (following 111.♖c5 ♖d8−+ the white rook is denied access to the c7-square)

111...♗d6! And here comes the final finesse. Not only does Black interpose along the sixth rank, disconnecting the white rook from its defensive duties, but also denies it access to the d6-square that it could use to unsaddle the black king from its key position.

112.♔h6 ♗f4+ 113.♔h5 ♖h7+−+ and checkmate next move.

Likewise, 99.♔h4? fails along the same lines to 99...♔f5! 100.♖b5+ ♗e5 101.♔h3 ♖g3+! 102.♔h4 (102.♔h2? ♖b3+−+ winning the rook) 102... ♖a3! (with the same idea of nudging the white rook) 103.♖d5 (103.♖c5 ♖a2−+ and White can avoid getting checkmated only at the cost of his rook; the black bishop cannot be unpinned: 103.♖b1 ♗f6+ 104.♔h5

♖h3#) 103...♖a8 104.♔h3 ♖a2−+ and it is game over.

The above lines give a vivid demonstration of how challenging the defense can be for the weaker side if the stronger side's pieces get to optimal positions.

99...♖g3+ 100.♔e2 ♖a3 101.♖c4

The immediate regrouping of the white rook with 101.♖b8!? to check the opponent's king from the rear is also possible.

101...♗e3 102.♖c8

102.♖b4!? was also fine: 102...♗d4 103.♖b8 ♔e4 104.♖e8+ ♗e5 105. ♖e7 ♖a2+ (105...♖b3 106.♖e8!?) 106. ♔e1, and we have essentially reached the position from which we started analyzing this endgame, but turned clockwise downwards. In front of us is the same picture of two files separating the opponents' kings, of the pinned bishop, and of the black rook cutting off the white king.

106...♔d4 (106...♔f4 107.♔d1! ♗d4 108.♖e2!) 107.♔f1! ♗f4 108. ♖e2!=.

102...♗d4 103.♖e8+ ♔d5 104. ♖d8+

Black realizes his opponent's awareness of the key drawn position and attempts to find another way to fight for more.

104...♔c4

104...♔e4 105.♖e8+ ♗e5 106.♖e7!? transposes to the positions reviewed earlier.

105.♖c8+

105.♖d7!? was worth considering: 105...♖a2+ 106.♔f3 ♔d3 107.♖b7 ♖f2+ 108.♔g3 ♔e4 109.♖b4 ♖f1 110. ♔g4 ♖g1+ 111.♔h4= and we are back to the initial position but 15 moves later.

105...♗c5 106.♖e8 ♖h3 107.♖c8 ♖e3+ 108.♔d2

It was also a good plan to divert the king away from the black army with 108. ♔f1!?

108...♖e7 109.♔c2 ♖e2+ 110.♔d1 ♖h2 111.♔c1

Yet again we see a typical defensive position with two files separating the opposite-placed kings. Lowering his guard could backfire after 111.♖c7? ♔d3! 112. ♖d7+ (112.♖xc5 ♖h1#) 112...♗d4 −+.

111...♔d4 112.♔b1!

Heading in the opposite direction!

112...♗b4 113.♖c2! ♖h8 114.♖f2

114.♔b2!? looked interesting

114...♖c3 115.♖c2+ ♔d3

Black gets nothing from 115...♔b3 116.♖b2+ ♔a4 117.♔a2=.

116.♖f2 ♗c3

117.♖f3+!

The slow 117.♖g2? fails again to 117...♖h1+ 118.♔a2 ♔c4 119.♔a3 (119.♖g4+ ♗d4−+) 119...♖h8! 120. ♔a2 ♖a8+ 121.♔b1 ♖a1+ 122.♔c2 ♖a2+−+, winning the rook.

117...♔d2

In case of 117...♔c4 118.♔c2 ♖h2+ 119.♔d1 ♖d2+ 120.♔e1!= the white king has no fear of placing himself in discovered check.

118.♖f2+

White could go for 118.♔a2 ♔c2 119.♖f2+ ♗d2 120.♖f3= and Black cannot win despite the regrouping of his pieces and reducing the number of files separating the kings down to one. The white rook safeguards its king from the enemy rook's checks from the top of the a-file, and the other part of this file is inaccessible to the black rook.

118...♔e3 119.♖f7 ♖h2 120.♔c1 ♗d4 121.♖f8

121.♔b1!? ♔d3 122.♖f3+!= was worth playing.

121...♔d3 122.♖f3+

The passive defense 122.♖f1? fails to 122...♖c2+! 123.♔b1 (123.♔d1 ♖a2 124.♖f3+ ♗e3−+) 123...♖b2+! 124.♔c1 (124.♔a1 ♖f2+−+) 124... ♖b8 125.♖d1+ ♔c3 126.♖e1 (126. ♖f1 ♗e3+ 127.♔d1 ♔d3−+) 126... ♖a8 127.♔b1 (127.♔d1 ♔d3−+) 127...♔b3! 128.♔c1 ♖a1+ 129.♔d2 ♗c3+ 130.♔d3 ♗xe1!−+, avoiding the cunning checkmating trap set by his opponent.

122...♗e3+ 123.♔b1 ♖e2!

It is to be noted that Black's strategy has achieved certain success over the past ten moves. One should bear in mind that the game has already surpassed 100 moves. Consequently, the defending side, among other things, is under additional pressure from both lengthy defense fatigue and a possible lack of time on his clock. At the same time, similar endgames highlight the importance of keeping in mind the 50-move rule and diligently counting the number of moves made. It has happened more than once in such endgames that the defending side claimed a draw under this rule even in a lost position. Even a saving chance like that is not to be missed.

124.♖f5?!

This is not yet a decisive error, but a first step towards losing. The rook is not ideally placed on the fifth rank due to the unavailability of some squares controlled by the bishop.

124.♖f8!? was a better idea: 124...♖e1+ (124...♔c4 125.♖c8+ ♗c5 126.♔c1=) 125.♔a2 ♔c4 126.♔b2 ♗d4+ 127.♔c2 ♖e2+ 128.♔b1! (128.♔d1? ♔d3 129.♖f3+ ♗e3−+) 128...♗c3 (128...♔b3 129.♖b8+!) 129.♖b8! ♔d3 (129...♖e1+ 130.♔c2!) 130.♖f8! (130. ♖g8? ♗e5−+) 130...♗e5 131.♖f3+!= and Black cannot rearrange his forces to create checkmating threats.

124...♔c3

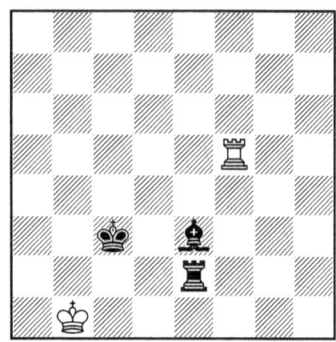

125.♖e5?

And this one is a blunder. 125.♖b5? was also losing, to 125...♗d4 126.♖b8 ♔d3 127.♖c8 (127.♖b3+? ♗c3−+; 127.♖b4 ♖h2 128.♖b5 ♖h8 129.♔a2 ♔c4 130.♖b7 ♖a8+ 131.♔b1 ♔d3 132.♔c1 ♖h8 133.♔b1 ♖h1+ 134.♔a2 ♖a1+ 135.♔b3 ♖b1+−+) 127...♖b2+! 128.♔c1 ♖a2! 129.♔d1 (129.♖b8 ♖h2 130.♔b1 ♖h1+ 131.♔a2 ♖a1+ 132. ♔b3 ♖b1+−+, winning the rook) 129...♖f2! 130.♖e8 ♗f6! We have already seen a similar winning maneuver.

131.♖e6 (likewise, 131.♔e1 fails to 131...♖f5 132.♔d1 ♗h4 133.♔c1 ♖b5−+) 131...♗c3! 132.♖d6+ ♗d4 133.♖e6 ♖d2+! 134.♔e1 ♖a2 135.♔f1 ♖f2+! 136.♔e1 ♖f5! 137.♔d1 ♗e5! 138.♔e1 ♗c3+ 139.♔d1 ♖f1+ 140. ♖e1 ♖xe1#.

125.♖f8! ♖b2+ 126.♔a1 ♗d4 127. ♖c8+ would have kept the draw. It was also fine to go for 127.♖f3+ ♔b4 (127... ♔c4 128.♖c3+!=) 128.♖f4 ♖d2+ 129. ♔b1 ♔b3 130.♖f3+ ♗c3 131.♔c1 ♖e2 (131...♖a2 132.♔d1) 132.♖d3 ♔c4 133.♖h3=.

127...♔d2 (127...♔d3 128.♖c3+!=; 127...♔b3 128.♖b8+=) 128.♖d8! ♖b4+ (128...♔d3? 129.♖xd4+ ♔xd4 130. ♔xb2=) 129.♔a2 ♔c2 130.♖c8+ ♗c3 131.♔a3 (131.♖a8? ♖b1−+) 131...♖b5

(131...♖b7 132.♖c4=) 132.♖c4 ♔d3 (132...♖b8 133.♔a4=; 132...♖b1 133. ♔a4=) 133.♖c8=.

125...♖b2+ 126.♔a1 ♗d4!−+ 127. ♖h5

White loses the game after both 127. ♖e1 ♖b4 128.♔a2 ♖a4+ 129.♔b1 ♔b3 130.♔c1 ♗c3−+ and 127.♖e8 ♖d2 128.♖c8+ ♔d3+! 129.♔b1 ♖b2+ 130. ♔c1 ♖a2 followed by the plan seen earlier: 131.♔d1 (131.♖b8 ♖h2 132. ♔b1 ♖h1+ 133.♔a2 ♖a1+ 134.♔b3 ♖b1+−+) 131...♖f2! 132.♖e8 ♗f6! 133.♖e6 ♗c3 134.♖d6+ ♗d4 135.♖e6 ♖d2+! 136.♔e1 ♖a2 137.♔f1 ♖f2+! 138.♔e1 ♖f5! 139.♔d1 ♗e5!−+.

127.♖c5+ is no longer of any help: 127...♔d2! (127...♔d3? 128.♖c3+!=) 128.♖d5 ♖b4+ 129.♔a2 ♔c2 130.♔a3 (130.♖a5 ♗c3 131.♔a3 ♖b2+ 132.♔a1 ♖b1+ 133.♔a2 ♖a1#) 130...♖c4 131. ♖a5 ♗c5+ 132.♔a2 ♖c3 133.♖a4 ♗d6 134.♖a6 (134.♔a1 ♔b3!−+) 134...♗b4 135.♖a8 (135.♖a4 ♖b3−+) 135...♖c6 136.♖a4 (136.♖a7 ♖b6−+) 136...♖b6 137.♖a8 ♗c3 138.♖a7 ♖b1−+ and the mating trap has snapped shut.

127...♖e2?

Reciprocating the blunder. The winning continuation was 127...♖b4!? 128.♖h3+ ♔c4+ 129.♔a2 ♖b2+! 130.

♔a3 ♖b1! and again implementing the winning plan that we know: 131.♔a4 ♖b8 132.♖h5 ♖b2! 133.♖h3 ♗f2! 134. ♖f3 ♗c5! 135.♖f4+ ♗d4! 136.♖f3 ♖b4+! 137.♔a3 ♖b6! 138.♔a2 ♖b2+ 139.♔a3 ♖e2! 140.♔a4 ♗e3!−+.

128.♔b1?

White's inner strength had abandoned him completely by this moment, and he missed the opportunity to save the game. 128.♖h3+! channeled the game back to a draw: 128...♗e3 (128...♔c4+ 129.♔b1 ♗c3 130.♖h7 ♔b3 131.♖b7+ ♗b4 132.♖c7=) 129. ♖h8=.

128...♖e1+! 129.♔a2 ♔c4!

White resigned because his king is defenseless against the mating threat.

Example No. 81
Vladimir Zakhartsov − A. Barseghyan
Chelyabinsk 2022

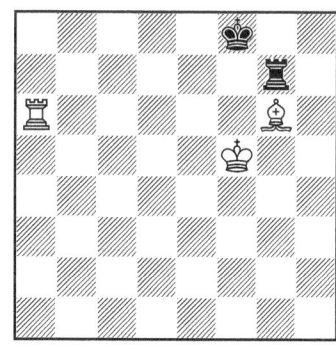

White to move

A rook and bishop versus rook endgame has already lasted over 30 moves. White has used this time to edge the black king to the bottom rank and is now looking for an opportunity to arrange his pieces ideally and complete the mating net prior to exceeding the fifty-move limit.

100.♔g5

Waiting for his opponent to go wrong. 100.♔f6 ♖f7+!= yields nothing, when the rook is not to be touched because of stalemate.

100...♔e7?

Being in a hurry to improve his king's position, Black overlooks White's winning maneuver. He needed to move the rook first, with his king running away from a dangerous position only afterwards: 100...♖c7 101.♗f5 (101. ♔f6 ♖f7+!=; 101.♖e6 ♖e7=) 101... ♔e7=.

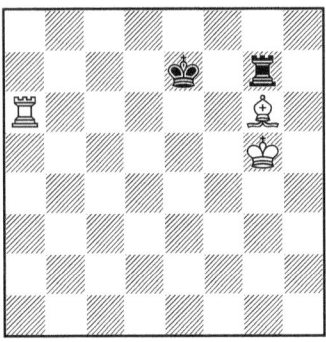

101.♖b6?

White played this move too quickly. He misses the chance provided by his opponent. 101.♖a7+! was winning: 101...♔f8 102.♖a8+! ♔e7 103.♔h6! ♔f6 104.♖a6++−, and the black rook falls.

101...♖g8 102.♔f5 ♖g7 103.♖a6 ♔f8 104.♔f6 ♖f7+! 105.♔g5 ♖c7

Of course not 105...♖g7? 106.♖a8+ ♔e7 107.♔h6+− and the black rook is in a deadly trap again.

106.♖e6 ♖e7 107.♖c6 ♖a7 108. ♖f6+

A stalemate comes to Black's rescue once again after 108.♔f6 ♖f7+!

108...♔g7!

There is no doing without this precision. Both 108...♔e7? 109. ♖f7++− and 108...♔g8? 109.♔h6 ♖b7 110.♗c2 ♖b8 111.♗f5 ♖e8 112.♗e6+ ♔h8 113.♔g6 ♖a8 114.♖f1+− are bad.

109.♖e6 ♖c7 110.♗f5 ♔f8 111. ♔g6 ♖g7+ 112.♔h6

White's winning dreams also evaporate after 112.♔f6 ♖f7+ 113.♔e5 ♖e7=.

112...♖e7 113.♖a6 ♖c7 114.♖e6 ♖e7 115.♖c6 ♖a7 116.♔g6 ♖c7

and, realizing that the 50-move limit was about to be reached, White exchanges off the rooks in a pointed manner.

117.♖f6+ ♖f7 118.♖xf7+ ♔xf7

with a draw agreed.

Example No. 82
B. Jobava − J. Moussard
Catez 2022

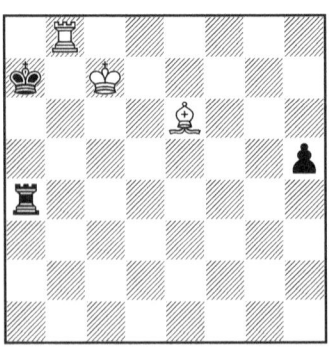

Black to move

The black king has already been pushed on to the rook file, while his white counterpart is located as close as possible, which allows the stronger side to tighten the mating noose around his opponent's neck. Only precise play can save the black king from execution.

94...♖a3?

Black fails to cope with the task.

94...h4? would have failed on the spot to 95.♗d5 ♔a6 96.♗c6+−.

94...♖a1? was not a saving move either: 95.♖b7+! ♔a8 (95...♔a6 96.♗c4+ ♔a5 97.♖a7++−) 96.♖b4 ♖a7+ (96...♖c1+ 97.♗c4 ♖a1 98.♗d5+ ♔a7 99.♖b7+ ♔a6 100. ♗c4+ ♔a5 101.♖a7++−) 97.♔c8 ♖a1 (97...♖a3 98.♗c4! ♔a7 99.♖b7+ ♔a8 100.♗d5+−) 98.♖b8+ ♔a7 99.♖b7+ ♔a8 (99...♔a6 100.♗c4+ ♔a5 101. ♖a7++−) 100.♗d5! ♖c1+ 101. ♖c7++−.

94...♖a5? is equally bad: 95.♖b7+! ♔a8 (95...♔a6 96.♗c4++−) 96.♖b1 ♖c5+ (96...♖a7+ 97.♔c8 ♖a5 98.♗d5+! ♖xd5 99.♖a1++−) 97.♔b6 ♖e5 (neither can Black find his way out of the mating net following 97... ♖c2 98.♖d1 ♖b2+ 99.♔a6 ♔b8 100. ♖c1 ♔a8 101.♖c8+ ♖b8 102.♗d5#) 98.♗d7 ♖e2 99.♖f1 ♖b2+ 100.♗b5+−.

The way to go is 94...♖e4!

a) 95.♖b6

95...♖e5! This resource is of utmost importance. Both 95...h4? 96.♗d5+− and 95...♖d4? 96.♖b5 ♔a6 97.♖xh5 ♖a4 98.♖c5 ♖a1 99.♗c4+ ♔a7 100. ♗d3 ♖a3 101.♖c4 ♖a1 102.♖b4 ♖c1+ 103.♗c4 ♖a1 104.♗b5 ♖a3 105.♖b1! ♖a2 106.♗c6 ♔a6 107.♖b8 ♔a5 108. ♖a8++− are bad.

96.♗d7. Following 96.♗c6 h4 97.♗c8 ♖e7+! 98.♗d7 ♖e5! 99.♖c4 ♔a6 100.♔c6 ♖a5 101.♖xh4 ♖a1 102. ♗e6 ♖c1+ 103.♗c4+ ♔a5 104.♔c5 ♖b1 105.♖h8 ♖b5+! 106.♔c6 ♖b2= the position is a draw.

96...♖c5+ 97.♗c6 ♖g5 98.♖b1 ♔a6! 98...♖g7+? fails to 99.♗d7 ♖g6 100.♖f1 h4 101.♗e8! ♖g7+ 102.♗f7 ♔a6 103.♔c6 ♔a5 104.♔c5 ♔a6 105. ♖a1+ ♔b7 106.♗d5+ ♔b8 107.♖a8+ ♔c7 108.♖a7++−.

99.♖a1+ (99.♖b4 ♖g4!?) 99...♖a5 100.♖f1 ♖g5= and Black holds a draw;

b) There is no checkmate following 95.♖b1 ♖xe6 96.♖a1+ ♖a6=;

c) A draw results from both 95.♗d7 ♖c4+ 96.♗c6 ♖xc6+ 97.♔xc6 ♔xb8 98.♔d5 h4 99.♔e4 h3 100.♔f3 h2 101. ♔g2=;

d) and 95.♗d5 ♖e7+ 96.♔d6 ♔xb8 97.♔xe7=;

e) In case of 95.♖e8 ♖e1 96.♔c6 ♖c1+! 97.♔b5 ♖b1+ 98.♔c5 ♖c1+ 99.♗c4 h4!?= the mating noose unties;

f) 95.♖b7+ is of no help: 95...♔a6! 96.♗d7 ♖c4+ 97.♗c6 h4 98.♖b1 (98. ♖b8 ♔a5) 98...♔a5= and the black king breaks free.

95.♗c4! ♖g3

95...♖a4 loses on the spot to 96.♗d5 ♔a6 97.♗c6+−.

Black is also in bad shape after 95... ♖c3 96.♖b4 ♖a3 97.♗b5 h4 (97... ♖c3+ 98.♗c6 ♖a3 99.♖b8+−; 97...♖a1

98.♗c6 ♚a6 99.♖b8 ♚a5 100.♖a8++−)
98.♖xh4 ♖a1 (98...♖c3+ 99.♗c6 ♖a3
100.♖h8+−) 99.♗c6 ♚a6 100.♖h8 ♚a5
101.♖a8++− winning the rook.

96.♖b7+! ♚a8 97.♖b6! ♖a3

97...♖g7+ leads to checkmate:
98.♚c8 h4 99.♖a6+ ♖a7 100.♗d5#.

98.♖b8+ ♚a7 99.♖b7+! ♚a8

100.♚b6! Regrouping the king to create new mating threats.

100...♖a1

There is no saving the game either after 100...♖g3 101.♖e7! ♖g6+ 102. ♗e6+−. 100...♖e3 101.♗d5+− is equally bad.

101.♖h7   ♖b1+   102.♗b5 and Black resigned in the face of inevitable checkmate.

Among other matters, the above rook and bishop versus rook endgame examples show the practical challenges even for professional chess players in terms of defending for the weaker side or finding the right solutions in already winning positions for the stronger side.

We now move to reviewing rook and knight versus rook endings. A major difference from endgames with an extra bishop is that it is far more difficult for the rook and knight tandem to drive

the weaker side's king from the center and into a corner. However, if it does come about, or a structure with such a misplaced king is already in place in the starting position, the chances of winning increase dramatically. When supported by their king, a rook and knight may in cases be no less productive in constructing mating nets than a rook and a bishop. The example below demonstrates this.

Example No. 83
S. Mamedyarov − B. Gelfand
Pamplona 2004

Black to move

Black has cornered the white king and now finishes him off.

66...♖d6!

Only here. Not only does this square provide the rook with an additional opportunity of challenging the white king along the h-file, but also of performing vital defensive duties.

67.♖a2

The following line highlights the advantage of placing the black rook on the sixth rank: 67.♖f7 ♚g3 68.♖g7+ ♘g6!−+, and White cannot stop checkmate along the home rank.

Black also completes the mating net after 67.♖a3+ ♚f2 68.♖a2+ ♘e2−+.

67...♖h6+

67...♔g3 68.♖a3+ ♔f2 69.♖a2+ ♘e2−+ was a winner, too.

68.♖h2

68.♔g1 ♘e2+−+ is no better.

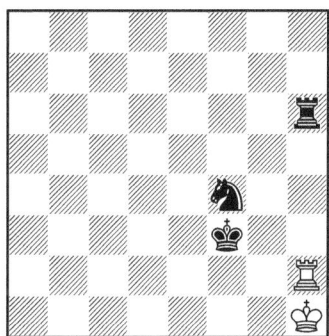

68...♘h3!

The final chord. White resigned in the face of 69.♖a2 ♘f2+ 70.♔g1 ♖h1#.

The following example comes from a game between two of history's greatest players.

Example No. 84
J. Polgar − G. Kasparov
Dos Hermanas 1996

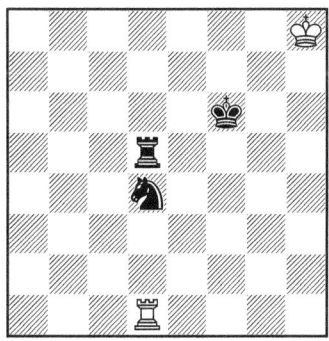

White to move

Black is close to achieving complete coordination of his pieces. It remains to bring the knight over to the enemy king,

and the mating net will begin to wrap around it.

79.♖a1?

White counts on adding to her rook's range of defensive abilities so that it can hassle the black king with side checks. 79.♔g8? fails to 79...♖g5+ 80.♔h8 (80. ♔f8? ♘e6+ 81.♔e8 ♖g8+ 82.♔d7 ♖d8+−+ winning the rook; 80.♔h7 ♘f5 81.♖h1 ♔f7 82.♖h2 ♖g3! 83.♖h1 [83.♖h5 ♘e7−+] 83...♖f3 84.♖h2 ♘e3 85.♖h4 [85.♖h1 ♘g4 86.♖h4 ♖g3 87.♔h8 ♘f6−+] 85...♖g4! 86.♔h8 [86.♖xg4 ♖h3+−+] 86...♘f6−+ and the white king is doomed.)

80...♘f5 81.♖h1. 81.♖f1 is no better: 81...♔f7 82.♖h1 ♖g2 83.♖h7+ (83.♔h7 ♘g3 84.♖h4 ♘e4!−+) 83...♔f8 84.♖h1 ♘d6−+, with checkmate soon after.

81...♔f7 82.♖h2 ♖g3! 83.♔h7 ♖f3! Gearing up for the decisive regrouping of his knight.

84.♖h1 ♘e7 85.♔h6 ♖f5! 86.♔h7 ♘g8 87.♔h8 ♘f6 88.♖h6 ♖g5 89.♖g6 ♖h5+−+.

79.♔h7? ♖h5+ 80.♔g8 ♖g5+−+ transposes to the above line.

Neither does 79.♖h1? solve any problems: 79...♘f3! 80.♖h6+ (80.♔h7 ♖d7+ 81.♔h6 ♖d8 82.♔h7 ♘g5+ 83.♔h6 ♖h8#) 80...♔f7! 81.♖h7+ (81. ♔h7 ♘g5+ 82.♔h8 ♖d8#; 81.♖h1 ♔g6−+; 81.♖h3 ♖d8+ 82.♔h7 ♘g5+−+) 81...♔g6 82.♖g7+ ♔f6

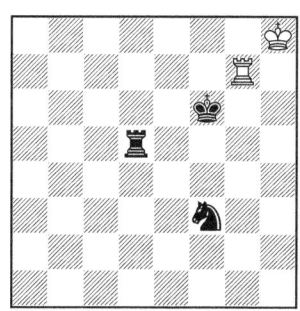

a) 83.♖g3 ♘g5−+ and the white king is in for checkmate.

The following lines end up in checkmate again.

b) 83.♔h7 ♘g5+ 84.♔h6 ♘f7+ 85.♔h7 ♖h5+ 86.♔g8 ♖h8#;

c) 83.♔g8 ♖d8+ 84.♔h7 ♘g5+ 85.♔h6 ♖h8+ 86.♖h7 ♖xh7#;

d) 83.♖a7 ♖d8+ 84.♔h7 ♘g5+ 85.♔h6 ♖h8+ 86.♖h7 ♖xh7#;

e) White is also doomed in case of 83.♖g2 ♖d4! 84.♖f2 (84.♔g8 ♖d8+ 85.♔h7 ♘g5+ 86.♔h6 ♖h8#; 84.♔h7 ♘g5+ 85.♔g8 ♖d8#) 84...♔g6 85.♖g2+ ♘g5−+.

Only 79.♖f1+! would have kept White in the game: 79...♘f5. The white rook never stops pursuing the black king following 79...♔g6 80.♖g1+! ♔h6 81.♖h1+!.

80.♖f2. White's rook pins the enemy knight and is also on alert to deliver checks if the black king walks to the g- or h-files.

80...♖d3 (80...♔f7 81.♖f1!; 80...♔g6 81.♖g2+!; 80...♖d1 81.♔g8! ♖a1 82.♖f4! ♖a2 83.♖f1!)

81.♔g8! Yet another only move. 81.♖f1? fails to 81...♔g6 82.♖g1+ ♘g3−+, while after 81.♔h7? ♖g3 82.♖f1 ♖g5! 83.♖f2 ♔f7 84.♖h2 ♖g3! 85.♖h1 ♖f3! we again witness

the above-mentioned winning plan in action: 86.♖h2 ♘e3 87.♖h4 ♘g4!−+.

81...♖a3. Both 81...♔g6 82.♖g2+ ♘g3 83.♔f8! and 81...♖g3+ 82.♔f8! ♖a3 83.♔e8 allow the white king out of the mating trap.

82.♖f1! ♖a2. This is a key position that the defending side should keep in mind.

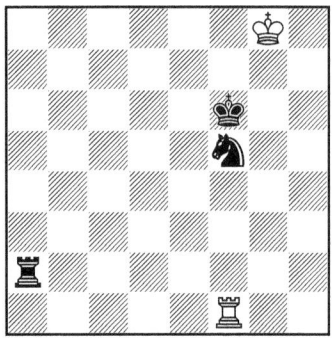

83.♖f4! The only move yet again. Both 83.♖f3? ♔g6−+ and 83.♖h1 ♘e7+ 84.♔h7 ♖f2 85.♔h6 ♘f5+ 86.♔h7 ♔f7−+ lose the game.

83...♖a1 (83...♔g6 84.♖g4+!; 83...♔g5 84.♖b4!) 84.♖f2!= and White holds the ground.

79...♘e6! 80.♖a6

80.♖f1+ ♔g6 81.♖g1+ ♘g5−+ would have lost on the spot.

White is also in grim shape after 80.♖a8 ♔g6 81.♔g8 (81.♖g8+ ♔f7−+) 81...♖d6 82.♖b8 ♘g5 83.♔f8 (83.♖a8 ♘h7 84.♖b8 ♘f6+ 85.♔f8 [85.♔h8 ♖d7 86.♖b7 ♖d8#] 85...♖d7 86.♖b7 ♘h7+−+) 83...♖e6 84.♔g8 ♘h7 85.♔h8 ♘f6 86.♖f8 ♖e7 87.♖f7 ♖e8+!−+.

80...♔f7 81.♖a7+ ♔g6 82.♖a8

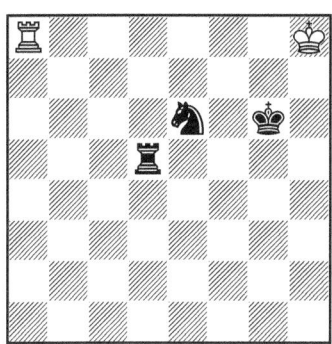

82...♖d7

White could also get the upper hand via 82...♖d6!? 83.♖g8+ (83.♔g8 ♘c7 84.♖b8 ♘d5 85.♔f8 ♖d7−+) 83...♔h6 84.♖a8 ♘g5 85.♔g8 ♔g6 86.♔f8 ♖e6! 87.♔g8 ♘h7 88.♔h8 ♘f6−+.

83.♖b8

Black completes weaving the mating net following 83.♔g8 ♘c7 84.♖b8 ♘d5−+.

Also, in case of 83.♖g8+ ♔h6 84.♖b8 ♘f4 85.♔g8 ♘g6 86.♖b7 ♘e7+!−+, the stalemate idea fails to work for White.

83...♖c7 84.♔g8 ♖c5 85.♖a8

Nor is 85.♖e8 ♖c6 86.♖b8 ♘g5 87.♔f8 ♖e6 88.♔g8 ♘h7−+ any better than the text.

85...♖b5 86.♔h8

Black triumphs in line with the patterns seen earlier after 86.♖c8 ♖b7

87.♔h8 (87.♖a8 ♘c7 88.♖d8 ♘d5−+; 87.♖e8 ♘c7 88.♖d8 ♘d5−+) 87...♖b6

(the position after White's 87th move was reached via a different move order in the actual game, and Kasparov's 87...♘c7! played was equally strong) 88.♔g8 ♘g5 89.♔f8 ♘e6 90.♔g8 ♘h7−+.

86...♖b7 87.♖c8

87.♔g8 falls to checkmate: 87...♘c7 88.♖d8 ♘d5! 89.♖xd5 (89.♖d6+ ♘f6+−+; 89.♔f8 ♖f7+ 90.♔e8 ♘f6#) 89...♖b8+ 90.♖d8 ♖xd8#.

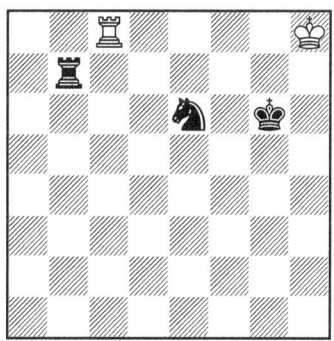

87...♘c7! 88.♖g8+

White also loses in case of 88.♔g8 ♘d5−+.

88.♔h6 89.♖g1 ♖b8+ 90.♖g8 ♘e8! and White resigned in the face of 91.♖f8 ♔g6 92.♖g8+ ♔f7.

Example No. 85
J. Lopez Martinez − V. Mikhalevski
La Roda 2022

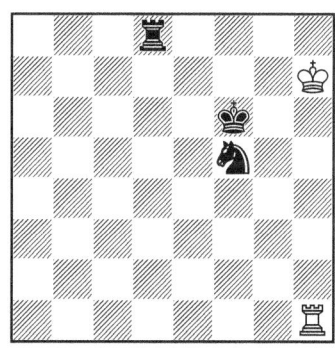

White to move

What we see in front of us is virtually a deja-vu of the Polgar – Kasparov game but over a quarter of a century later. As in the predecessor game, the Spanish grandmaster, playing White, also failed to demonstrate the way to a draw.

118.♖a1?

As we already know, the correct plan is to keep the rook on the f-file. Reaching a draw takes 118.♖f1! ♖a8 119.♖f2 ♖a1 120.♔g8!= .

118...♖d7+! 119.♔h8

119.♔g8 fails on the spot to 119...♘h6+ 120.♔h8 (120.♔f8 ♖d8#) 120...♘f7+ 121.♔g8 (121.♔h7 ♘g5+ 122.♔h6 ♖h7#) 121...♖d8+ 122.♔h7 ♖h8#.

119...♖d4

119...♖d3!? is more precise.

120.♖f1

White is checkmated after both 120.♔h7 ♖h4+ 121.♔g8 ♘e7+ 122.♔f8 ♖h8# and 120.♔g8 ♘e7+ 121.♔f8 (121.♔h8 ♖h4#) 121...♖d8#.

Black wins with already known patterns in case of 120.♖h1 ♔f7 121.♔h7 ♖g4 122.♖h2 ♖f4 123.♖h1 ♘g3 124.♖h2 ♘e4 125.♔h6 ♖g4 126.♔h5 (126.♖h1 ♘f6 127.♖g1 ♘g8+!−+) 126...♘f6+ 127.♔h6 ♖g6#.

120...♔g6 121.♖g1+ ♔f7 122.♖h1 ♖d3 123.♔h7

123.♖h7+ ♔g6−+ is game over.

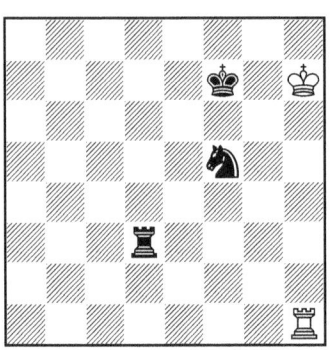

123...♖d7?

This is a blunder that throws the win away. Black needed to take control over the f-file, limiting the opposing rook's ability to deliver checks, and then reroute his knight to construct mating structures. We have also seen this key maneuver in various forms in the previous example:

123...♖f3!? 124.♖h5 (124.♔h8 ♘e7 125.♖h7+ ♔f8 126.♖h1 ♘g8 127.♔h7 ♔f7 128.♔h8 ♘f6−+; 124.♖h2 ♘e7 125.♔h6 ♖f5! 126.♔h7 ♘g8 127.♖h1 ♖g5 128.♖f1+ ♘f6+−+) 124...♖f1 125.♖h3 ♘e7 126.♔h6 ♖f5! 127.♔h7 ♘g8 128.♖h1 ♖g5 129.♖f1+ ♘f6+ 130.♔h6 (130.♔h8 ♖g8#) 130...♖g6#.

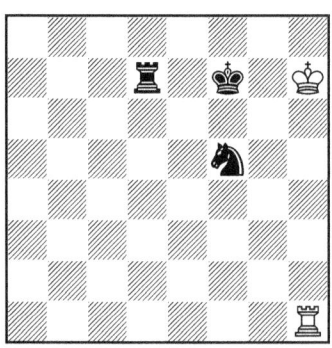

124.♔h8?

White misses the opportunity provided by his opponent. 124.♖f1! would have led to a drawn position yet again: 124...♔f6+ 125.♔h8 ♖a7 126.♖f2 ♖a1 127.♔g8! (both 127.♖f3? ♔g6−+ and 127.♖f4? ♔g6 128.♖g4+ ♔f7−+ lose the game) 127...♖b1 128.♖f4!=.

124...♔f6?

It was necessary to go back to the winning plan one more time with 124...♖d3 125.♔h7 ♖f3!−+.

125.♖a1?

A lack of command of similar endgames and likely fatigue from having to fight back over a long time takes its toll on White's play. As we already know, 125.♖f1!= is the way to go.

125...♖d3! 126.♖h1

Black finishes the mating net after both 126.♖a7 ♖h3+ 127.♖h7 ♘h6 128. ♖a7 ♘f7+ 129.♔g8 ♖h8# and 126. ♖a6+ ♔f7 127.♖a7+ ♘e7−+. 126. ♖f1 ♔g6 127.♖g1+ ♘g3−+ makes no difference.

126...♔g6 and White resigned in the face of 127.♖g1+ ♘g3.

And, finally, wrapping up this section is an example in which the weaker side achieved a draw with precise defense.

Example No. 86
H. Gabuzyan– S. Sargsyan
Yerevan 2022

White to move

Unlike the previously analyzed rook and bishop endgames, in which the opposing king's placement in the middle of the rank or file gives the stronger side's rook both sides of the rank or file to create mating threats, a rook and a knight profit from having the defending side's king pressed into a corner with a mating net in store for him there.

80.♖h4!

Resorting to a pin to fend off Black's concrete threat. 80.♖h1? fails on the spot to 80...♘b3+ 81.♔a4 ♖a6#

80...♖e6 81.♖g4!

White marks his time, maintaining the pin to restrict the opponent's knight.

81...♖h6 82.♖e4 ♖h1

Black attempts to regroup his pieces.

83.♖g4 ♖h2 84.♔b6!

White exploits the opportunity to evacuate his king out of the risky area.

84...♖f2 85.♖h4 ♔d5 86.♖h5+ ♘f5 87.♖h1 ♖b2+ 88.♔c7 ♖d2 89.♖h5

Restricting the black knight's activity with a pin yet again.

89...♖c2+ 90.♔b6 ♔e6 91.♖h1 ♖c3 92.♖h5 ♘d4 93.♖h6+ ♔d5 94.♖h5+ ♔d6 95.♖h6+ ♘e6

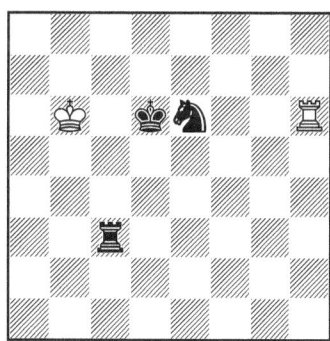

96.♔b5!

Preventing the opponent from cutting off his king on the very edge of the board.

96...♖c1 97.♔b4 ♔e5 98.♖h5+ ♔e4 99.♖h4+ ♘f4 100.♔b5 ♔e5 101. ♖h8 ♘e6 102.♖h5+ ♔d6 103.♔b4 ♘c5 104.♖h6+ ♔d5 105.♖h5+ ♔d4 106.♖h4+ ♘e4 107.♔b5

Taking care to avoid having his king pressed to the edge of the board yet again.

107...♖c5+ 108.♔b6 ♖e5 109.♔c6 ♔c4 110.♖f4 ♖e6+ 111.♔d7

and, realizing the futility of further attempts to play for a win, Black goes for the exchange of rooks

111...♔d5 112.♖f5+! ♖e5 113. ♖xe5+ ♔xe5. Draw.

We now turn to over-the-board examples of struggle between a rook and minor piece versus a pair of minor pieces.

Example No. 87
F. Klein — J. Werle
Germany 2020

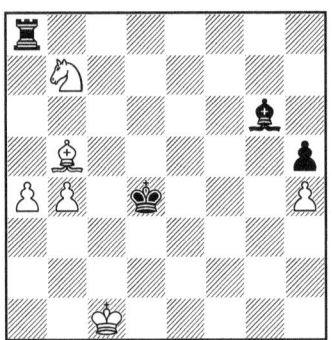

White to move

White has a pair of connected passed pawns for the missing exchange. However, Black has a very active king and is capable of building mating threats to its white counterpart.

40.♔b2?

White's choice of king route is wide of the mark. Both 40.♘c5? ♔c3 and 40.a5? ♔c3 are obviously bad.

White should have sidestepped the mating ideas by directing his king to the center instead: 40.♔d2! ♖f8 (40...♖c8 41.♘c5=) 41.♔e2 ♖f2 (the white passed pawns generate enough counterplay after 41...♖f4 42.b5 ♖xh4

43.b6 ♔d5 44.a5=) 42.♘d6 ♖h2 (42... ♗d3 leads to equality after 43.♘b5+ ♗xb5 44.axb5=) 43.♘b5+ ♔e5 (43... ♔d5 44.a5 ♖xh4 45.a6 ♖xb4 46.a7 ♖a4 47.♘c3+ ♔c6 48.♘xa4 ♔b7=) 44.a5 ♖xh4 (44...♗f7 45.♘c3 ♗c4 46.b5 ♗xe2 47.♘xe2 ♖xh4 48.b6 ♔d6 49.♘g3=) 45.a6 ♖xb4 46.a7 ♗e4

(46...♖a4 47.♗f3 ♗e4 48.♗xe4 ♖xa7! [48...♔xe4? 49.♘c3++−] 49.♘xa7 ♔xe4=)

47.♘c3 ♖b2+ (47...♗a8 48.♗xh5 ♖b7 49.♗f3 ♖d7+ 50.♔e3=) 48.♔e3 ♖b3 (48...♗a8 49.♗f3 ♖b3 50.♗xa8 ♖xc3+ 51.♔d2 ♖a3 52.♗f3 ♖xa7 53.♗xh5=) 49.♔d2 ♗c6 50.♗xh5 ♖a3 51.♗e2 ♖xa7= and Black has failed to disorganize the opponent's pieces and create problems for the white king, which means that the position is drawn.

40...♖f8!

And now the white king falls under a mating attack.

41.♘d6

Neither 41.a5 ♖f2+ 42.♔a1 (42. ♔a3 ♗f7−+; 42.♔c1 ♖c2+ 43.♔d1 ♔e3 44.♘c5 ♖b2−+) 42...♔c3 43.a6 ♖d2 44.♗a4 ♗f7 45.♘c5 ♔xb4 46.a7 ♗d5 47.♘b3 (47.♗b3 ♗f3−+) 47... ♖h2−+, nor 41.♘c5 ♖f2+ 42.♔a1 (42.♔b3? ♗f7+ 43.♔a3 ♖a2#) 42... ♔c3−+ are any better than the text.

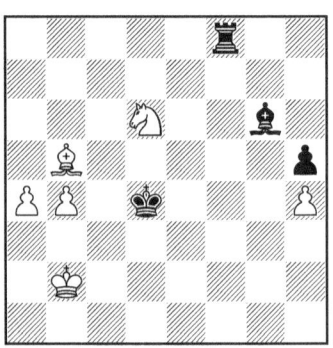

41...♖f6!

Displacing the knight to a worse pasture.

42.♘c4 ♖f2+! 43.♔c1

Neither 43.♔a3 ♗f7 44.♘b2 ♖f3+ 45.♗d3 ♗c4−+, nor 43.♔a1 ♔c3−+ make any difference now.

43...♔c3! 44.♔d1

White loses anyway after 44.♘e3 ♔xb4−+.

44...♖f1+ 45.♔e2 ♗d3+ and White resigned.

Example No. 88
K. Dragun − S. Sevian
Saint Louis 2022

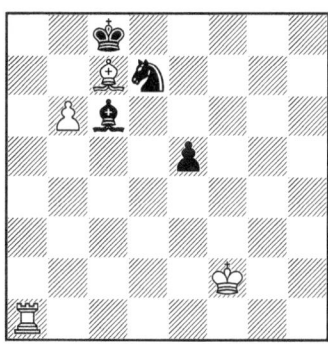

White to move

At first glance, conversion of his material advantage should pose no problems for White. To achieve this he should bring his king into play.

67.♔e3?

This is too blunt. 67.♔e2 ♗b5+ 68.♔d2? would have landed White with the same problems as in the game. 68.♔e3? is no better: 68...♔b7 69.♖b1 ♔c6 70.♖c1+ ♔b7=.

68.♔e1! is correct and now 68...♔b7? runs into 69.♖a7+! ♔c6 70.♗d8 ♘xb6 71.♖c7+ ♔d5 72.♖b7+−, and Black has no saving check.

68...♔b7! 69.♖a7+ (69.♖b1 ♔c6! 70.♖c1+ ♔b7) 69...♔c6 70.♗d8 ♘xb6 71.♖c7+ ♔d5 72.♖b7 ♘c4+!=.

It was necessary to restrict the black king first with 67.♖a7! ♘f6 (if Black marks time with 67...♗b7 68.♔e2! ♗c6 69.♔d3 ♗d5 70.♔c3 e4 71.♔b4 e3 72.♔b5 e2 73.♗g3 ♗b7 74.♖a3+− White brings his king to his pawn to free up his pieces for decisive action. Likewise, 67...e4 68.♔e3+− makes no difference), and reroute the king to the queenside only afterwards: 68.♔e2! (68.♗xe5? ♘g4+) 68...e4 (68...♘d5 69.♗xe5! ♗b7 70.♗d4+−) 69.♔e3 ♗b7. Both 69...♘d5+ 70.♔d4 e3 71.♗g3 ♗b7 72.♖a5! ♘xb6 73.♖c5+ ♔d8 74.♗c7++−, and 69...♘d7 70.♔d4+− lose the game.

70.♖a5! ♔d7. 70...♘d5+ is also bad for Black: 71.♔d4 ♘xc7 72.♖c5+−, whereas after 70...♗c6 71.♔d4 ♘d7 72.♖a1 ♔b7 73.♖a7+! ♔c8 74.♔c4 e3 75.♗f4 e2 76.♖c7+ ♔d8 77.♗g5+ ♔e8 78.♗h4 ♘xb6+ 79.♔c5+− Black ends up dropping a piece.

71.♔d4! e3

72.♖c5! (72.♔xe3? ♘d5+=) 72...e2 (72...♗c6 73.♖g5+−) 73.♗g3 ♘e4 74.♖c7+ ♔e6 75.♗h4! ♘d6 76.♖e7++−, winning a pawn.

67...♘f6!

Now Black exploits the white king's misplaced position not only to put pressure on the pawn, but also to attack the white bishop with a fork.

68.♗xe5?!

Transposing to another type of endgame, which proves to be a draw. 68.♖c1 ♘d5+ 69.♔e4 ♔b7= is of no help because the white pawn is doomed.

68.♖a7 would still have retained winning chances: 68...♘d5+ 69.♔d2 ♗b7 70.♖a1 ♗c6 (70...♘xc7? 71.♖c1+−) 71.♖c1 ♔d7 72.♖g1 ♔c8! (72...♘xc7? 73.♖g7++−) and now in case of 73.♖g7 ♔b7! 74.♗d8+ ♔c8 75.♖g6 ♔b7! 76.♖g1 ♔c8! (76...♘xb6? 77.♖b1+−) 77.♖c1 ♔d7! we see how White runs into problems keeping his pawn alive, but 73.♗xe5! ♘xb6 74.♔c3 is stronger, and this ending gives White substantial practical winning chances, as we are going to see in the next example.

68...♘d5+ 69.♔d4 ♘xb6 70.♔c5 ♘d7+!

70...♔b7? fails to 71.♖b1+−.

71.♔xc6 ♘xe5+ 72.♔d6

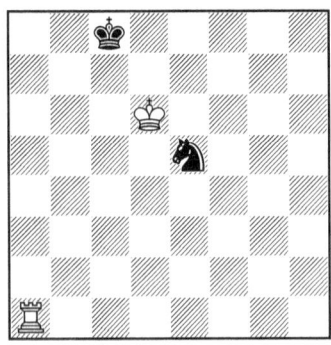

72...♘d7!

The only move that holds a draw.

Both 72...♘f7+? 73.♔e7 ♘e5 74.♖c1+ ♔b7 75.♔d6 ♘f7+ 76.♔e6 ♘d8+ 77.♔d7 ♘f7 78.♖c5+−,

and 72...♘c4+? 73.♔d5! ♘e3+ (73...♘b6+? 74.♔c6 ♘d7 75.♖a8+ ♘b8+ 76.♔b6+−) 74.♔e4 ♘g4 (74...♘c4 75.♖c1+−) 75.♖a6 ♘f2+ 76.♔e3 ♘g4+ 77.♔f4 ♘f2 78.♖d6+− would have lost the game because the black knight has departed from its king and is doomed in both cases.

73.♖a7 ♘b8!

73...♘b6? 74.♔c6+−.

74.♖a2 ♘d7 75.♖a1 ♘b8!

Then White persisted for ages in unsuccessful attempts to make Black go wrong.

76.♖h1 ♔b7 77.♖b1+ ♔c8 78.♖b3 ♘d7 79.♖c3+ ♔d8 80.♖c1 ♘f8 81.♖e1 ♘d7 82.♖a1 ♔c8 83.♖b1 ♘b8 84.♖c1+ ♔b7 85.♖c2 ♘a6 86.♖b2+ ♔c8 87.♖b5 ♘b8! 88.♖a5 ♔b7 89.♖a2 ♘a6 90.♖b2+ ♔c8 91.♖b3 ♘b8! 92.♖b6 ♘d7 93.♖c6+ ♔d8 94.♖c7 ♘f8 95.♖e7

95.♖a7 ♔e8!= is a draw, too.

95...♘g6 96.♖f7

96.♖g7 ♘f8!= makes no difference to the evaluation.

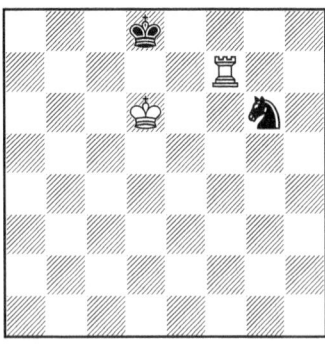

96...♔e8!

Not only defending against a potential checkmate along the bottom rank, but also rushing to his knight's rescue.

97.♖f6 ♘f8

and White finally recognized the futility of his attempts to prevail in this ending.

98.♖xf8+ ♔xf8 and a draw agreed.

Example No. 89
F. Vallejo Pons – M. Carlsen
Karlsruhe 2019

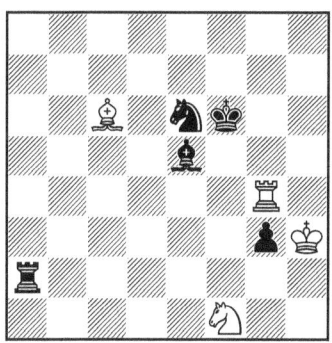

Black to move

This time we begin not with the rook and minor piece vs. two minor pieces endgame itself, but with the move prefacing it so as not to miss a classy idea from the world champion.

48...g2!

Black gives up his last pawn in exchange for more valuable material. The position is ripe for taking a committal decision about what material balance to choose for the final endgame type. And now it is up to White to select the lesser evil.

Black gains nothing from 48... ♘g5+? 49.♔h4.

49.♗xg2

49.♖xg2? ♘f4+ fails on the spot because White drops an entire rook.

Or 49.♘e3 ♖a3. The endgame is also winning following 49...♘f4+ 50.♖xf4+ (50.♔h4 ♖a3! 51.♘d5+

♘xd5 52.♗xd5? ♗g3+!–+) 50...♗xf4 51.♘xg2 ♗d6–+.

50.♖xg2 (50.♔xg2 ♖xe3–+) 50... ♖xe3+ 51.♔g4 ♘d4

The current material balance is rook and two minor pieces versus rook and minor piece with no pawns on the board. Overall, this balance is considered drawish. However, in this particular position White experiences problems with his king, which proves decisive in assessing the position as winning for Black.

52.♗b7. 52.♗d5? fails to 52...♘f5 53.♗a2 (53.♖f2? ♖g3+ 54.♔h5 ♖g5#; 53.♗b7? ♖b3–+) 53...♘h6+ 54.♔h4 (54.♔h5 ♖h3#) 54...♗g3+! 55.♔h5 (55.♖xg3 ♘f5+–+; 55.♔h3 ♗f4+ 56.♔h4 ♖e1–+) 55...♔g7–+, and Black has woven a mating net for the white king.

52...♘f5! 53.♗c8 ♘d6 54.♗d7 ♖c3! 55.♖f2+ ♔e7 56.♖e2 (White is doomed following 56.♗f5 ♖g3+ 57.♔h4 ♘c4 58.♗h3 ♘e3–+) 56...♘c4 57.♗b5 ♘e3+ 58.♔f3 ♘f5+ 59.♔f2 ♗f6–+. The white king seems to have fled from the danger zone. However, a second wave of attack by the regrouped black figures is about to come.

For example, 60.♖d2 ♗d4+ 61.♔e2 ♗c5 62.♖b2 ♖h3 63.♔d2 ♔e5 64.♖b1

♘d6 65.♗d3 ♔d4 66.♗g6 ♘c4+ 67.♔e1 ♖h6! 68.♖d1+ ♔e5 69.♗f7 ♖h1+ 70.♔e2 ♖h2+ 71.♔e1 ♘e3−+ and Black gets the upper hand.

49...♘f4+ 50.♖xf4+

50.♔h4? is bad: 50...♘xg2+ 51.♔h5 (51.♔h3 ♘f4+!) 51...♘f4+ 52.♔h4 ♖a8! 53.♔g3 (53.♖g1 ♖h8+ 54.♔g3 ♘e2+−+) 53...♖a3+ 54.♔f2 ♗d4+ 55.♔e1 ♔f5 56.♖g8 ♖a1+−+.

50...♗xf4−+

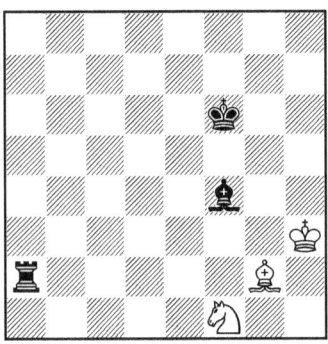

The material balance currently on the board is also considered to be drawn. However, in evaluating a particular endgame the weaker side's king's position and piece activity again come to the forefront. In fact, White is up against significant challenges here. His king is under attack, while his pieces are hard to coordinate.

51.♗f3 ♗b8! 52.♘g3 ♔g5! 53.♘e2

53.♘e4+? loses quickly to 53...♔f4 54.♗h1 ♖a3+ 55.♔h4 ♗a7 56.♗g2 (56.♘g5 ♗f2+ 57.♔h5 ♖a5−+) 56...♖a2 57.♔h3 ♖a6−+.

53...♗c7! 54.♔g2

There are no alternative moves: 54.♘d4? ♖h2#; 54.♗g4? ♖a3+.

54...♔h4! 55.♔f2 ♗b6+! 56.♔e1

Keeping the king on the flank is of no help either: 56.♔g2 ♗e3 57.♔h2 ♖a1

58.♔g2? ♖e1 59.♔h2 (59.♘c3 ♖g1+ 60.♔h2 ♖c1 61.♘e4 ♖c2+ 62.♔h1 ♗a7 63.♗g2 ♖c1+ 64.♔h2 ♗b8+ 65.♘g3 ♗xg3#) 59...♖f1 60.♗d5 ♖f2+−+.

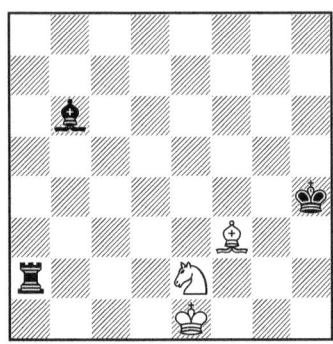

56...♗e3!

Rerouting the bishop to a stronger outpost.

57.♔d1 ♔g5 58.♗e4

58.♘c3! is more precise.

58...♔f6 59.♗f3 ♔e5 60.♗g2 ♔d6?!

The world champion has played superbly up to this moment, but now deviates from the precise winning plan. 60...♗d2! is correct: 61.♗f3 ♗b4 62.♗g2 ♔f6! 63.♗f3 ♔g5! 64.♔c1 (64.♗g2 ♔g4−+) 64...♗d2 65.♔b1 ♗a3 66.♔a1 ♗c5 67.♔b1 ♖d3! 68.♗c6 ♖e3 69.♘c1 ♗a3 70.♘a2 ♖b3+ 71.♔a1 (71.♔c2 ♖b2+−+) 71...♗d6 −+ and Black wins.

61.♗e4 ♔c5 62.♗f5

62.♗f3! is stronger, setting the following trap: 62...♔c4? 63.♗d5! ♔xd5 64.♘c3+=.

62...♖d2+ 63.♔e1 ♖d8 64.♗e4

64.♔f1? is bad: 64...♖f8 65.♘g3 ♗f4 66.♘e4+ ♔d4 67.♗g6 (67.♗h7 ♔e3 68.♔g2 ♖f7 69.♗g6 ♖g7−+) 67...♔e3 68.♔g2 (68.♔e1 ♖g8−+) 68...♖g8−+.

64...♔c4 65.♔f1

65.♘g3! is tougher.

65...♖f8+

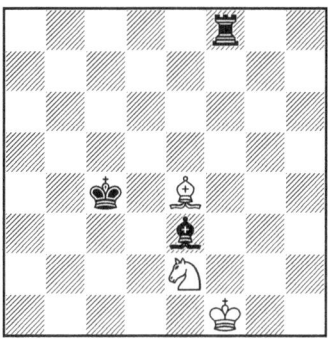

66.♔e1?

This is an erroneous decision. The correct continuation was 66.♔g2! ♖f2+ 67.♔h1! with a cute stalemate idea 67...♖xe2? (67...♔b4 68.♗d3! and the black king cannot become part of a full-fledged fight) 68.♗d3+! ♔xd3=.

66...♗f2+! 67.♔d2

67.♔f1 also failed to 67...♗c5+ 68.♔e1 (68.♔g2 ♖f2+−+) 68...♗b4+ 69.♔d1 ♖d8+ 70.♔c1 ♗e7 71.♔c2 (71.♘f4 ♗g5−+; 71.♘g3 ♗g5+ 72.♔b2 ♖d2+ 73.♗c2 ♗f4 74.♘e4 ♖h2 75.♔b1 ♖h1+ 76.♔a2 ♗e5 77.♗b1 ♔b4−+) 71...♗g5−+.

67...♖d8+! 68.♔c2

68.♔c1? ♗e3+ 69.♔b1 ♖d1+ 70.♔c2 ♖d2+−+ is bad.

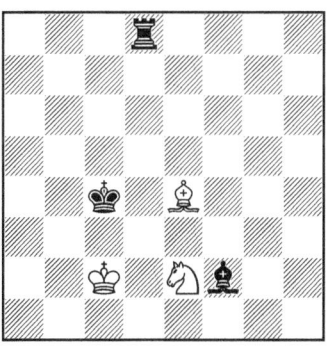

68...♗e3!

Paving the way for infiltration of the black rook along the d-file.

69.♗f3

There is no good move for White now.

69.♘c1 ♖d2+ 70.♔b1 ♖d1−+, 69.♘c3 ♖d2+−+, 69.♘g3 ♖d2 70.♔b1 ♔b3 71.♗f3 ♖b2+ 72.♔a1 ♗d4 73.♘f5 ♖a2+ 74.♔b1 ♖a1#, and 69.♔b1 ♖d1+ 70.♔b2 ♖d2+−+ all lose the game.

69...♖d2+ 70.♔b1 ♔b3! 71.♘c1+

Or 71.♘g3 ♖b2+ 72.♔a1 ♗d4 73.♗d5+ ♔a3−+.

71...♔a3 72.♘e2 ♖b2+ 73.♔a1 ♖b8 and White resigned in the face of the black bishop's transfer to the a1-h8 diagonal with a crushing effect.

Lessons from my Career

Example No. 90
A. Mista − A. Galkin
Plovdiv 2008

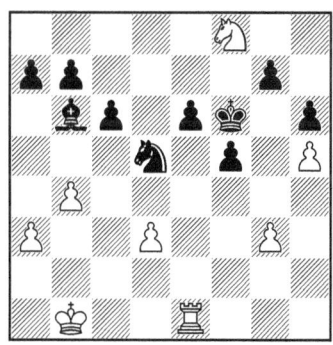

Black to move

Black has a bishop, a pair of pawns and very active pieces for the exchange. Obviously, if he succeeds in coping with his opponent's concrete threats he will enjoy substantial winning chances.

37...♗e3!

Stifling the rook's pressure along the e-file. The pawn move 37...e5 walks into the 38.♘d7+ fork .

Meanwhile, in case of 37...♗f2?! 38.♖xe6+ ♔f7 39.♖e5! (39.♖e2 ♘c3+) 39...f4 (39...♗xg3 40.♖xf5+ ♘f6 41.♘g6 ♔e6 42.♖f3 ♘xh5 43.♘f8+ ♔e7 44.♘g6+=) 40.♖f5+ ♘f6 (40...♔e8? is an error because of 41.g4!) 41.♖xf4 ♗xg3 42.♖f3 ♔xf8 43.♖xg3 ♘xh5 44.♖f3+ ♘f6 45.♔c2 ♔f7 (45...h5 46.♔c3 h4? 47.♖f4 h3 48.♖h4) 46.♔c3 g5 (46...h5 47.♔d4!) 47.♔d4 ♔e6 (47...♔g6 48.♔e5 ♘g4+ 49.♔e4 h5 50.♖f8=) 48.♖e3+ ♔d6 49.♖f3= the activity of the white pieces is sufficient for equality.

38.♖f1

After 38.♘d7+ ♔e7 39.♘c5 (39.♘e5 ♗f2−+) 39...b6!? 40.♘b3 ♗f2 41.♖c1 ♔d6−+ or 38.♔c2 ♔f7!? 39.♘d7 ♗f2−+ Black wins yet another pawn.

38...♗d4!

38...e5? is premature yet again: 39.♘d7+! ♔e6 40.♘f8+=.

39.♖e1

Both 39.♔c2? ♘e3+−+ and 39.♘d7+ ♔e7!? 40.♘c5 b6 41.♘b3 ♗e5 42.♖f3 (42.♖g1 ♘f6−+) 42...♘f6 43.♖e3 ♘g4 44.♖f3 ♔d6 45.d4 ♗f6 46.♔c2 ♗g5 47.♔d3 ♘f6−+ are bad.

39...e5!

39...♔e7? is wrong because of 40.♘xe6 ♗c3 (40...♗f2 41.♖f1) 41.♖e2.

40.♘d7+ ♔e6 41.♘xe5?

White fails to see the trap set by his opponent. His position is bad following 41.♘f8+ ♔e7 42.♘g6+ ♔f6∓.

It was worth going for 41.♘c5+ ♗xc5 42.bxc5 ♘f6 43.d4 (43.♖h1? ♘d7 44.♖c1 ♔f6 45.♔b2 ♔g5−+) 43...e4 44.♖h1 (44.♔c2? ♘xh5 45.g4 fxg4 46.♖xe4+ ♔f5 47.♖e5+ ♔f4 48.♖xh5

g3 49.♖h1 g2 50.♖d1 ♔g3−+) 44...♔d5 45.♖f1 ♔xd4 46.♖xf5 b5!? 47.cxb6 (47.♔c2? a5 48.♔d2 b4 49.axb4 axb4 50.♔c2 e3−+) 47...axb6∓, but White's position looks difficult here as well.

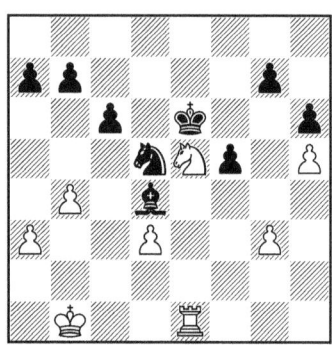

41...♗c3!

A strong intermezzo. Now the white rook is in for a fork in the line 42.♖e2 ♗xe5 43.d4 ♘c3+. Therefore, White resigned.

We now review examples from grandmaster games in which the rook and minor piece tandem opposes a pair of rooks.

Example No. 91
S. Brynell – B. Heberla
Sweden 2020

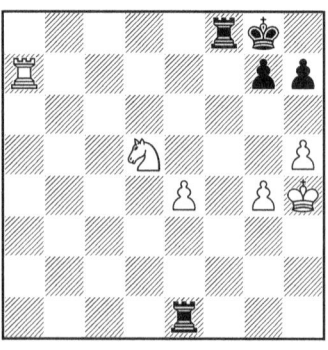

White to move

Black is material up. However, pawns on the same flank and overall activity of White's pieces offer the latter player hope of a satisfactory outcome in this game. It only remains to find the right path.

58.♖e7?

In defending his pawn White does not fully realize the challenges his king is up against. 58.h6?! is underwhelming too: 58...♖h1+ 59.♔g3 (59.♔g5 gxh6#) 59...♖xh6 60.♘e7+ ♔h8 61.♘f5 ♖g6!? and Black should convert his material advantage.

It was necessary to start generating counterplay even at the cost of a pawn: 58.♘e7+! ♔h8 (58...♔f7? 59.♘g6+) 59.e5! ♖xe5 (59...h6? fails to 60.♘g6+, while the checks are of no help either: 59...♖h1+ 60.♔g3 ♖g1+ 61.♔h3=) 60.♘f5 ♖e4 (60...g6 61.hxg6 hxg6 62.♘h6=; 60...♖g8 61.♘d6=; 60...♖e1 61.♘xg7 ♖e4 62.h6!?)

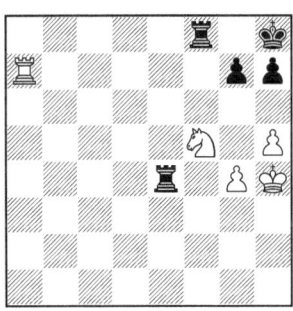

61.h6! Shattering the black king's pawn cover. 61.♘xg7?! is dubious: 61...♖ff4 62.♔g5 (62.h6 ♖xg4+ 63.♔h5 ♖h4+ 64.♔g5 ♖eg4+ 65.♔f5 ♖a4) 62...♖xg4+ 63.♔f6 ♖ef4+ 64.♘f5 ♖g8 65.♖a5 ♖f1.

61...g6. In case of 61...gxh6 62.♘xh6 ♖e1 (62...♖b4 63.♖c7!?; 62...♖fe8 63.♘f7+ ♔g8 [63...♔g7 64.♘d6+

♖8e7 65.♘f5+=] 64.♘h6+=) 63.♔g5= the white pieces' activity makes it hard for Black to improve his position further.

62.♘d6 ♖e2 (62...♖e6? is an error that already turns the tables in White's favor following 63.♘f7+ ♔g8 64.♘g5, while 62...♖ef4 63.♔g5 ♖f1 64.♖g7 ♖1f2 65.♖a7 transposes to the main line) 63.♘f7+ ♔g8 64.♘d6 (64.♘g5? ♖h2+ 65.♔g3 ♖xh6−+ is bad) 64...♖h2+ 65.♔g5 ♖hf2 66.♖g7+ ♔h8 67.♖a7= and White has sufficient counterplay to make a draw.

58...h6!

Closing the entry point for the white king, namely the g5-square.

58...♖f3?! is premature: 59.♖e8+ ♔f7 60.♖e7+ ♔f8 61.♖e5 h6 (61...♖h1+?! 62.♔g5 h6+ 63.♔g6 ♖g1 64.♔h7! ♖xg4 65.♘e7 ♔f7 66.♘g6 ♔f6 67.♖e8= yields nothing, too) 62.♖f5+ ♖xf5 63.exf5 and the resulting endgame is drawn.

59.♖e5

59.e5 ♖f3 60.♖e8+ ♔h7 61.g5 ♖e4+−+ loses on the spot. 59.♘c7 ♖f3 60.g5 ♖f4+ 61.♔g3 hxg5−+ is also underwhelming.

Likewise, the white king is denied a safe haven following 59.♔g3 ♖g1+ 60.♔h3 (60.♔h2 ♖xg4−+) 60...♖f3+ 61.♔h2 ♖xg4−+.

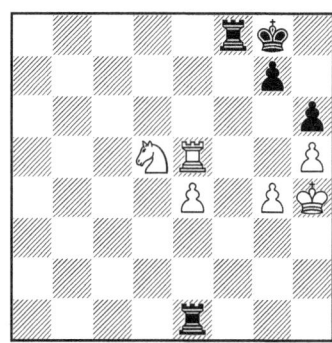

59...♖h1+!

Regrouping the rook with checks. 59...♖f3 60.g5! would be weaker.

60.♔g3 ♖g1+! 61.♔h4

Both 61.♔h2 ♖xg4 62.♘e7+ ♔h7 63.♘g6 ♖f2+ 64.♔h3 ♖g5 65.♖xg5 hxg5 66.e5 ♔h6 67.♔g4 ♖g2+ 68.♔f3 ♖g1 69.♔f2 ♔xh5!−+ and 61.♔h3 ♖f3+−+ lead to failure.

61...♖f2! 62.♔h3 ♖f3+ 63.♔h4

Instead of suffering in a hopeless position after 63.♔h2 ♖xg4−+, White opts to get checkmated.

63...♖h1#.

The following example from a grandmaster game illustrates how important it is to correctly evaluate the transition from a more complex ending to a less complex one when prosecuting your advantage.

Example No. 92
M. Matlakov − V. Potkin
Sochi 2022

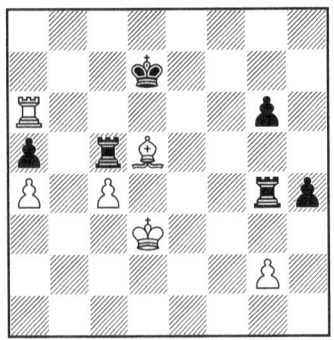

Black to move

Black is the exchange up. White can only counter this with the good position of his bishop and overall activity of his pieces. The evaluation is obvious — White has to fight for a draw.

46...♖xd5+?

Black decides against defending against the bishop check on e6, but returns his extra exchange for the prospect of two connected passed pawns in the rook ending. However, it proves insufficient to get the upper hand in this particular position.

Black needed to play 46...♔c7! 47.♖a7+ (the rook ending is already winning for Black in case of 47.♔e3 g5 48.♔f2 ♖xd5 49.cxd5 ♖xa4−+) 47...♔d6 48.♖a6+ ♔e5 49.♖e6+

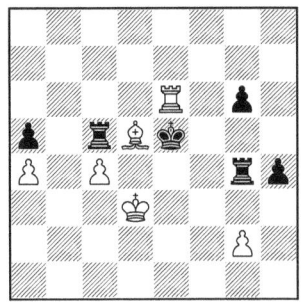

49...♔f5! 49...♔f4? is bad: 50.♖e4+ ♔g3 51.♖xg4+ ♔xg4 52.♔d4 ♖c7 53.♔e5 ♔g3 54.♔d6 ♖c8 55.c5 ♖d8+ 56.♔e6 ♖xd5 57.♔xd5 ♔xg2 58.c6 h3 59.c7 h2 60.c8=♕ h1=♕ 61.♕c2+ ♔g3+ 62.♔e5 ♕h5+ 63.♔f6= with a drawn ending.

50.♖e8 ♔f6 51.♖e6+. 51.♖f8+ is no better: 51...♔e5 52.♖e8+ ♔d6 53.♖e6+ ♔c7 54.♖a6 (54.♖e7+ ♔d8 55.♖a7 g5!?) 54...g5!

51...♔g7 52.♖e7+ ♔h6 53.♖b7. 53.♖a7 g5 54.♖a6+ ♔g7 55.♖a7+ ♔f6 56.♖a6+ ♔e5 57.♖e6+ ♔f5 58.♖e2 ♖f4!? gives the black pieces a substantial boost in activity.

53...♖c8!? 54.♖a7. While White is busy eliminating the pawn, Black finds time to launch an attack with his rooks

on the opponent's king: 54.♖b5 ♖d8!?
55.♔e2 ♖g3 56.♖xa5 ♖a3 57.♔f2
♔g5! 58.♗e4+ ♔f4 59.♗xg6 ♖d2+
60.♔g1 ♖a1+ 61.♔h2 h3!−+ 62.♔xh3
♖h1#.

54...♖d8 55.♔e3 (both 55.♖xa5
♖xg2−+ and 55.♔e2 ♖e8+ 56.♔d3
♖e5!? 57.♖xa5 ♖xg2−+ are bad)

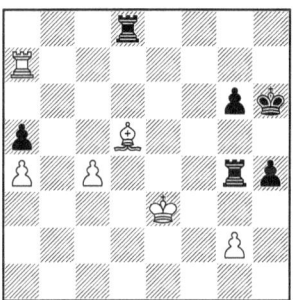

55...g5!? It is time to move the pawn
forward.

56.♖xa5. The white king is again
in dire straits following 56.♖a6+ ♔g7
57.♖a7+ ♔f6 58.♖a6+ ♔e7 59.♖a7+
♔d6 60.♖a6+ ♔c5 61.♖xa5+ ♔b4
62.♖a7 ♖g3+ 63.♔f2 ♖f8+ 64.♔g1
♖f4−+.

56...♖g3+ 57.♔e2 (57.♔f2 g4
58.♖a6+ ♔g5 59.♖e6 ♖f8+ 60.♔e2
♖a3−+) 57...g4−+ and Black's passed
pawn should seal the outcome of the
game.

47.cxd5 g5

Or 47...♖xg2 48.♖xa5 ♔d6. White
also holds his ground after 48...h3
49.♖a7+ ♔d6 50.♖h7 ♖a2 (50...h2
51.♔e4=) 51.♖h6 ♔xd5 52.♔e3 (52.
♖xg6? loses to 52...♖a3+ 53.♔c2 h2
54.♖h6 ♖a1−+)

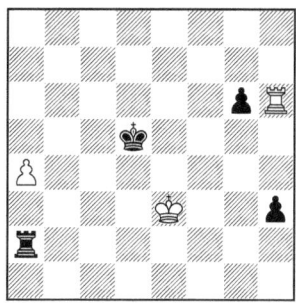

a) 52...♔e5 53.♔f3 ♔f5 (53...h2
54.♔g3=) 54.♖xh3= with an easy draw;

b) 52...h2 53.♔f4 ♖xa4+ 54.♔g3
♖a2 55.♖xh2 ♖xh2 56.♔xh2 ♔e4
57.♔g3 ♔f5 58.♔f3=;

c) 52...♖xa4 53.♖xg6 ♖h4 54.♖g1=;

d) 52...g5 53.♖h5=

whereas 48...g5 transposes to the
game.

49.♖a8 ♔xd5 50.a5 ♔c6 51.♖b8!
♔c7 (51...g5 52.a6 ♖a2 53.♖g8 ♖a5 54.a7
♔b7 55.a8=♕+ ♖xa8 56.♖xg5=) 52.♖b1
g5 (52...h3 53.♔e4 g5 54.a6=) 53.a6 ♖a2
54.♖b7+ ♔d6 55.♖g7 ♖a5 56.a7= and
White achieves a draw here too.

48.♖xa5 ♖xg2

Black cannot improve his position
following 48...♔d6 49.♖b5 ♖xg2 (49...
♖xa4 50.♔e3 g4 51.♖b8=) 50.♔e4 ♖e2+
51.♔f5 ♖e5+ 52.♔g4 ♖xd5 53.♖b6+
♔c7 (53...♔c5 54.a5=) 54.♖h6=.

49.♔e4!? h3

White is also in time with saving counterplay after 49...g4 50.♖a7+ ♔d6 51.♖a6+ ♔c7 52.♖h6 h3 53.a5 h2 54.♔f4 g3 55.d6+ ♔c6 56.a6 ♖g1 57.a7 ♔b7 58.d7 ♖d1=.

50.♖a7+ ♔c8

50...♔d6 51.♖a6+! ♔c5 52.♖c6+ ♔b4 53.♖h6= yields nothing, too.

51.♖h7 ♖g4+

51...g4 52.♔f4 h2 53.a5 g3 54.a6 ♔b8 55.d6= leads to mass liquidation yet again.

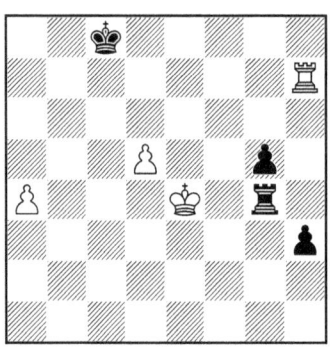

52.♔f3!

52.♔f5? ♖h4−+ loses the game. There is no eliminating the black pawn with 52.♔e3 ♖xa4 53.♖xh3? ♖a3+−+.

52...♖xa4 53.♔g3!

53.♖xh3? blunders to 53...g4+−+.

53...g4

The position after 53...♖a3+ 54.♔g4= is a draw.

54.d6 ♖d4 55.♖c7+! ♔d8 56.♖h7 ♖e4

Bringing the king closer to the action promises nothing to Black either: 56...♔e8 57.♖e7+ ♔f8 58.♖h7 (or 58.♖e1) 58...♔g8 59.♖a7 ♖xd6 60.♔xg4 h2 61.♖a1 ♖g6+ 62.♔h3 ♖g1 63.♖a8+! ♔f7 64.♔xh2=.

57.♔h4

It was also fine to mark time with the rook: 57.♖g7=.

57...♔e8

The black pawns drop in case of 57...h2 58.♔g3=.

58.♔g3 ♖d4 59.♖e7+ ♔f8 60.♖e1 ♔f7 61.d7 ♔f6 62.d8=♕+! ♖xd8 63.♔xg4 and a draw was agreed.

Example No. 93
V. Iordachescu − S.P. Sethuraman
Sharjah 2021

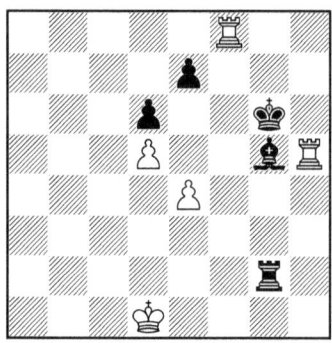

White to move

Despite being an exchange up, it is hard for White to break down Black's defense. Firstly, there are very few pawns on the board. Secondly, the pawns are arranged in a way that defies creating a passer for now. Further, the chain of black pawns is hard to undermine because defending its root e7-pawn is simple for the bishop. Besides, the black king is always ready to take care of it as well.

62.♖hh8?

White attempts to establish as much coordination as possible between his rooks so as to develop an initiative against his opponent's king and bishop. However, he misses his opponent's saving counterplay.

He needed to send his rook in a different direction instead: 62.♖h1!? ♔g7 (White wins after the bad 62...

♖d2+ 63.♔e1 ♖d4? 64.♖g8+ ♔f6 65.♖f1++−, and in case of 62...♖g4 63.♖e1 ♔g7 64.♖ff1 ♖g2 65.♖e2 ♖g3 66.♔c2 the white king also breaks his chains) 63.♖f5 ♗f6 (63...♔g6 64.♖h8!? ♔g7 65.♖c8 ♗f6 66.♔c2 ♖g4 67.♖e2 ♔f7 68.♖f3 ♖g1+ 69.♔c2 makes no difference) 64.♖hf1 ♖a2

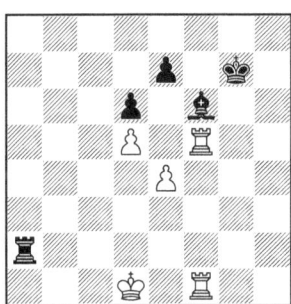

65.♖5f2! It is necessary to lift the restriction stopping the white king from joining the game.

65...♖a4 66.♖f4 ♖a2 67.♖1f2! ♖a3 68.♔e2 ♖a2+ 69.♔d3!? His opponent's solid defense is a hard nut for White to crack without his king's assistance. The ideal route for the white king is c4−b5−c6−d7−e6, with a follow-up combination of creating mating threats to the black king and a winning exchange sacrifice. Black's plans clearly exclude total submission and negligence in the face of imminent defeat. Black will do his best to derail White's plans.

69...♖a3+ 70.♔c4 ♖c3+ 71.♔b4!? ♖e3. Both 71...♔f7? 72.♖xf6++− and 71...♖c5? 72.e5 ♗xe5 73.♖g2+ ♔h6 74.♖h4# lose on the spot.

72.♔b5 ♖c3 73.♖g4+!? ♔f7 74.♖a2 ♖c1 75.♖a4 ♖c5+ (75...♖c2 76.♖c4 ♖b2+ 77.♔c6 ♔e8 78.♖g8+ ♔f7 79.♖a8!?) 76.♔b6 ♖c1 77.♖g2 and White's second rook should help

displace the black rook from the c-file, followed by resuming the white king's progress towards the black pawns. White will enjoy decent practical chances to win the game afterwards.

62...♖d2+! 63.♔e1

The pawn drops following 63.♔c1 ♖xd5+ 64.♔c2 ♖e5=.

63...♖d4!

Now Black piles up on the weak link in his opponent's pawn chain.

64.♖fg8+ Likewise, 64.♖hg8+ ♔h6! makes no difference to the evaluation, although 64...♔h5? is an error: 65.♖f5 ♖xe4+ 66.♔f2 ♖f4+ (White wins the pawn ending following 66...♖g4 67.♔f3 ♖g1 68.♖gxg5+! ♖xg5 69.♔f4! ♖xf5+ 70.♔xf5+−) 67.♔xf4 ♗xf4 68.♔f3 ♗g5 69.♔e4 ♔g4 70.♖g7! ♔h4 71.♔f5 ♗f6 72.♖f7+− and Black cannot stop the decisive exchange sacrifice.

65.♖f1 ♖xe4+ 66.♔d1 ♖h4!=.

64...♔f6 65.e5+

65.♖f8+ ♔g6! leads to a repetition of moves. Giving up a pawn for nothing with 65.♔e2 ♖xe4+ 66.♔d3 ♖e5= leaves White with no winning chances.

65...dxe5 66.♖f8+ ♔g6 67.♖hg8+ ♔h6!

67...♔h5? is underwhelming again: 68.♖f5! ♖g4 69.♖xe5 ♔h4 70.♔e2.

68.♖f1

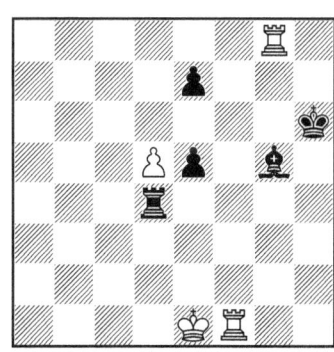

68...♖g4!

A defensive resource of utmost importance. 68...♖h4? would have failed to 69.♖g1! ♗f6 (Black is also in bad shape after 69...♖h5 70.♔e2 e4 71.♖g2 e3 72.♔f3 ♖h3+ 73.♔g4 ♖h4+ 74.♔f5 ♖f4+ 75.♔e5+−) 70.d6+−.

68...♗h4+? 69.♔e2 ♔h7 (69...♖xd5? 70.♖h8+ ♔g5 71.♖g1++−) 70.♖g2 ♖e4+ (70...♖xd5 71.♖h1 ♖d4 72.♖gh2+−) 71.♔d3 ♖d4+ 72.♔e3 ♔h6 73.♖h1 ♔h5 74.♖g7 ♖xd5 75.♖h7++− leaves no hope either.

Useless checks only urge the white king towards a superior outpost: 68...♖e4+? 69.♔d1! ♖d4+ 70.♔c2.

69.♔e2

69.♖h1+? ♗h4+ does not work because in addition to the white king being in check, the white g8-rook is en prise as well.

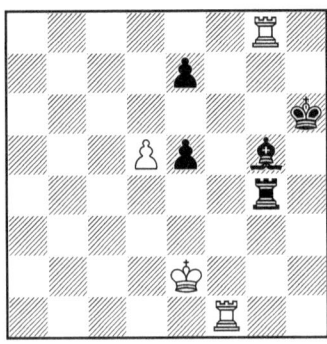

69...♔h7!

The king should help himself out of the mating trap.

70.♖ff8 e4! 71.♖h8+ ♔g6 72.♖hg8+

The check from the fellow rook yields nothing as well: 72.♖fg8+ ♔f6=.

72...♔h7 73.♖h8+ ♔g6 74.♖hg8+ ♔h7

White lacks any real means of improving his position.

75.♔f1 e3 76.♖h8+ ♔g7 77.♖hg8+ ♔h7 78.♖h8+ ♔g7 79.♖hg8+ ♔h7 80.♖h8+ ♔g7 and the opponents agreed a draw.

We now consider two more examples with the rook and minor piece belonging to the stronger side.

Example No. 94
D. Dubov – L. Dominguez
Berlin 2022

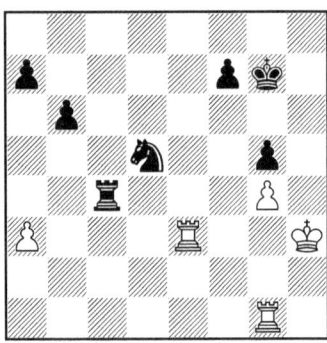

White to move

Black has a pair of pawns for the missing exchange. Besides, his pieces are very active, while his opponent is saddled with pawn weaknesses. The pair of rooks is far from establishing any sort of coordination as yet. It is clearly White who has to fight for a draw in this ending.

43.♖f3?

In removing the rook from en prise, White choses the wrong place for it. The rook is misplaced here and takes away the vital f3-square from his king.

43.♖e5!? deserved consideration, then 43...♘f4+ 44.♔h2 (44.♔g3? fails to 44...♖c3+ 45.♔f2 ♘d3+−+) 44...♖c2+ 45.♔h1! (45.♔g3? ♖c3+ 46.♔h2

♖h3#) 45...♔g6 46.♖d1 and the white rooks gain room to maneuver.

46...♖c3. White also maintains the balance after 46...♖g2 47.♖d6+ f6 48.♖f5 ♖xg4 49.♖fxf6+ ♔g7 50.♖f5=.

47.♖e7 ♖xa3. 47...♖h3+ 48.♔g1 ♖g3+ 49.♔f2 ♖xg4 50.♖d6+ f6 51.♖xa7= is harmless as well.

48.♖dd7 ♖h3+ (48...f6? loses to 49.♖g7+ ♔h6 50.♖h7+ ♔g6 51.♖dg7#) 49.♔g1 ♖g3+ 50.♔f2 ♖xg4 51.♖xf7 and White holds his ground despite being material down: 51...a5 52.♔f3 ♖g1 53.♖f8 g4+ 54.♔e3 (54.♔xf4? blunders to 54...♖f1+ 55.♔xg4 ♖xf8 56.♖d6+ ♖f6−+) 54...♘h3 (54...♖e1+ 55.♔f2 ♖e4 56.♖d6+= yields nothing either) 55.♖d6+ ♔g5 (55...♔g7 56.♖b8=) 56.♖xb6=.

It was also fine to go for 43.♖b3 ♘f4+ 44.♔h2 ♖c2+ 45.♔h1 ♘g6 46.♖e1!?, and active counterplay should help White achieve a draw.

43...♖c2! 44.♔g3

44.♖d1? fails miserably to 44...♘f4+ 45.♔g3 ♖g2#.

Both 44.♖ff1 ♘f4+ 45.♔g3 ♖c3+ 46.♖f3 (46.♔h2 ♖h3#) 46...♘e2+−+ and 44.♖gf1 ♘f4+ 45.♖xf4 (45.♔g3 ♖g2#) 45...gxf4 46.♖xf4 ♖c3+−+ lead to failure.

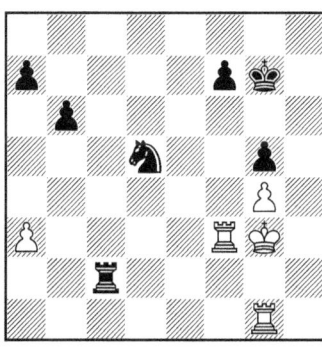

44...♘f4!

Mounting threats against both the white king and the misplaced white rooks.

45.♖xf4

Attempting to bail out in the rook ending. White is checkmated after 45.♖f2? ♖c3+ 46.♔h2 (46.♖f3 ♘e2+−+) 46...♖h3#.

45...gxf4+ 46.♔xf4

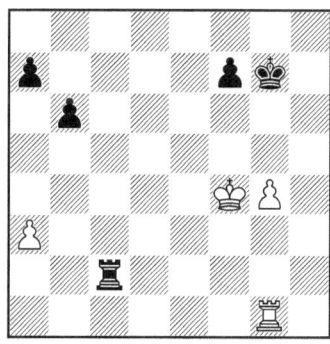

46...♖c3!

Yet another precise move. White could have still put up some fight following 46...♖c4+ 47.♔f5 ♖a4 48.♖g3.

47.♖a1

47.a4 drops the pawn to 47...♖c4+−+.

47...♖c4+! 48.♔g5 ♖a4!

Black has forced the white rook into a passive position.

49.♔h5 ♖a5+ 50.♔h4

50.g5 f6−+ drops a pawn, this time on the kingside.

50...♔g6

White is doomed and, no longer capable of marking time passively in the face of the worse to come, gives up yet another pawn.

51.♖c1 ♖xa3 52.♖c6+ f6 and, having delivered a check from his deathbed, White threw in the towel.

Example No. 95
E. Iturrizaga – T. Stoyanov
Catez 2022

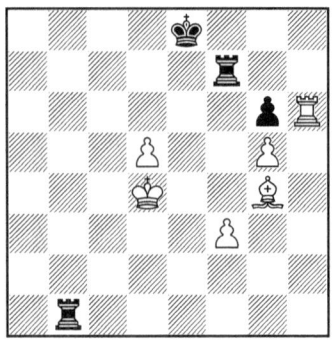

Black to move

In terms of material, White has a bishop and a pair of pawns for a rook, which even exceeds the rook equivalent. Besides, the only remaining black pawn is weak and is likely to perish soon. The black king is also misplaced and faces mating attacks in various lines. Further, the white pieces are very active, and the black rooks have so far no way of attacking the white pawns. Black is in for a grueling defense.

43...♔e7?

Black steps up with his king and sacrifices the pawn in the hope of generating active play against the opponent's king.

An attempt to switch to passive defense also backfires for Black 43...♖g7? 44.♔e5! ♖b6 (44...♔e7 45.d6+ ♔f7 46.♗e6++−; 44...♔f7 45.♗e6+ ♔e7 46.d6++−) 45.♗e6 ♔e7 46.f4!? ♖a6 (46...♖d6 47.♖h8 ♖d8 48.♖xd8 ♔xd8 49.♔f6 ♖a7 50.♔xg6+−) 47.♖h8 ♖b6 48.♖a8+− with a decisive initiative. Likewise, 43...♖b6? 44.♔c5 ♖a6 (44...♖fb7 45.d6+−) 45.d6 ♖a5+ 46.♔b6+− is bad.

It was necessary to play 43...♖d1+! 44.♔c5

(Black holds the position following 44.♔e5 ♔e7! 45.♖xg6 ♖e1+ 46.♔d4 ♖f4+ 47.♔d3 [47.♔c5 ♖c1+ 48.♔b6 ♖b4+ 49.♔a7 ♖d1 50.♖e6+ ♔f8 51.♖d6 ♖b5 52.♗e6 ♖db1 53.f4 ♖b7+ 54.♔a6 ♖b8 55.♔a7 ♖8b7+=; 47.♔c3 ♖d1 48.♖e6+ ♔f8 49.d6 ♔g7 50.♖e7+ ♔g6 51.d7 ♔xg5 52.♖e8 ♖fd4=] 47...♖d1+ 48.♔e3 ♖fd4

49.♖e6+

[49.♗e6 ♖1d3+ 50.♔f2 [50.♔e2 ♖d2+!] 50...♖f4 51.♔e2 [51.♔g2 ♔e8!] 51...♖fxf3 52.d6+ ♖xd6 53.♔xf3 ♖xe6= is harmless]

49...♔f8 50.♖f6+ ♔g7 51.♗e6 ♖1d3+ 52.♔f2

52...♖d1!? And it is unclear how White is supposed to set his multiple passed pawns in motion.

53.♖f5 [53.f4 ♖4d3!] 53...♖1d2+ 54.♔g3 ♖d1!? 55.♖e5 ♖g1+ 56.♔f2 ♖gd1!? [56...♖dd1? 57.♗h3! ♖h1 58.♗f5] 57.♖e4

a) 57...♖4d3!?

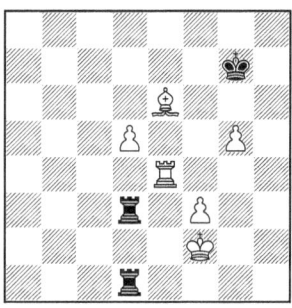

58.f4 ♔g6! Black's piece activity proves sufficient compensation in this ending. For example, 59.♖e3 ♖d4 60.♖f3 ♖a1!? 61.♔g2 [61.f5+ ♔xg5 62.f6 ♖dd1=; 61.♔g3 ♖g1+!; 61.♔e3 ♖ad1!] 61...♖e1 62.♖f2 [the line 62.f5+ ♔xg5 63.f6 ♖d2+ 64.♔f2 ♖xf2+ 65.♔xf2 ♖xe6 66.dxe6 ♔xf6 67.e7 ♔xe7= ends in a total liquidation] 62...♖a1!? [62...♖e3? 63.f5+ ♔xg5 64.f6] 63.♔g3 ♖d3+ 64.♖f3 [64.♔g4 ♖g1+ 65.♔h4 ♖h1+ 66.♔g4 ♖g1+=] 64...♖g1+ 65.♔f2 ♖f1+! 66.♔xf1 ♖xf3+ 67.♔e2 ♖xf4=;

b) 57...♔g6? fails to 58.♖xd4 ♖xd4 59.♔e3+−;

c) 57...♖xe4? is also bad: 58.fxe4 ♔g6 59.♔e2 ♖a1 [59...♖b1 60.d6 ♔xg5 61.e5 ♔f4 62.♗b3! ♖b2+ 63.♔e1 ♖xb3 64.d7 ♖d3 65.e6+−] 60.d6! ♔xg5 61.e5 ♔f4 [61...♔g6 62.♔e3 ♔g7 63.♔d4 ♔f8 64.♗d7+−] 62.d7 ♖a8 63.♗d5! ♖d8 64.e6+−).

44...♖c1+ 45.♔d6 ♖a1! 46.♖h8+ (the pawn cannot be captured: 46.♖xg6? ♖a6+, and in case of 46.♗e6 ♖xf3 47.♖xg6 ♖ff1!? 48.♖g8+ ♖f8 49.♖g7

♖a6+ 50.♔e5 ♖f1 Black manages to hold) 46...♖f8 47.♖xf8+. Black keeps holding the position after 47.♖h2 ♖f7!? 48.♖c2 ♔f8! 49.♖c3 ♔g7 50.♗e6 ♖fa7 51.♖c8 (51.♖c7+ ♖xc7 52.♔xc7 ♔f8 53.d6 ♖a7+ 54.♔b6 ♖a3 55.♗d5 ♖c3 56.♗c6 ♖d3 57.♔c7 ♔f7) 51...♖f1!?

47...♔xf8 48.♔e6 ♖e1+ 49.♔f6 ♖d1 50.♗e6 (50.♔xg6 ♖xd5=) 50...♖f1 51.♔xg6 (51.♗g4 ♖d1=) 51...♖xf3 52.♔h6 (52.d6 ♖d3 53.d7 ♔e7 54.♗f5 ♖f3=) 52...♖f2! 53.g6 ♖h2+ 54.♔g5 ♔e7 55.g7 ♖g2+ 56.♗g4 (56.♔h6 ♖h2+=) 56...♔f7 57.d6 ♔xg7 58.d7 ♖d2=.

44.♖xg6 ♖d1+ 45.♔c5! ♖c1+ 46.♔b6! ♖b1+

46...♖f8 fails to 47.♖e6+ ♔d8 48.♖c6!? ♖b1+ (48...♖xc6+ 49.dxc6 ♖f7 50.g6 ♖g7 51.♗e6+−) 49.♔c5 ♖c1+ 50.♔d6+−.

47.♔c7 ♔e8+

The checks run out and the white passed pawns seal the game in case of 47...♖c1+ 48.♖c6 ♔f8+ 49.♔d6+−.

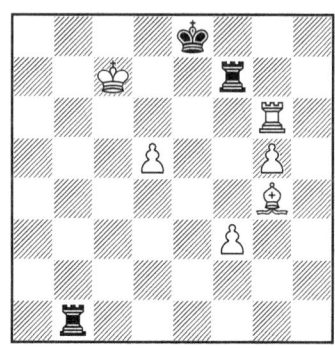

48.♔c6!

A precise move. 48.♔d6? loses to 48...♖b6+−+, and 48.♔c8? ♖a1= is also bad.

48...♖c1+ 49.♔d6! ♔f8 50.♗e6 ♖g7

The black rook has no other retreat: 50...♖xf3 51.♖g8#.

51.♖f6+ ♔e8 52.♖h6. The mating trap snaps shut and Black resigned.

We wrap up by moving to the last material ratio to be analyzed, in which the rook and minor piece tandem opposes a queen.

We begin with a simple example that clearly shows the queen as being far more maneuverable and stronger than any other piece on the board. An active queen controls the entire board and is always poised to deliver various tactical blows.

Example No. 96
A. Pashikian − D. Khismatullin
Minsk 2017

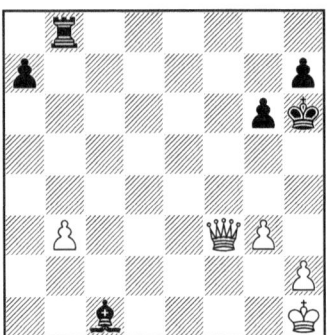

White to move

Should Black manage to establish coordination between his rook and bishop, he can count on holding this endgame. However, his pieces are uncoordinated at the moment, and his king may be exposed to an attack. This is exactly what White exploits.

37.♕c3!
Attacking the first time.
37...♗g5
The alternative bishop retreat also loses, to 37...♗a3 38.♕e3+ g5. The rook falls both to 38...♔h5 39.♕e5++− and to 38...♔g7 39.♕xa7++−.

39.♕e6+   ♔h5   (39...♔g7
40.♕e5++−) 40.g4+ ♔h4 41.♕e1+
♔xg4 (41...♔h3 42.♕g3#) 42.♕g3++−
with decisive material gains.
38.h4!
Attacking the second time.
38...♗d8
The bishop drops to 38...♗e7
39.♕e3++−.

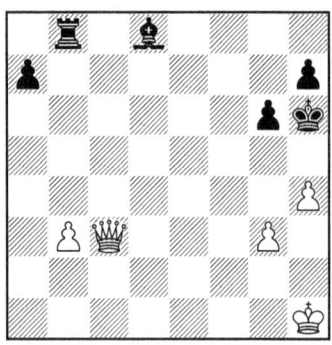

39.♕e3+!
Delivering the first check.
39...g5
Black loses the rook in case of 39...
♔h5 40.♕e5++−.
40.♕e6+!
Delivering the second check.
40...♔h5
40...♔g7 41.♕e5++− is no better than the text.

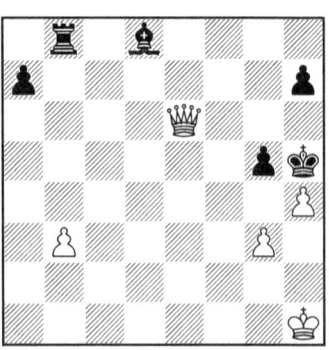

41.♔g2!

The white king also intends to take part in the hunt after his black counterpart. Black resigned in the face of the checkmate coming after 41...a5 42.g4+ ♔xh4 43.♕f7 ♔xg4 44.♕f3+ ♔h4 45.♕h3#.

The following example from the 2017 European Championship allows us to analyze a number of important theoretical positions and techniques in which a rook with one or more pawns can successfully hold a queen to a draw. I am sure that many players will find it interesting to get to know such positions.

Example No. 97
B. Bok – T. Kantans
Minsk 2017

Black to move

On the one hand, the presence of only a few pawns on the board and his pieces standing compactly side by side and protecting each other points to Black's ability to hold this endgame. However, there is a concrete problem of the white e-pawn's advance, upon which the black pieces will lose their coordination and run short of space, while the black king may become exposed to attacks.

44...♔f7?

This natural move is a poor decision. 44...e6? 45.♕b6 ♔f7 (45...♖xe4 46.♕b7++−) 46.♕a7+ ♔g8 47.♔f3!+− transposes to 44...♔f7 and the position given below.

The king was best assigned to a different square with 44...♔f8! 45.♕b7! (45.e5? ♗xe5; 45.♕b8+? ♔f7 46.e5? g5!) 45...♔f7!

(Both 45...♔g7? 46.e5 ♗xe5 47.♕xe7++− and 45...e6? 46.♕h7 ♖d1 [46...♖xe4 47.♕xg6+−] 47.♔f3 ♖g1 48.♕d7 ♗h4 49.♕xe6 ♖g3+ 50.♔e2 ♔g7 51.e5+− are bad. The bishop falls to 45...♔e8 46.e5 ♗xe5 47.♕b5++−.)

46.♔f3! (46.♕b3+? e6!=; 46.♕c7? ♖xe4=) 46...♗h4!? (46...♖d3+ 47.♔e2 ♖d4 48.♔e3!? makes no sense; 46...♖d8 47.e5 ♗h4 results in a transposition) 47.e5 (47.♔e3 ♖d8!?)

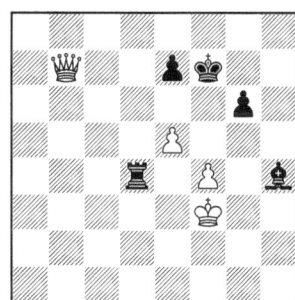

47...♖d8!?

(Both 47...♔g7? 48.♔g4 and 47...g5? 48.♕b3+! ♔g7 49.♔g4! ♖xf4+ 50.♔h5+− are bad and expose the black king to a decisive attack.

The continuation involving a preliminary check also looks interesting: 47...♖d3+ 48.♔g4 [48.♔e4 ♖d8!] 48...♗f2 49.e6+ [49.f5? fails to 49...♖g3+ 50.♔f4 g5+ 51.♔e4 ♖e3+ 52.♔d5 ♗g3 53.e6+ ♔f6=] 49...♔f6 [49...♔xe6?

50.♕e4++−; 49...♔f8? 50.♕b2 ♖g3+ 51.♔h4 ♖f3+ 52.♔g5 ♖g3+ 53.♔h6 ♖h3+ 54.♔xg6 ♖g3+ 55.♔f5+−] 50.♕b2+ ♗d4 51.♕b5 ♖d1! [Both 51...♖e3? 52.♕e8 ♔xe6 53.♕c6+ ♔f7 54.♕d5++− and 51...♖d2? 52.♕g5+ ♔xe6 53.f5+ gxf5+ 54.♕xf5+ ♔d6 55.♕f4++− are bad] 52.♕a4! [52.f5? ♖g1+ 53.♔f4 ♖g5!?] 52...♖d2! [52...♖d3? 53.♕e8 ♔xe6 54.♕xg6++−] 53.♕e8 ♔xe6 54.♕c8+ [The position arising after 54.♕xg6+ ♗f6= is a draw.] 54...♔f7 55.♕c1 ♗e3! [55...♖g2+? 56.♔h3; 55...♖d3? 56.♕c4+] 56.♕c3

56...♗xf4!   Eliminating   his opponent's last pawn. 57.♕c4+ ♔g7 58.♕xf4 [58.♔xf4 g5+!? 59.♔xg5 ♖d6= is also a draw] 58...♖d6= with a drawn position.)

48.♕e4! (The position following 48.♔g4 ♖h8! is a fortress) 48...♖h8 (48...♔g7? 49.f5 ♗g5 50.♔g4+−) 49.f5 (49.e6+? ♔g7=) 49...♗g5 (Black fails to keep his position together following 49...gxf5? 50.♕xf5+ ♔g7 51.♕g4+ ♔f8 52.♕g6 e6 53.♕xe6 ♗e7 54.♕g6 ♖g8 55.♕f5+ ♔e8 56.♕c8+ ♔f7 57.e6+ ♔g7 58.♕c7 ♔f6 59.♕f4+ ♔xe6 60.♕c4++−; 49...♔g7? 50.♕g4 ♖h6 51.fxg6+− is bad, too.)

a) 50.♕d5+ ♔g7 51.♔g4 (51. fxg6? ♔xg6=; 51.f6+ ♗xf6! 52.exf6+

♔xf6!=) 51...♗h4 52.f6+ (52.fxg6 ♔xg6 53.♕e6+ ♔g7=) 52...♗xf6! 53.exf6+

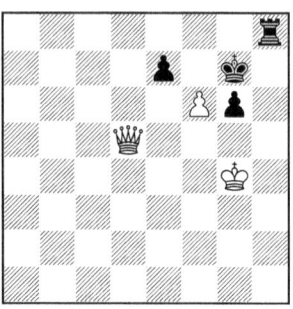

53...exf6!=. This time 53...♔xf6? fails to 54.♕f3+ ♔g7 55.♕c3+ ♔g8 (55...♔h7 56.♕c7+−) 56.♔g5!+−.

54.♕d7+ ♔g8 55.♕d8+ (55.♕e7 ♖h5 56.♕xf6 ♖h7! makes no difference) 55...♔g7 56.♕e7+ ♔g8 57.♕xf6

57...♖h7! This is the only move to hold a draw.

58.♕d6 (58.♕xg6+? ♖g7=; 58.♔g5? ♖h5+! 59.♔xg6 ♖h6+!=; 58.♔f4? ♖f7=) 58...♔g7 59.♕e7+ (59. ♕e6 ♖h5=; 59.♔g5 ♖h5+=) 59...♔g8! (59...♔h6? 60.♕f8+ ♖g7 61.♕f4+ ♔h7 62.♕h2+ ♔g8 63.♔g5+−) 60.♕f6 ♖f7!= and the position is a fortress;

b) Not 50.♔g4? ♖h4+;

c) 50.e6+? ♔g7 51.♕d4+ ♗f6 52.♕g4 ♖h6= is bad;

d) Likewise, 50.f6? ♗xf6 51.exf6 ♔xf6! is no winner (51...exf6? goes down to 52.♕c4+ ♔g7 53.♕c7+ ♔h6 [53...♔g8 54.♕d8+ ♔g7 55.♕e7++−] 54.♕d6+−) after 52.♕d4+ (52.♔g4 ♖h5=) 52...e5 53.♕d6+ ♔f7! 54.♔e4 (54.♕xe5 ♖h5=) 54...♖h4+ 55.♔xe5 ♖h5+!=

45.♕b7! ♗g7?!

A relatively better continuation was 45...♔f8 46.♕a7! Both 46.e5? ♗xe5 and 46.♕b8+ ♔f7 47.e5? g5! 48.exf6 (48.♕b3+ ♔g6 49.♕b1+ ♔h6 50.♕h1+ ♔g6 51.exf6 ♖xf4+ 52.♔g3 exf6=) 48...♖xf4+ 49.♔xg5 ♖xf6= are bad and lead to a theoretically drawn position.

46...♔f7. Black drops the rook to 46...♖xe4? 47.♕a8++−, while after 46...♖d8 47.e5! ♗g7 48.♔g5! ♔f7 49.♕a2+ e6 50.♕a7++− White manages to get to the black king.

47.♕c5! Paving the way for the pawns to move.

47...e6 (The alternatives collapse on the spot: 47...♖d2? 48.e5 ♗g7 49.e6+! ♔xe6 50.♕e3++−; 47...♖d1? 48.e5 ♗g7 49.♕c4+ ♔f8 50.♕c8+ ♔f7 51.e6+ ♔f6 52.♕g8+−; 47...♖d8? 48.e5 ♗g7 49.♕c4+ ♔f8 50.♔g5+−.)

48.♕a7+! 48.e5? is an error: 48...♖d5 49.♕c7+ ♗e7, and Black has built a fortress.

48...♔g8 (Both 48...♔e8? 49.♕h7+− and 48...♔f8? 49.e5 ♗xe5 50.♕c5++− lose the game.)

49.♔f3! There is no doing without the king's assistance. 49.♕b8+? is bad: 49...♔f7 50.e5 ♖d8! 51.♕b7+ ♗e7 52.♕h1 ♔g7=.

49...♖d3+ 50.♔e2 ♖d4. 50...♖d8 is also of no help: 51.e5! ♗h4 (51...♗g7 52.♕e7 ♖f8 53.♕xe6+ ♔h7 54.♕d7 ♖xf4 55.e6+− and the passed pawn will win the rook) 52.♔f3! ♖d5 53.♕a4! ♔f7 54.f5 exf5 55.♕xh4 ♖xe5 56.♕h7+ ♔f6 57.♕h8+ ♔e6 58.♕g7+− and Black fails to build any drawn position.

51.♔e3! (51.e5? ♖xf4 52.exf6 ♖xf6, reaching a drawn position yet again: 53.♕e7 ♖f5 54.♔e3 ♔h8 55.♔e4 ♔g8 56.♕xe6+ ♔g7=) 51...♖d8 (51...♗g7 52.♕e7+−) 52.e5 ♗h4 53.♔f3+− also leads to a lost position for Black. White is poised to attack the bishop with his king and take Black's shaky structure apart.

46.♕b3+! ♔f8

46...e6 47.♕b7+ ♔g8 is of no help either. The black king falls into captivity in case of 47...♔f8 48.♔g5 ♖d3 (48...♖d1 49.♕a8+ ♔f7 50.♕a7+ ♔f8 51.♔xg6+−; 48...♖d2 49.♕b4++−) 49.♕c8+ ♔f7 50.♕c7+ ♔f8 51.f5! gxf5 52.♔g6+−.

48.♔g5! ♖d2 49.♕e7 ♖g2+ 50.♔h4 ♔h7 51.♕xe6+−.

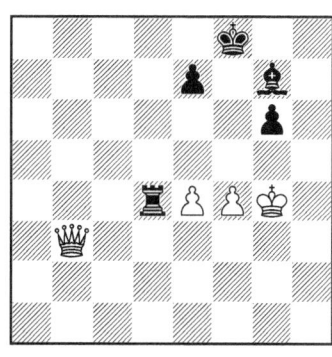

47.♔g5!

The white king assaults the enemy's fortifications.

47...e5

The rook drops when saving his own pawns in case of 47...♖d6 48.e5 ♖c6 49.♕d5 ♖a6 50.♕b7 ♖e6 51.♕a8+ ♔f7 52.♕d5 ♗h8 53.f5 gxf5 54.♔xf5+−.

48.♕b8+ ♔f7

48...♔e7 49.♔xg6+− is equally hopeless.

49.♕c7+ and Black resigned.

Lessons from my Career

Example No. 98
G. Kaidanov − A. Galkin
Moscow 2003

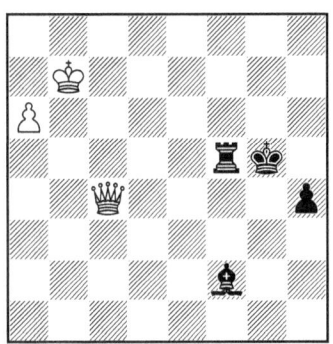

White to move

The material balance is queen versus rook and bishop. Each side has big plans for his remaining pawn. White's previous actions involved the queen taking control of the f7-square, from which the black rook wanted to control the 7th rank.

88.a7?

White's rush to collect the bishop is an error.

It was correct to regroup the queen first to discourage the black passed pawn from advancing, followed by returning the king to the kingside to support the queen and create deadly threats to the opponent's king. 88.♕g8+!? ♔f4 (88...♔h5 goes down to 89.a7 ♗xa7 90.♔xa7 h3 91.♕g3+−) 89.♕g2! ♗e3 (89...♔e5 90.♔c6 ♔f6+ 91.♔b5 ♖f5 92.♔c4 ♔f6 93.♔d3 ♖f4 94.♕b7+−)

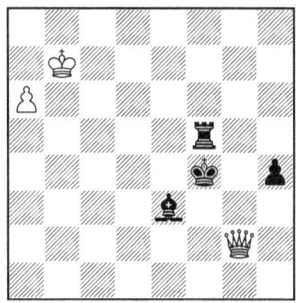

90.♔c6! Time for the king to start its campaign (90.a7? fails to 90...♖f7+=) 90...♖f6+ (90...♖h5 91.♕f1+ ♔g5 92.♕a1+−) 91.♔d5 ♖f5+ (91...♖xa6? drops the rook to 92.♕f1++−) 92.♔c4 ♖g5 93.♕c6 h3. 93...♖c5+ is bad after 94.♕xc5 ♗xc5 95.♔xc5 h3 96.a7 h2 97.a8=♕+− and the newly-promoted queen keeps the black passed pawn's promotion square under control.

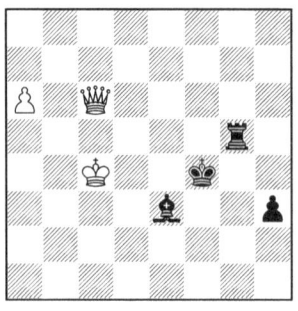

94.♕h6 ♔g4 95.♕e6+! ♔f4 96.♕xh3+− and White has destroyed

the black pawn to see his own passer secure him a win.

88.♕f1!? ♖f7+ was an alternative way to implement the same idea. White also secures a gradual victory with 88...♗e3 89.♕h3 ♗d4 90.♕b3 ♖e5 91.♕g8+ ♔f4 92.♕f7+ ♖f5 93.♕c4 ♔e3 94.a7 ♗xa7 95.♔xa7 ♖f4 96.♕c3+ ♔f2 97.♕h3+−.

89.♔c8 ♖f6 (89...♖f5 90.♕g2+ ♔h5 91.♔d7+−; 89...♖f8+ 90.♔d7 ♖f7+ 91.♔e8 ♖f6 92.♕g2+ ♔h5 93.♕d5+ ♔h6 94.♕d8 ♔g6 95.♕d7+−) 90.♕g2+ ♔h5 91.♕g7 ♖f4 (both 91...♖xa6 92.♕f7++− and 91...♖c6+ 92.♔b7 ♖b6+ 93.♔c7 ♖g6 94.♕f7 ♗b6+ 95.♔b7 h3 96.♕f5++− lose the game) 92.♔d8!

92...♗b6+. In case of 92...h3 93.a7 ♗xa7 94.♕xa7 ♔h4 95.♕g1 ♖g4 96.♕f2+ ♖g3 97.♔e7! ♔g4 98.♕d4+ ♔f3 99.♕d5+ ♔g4 (99...♔f2 100.♕h1+−) 100.♕e4+ ♔g5 101.♔e6! h2 102.♕e5+ ♔g4 103.♕f5+ ♔h4 104.♕h7++− the white queen and rook tandem forces Black to part with the pawn.

93.♔e8 ♗d4. Black gains nothing from delivering checks: 93...♖e4+ 94.♔f7 ♖f4+ 95.♔e6+−.

94.♕h7+ ♔g4 95.a7 ♗xa7 96.♕xa7 h3 97.♕g1+! ♔f3. 97...♔h4 goes down

as well to 98.♔e7 ♖g4 99.♕f2+ ♖g3 100.♔f6 ♔g4 101.♕f5+ ♔h4 102. ♕f4+ ♖g4 103.♕f2+ ♔h5 104.♕e3 ♔h4 105.♔f5 h2 106.♕f2+ ♔h3 107. ♕f3+ ♖g3 108.♕f1+ ♔h4 109.♕e1 ♔h3 110.♔f4 ♖g1 111.♕c3+ ♔g2 112. ♕f3#.

98.♕h2 ♔g4 99.♔e7! ♖f3 100.♔e6 ♖g3

101.♔e5! and the white king steps in just in time to assist his queen: 101... ♖g2 102.♕f4+ ♔h5 103.♔f5 h2 104. ♕f3++−.

88...♗xa7 89.♔xa7 h3!

It now turns out that the threat of the passed pawn's advance provides sufficient counterplay for Black to make a draw.

90.♕e4

90.♕d3 ♔g4!= is not superior to the text.

In case of 90.♕e2 ♖f4 91.♔b6 (91. ♕h2 ♔g4 92.♔b6 ♖f3 93.♔c5 ♖g3 94.♔d4 ♖g2=) 91...♖g4 92.♔c5 ♖g2 93.♕d3 (93.♕e5+ ♔g4=) 93...♔g4! (93...h2? 94.♕d5++−) 94.♔d4 h2= the white king is never in time to help his queen mount serious threats against the opponent's king.

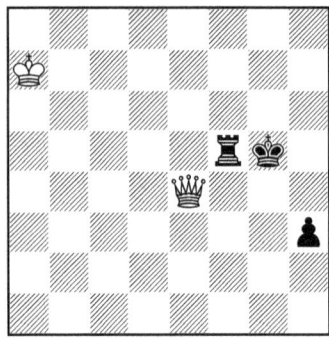

90...♖f4!

Lifting the restrictions imposed by the white queen along the fourth rank.

91.♕e7+

91.♕e3 ♔g4!= is no game changer.

Meanwhile, following 91.♕e1 ♖f3 92.♕g1+ ♔h4 93.♔b6 ♖g3 94.♕f2 ♔g4 95.♔c5 ♖g2= the pawn resumes its progress.

91...♔g4 92.♕g7+ ♔f3

93.♕h6

The game also peters out to a draw following 93.♕g1 ♖a4+!? 94.♔b6 ♖a2 95.♔c5 h2 96.♕h1+ ♔g3 97.♔d4 ♖g2 98.♔e3 ♖g1 99.♕f3+ ♔h4 100.♕f4+ ♔h3 101.♕h6+ ♔g3 102.♕g5+ ♔h3 103.♕h5+ ♔g3 (103...♔g2? 104.♕f3#) 104.♕f3+ ♔h4 105.♕f4+ ♔h3=.

93...♔g3 94.♕g5+ ♖g4 95.♕e3+ ♔g2 96.♕e2+ ♔g3

The black king is now well-positioned to secure his passed pawn's advance. 96...♔h1? 97.♕f3+!+− (97.♕xg4? h2= with a theoretical draw) is a blunder that costs Black the game.

97.♕e1+

Likewise, 97.♔b6 h2 98.♕f1 ♔h4= makes no difference for the evaluation.

97...♔g2 98.♕e2+ ♔g3 and White recognized the futility of his attempts to win. Draw.

Example No. 99
JK. Duda − J. Lopez Martinez
Minsk 2017

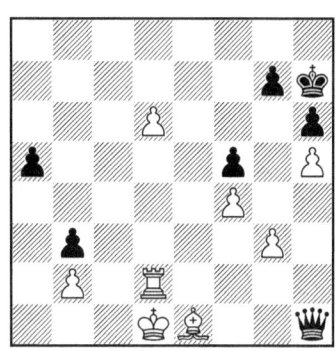

Black to move

White has decent counterplay by threatening to promote the passed pawn, supported by the rook from behind. Therefore, Black should be vigilant so as not to miss the moment when keeping the white foot-soldier at bay becomes no longer possible. Meanwhile, the black queenside pawns have advanced quite far. This enables Black to fight for victory by generating concrete threats.

56...♕xh5+?

Capturing the pawn with the idea of making it in time to hold the white passed pawn. Winning the game took resorting to concrete measures against his opponent's king: 56...a4! 57.d7 ♕f3+ 58.♔c1 (58.♖e2 a3! 59.d8=♕ axb2−+ and White has no defense despite a huge material advantage) 58...♕c6+ 59.♔d1. 59.♔b1 gives the game away to 59...♕e4+ 60.♔c1 ♕xe1+ 61.♖d1 ♕e2 62.♖d2 ♕c4+ 63.♔d1 ♕f1#.

59...a3!

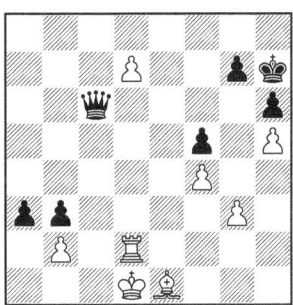

60.bxa3

(Queening the pawn with 60.d8=♕ goes down to 60...♕f3+ 61.♔c1 [61. ♖e2 axb2−+] 61...a2! 62.♕a5 ♕e4! 63.♔d1 ♕b1+ 64.♔e2 a1=♕ 65.♕xa1 ♕xa1 66.♔f2 ♕a7+ 67.♔f1 ♕a8−+ and the h5-pawn is doomed)

60...b2! Securing the exchange of White's powerful passed pawn.

61.♖xb2 ♕xd7+ 62.♖d2. White is in bad shape after both 62.♔c2 ♕a4+ 63.♖b3 ♕e4+ 64.♔d2 ♕g2+ 65.♔d1 ♕h1 66.a4 ♕d5+ 67.♔c2 ♕e4+ 68.♔d2 ♕xa4−+ and 62.♗d2 ♕a4+ 63.♖c2 ♕xa3 64.♗c3 ♕b3 65.♗e5 ♔g8!−+.

62...♕f7 63.♖d3 (63.a4 ♕b3+ 64.♔e2 ♕xa4−+; 63.♖h2 ♕b3+ 64.♔e2 ♕xa3 65.♔f2 ♕d3 66.♔g1 ♕e3+ 67.♗f2 ♕f3 68.♗e1 ♔g8−+ and the black king joins the fray to decisive effect) 63...♕xh5+ 64.♔c2. White also loses the game in case of 64.♔c1 ♕e2 65.♖d1 ♔g6!? 66.a4 ♕c4+−+.

64...♕e2+ 65.♗d2 ♕e4 66.♗e3 (66. ♔c3 ♔g6!?) 66...♕c6+ 67.♖c3 ♕g2+ 68.♗d2

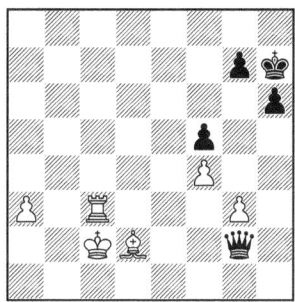

68...♔g6! The king is a full-fledged actor in endgame play and his productive participation can seal the game's outcome.

69.a4.

(The pawn drops to 69.♔c1 ♔h5 70.a4 ♕h1+ 71.♔b2 ♕d1−+; 69.♖d3 is no better: 69...♔h5 70.a4 ♕c6+ 71.♔b3 ♕a6 72.♖e3 [72.♖c3 ♕e6+ 73.♔b2 ♕d7−+] 72...♕b6+ 73.♔c4 [73.♔a3 ♕d4 74.♗c1 ♕a1+−+] 73...♕c6+ 74.♔b3 [74.♔b4 ♕d6+ 75.♔c3 ♕a3+−+] 74...♕d5+ 75.♔c3 ♕a5+−+)

69...♕e4+ 70.♔b3 ♕d5+ 71.♔c2 ♕a2+−+ with a technically winning endgame.

57.♖e2?

The Polish grandmaster returns the error. 57.♔c1? ♕h1 58.♔d1 (58.d7 ♕xe1+ 59.♖d1 ♕e2 60.♖d2 ♕c4+−+) 58...a4!−+ is also bad.

Reaching a draw required 57.g4! ♕xg4+ (57...fxg4 58.d7 g3+ 59.♔c1 ♕c5+ 60.♔d1=) 58.♔c1! ♕g1 (58...♕xf4 59.d7 ♕c4+ 60.♔d1 ♕g4+ 61.♔c1=) 59.♔d1 ♕g4+ (59...♕b6? 60.d7 ♕d8 61.♖d3!? a4 62.♗a5 ♕xa5 63.d8=♕) 60.♔c1=

and Black has nothing better than repeating moves.

57...♕f7 58.♗c3

Or 58.♖d2 ♕d7 59.♖d3 a4 60.♗c3 (60.♗b4? ♕c6 61.♗c3 ♕g2−+) 60...g5!? 61.♔d2 (61.♗e5 ♔g6!) 61...♔g6 62.♗e5 h5!? 63.fxg5. White loses following 63.♖c3 h4 64.♖c7 ♕b5 65.♖g7+ ♔h6 66.fxg5+ ♔h5−+.

63...♕xg5 64.♖d4. 64.♖c3 is no better: 64...♕b7 65.♖d3 ♕g2+ 66.♔c3 ♕c2+ 67.♔d4 ♕xb2+ 68.♔d5 ♕e2−+; 64.♗f4+ ♔f6! only improves the black king's position

64...♔g6 65.♗f4. The black pawns seal the game following 65.♖d3 ♔f7 66.♖c3 ♕b5 67.♖c7+ ♔e6 68.♖e7+ ♔d5 69.♗f4 (69.d7 ♕b4+−+) 69...♕b4+ 70.♔e2 a3−+.

65...a3! 66.bxa3 ♕a7−+ and Black wins again.

64.♔e2 gxf4 65.♗xf4 (65.gxf4 h5−+) 65...a3! 66.bxa3 (66.♖xb3 a2 67.♖a3 ♕b5+−+) 66...b2 67.♖b3 ♕c6 68.♖xb2 ♕g2+−+ and Black is winning.

59.♖d2 ♕h1+

59...♕f3+ 60.♔e1! ♕xg3+ (60...♕e3+ 61.♔f1) 61.♔e2= also leads to a draw.

60.♔e2 ♕g2+

60...♕e4+? loses to 61.♔f2+−.

61.♔e3   61.♔d1? blunders a checkmate to 61...♕f1#.

61...♕xg3+?

Black is carried away with grabbing the opponent's pawns. 61...♕e4+? fails again to 62.♔f2+−.

The way to save the game is 61...♕g1+! 62.♔f3 (62.♔d3 ♕b6 63.d7? ♕e6! 64.d8=♕ ♕e4#; 62.♖f2? ♕xg3+ 63.♖f3 ♕g6) 62...♕f1+ 63.♔e3 ♕g1+= with an inevitable draw.

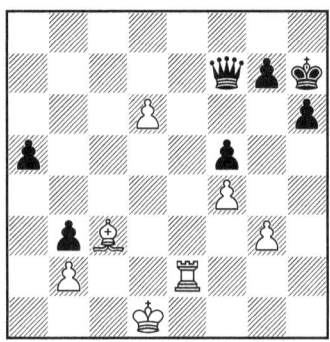

58...♕d5+?

Yet another mistake by Black. White is also fine after 58...a4?! 59.♖e7 ♕d5+ 60.♔e2.

Black needed to play 58...♕d7! 59.♖d2 (59.♖e7? ♕xd6+−+; for 59.♗e5 a4 60.♖d2 g5 61.♖d3 ♔g6 see the line with 58.♖d2) 59...a4 60.♔e1 (60.♗e5 g5!?; 60.♔c1 g5!?) 60...g5!? 61.♗e5 ♔g6 62.♔f2 ♕f7 63.♖d3 ♔e6

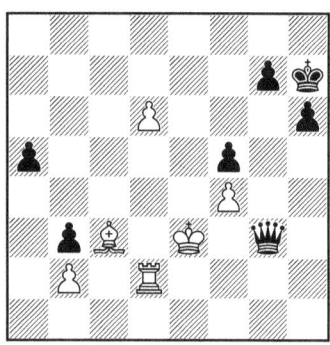

62.♔d4!+−

Now the tables turn drastically in White's favor.

62...♕xf4+

62...♕g1+ 63.♔c4 ♕f1+ 64.♔c5 ♕g1+ 65.♔c6+− is of no help either.

63.♔c5! a4

63...♕e3+ 64.♔b5! (64.♖d4? ♕e5+ 65.♖d5 ♕e3+ 66.♔b5? ♕e6; 64.♔c6? ♕e6 65.♔c7 ♕c4+) 64...♕e8+ 65.d7

♕d8 66.♗xa5+− results in the pawn queening.

64.d7! ♕e3+

In case of 64...♕c7+ 65.♔b4 ♕b6+ (65...♕d8 66.♔xa4 f4 67.♗a5+−) 66.♔a3 ♕c5+ 67.♗b4 ♕g1 68.♔xa4!+− the white king is out of the woods, and Black is doomed.

65.♔b5 a3 66.d8=♕ a2 67.♕d7!? ♕xd2

The line 67...♕g5 68.♗xg7! a1=♕ (68...♕xg7 69.♕xf5++−) 69.♗e5+ ♔g6 70.♕e8+ ♔h7 71.♖d7++− ends in a checkmating attack, too.

68.♕xg7#.

This is a highly instructive endgame about adequate evaluation and aligning your decisions in accordance with changes occurring during the game.

We wrap up the book by analyzing a couple of instructive examples from the tournament games of world champion Magnus Carlsen, in which he confidently outplays his famous opponents with the rook and knight tandem versus a queen.

Example No. 100
M. Carlsen – D. Navara
Biel 2018

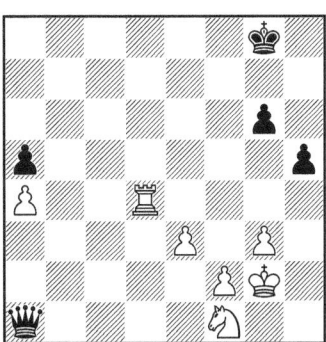

Black to move

White has a rook, a knight and a pawn for a queen. His king is reliably shielded against his opponent's checks. The rook takes up a centralized position, which enables it both to defend its queenside pawn and participate in an attack on potentially weak black pawns. White's further plans include improving his knight's position.

43...g5?!

Black moves his kingside pawns without any special reason, thereby saddling himself with more weaknesses. It was logical to post the queen to a more active square and follow it up by simply marking time with precise moves. White can either determine that he has no way to fight for a decisive advantage, or push his passed e-pawn forward, thus providing Black with dangerous counterplay. 43...♕c1!? 44.♘d2 ♕c6+ 45.♘e4 ♔g7=.

44.♘d2 g4

44...♔g7!? deserved consideration: 45.♘e4 (45.♘f3 ♔f6) 45...♔g6!? 46.♖d6+ ♔g7 47.♖d4 (47.♘xg5?! ♕xa4) 47...♔g6= and White finds it hard to get at his opponent's weaknesses here too.

45.♘e4

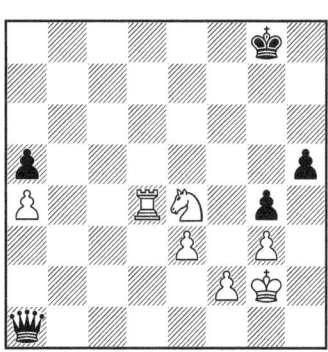

45...♕c1?

Just a blunder. 45...♔g7 was correct: 46.♘c5 ♕a2! 47.♘d3 ♕e6 48.♘f4 ♕e8!? 49.♔h2 (49.e4?! ♕e5 50.♖c4? h4∓; 49.♖c4 ♕e5!?) 49...♔h6!? 50.♖d6+ (50.e4?! h4! 51.gxh4? ♕e5; 50.♔g1 ♔g7 51.♔f1 ♔h6=) 50...♔g7 51.♖d4 ♔h6= and Black keeps his pawns alive.

46.♘f6+! ♔f7 47.♘xh5 ♕c6+ 48.♔g1 ♕c1+ 49.♔h2 ♔g6

49...♕c2? 50.♖f4+ ♔e6 51.♘f6+− is bad and blunders yet another pawn to White.

50.♘f4+ ♔f6 51.♘g2!

51.♘d5+ ♔e6! is harmless.

51...♔g5?!

51...♕c8!? 52.♘h4 ♔e5 was a better plan.

52.♖f4 ♕d1 53.♘h4

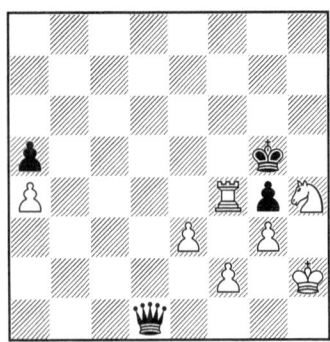

53...♕c2?!

Yet another inaccuracy. 53...♔h6! is a superior continuation: 54.♘f5+ ♔h7! (54...♔g5? 55.♘d4! ♔h6 56.♘c6 ♕d5 57.♘e7 ♕d1 58.♘g8+ ♔g7 59.♘f6+−) 55.♔g2 (55.♖d4 ♕c2 56.♖f4 ♕d1!) 55...♕d5+ 56.e4 ♕c6! 57.♖xg4 ♕xa4 58.♖g7+ ♔h8, and Black generates counterplay thanks to his passed pawn's advance.

54.♘f5 ♕d3?

Black has mishandled this endgame. 54...♕a2? failed to 55.♘d6 ♔h6 56.♘e8 ♕c2 57.♘f6+−.

Instead, Black needed to throw a wrench into the white knight's decisive transfer with 54...♕d1!? 55.♘d4 ♕d2 (55...♕xa4? 56.♘e6+) 56.♘e6+ ♔h6 57.e4 ♕b2 58.♔g2 ♕e5 59.♘d8 ♕e8 60.♘f7+ ♔g7 61.e5 ♕c6+ 62.♔g1 ♕d5.

55.e4!

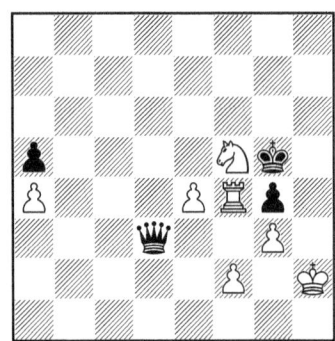

55...♕d7?

Both 55...♕e2? 56.♘e3+− and 55...♕c2? 56.e5 ♕c5 57.♘e3 ♕xe5 58.♖f5+ ♕xf5 59.♘xf5 ♔xf5 60.♔g2 ♔e4 61.f3+ gxf3+ 62.♔f2+− are bad.

55...♕f6! would have retained some chances: 56.♘e3+ (56.♖xg4 ♕c2!) 56...♔e6 57.♘xg4 (57.♖xg4 ♕d4! 58.e5 ♕xe5) 57...♕c2 58.e5 ♕h7+ 59.♔g2, although here, too, White should gradually set his pawns into decisive motion. For example, 59...♕b7+ 60.f3 ♕b2+ 61.♔h3 ♕a1 62.♔h4 ♕h1+ 63.♔g5 ♕c1 64.♔h6 ♕g1 65.♔g7 ♕xg3 66.♖f6+ ♔e7 67.♖f7+ ♔e6 68.♔f8+−.

56.e5! ♕h7+

Black loses the pawn ending arising after 56...♕xf5 57.♖xf5+ ♔xf5 58.♔g2

♔xe5 59.f3 gxf3+ 60.♔xf3 ♔f5 61.♔e3 ♔g4 62.♔d4 ♔xg3 63.♔c5 ♔f4 64.♔b5 ♔e5 65.♔xa5 ♔d6 66.♔b6 ♔d7 67.♔b7+−. 56...♕e6 57.♘e3+− is equally insufficient.

57.♔g1 ♕g6

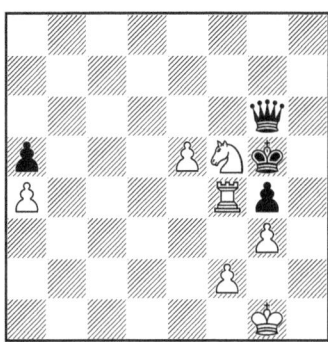

58.♘d6!

A precise move. Following the erroneous 58.♘e3? ♕b1+ 59.♔g2 ♕b7+ 60.♔h2 ♕h7+ 61.♔g1 ♕b1+ perpetual check can be stopped only at the cost of ruining the knight's position.

58...♕e6?!

Black still has a totally lost position after the computer's first line 58...♕b1+ 59.♔g2 ♕a2 60.♘e4+ ♔g6 61.♘f6 ♔f7 62.♘xg4+ ♔e6 63.♔h3 ♕a1 64.♔h4+−.

59.♖f5+

59.♘f7+ ♔h5 (59...♔g6 60.♖f6++−) 60.♖f6 ♕b6 61.♖h6+!+− was an alternative way to win the game.

59...♕xf5

Black may resign after 59...♔g6 60.♖f6++−.

60.♘xf5 ♔xf5 61.f4! gxf3 62.♔f2 ♔xe5 63.♔xf3 ♔f5 64.♔e3 and Black resigned.

Example No. 101
M. Carlsen − I. Nepomniachtchi
Dubai 2021

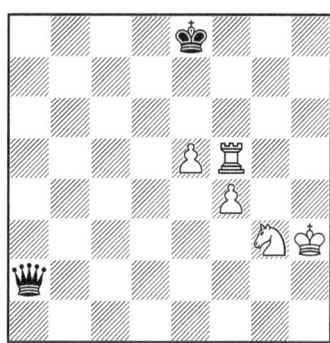

Black to move

This is perhaps the key moment in one of their world championship match games − in round 6 after five draws. A long seesaw struggle resulted in the reigning champion outplaying his opponent and reaching an endgame which takes precise defense for Black to achieve a draw.

130...♕e6?

And the challenger failed to do the job here. Saving the game requires that Black prevent the white pieces from getting coordinated and pushing his pair of passed pawns.

The way to go is 130...♕b1!? 131.e6 (131.♔g4 ♕d1+! 132.♔g5 ♕g1! promises White nothing. In case of 131. ♖f6 ♕e1! 132.e6 [132.f5? is wrong: 132...♕xe5 133.♖e6+ ♕xe6 134.fxe6 ♔e7=, 132.♔g4 ♕d1+ 133.♔f5 ♕d3+ 134.♘e4 ♕h3+ 135.♔g6 ♕d3= is of no help] 132...♔e7 133.♖g6. The following line ends in a cute stalemate: 133.♖h6 ♕e3 134.♔g4 ♕g1 135.f5 ♔d6!? 136. ♖h7 ♕d4+ 137.♔h3 ♕f4! 138.♖d7+ ♔e5! 139.e7 ♕h6+ 140.♔g4 ♕f4+ 141.♔h5 ♕g5+! 142.♔xg5=

133...♕b1 134.f5 ♕a1 135.♔g4. 135.♖h6 ♕g7!? 136.f6+ ♕xf6 137.♖xf6 ♔xf6= only leads to a draw.

135...♕d1+ 136.♔g5 ♕d4 137.♖g8 [137.♔h6 ♕h8+!; 137.♘h5 ♕e3+ 138. ♔g4 ♕e2+ 139.♔h4 ♕e4+=] 137... ♕e3+ 138.♔h5 ♕c3 139.♔h4 [139. ♘e4? ♕f3+] 139...♕d4+ 140.♔g4 ♕f6+ 141.♖g5 ♕d4+ 142.♔h3 ♕a1 143.♖h5 ♕c3 144.♖h7+ ♔f6 145.♖f7+ [a drawn position involving stalemate ideas arises after 145.e7 ♕e3!? 146.♔g4

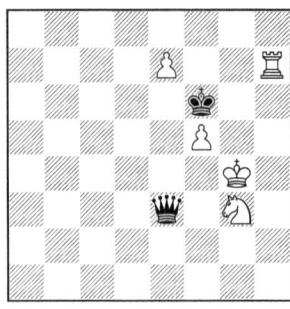

146...♕f4+!=] 145...♔g5 146. e7 ♕h8+ 147.♔g2 ♕b2+ 148.♔h3 ♕h8+= and there is no avoiding a perpetual check)

131...♔e7!? 132.♖e5 ♕h7+ 133. ♖h5. 133.♘h5 is no better: 133... ♕d3+ 134.♔h4 ♕d4 135.♔g5 ♕g1+ 136.♔h6 ♕d4 137.♔g6 ♕xe5! 138. fxe5 ♔xe6= and the last white pawn perishes.

133...♕d3 134.f5 ♕c3 135.♖h7+ ♔f6 136.♖f7+. There is no way of improving the position in case of 136. e7 ♕e3=, while following 136.♔h4 ♕b4+ 137.♔h5 ♕f4 138.♖f7+ ♔e5 139.e7 ♕f3+ 140.♔h6 (140.♔h4 ♕f4+ 141.♔h3 ♕h6+ 142.♔g2 ♕d2+=) 140...♕f4+ 141.♔h7 ♕h4+ 142.♔g8 ♕xg3+ 143.♔f8 (143.♖g7 ♕b3+ 144. ♔f8 ♕a3=) 143...♕a3= Black holds the position via pinning.

136...♔g5 137.e7 ♕h8+ 138.♔g2 ♕b2+= and a draw is inevitable.

131.♔h4!+−
And Black's position is lost.
131...♕h6+?!
The relatively better 131...♕a2 132. ♘h5! ♕h2+ 133.♔g5 ♕g1+ 134.♔h6 ♔e7 135.♖g5 ♕b6+ 136.♔h7 ♕e3 137.♔g7 ♔e6 138.♖g6+ ♔e7 (138... ♔f5 139.e6 ♕a7+ 140.♔h6+−) 139. ♘f6! ♕f3 (139...♕xf4? 140.♘d5+) 140.♘g8+ ♔e8 141.♖e6+ ♔d7 142. ♖f6 ♔e8 143.f5 ♕g3+ 144.♔h7! ♕h2+ (144...♕xe5 145.♖e6++−) 145.♖h6 ♕f4 146.♖e6+ ♔d8 147.♘h6+− still loses.

132.♘h5 ♕h7
Black is also in a grim situation following 132...♔e7 133.♖f6 ♕h8 134.♔g5! ♕g8+ 135.♖g6 ♕d5 136.

♘f6 ♕g2+ 137.♔h6 ♕h2+ 138.♔g7
♕c2 (138...♕xf4 139.♘d5++−) 139.
♘d5+ ♔d8 140.♔f7 ♕f5+ (the queen
drops to 140...♕c4 141.♖d6+ ♔c8 142.
♖c6+ ♕xc6 143.♘e7++−) 141.♘f6
♕xf4 142.♖g8+ ♔c7 143.e6 ♕c4 144.
♖g5 ♕b3 145.♖d5+− and there is no
stopping the white passed pawn.

133.e6! ♕g6

The queen falls both to 133...♕xf5
134.♘g7++− and 133...♔e7 134.
♖f7++−.

Meanwhile, Black is also doomed
after 133...♔e7+ 134.♔g4 ♕b7 (134...
♕a7 135.♖d5 ♕g1+ 136.♔f5 ♕b1+
137.♔f6 ♕a1+ 138.♖e5+−) 135.
♖d5!+−.

134.♖f7! ♔d8

The pawn ending is lost following
134...♕xe6 135.♘g7+ ♔xf7 136.♘xe6
♔xe6 137.♔g5 ♔f7 (137...♔e7 138.
♔g6+−) 138.♔f5+−. 134...♕h6 135.
f5+− is not a game changer either.

135.f5 ♕g1 136.♘g7

and Black resigned in the face of
136...♕h2+ 137.♔g5 ♕g3+ 138.♔h6
♕h2+ 139.♔g6 ♕g3+ 140.♔h7 ♕h4+
141.♔g8.

Index of Names
Numbers indicate the example